Attention

Attention All Shipping

A Journey Round the Shipping Forecast

Charlie Connelly

W F HOWES LTD

This large print edition published in 2007 by
W F Howes Ltd
Unit 4, Rearsby Business Park, Gaddesby Lane,
Rearsby, Leicester LE7 4YH

1 3 5 7 9 10 8 6 4 2

First published in the United Kingdom in 2004
by Little, Brown

A CIP catalogue record for this book is available
from the British Library

ISBN 978 1 40740 541 4

Typeset by Palimpsest Book Production Limited,
Grangemouth, Stirlingshire
Printed and bound in Great Britain
by Antony Rowe Ltd, Chippenham, Wilts.

For Aunt Joan

CONTENTS

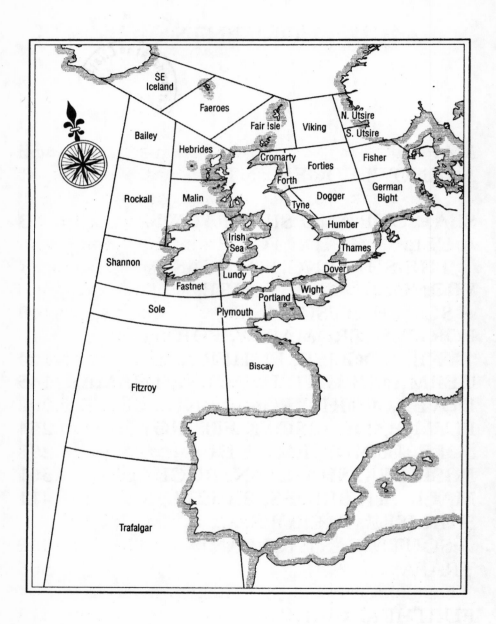

ACKNOWLEDGEMENTS

I sought the advice and opinions of many wise people in the preparation and execution of this book, but still went ahead and wrote it anyway. Sincere thanks to Alan Samson for his encouragement and faith from the book's very inception, to Richard Beswick and particularly Sarah Shrubb for all their advice and input, and to Lizzy Kremer for being the world's greatest agent. Special thanks also to Hilary Hale.

Big thanks are due to Andy Yeatman and Martin Rowley at the Met Office, and Jane Watson, David Anderson and Nikki Richardson at BBC Radio 4.

Daphne Caine at the Isle of Man government's Department of Tourism (www.gov.im/tourism/) was helpful way beyond the call of duty, while I am also particularly indebted to Lisa Morgan at Braathens (www.braathens.no) and Bill Tinto at Scotia Travel (www.scotiatravel.com) for their assistance.

Thanking everyone who helped to make my job easier would take up a whole extra volume, but Wenche Ringstrand, Jo Heuston, Julie Robson and Clive Ramage, Brian Rees, Donald and Eileen

Cowey, Mike With, David and Nessie Taylor, Matt Wright, Campbell Scott, Lew and Prince Michael of Sealand, Tim Bennett, the Broadstairs Babes, Sam Lacey, Mum and Dad, Roy and Sandy Sands, Hugh MacDonald, J.R. Daeschner, Lola Brown, Mick Collins, Paul and Emma s'Jacob, Tim and Elizabeth O'Brien, Douglas Greig, Helen Carter and Emma Murray all provided invaluable assistance, encouragement and in some cases terrific travel companions. There are many people I haven't mentioned here by name, mainly because I am completely disorganised and forgot, but a great big 'Thanks, folks' and a (strictly metaphorical) round of drinks to everyone.

Special thanks and much, much love to Katie for putting up with my frequent absences, rank disorganisation and chronic untidiness. As usual, I couldn't do it without you.

SEA, SOUP AND SILVERTOWN

The solemn, rhythmic intonation of the shipping forecast is as familiar to us as the sound of Big Ben chiming the hour. Since its first broadcast in the 1920s it has inspired poems and songs in addition to its intended objective of warning generations of seafarers of impending storms and gales.

Sitting at home listening to the shipping forecast can be a cosily reassuring experience. There's no danger of a westerly gale eight, veering south-westerly increasing severe gale nine later (visibility poor) gusting through your average suburban living room, blowing the Sunday papers all over the place and traumatising the cat. The chances of squally showers, moderate or good becoming poor later, drenching your new sofa and reducing the unbroken two-year run of *Hello!* magazines under the coffee table to a papery pulp are frankly slim unless there's a serious problem with your radiators. There's definitely something comforting about the fact that although some salty old sea dog in a draughty wheelhouse somewhere will be buttoning his sou'wester even tighter at the news

3

there are warnings of gales in Rockall, Malin and Bailey, you can turn up the central heating and see if there's a nice film on the telly. *The Cruel Sea*, perhaps.

Oddly comforting though the shipping forecast is, to most of us it is totally meaningless. A jumble of words, phrases and numbers which could be thrown into the air, picked off the floor and read out at random and most of us wouldn't be any the wiser. It has, however, accompanied most of our lives from childhood, a constant, unchanging cultural reference point that goes back further than *Coronation Street*, the Ovalteenies and even the Rolling Stones. No one, not even the most committed mariner, listens to all four broadcasts every day. In fact very few of us make a point of listening to the shipping forecast. But it's always there, always has been, always will be, lodged inexplicably in our subconscious. Stop anyone in the street and ask them to name as many of the areas as possible and the chances are they'll get through about half a dozen before even pausing for breath. I guarantee Dogger and Fisher will be two of them as well. Ask them how they know these things, and you're likely to receive in response a gaze into the middle distance, a slight furrow of the brow and a 'Well, er, dunno really . . .'.

For me as a small boy, when the shipping forecast came on the kitchen radio just before six o'clock in the evening it meant that my tea was nearly ready. It didn't mean any more than that;

just a hotchpotch of incomprehensible words that acted as a Pavlovian bell to my tastebuds. In fact, it's only recently that the words 'Forties', 'Cromarty' and 'Forth' have stopped causing me to salivate slightly and think of Findus Crispy Pancakes.

If anything, the sound of the shipping forecast made me think of being safe at home. It also necessitated at least one visit to Greenwich Hospital when the familiar words prompted an uncontrolled hunger-inspired scamper of stockinged feet across polished kitchen lino that was interrupted at full tilt by an unfortunately positioned domestic appliance. Stitches were required. Come to think of it, I could probably blame the shipping forecast for the scar on my forehead that scuppered an otherwise inevitable modelling career.

Childhood visits to casualty aside, for me the shipping forecast retains a soothing, homely aspect to it, which is strange when you think that its contents are anything but soothing and homely. But as I grew up and began to sprout hair in places I'd never considered before, and began to live in places I'd never considered before, catching the shipping forecast on the radio would always be a comforting experience. The forecast itself might be telling me otherwise, but hearing it meant that everything was all right. No matter how bad things got, no matter how dubious any career or romantic issues became, not to mention global events, the knowledge that the shipping forecast was still going out four times a day, regular as clockwork, meant that everything would be fine. Not, perhaps, for the good people of Hebrides when they heard severe gale nine was heading their way in the next few hours, but the great scheme of things was generally all right. Oh, and my fish fingers were nearly ready.

I was up working late one night. In my dark office, a lamp cast a pool of light across my desk while the orange glow of a streetlight filtered through the slats of my window blind. I slumped back in my chair and placed my feet on the desk. By rights the next line should be 'I was about to pour myself another bourbon when in walked this blowsy broad and I knew I had my next case'. Instead, I was wrestling with an article about football in an obscure eastern-European backwater with the radio on quietly so as not to wake the slumbering form in the bedroom next door.

As I gazed glassy-eyed at a flashing cursor on an otherwise unblemished white screen a report came on the midnight news. The British fishing industry was in crisis – it was running out of fish. A combination of the European Common Fishing Policy, which allowed EEC members wide fishing rights, overfishing of young cod and a rise in sea temperatures making breeding conditions difficult had meant that the trawlers which put out to sea all around these islands were coming back practically empty. The battered fillets dunked into the hot fat at your local Master Fryer were more likely to come from Icelandic than British fleets. The entire industry was on its uppers, and the European Union was proposing a ban on cod fishing to allow stocks to rise again.

Sitting there in that puddle of weak light I looked out of the window where a slight drizzle had begun to speckle the pane from the darkness beyond. Trawlers would be out at sea now, hauling in nets barely half full with immature fish, the fishermen not knowing whether men in suits in Brussels were about to bring their livelihood to an end with a flourish of signatures on the bottom of a document so sesquipedalian as to induce headaches and drooling in all who attempted to read it.

The clock ticked around towards one o'clock and eastern-European football was becoming no more alluring. The murmur of voices on the radio then gave way to a calming piece of music, all rising and falling strings and a lilting melody, before the familiar recital began:

And now the shipping forecast issued by the Met Office at 0015 on Thursday the seventeenth of October . . .

There were warnings of gales in North Utsire, South Utsire, FitzRoy, Sole, Fastnet, Shannon, Rockall, Malin, Hebrides, Bailey and South-east Iceland. Brrr, I thought. Glad I'm in here. The fortunes of Ukraine's representatives in the UEFA

Cup suddenly seemed far more appealing. Those trawler men would be at sea in these gales. Homely and comforting though the forecast remained, for the first time I began to realise that there was much more at stake here than just my feeling cosy and reminiscing about Alphabetti Spaghetti. I slept restlessly that night.

The next day I went to Greenwich, where it's probably appropriate that time seems to have a quality of its own. While the rest of London hurtles around at a pace that can make your nose bleed, the Greenwich day slows almost to a halt among the amiable jumble of shops, pubs and historic buildings on the southern shore of the Thames. Maybe it's because time, or at least our attempts at harnessing it, is manufactured here. Outside the Royal Observatory, the home of Greenwich Mean Time, a brass strip runs through the tarmac representing zero degrees longitude. Tourists can hop back and forth across the line, jumping from the eastern hemisphere to the west, bouncing around the centre of time.

Perhaps the sense of timelessness stems from the fact that Greenwich is now out of step with time. Where once it was the heart of the maritime world, today it is a nautical anachronism, a museum to Britain's seafaring rise and fall. Shops sell ropes, clocks and bells, but they are ornaments for mantelpieces rather than wheelhouse necessities, sold to tourists at inflated prices. The architectural centrepieces of Greenwich, the Inigo Jones-designed

Queen's House and Christopher Wren's Royal Naval College, were once of huge importance to Britain as a maritime power. The former meant that explorers such as Martin Frobisher and Sir Walter Ralegh were regular visitors – Ralegh famously laid his cloak over one of Greenwich Park's puddles in order that Elizabeth I would not soil the royal shoes, an even greater act of chivalry when you consider that it probably said 'hand wash only' on the label – while if the First World War was won on the playing fields of Eton, Britain's great naval victories had their basis in the ornate but draughty classrooms of a former nautical poorhouse.

Today the Queen's House has not been home to a monarch for more than two hundred years and forms part of the National Maritime Museum. The Naval College had been conceived as a refuge for destitute and invalid sailors left on the streets at the conclusion of the naval wars of the seventeenth and eighteenth centuries. It had housed around three thousand sailors before being taken over by the Royal Navy and converted to academia in the nineteenth century. In 1997, the college was moved to the Royal Airforce College at Cranwell, and Greenwich's last working link with the sea was gone, its decline mirroring that of Britain as a maritime nation. A short way along the river the great royal shipyards of Deptford and Woolwich, which produced legendary vessels like Henry VIII's *Great Harry* and Charles I's *Sovereign of the Seas*, are long, long gone.

Having lived in or near Greenwich for most of my life I like to spend time in Greenwich Park. Sitting on a bench under General Wolfe's statue offers one of London's most dramatic and detailed panoramas, with the city landscape at its sharpest after an autumn shower has rinsed clean the air. With St Paul's Cathedral and the Tower of London far off to the left and the Millennium Dome to your right, Greenwich can appear physically to be at the very centre of London history, something that certainly suits my Greenwich-centric view of the world anyway. It has grown from an ancient fishing community to become the focus of both British royal and global maritime life, and when you look down from beneath Wolfe's startled expression (as if he has just been goosed unexpectedly by an elderly aunt) the look of Greenwich betrays much of its former glory and its struggle for a place in the modern city.

On a walk through the park, the paths wet and shiny in the wintry late-afternoon sun that shoots between skeletal trees from behind the Royal Observatory, it's easy to take the peace for granted. Barely a hundred yards from the park gates, just the other side of the immaculate classical lines of the Queen's House, runs one of London's most fearsome one-way systems, where traffic thunders day and night to remind you that you are actually in a twenty-first-century city.

Once you're through the covered market and have passed the Spanish Galleon and Gipsy Moth pubs, the spindly masts and rigging of the *Cutty Sark* make an incongruous foreground to the silvery skyscrapers of Canary Wharf on the other side of the river.

Placed in dry dock by the river at Greenwich half a century ago, the famous old tea clipper still gives off a musky whiff of the lapsang suchong that used to pack its holds. A glance into the concrete crater in which this noble old ship sits, not to mention onboard encounters with the spooky mannequins representing life on board in the glory days of sail, serves only to underline further how Britain's maritime dominance is a thing of the past. Where the proud figurehead at the bows once led the way, rising and falling through crashing waves, today she overlooks nothing more than an expanse of paving stones. If you examine her expression there appears to be a desperation in her eyes as she reaches out for the river fifty short but impassable yards away.

Walking beyond the *Cutty Sark* and past the pleasure-boat terminal takes you to the footpath along the river itself. You pass the old Naval College, stepping to one side at the Queen's Steps to allow cyclists through. The college was built by Sir Christopher Wren in two symmetrical halves because Queen Mary wanted the view of the river from the Queen's House undisturbed – the distance between the two sections is exactly the width of the Queen's House. Hence from the Queen's Steps you look right through the college to the Maritime

Museum and the park beyond, and then up the hill to the Royal Observatory.

At these steps Martin Frobisher stopped off for an audience with Elizabeth I on his way from Deptford to search for the North-west Passage, and here is where Nelson's body arrived back from Trafalgar pickled in a barrel of brandy. Transferred to a coffin, he was taken from the ship to lie in state in the Naval College's Painted Hall before being rowed upriver for a state funeral. His blood-stained uniform now resides in a glass case at the Maritime Museum.

Before long you arrive at the Trafalgar Tavern, a big old draughty Georgian building of fading grandeur where Dickens dined regularly and whither parliament would decamp for an annual whitebait dinner. Beyond the Trafalgar, along the river, you pass the tiny, whitewashed seventeenth-century Seamen's Hospital, in turn dwarfed by an enormous power station wholly out of place on the otherwise dignified Greenwich riverside. Its huge but now redundant jetty passes over your head and thumps into the river next to you with a defiant belligerence out of line with the genteel hospice next door. A new complex of luxury apartments is being built beyond – prior to construction the old British Sailor pub had stood here, derelict and half demolished, letters missing from its name and the red-bearded sailor on its sign looking faintly embarrassed.

We've reached our destination now, and one of my favourite places in London. The Cutty Sark pub is a good half mile from the ship that gave it its name, but that doesn't seem to matter. Inside it is dark and timbered, snugs here and barrel stools there. A grand wooden staircase sweeps up through the centre, and I like to sit and look out at the river from the huge first-floor bay window. Here it's easy to be lulled into Greenwich time, where the days pass more slowly than anywhere else in London. It's late afternoon and the pub is all but empty. The weak, wintry sun is still leaking from behind the Observatory and occasionally will be caught by the brown sails of an old Thames sailing barge making its way along the river. Hundreds of these used to buzz around the east coast carrying cargoes of all descriptions right up to the middle of the twentieth century. There are no working barges now but a handful are maintained by a dedicated band of enthusiasts, some still making their dignified way up the Thames for the benefit of tourists, their dark old hulls and brown sails almost lost beneath the huge glinting skyscrapers of Docklands beyond.

If you sit to the left of the window you can see the Millennium Dome looming large on the Greenwich peninsula, and the Thames barge soon disappears behind it. You have to crane your neck a little, but off to the far right you can just make out the two slim, black-tipped silver chimneys of the Tate & Lyle sugar refinery in Silvertown. And Silvertown is where this journey really begins.

From the turn of the twentieth century until its destruction during the Second World War, my great-grandparents, Harry and Nelly, ran the Royal Victoria & Albert Docks Shipping Laundry at the heart of the London docks in Constance Street, Silvertown.

An industrial and residential district in east London, Silvertown took its name from the Samuel Winkworth Silver Rubber Works established in the 1850s and quickly grew from empty boggy marshland into a major industrial area. It was poor, despite the presence of the three huge royal docks that made Silvertown, with the docks to the north and the Thames to the south, an island. The docks were a major terminus for global shipping particularly during the days of the British Empire, and all sorts of exotic craft, people and cargo passed through this part of London. I have on the wall above my desk an old black-and-white photograph of my late uncle as a little boy reaching out in wonder to touch the outstretched trunk of a baby elephant peering out of a crate destined for who-knows-where.

Silvertown was often rough and occasionally tragic. In 1917, fifty tons of TNT exploded at the Brunner Mond chemical works in west Silvertown, killing seventy, injuring hundreds more and destroying much of the area in an explosion that was heard as far away as Norwich. The blast blew in the windows and tossed my grandmother from her cot, and my great-grandmother opened up the laundry as a temporary refuge for the injured and homeless. Their business shipping laundry had started by sheer chance. 'Dad was always out of work,' my Great-aunt Joan once told me. 'Well, everyone was in them days. But one day Mum said to Dad, "Go down the docks and see if there's any washing." Now, the big liners had their own laundry, all run by Chinamen, you know, but on the odd smaller ship the men had to do their own washing.

'Well he came back with six white stewards' jackets that had to be starched. Course, they hadn't got any bleedin' soap, had they? So Dad had to go next door to the neighbour and borrow thruppence. They bought a penny bar of Sunlight soap, a penn'orth of starch and a penny for the gas to heat the water, and the old girl scrubbed up these jackets, starched them and pressed them. Dad took them back, got probably a tanner for each of them and it all started from there. The old man used to stand there on the dockside and they'd all bring their stuff out to him.

'When you took the laundry back to the ships you didn't get paid. The captain signed your chit to say it was all correct and you took it up to the shipping office in London. Of course, your great-granddad liked that bit on the ship because they'd all be saying, "Have a drop of rum, Harry, have a drop of beer."'

Harry always volunteered to take the laundry back to the ships because with his reputation as a bit of a comedian he was guaranteed an invitation to stay for a tipple with the sailors, an invitation he accepted heartily. At least once a month the ship would sail with him aboard, necessitating his being put off at Tilbury by the Thames pilot.

'One day though, during the First World War, the bloody boat kept going, didn't it? Him and his mate the greengrocer, who was also having his chit signed, ended up sailing for the other side of the bloody world. Mum was expecting at the time, as she usually was, but the old man had been shanghaied. He went all over the place, the Dardanelles, everywhere.'

Harry was put to work in the galley, and had the misfortune to be carrying a huge vat of boiling soup at the moment the ship was torpedoed. The soup spilled all over his leg, and the ship's surgeon had to be called from more conventional military injuries to declare that the extent of the burns meant Harry's leg had to come off. Overhearing that, my great-grandfather, understandably rather partial to his lower limbs due to their crucial role in propelling him to the pub, decided to jump ship.

'He literally went over the side and swam for it,' said Joan. 'He'd seen this bit of ground not far off, this island where they'd anchored to inspect the damage, and him and his mate the greengrocer swam out, and it was the bloody Falklands, wasn't it? I didn't know this until the Falklands War started and my sister, Win, told me, and how they had to wait there until another boat pulled in and they could get home.'

No one alive today knows how he did it, but several months after his inebriated departure my great-grandfather arrived back at Silvertown station with all limbs still attached. As his train pulled in, through the steam on the opposite platform he saw my great-grandmother dressed in her Sunday best waiting to board a train. Harry hurried across the footbridge, convinced that during his lengthy, unannounced absence she'd found herself a new man, only to find that the baby born after he'd left was gravely ill with dysentery in Bethnal Green Hospital. They travelled there together and made it just in time to be present when their child died.

Despite having grown up with a wealth of such tales, I realised only recently that I'd never been to Silvertown. With the wind at my back and the aid of a sturdy catapult, I could probably twang a pebble across the river into Silvertown from my bedroom window so I had little excuse not to go. Consumed by family nostalgia one afternoon, I pulled out a street map and discovered that although Silvertown had been flattened in the blitz (mostly on one horrific Saturday afternoon in 1940, which necessitated my grandparents fleeing the area on a motorcycle with fires raging and bombs falling around them, my grandmother riding pillion with my infant mother in her arms), a truncated Constance Street was still there.

There were spots of rain in the wind as I boarded the Woolwich Free Ferry, which has shuttled people and vehicles across the Thames since 1889. On a warm summer evening in 1940 my mother had been born on the ferry; the nearest maternity hospital to Silvertown was over the water at Woolwich and hence she made a spectacular entrance halfway across the river.

Peering between the whitewashed ironwork of the foot-passengers' deck as we chugged across the river, I could see the titanium-coated shells of the Thames Barrier and the gently decomposing Millennium Dome across the choppy, rain-pocked waters. Small bullets of water stung my face as I took in the magnificent riverside panorama of London from this century-old aquatic vantage point.

When we reached the north side of the Thames, a cheerfully weather-beaten man in oilskins and a West Ham United ski-hat unhooked the chain at the front and I began a walk along the river to Silvertown. Constance Street was there all right, but would be unrecognisable to my ancestors today. A small row of shops, no more than twenty years old and nearly all boarded up, gave way to a new-looking council estate. I knew the laundry had been at number 16, so counted the shops. The last in the row was a disused British Legion at number 14. The empty paved space next to it, where some leaves and crisp packets did circuits in the wind, was clearly the site of the old laundry. I was, erm, home.

Back at the end of the street was an abandoned old pub. Clearly grand in its day, it had no name, no painted sign, and the windows were covered with metal grilles. This could have been Cundy's, one of the pubs to which my grandfather repaired for his nightly pots of beer.

'When Dad died there were more wreaths from bleedin' pubs than there were from family,' laughed Joan when I asked her about Harry. 'The Rose and Crown, the Queen Victoria, Cundy's at the top of the road, the Three Crowns, the Royal Albert at North Woolwich, the Queen's Head; all wreaths from bloody pubs!'

As I walked past the pub I thought I heard something – music from within. It was then that I noticed that the metal grille over a side door was half raised. Despite every apparent effort to make it seem otherwise, the pub was open. I ducked under the grille and went inside. It was an old-fashioned, high-ceilinged Victorian pub with threadbare carpets and faded flock wallpaper. Weak sunshine streamed through the grilles, flecks of dust floating gracefully in the thin beams of light. A few old men with wispy white hair and shabby overcoats squinted through rheumy eyes at pints of Guinness on the tables in front of them. I ventured to the bar across a carpet so old it shone as if polished and slid to a halt like a novice ice-skater wobbling to the barriers. A friendly man in his forties wearing a grubby tracksuit poured me a Guinness, and I asked what the pub was called.

'The Railway Tavern,' he said. My heart sank a little, until he added, 'But everyone around here knows it as Cundy's.' This was it, this was the right place – Harry's local. In addition, it was a famous dockland pub: during the Great Dock Strike of 1889 Eleanor Marx, wife of Karl, organised strike meetings in Cundy's.

'Cundy owned the place in the early years, when I was a kid. And ooh, he was a sod,' Great-aunt Joan explained to me later. 'Dad would make his first move up to Cundy's for a couple of pints before he'd start doing the rounds of all the other pubs and usually end up back there. He used to tell me, "Old Cundy knows when I've had a few." Dad used to give him a pound and it would be, what, fourpence a pint in those days, and he'd only get change back from ten shillings. The old man marked his pound note one night, and Cundy gave him change from ten shillings. Dad says, "I gave you a pound," so he said, "No you didn't," and Dad's got a policeman from outside. He checked the till and there's this marked pound note, and Dad never went into Cundy's again from that day on.'

I sat at a table in the corner and looked at the pictures around the walls. They showed the docks in their heyday: forests of cranes dipping their heads over the decks of enormous vessels, cockney stevedores milling around cavernous containers, vast liners like the *Mauretania* nosing into the Royal Docks, the largest inland acreage of dock water in the world.

In my grandmother's day, Silvertown was like an island; with the docks to the north and the Thames to the south, you had to cross water to leave. It even had an island mentality. Right up until her death my grandmother was suspicious of anyone not from Silvertown, even though she never returned there to live after being bombed out. Cockneys in general were just about okay, but anyone else was dodgy and not to be trusted. 'You've got dock water in your veins, boy, and don't you ever forget it,' she'd warn me.

It struck me that, a few ferry trips and the odd session on a pedalo aside, my own seafaring experience was not nearly as impressive as it should have been, given the nature of the fluid apparently coursing through my arteries. Even my grandfather was a seafarer, although more intentionally than his father-in-law. Charlie wasn't a particularly successful sailor, however, and his fishing boat would regularly have to be rescued. Rarely would an expedition with Great-aunt Joan's husband, also called Charlie, end without misnap.

'We went out one day, me and the two Charlies, down to Folkestone because they had to do a bit of tinkering with the engine,' Joan would tell me. 'They decided to take the boat out and there's me sitting in nothing but a cotton frock, three or four miles out to sea. And the waves are getting up and the boat's rocking from side to side, and we're having to sit with our feet out, braced against the side.

'So all of a sudden we're in a calm bit, and your granddad says, "You all right, Joan? Do you want a rod and line?" and gives me a line with a load of hooks all along it. "Chuck it over the side," he says. So, of course, silly cow, I do it, don't I, and within a minute I'm nearly over the side myself. "Pull it in," they're shouting, "pull it in." We pulled it in and there's bleedin' mackerel all along it. Mackerel's easy to catch – you can chuck a bit of silver paper in and get mackerel – and I'd got hundreds of 'em. Took about an hour to get these bloody things off and chuck them back in the water.

'So we're sitting there and it's cutting up a bit rough again, and fog's come down too. There's your granddad in the wheelhouse with his pipe, all happy, you know. My Charlie's down below tinkering away with the engine and all of a sudden there's this big "paaaaarp, paaaaaaarp", and it's only the bleedin' cross-Channel ferry about a hundred yards away, coming straight for us out of the fog. I looked at your granddad, and he's just standing there looking at this ferry going, "What's the matter with that silly so-and-so?" My Charlie's looked up from the engine, seen this bloody great thing coming for us and gone, "Jesus Christ, let's get a move on!" And the bow wave comes right over us. The ferry's gone by like a bloody ten-storey block of flats and your granddad's leaning out of the wheelhouse shaking his fist after this thing, going, "You silly bastard!"'

Sitting in the pub that day I thought of Joan's tales and realised that I'd probably been a bit of a let-down to the nautical side of the family. Not only had I just passed some of the family silver over Cundy's bar for the first time since the great marked-note scandal of nearly a century earlier, my ten-minute trip on the Woolwich ferry was probably about the most daring maritime escapade I had ever undertaken. I had never swum for an unknown land half the world away in order to save a blistered leg, nor had I taken on a cross-Channel ferry and lost. Indeed, about the closest I had ever come to being a seafarer was probably catching the shipping forecast on the radio late at night and thinking, Boy, I'm glad I'm in here and not out there.

I left Cundy's deep in thought. As I made the return journey south on the Woolwich Ferry I thought of the shipping forecast and the news bulletin I'd heard in the early hours of that morning. I was starting to realise just how much the forecast is part of the fabric of Britain. Those of us who don't work on the sea see it as a kind of poetry, almost a comfort blanket that the world is still turning as it should. Those who do put out to sea in craft large and small, the people who actually know what the announcer is on about, see it as something different, a friendly, helpful and above all useful voice. My grandfather would have listened to it. And by the sound of things, largely ignored it.

Yet familiar though the sea areas are by name

to the rest of us, and strangely comforting as their recital may be, few people give much thought to where they are or what they contain. The old pictures on Cundy's wall of ships departing for who-knows-where, with linen laundered by the scrubbed, shiny red hands of my own family, caused me to ponder how I could put right my nautical failings.

I strolled along the towpath back to Greenwich and parked at my favourite table in the Cutty Sark, looking out through the huge bay window at the Thames as the sun prepared to set. An idea was forming.

With a great-grandfather who once sailed to the Falklands by mistake (and became possibly the only man in British maritime history to be seriously wounded by soup), a mother born on the Woolwich Ferry and a grandfather whose boating misadventures left him on first-name terms with every lifeboatman in the South-east, there was only one thing for it: I would take more note of the shipping forecast than my ancestors and see the places it represents. Where were these curiously titled sea areas and what do they contain? These regions, mentally recited as soullessly as multiplication tables rote-learned at school, barged into my mind as I sat in my favourite boozer, and I felt sure that a little research would yield enough information to make an exploration of them worthwhile. Who, what or where was Utsire, of North and South fame? Who were

Fisher, Bailey and the most recent addition to the fold, FitzRoy?

Trawlers, container ships, barges, ferries, yachts, fishing smacks, lifeboats: the range of vessels that depends on an accurate maritime weather forecast is as wide as the ocean. What better way to continue the nautical legacy of my dock-watered bloodline than to explore the shipping forecast? I began to rue that I had never had my timbers shivered, barnacles blistered nor my deck pooped. To this hopeless landlubber Sole was what I had on the bottom of my shoe, Dogger Bank must be where golden retrievers kept their savings, and German Bight was something unpleasant contracted by my sleazier friends on a visit to Berlin.

Who on earth can hear phrases like 'low Latvia one thousand moving south-east and filling' and 'North Spain one thousand and thirty two losing its identity' and know what they actually mean? When I listened to the shipping forecast that night in my office my only claims to seaworthiness were the half-empty bottle of Captain Morgan in the kitchen and the battered copy of *Moby Dick* on my bookshelf. But out there somewhere on the swell were fishermen, trawler men, lifeboatmen and dredger skippers all tuning in, a range of sea-farers from the impeccably uniformed captain of a vast passenger ferry to the crusty old salt in his brine-spattered fishing boat, all of whom were depending on this strangely poetic mantra for their immediate safety.

My task was set. I would travel the shipping fore-cast, and I would do it within a year. It was October 17. Exactly one year hence, I decided, I would return to this table in the Cutty Sark pub situated at the heart of Britain's maritime heritage having conquered this broadcasting idiosyncrasy. I'd know how and why it's there, where it came from and what lies behind the mysterious names. It wasn't a voyage as spectacular or drink-fuelled as my great-grandfather's, but if I succeeded I could at least hold my head up as being a part of my family's nautical tradition.

I left the Cutty Sark that day with my mind full of lighthouses, fishing smacks and buoys. But to find out more about the shipping forecast than the sketchy list of names I had absorbed from the radio over the years, my first destination would not be a maritime one. I would have to plot a course to a place whose skyline is punctured not by masts but by office blocks. My ears would be assailed not by screeching gulls but by screeching brakes. My journey around the shipping forecast map would doubtless take me to some bizarre places, so a nondescript new town just outside the M25 provided a suitably abstruse first port of call.

A USER'S GUIDE TO
THE SHIPPING FORECAST

Try as you might, no matter how many times you listen to the shipping forecast, no matter how hard you concentrate, you won't ever hear a single mention of Bracknell. On a purely aesthetic level that pleases me greatly. Invoking the name of that tribute to the worst in British town planning doesn't really conjure up, say, the rolling blue against green of Shannon, nor is it as remote as Rockall (although after a couple of hours there you'll wish it was).

The extent of Bracknell's fishing industry is negligible unless you count tadpoles. Dolphins are rarely sighted. There is no cute, colourful quayside in Bracknell where you can have a pleasant summer pint watching boats bobbing in the water and small children being flipped over by mooring ropes. In fact, Bracknell's only real claim to liquid notability is as the home town of both Sharron Davies and David Wilkie, about whom you could say Bracknell is, heh heh, their 'alma water'.

Given its uncompromisingly landlocked location in Berkshire, just off the M4, and its status as the place where roundabouts go to die and where town planners should go to die – and quickly – Bracknell is as unlikely a place to start a voyage around the shipping forecast as you could imagine. Yet without Bracknell there would be no shipping forecast. Without Bracknell there would also be a lot of roundabouts milling around the countryside with nowhere to go, tramping over fields and dropping litter, but that is not something that concerns us here. No, it is Bracknell's vital importance to seafarers that had me striding purposefully through a soulless shopping centre dodging shiny-faced charity panhandlers in bibs while some children emptied a bottle of washing-up liquid into a fountain one overcast Wednesday afternoon.

Strange as it may seem, one can only imagine the chaos that might ensue in and around our waters if it wasn't for Bracknell and, more specifically, a very nice man called Martin and his small band of colleagues. This horrendous affront to architecture is the town the Met Office calls home, and it's from within an ugly office block reached via a graffiti-spattered underpass beneath a busy roundabout that the shipping forecast emanates.

Martin Rowley, a meteorologist of more than thirty years' standing, really is a very nice man. Quietly spoken and unassuming, Martin sits high up in a draughty, charmless building at a desk in front of four screens, each showing shifting weather patterns across the UK and Europe, and writes the shipping forecast we hear on the radio.

Having spent an hour or so in Martin's engaging company I left Bracknell with a deep sense of contented reassurance. This warm feeling was partly because I knew that it was unlikely that I would ever return to Bracknell as long as I live, but mostly because I knew that with Martin at the forecasting helm, the seafaring sons of Albion are in the safest of meteorological hands.

Martin had furnished me with a sheaf of papers, many annotated in his own handwriting, about its history, a bundle I read avidly while he put the finishing touches to his next forecast. It's more than eighty years since a specially prepared weather forecast for shipping was first transmitted in the UK. In fact it was in 1911 that gale warnings were first telegraphed to ships in the north Atlantic, but the origins of the shipping forecast go way back to the middle of the nineteenth century and the very foundation of the Meteorological Office. Indeed, the Met Office itself came about largely in response to the vast numbers of lives being lost in foul weather at sea, something that concerned Capain Robert FitzRoy greatly.

Most famous for captaining the *Beagle*, the ship from which Charles Darwin startled the world with his discoveries about evolution, FitzRoy was also the man who founded the Meteorological Office and the man directly responsible for the shipping forecast we know today. Born in 1805, the year of Trafalgar, FitzRoy was the second son of the second son of the third Duke of Grafton, the first Duke of Grafton having been the illegitimate son of Charles II. Keeping up? Good. His ancestors included a man described by Jonathan Swift as 'Grafton the deep, drunk or asleep', an admiral who instigated a sea battle with the French in the Caribbean on one of those rare historical occasions when Britain wasn't at war with France. Red-faced apologies were required all round. Another Grafton became prime minister, albeit temporarily, against his will and, apparently, accidentally. Politics was clearly a reluctantly entered arena in FitzRoy's family: an uncle managed to be an MP for twenty-five years without once rising to speak in the House of Commons.

Unsurprisingly, FitzRoy didn't fancy a career in politics, enrolling instead at the Royal Naval College in Portsmouth. As he was an excellent student, it wasn't long before he was being sent out to the Mediterranean and South America as a midshipman. So quick was his progress that FitzRoy was given command of the surveying ship *Beagle* at the age of just twenty-three, with orders to chart the coasts off South America.

Any excitement about this posting was soon dispelled when he discovered that his predecessor on the *Beagle*, a captain called Stokes, had committed suicide. When he boarded the ship for the first time and opened the log, FitzRoy found Stokes' last entry. 'The soul of a man dies in him,' it said. When he met the crew he found a jumpy, paranoid, sickly gang convinced that Stokes' ghost haunted the ship, and when the *Beagle* sailed for the first time under FitzRoy's command, it was into the worst storm for twenty years. The ship nearly capsized several times before running aground and drowning two crewmen.

On the bright side, things could only get better. And they did. The surveying mission was a success and FitzRoy won over the crew with his affable man-management and obvious gift for seaman-ship. FitzRoy brought four Tierra Del Fuegans home from the voyage in order to teach them Western skills, a dubious piece of anthropological research with mixed results. At his own expense FitzRoy planned to take them back again three years later, when he had the visionary idea of taking a naturalist with him. Volunteers were hard to come by, given the length of time at sea (five years, as it turned out) and dangerous waters involved, but eventually a young graduate called Charles Darwin was engaged and the *Beagle* sailed on December 27, 1831. Darwin and FitzRoy were not the only historically significant figures on board: the ship's hydrographer was a promising scientist called Beaufort, who would devise the scale by which wind speed is measured; the scale used by the shipping forecast to this day. It's only with hindsight that we appreciate the genius of FitzRoy. As well as his masterstroke in taking Darwin with him, an appointment that would change the entire course of natural history, and the presence of Beaufort, FitzRoy himself came up with a belter of a brainwave following an earthquake off Valdiria in February 1835. While the *Beagle* pitched and tossed on the swell, it was FitzRoy who deduced that 'tidal' waves were nothing of the sort, and it was the movement of tectonic plates that caused tsunamis.

When the *Beagle* docked first at Falmouth and then at Greenwich in October 1836, FitzRoy and the ship became immediate celebrities, the captain giving guided tours of his vessel on the Thames. He made it clear though that only 'respectable-looking people' could board via the accommodation ladder. The riff-raff had to take their chances climbing up ropes.

Perhaps against his better judgement, given the family history, FitzRoy accepted an invitation to stand for parliament as a candidate for Durham in 1841. Predictably, things soon went wrong. So soon, in fact, that the conduct of the election itself was called into question, resulting in FitzRoy being challenged to a duel by the man he defeated. Only a protracted exchange of letters and several frantic meetings between seconds prevented bloodshed. Two years later, however, FitzRoy was appointed governor of New Zealand. Like the *Beagle* commission, it was a tough job. Britain had never successfully subjugated New Zealand as it had its other colonial conquests, and it was known to be a lawless place involving shady dealings and even reports of cannibalism among the indigenous population. Although his governorship featured notable successes, FitzRoy alarmed officialdom in London by such outrageous acts as standing up for the natives in the face of harsh treatment by the settlers and generally acknowledging the native point of view, particularly when it came to land rights. It wasn't long before he was recalled.

Appointed superintendent of Woolwich Dockyard on his return, FitzRoy became a keen enthusiast for research into the application of steam power to ships, and was appointed to the Navy's first screw-driven steamship, HMS *Arrogant*, in 1849. A year later, however, he resigned, ostensibly on health grounds.

It was in his later years that FitzRoy made his most significant contributions to history. In 1853 a conference of leading maritime powers discussed the importance of meteorology at sea, and the British government allocated significant funds for research into weather prediction. All over the world, ships and lives were being lost in storms and gales, and as the shipping lanes became ever busier, the losses for want of weather information grew more numerous and more expensive. At the suggestion of the Royal Society, FitzRoy was put in charge and took to the job with energy and enthusiasm. The Meteorological Office was founded with FitzRoy at its helm.

He circulated new instruments among naval captains and collated their reports on humidity, wind, atmospheric pressure and temperature to compile charts of his own invention that he called 'wind stars', which showed primitive isobars. Soon he turned his attention to fishermen around the coasts of Britain, devising simple, easy-to-use barometers. Even the instruction manual he wrote in rhyming couplets for ease of memory.

When the *Royal Charter* went down in a storm off Anglesey in 1859 with the loss of all five hundred on board, one of more than two hundred vessels wrecked around Britain in just two weeks in the late summer of that year, FitzRoy's determination and frustration grew. He knew that more could be done to prevent such losses. The information was getting better, but lives would continue to be lost until that information could be disseminated quickly and efficiently. He set up twenty-four weather stations around Britain, which communicated their data to London via the new-fangled Morse code. From this information FitzRoy drew up the first synoptic charts, a method used to this day. The charts enabled him to give a fair estimate of weather patterns for the following couple of days and he issued these to the newspapers, which published the first 'weather forecasts', a term invented by Fitzroy himself.

Despite his herculean efforts, the forecasts were often inaccurate, and by the 1860s FitzRoy's health had begun to fail. He had lost his wife, Mary, in 1852 and his eldest daughter at sixteen, four years later. His mental health had also begun to suffer. Criticism of his forecasts served only to make him more stubborn in his resolve to succeed, but the frustration grew and grew. Finally, on April 30, 1865, FitzRoy went into the bathroom of his house in Upper Norwood, south London, and took a razor to his own throat.

It was years before FitzRoy attained anything like the recognition he deserved, but he is now held in the highest regard in meteorological circles. Martin and his colleagues are proud that when Finisterre was renamed in February 2002 it was FitzRoy whose name joined the shipping forecast.

'I know people were up in arms when the name changed, but there is no more deserving man than Robert FitzRoy, in my opinion,' said Martin. 'After all, he did start it all. And FitzRoy is now the only area on the shipping forecast map that is named after a person.'

Building on the pioneering work carried out by FitzRoy, meteorologists became more specific with their forecasts and by the time the shipping forecast first appeared in something approximating its current format, on January 1, 1924, forecasters were able to divide the waters around Britain into regions. At first there were just thirteen (going roughly clockwise from a 'midday' position on the British Isles they read Shetland, Tay, Forties, Humber, Dogger, Thames, Wight, Channel, Severn, Shannon, Mersey, Clyde, Hebrides): today there are thirty-one.

The bulletin, called *Weather Shipping*, was broadcast twice daily, at 9 a.m. and 8 p.m., from the Air Ministry in London with a range radius of some two thousand miles. Today it's broadcast on Radio 4 four times each day, at 0048, 0535, 1201 and 1754.

After some minor tinkering with the regions in the early thirties the service was disrupted for the duration of the Second World War. The explosion in British shipping traffic in the immediate post-war years necessitated a wider and more detailed forecast, and in 1949 it took the form with which we are familiar today. Indeed, the only changes to the sea areas since then have been the renaming of area Heligoland as German Bight in 1955, the introduction of North and South Utsire in 1984 and the renaming of Finisterre as FitzRoy in 2002. The names of the areas may seem incongruous to most of us, but to mariners there is a clear logic to them. Some are obvious, like Faeroes, Hebrides and Dover. Others are less so, but take their names from features that would be familiar to seafarers. Areas such as Bailey, Dogger, Viking and Fisher are named after sandbanks, for example, with Dogger coming from '*dogge*', an old Dutch word for fishing boat.

'We've come a long way from handwritten telegrams to coastal stations,' said Martin, gesturing at the hi-tech set up arranged in front of him.

'Knowing how important the shipping forecast is to mariners, there are strict rules that we have to follow. A new forecast is produced every six hours and the areas are always written in exactly the same order, starting with Viking and proceeding around

Britain in a broadly clockwise direction to South-east Iceland.'

Because of the strict timings at the BBC, Martin and his colleagues have to ensure that the forecast is as close to 350 words as possible, 370 for the late-night broadcast, which includes Trafalgar. The only exception is during winter when there are often strong winds in the west of Scotland, with forces ten and even eleven levering tiles from roofs, uprooting trees and playing havoc with hairpieces all across the Highlands. It strikes me that Scottish toupee wearers might be the forecasts' most avid winter listeners. It's in such extreme conditions that Martin and chums can use extra words as long as they notify the Beeb in advance.

'Although it sounds complicated the shipping forecast is very broad,' said Martin, intruding on the images of airborne wigs soaring over the Trossachs that were occupying my mind. 'All we do is give people an idea of wind speed, visibility and the prevailing conditions in each area. Anything more specific would be pointless really. Once I've written it the whole thing is checked meticulously before we e-mail it over to Broadcasting House, then it's out of our hands.

'All of us who write the shipping forecast are conscious of its significance. I come from north Cornwall, a seafaring coastline where everyone is aware of it. It's always been broadcast on easily available channels, from the old BBC Light Programme to Radio 4 today, and it's slipped almost imperceptibly into the national conscious-ness.

'Obviously Bracknell isn't a maritime location, so when I'm writing it I do try and imagine I'm taking a trawler out of Peterhead or on a ferry in the Solent. When I read my words back I wonder how it'll play to those people as, after all, it might have a great effect on the rest of their voyage. Yesterday, for example, we could have put gales up for Dover but didn't because it would have changed the oper-ating patterns for the ferries. If we're overcautious then the ferry companies would cancel all their services when they don't really need to.

'So although the sea isn't crashing against the windows over there, we are aware that we're doing more than just arranging certain words in a partic-ular order.'

No one has seen the changes in forecasting tech-nology over the last thirty years more than Martin Rowley. He wasn't quite delivering handwritten telegrams to coastal stations, but certainly remem-bers the storm cones (large canvas tubes hoisted at coastguard stations to indicate gale warnings) that were phased out by the seventies, something devised by FitzRoy himself more than a century earlier. But in these days of the Internet and satel-lite transmissions, is there really a future for the shipping forecast on mainstream British radio? Does anyone actually listen to it for the reason it's intended?

'Well, sometimes I think the BBC might like to

take it off,' he muses. 'It interrupts the commentary of the test cricket, for example. But there are people who still use it, and even the best satellite systems can go down, so it's vital that the information is freely available, albeit just as backup. The broadcast has probably become less important in recent years but I don't see it disappearing for that reason.'

As I negotiate the maze of underpasses and walkways back to Bracknell station I realise that in that very nice man, a man so nice that he named his personal meteorological website in tribute to his family's recently departed budgie, I have just met a poet. Martin Rowley and his colleagues may be restricted in the words they can use, but the phrases they slot together are blank verse of a mysteriously evocative nature. Even Seamus Heaney has used the shipping forecast as the basis for a poem, and I can't think of any other broadcasting mantra that has slipped into the public consciousness in the same way. Unless you start venturing into Pugh, Pugh, Barney McGrew, Cuthbert, Dibble, Grubb territory, and let's not do that.

The shipping forecast is evocative modern verse. That's why poets have borrowed from it, and why it's been chosen more than once as a Desert Island Disc. Now what I needed to do was visit the people who impart the solemn stanzas into our kitchens and cars. And, thankfully, that didn't involve going anywhere near Bracknell.

★   ★   ★

A few days after meeting Martin, I found myself disappearing into the art-deco wraparound façade of BBC Broadcasting House, a building whose exterior is actually reminiscent of a giant ocean liner, off Oxford Street in the centre of London. As soon as you enter reception the chaos of central London evaporates and you're taken in by an air of calm and benign confidence. In fact, if you're ever in the centre of London and are worried about something, I can heartily recommend a few minutes of aimless wandering around in Broadcasting House reception; it's like losing yourself in an enormous reassuring cuddle and you'll be right as rain in no time.

I'd come to see Radio 4 announcer Jane Watson. Jane had generously agreed to let me sit in with her on the noon broadcast of the shipping forecast as long as I promised not to get in the way or shout contentious political slogans from the corner of the room or anything.

'The midday forecast sees Jane break off from FM and take herself into long wave,' explained her boss, David Anderson, while Jane pored over the forecast printout from the Met Office. 'Now, she has exactly four minutes to run through the news bulletin and the shipping forecast, and then has to introduce the next programme at exactly the same time as the FM announcer. So she's got to read and listen to someone else at the same time to make sure they finish together, which is quite a skill.'

Eventually I was led into the studio where Jane sat at a huge console. She greeted me with a friendly smile and gestured at me to sit down. We had a few minutes before noon, so we chatted for a while about addressing the nation's seafarers.

'The way you read the shipping forecast varies depending on what time of the day it is being broadcast,' she told me. 'This one is quite fast and businesslike because it comes straight after a news bulletin and we only have three minutes by the time you've done the news headlines. Late at night it's a longer shipping forecast anyway because we have the coastal reports to do as well, so that one tends to be slower and more gentle. In some ways it shouldn't be, because if it was strictly for the people who need it, the people on the ships, you'd read it in the same manner all the time. In fact someone told me the other day that no sailor in his or her right mind would depend solely on listening to the shipping forecast, so maybe one reads the late-night broadcast as something for people to go to sleep to.'

Jane's favourite time to broadcast is the late-night edition that goes out at 0048. I realised that it was Jane's voice I had heard the night I'd been up late working and first began to think about the shipping forecast in a context other than childhood dinner gong.

'I think about everybody going to bed,' said Jane. 'I read it much more gently than the daytime broadcasts, and it's lovely, a time when the forecast is at its most poetic, whereas this one at midday is really just, Here it is, watch out, here comes the weather.'

The 0048 broadcast is the only one preceded by a piece of music, a snippet that has become synonymous with the forecast. The rising and falling cadences make up *Sailing By* by the twentieth-century British light-music composer Ronald Binge, who scored more than fifty films and television programmes for the BBC. Curiously Binge, a confidant of Mantovani, originally wrote the piece to accompany film of a hot-air balloon gliding over the Alps.

'Obviously you never totally forget the ships,' continued Jane. 'I'd never drift off into complete whimsy, but I do think that the people on the ships are tired and might need a bit of comforting as well. Especially in the winter, when the gales are really strong. You often get gale, force eight and severe gale nine, then sometimes storm force ten, violent storm eleven and hurricane force twelve. I think in the eight years I've being doing this I've had one hurricane force twelve and I was genuinely concerned. Even with violent storm eleven, which is quite common during the winter, the very words are disturbing. But I think that's still quite comforting for people at home, because they're tucked up in bed and they're hearing that it's absolutely blowing a gale somewhere out at sea.

'The names are fascinating too. I think as people are going off to sleep they try to picture those places. It always amazes me how interested people are in the shipping forecast. They often say, "Oh, I always used to listen to that when I was little," or "My dad has it on in the morning and it wakes him up." It's like pressing a magic button.

'I think it's poetry. It's not just a question of reading a list of words, you really have to let it flow through you. Without exception everybody who reads it loves reading it, and I think it's because we probably feel quite privileged to do it.

'Another interesting thing is how it comes up all the time on other programmes. I heard it once on *Prime Suspect* when Helen Mirren was getting up in the morning; it was there to let you know she was getting up at a certain time. It was even on *Floyd on Fish*. You can tell when they've got an actor to do it, because it's not quite the way it should be done. It's been on a rap record, *Desert Island Discs*; it seems to be one those things that people seem to hold dear. It even turns up in Alec Guinness's diaries, apparently. There are poems too: 'Shipping Forecast Donegal' by Sean Street, which was read out at Laurie McMillan's memorial service, is an absolutely beautiful piece.'

It seems then that the people who really hold the shipping forecast dear are people like me: people with no connection to it whatsoever. Since my moment of mild epiphany in Cundy's I'd made a point of listening out for it, but clearly there are stronger aficionados than me. Jane told me that she receives letters from people telling her she's read it too quickly. Or sometimes too slowly. When she first started reading, there was heated debate and correspondence about the pronunciation of the word 'temporarily' (it's 'temprally' rather than 'temp-or-airily', apparently). While proving that there are people who really have far too much time on their hands, this also demonstrates how the shipping forecast has immersed itself into broadcasting culture and onward into British consciousness. Indeed, Jane agrees with Martin Rowley that strictly speaking its broadcast isn't as important as it used to be.

'In all probability the shipping forecast doesn't actually need to go out,' she said. 'It's just become part of the BBC fabric. We get lots of letters about how we read, but these aren't people from ships, they're usually people miles even from the coast. But we certainly don't want it to end and I don't think it will because there would be an absolute outcry.

'Part of the appeal is its mystery, the names and curious phrases like "rain later, good". How can that be? We read it so it makes sense, but realise that many people aren't listening for that; it all rolls into one.'

By now the clock had ticked around towards noon and Jane gestured at me to don the headphones. I slipped the cans over my head in time to hear the lead into the news and, having reached below the desk and pushed the button that divides long wave from FM, Jane began to read the news headlines. Then the familiar mantra commenced:

> And now the shipping forecast issued by the Met Office at 1130 on Tuesday . . .

Jane had furnished me with a copy of the forecast and marked off the points where she should be at every thirty seconds in order to finish on time. I looked at the studio clock and she was bang on every one.

It was a strange feeling being present at the recital of something so familiar. A bit like being on the roof of the Apple building with the Beatles, or sitting at a Fawlty Towers dinner table watching John Cleese mentioning the war once but thinking he got away with it all right. Yet here I was, parked barely four feet from Jane while she enunciated, 'Thames, Dover, Wight, south-westerly veering north-westerly five or six, decreasing four. Rain then showers. Moderate with fog patches, becoming good.'

People may find their hands flying to their mouths when I say this, but the shipping forecast is not actually as complicated as it sounds. Each area forecast is divided into three sections: wind, weather and visibility. Hence in the 'Thames, Dover, Wight' forecast above, the first part gives the wind direction and speed (bit of a stiff breeze in this case. It's only when you get up to eight on the Beaufort Scale that you start telling people

45

it's going to be a bit tasty out there). The second part predicts the weather (a bit wet as it turns out, cows will be lying down) and finally there's the visibility forecast (bit foggy, but should be all right later, probably once the rain stops). 'Moderate' means you can see for about five nautical miles, 'good' means you can see beyond that and, in this case, could probably wave at French people. The forecast begins with gale warnings for areas that should expect winds of force eight and above, before a general synopsis of the weather approaching from the Atlantic, quoting pressure in millibars. Then we settle back for the area forecasts.

Although this was Jane's 'businesslike' rendition, with little room for aesthetics, the familiar phrases retained their lilting quality. It was roughly when Jane was revealing how Rockall should expect rain later, good becoming moderate, that I nearly fell off my chair in alarm. Suddenly, through the headphones, someone began calmly to describe how British men's tennis hopes had been scuppered again in some tournament somewhere. I sat bolt upright with a start. Jane must be getting this too, surely? Were there people at sea twiddling with their dials as rain lashed the wheelhouse window looking for weather news instead of how a skinny bloke with too many teeth can't hit a ball over a net properly? I didn't know how I'd done it but I knew this had to be my fault. I hadn't touched anything, I'd sat quietly in the corner, double- and triple-checking every thirty seconds that my phone really was switched off, yet somehow I had ruined the shipping forecast. My mouth was opening and closing in horror. I looked at Jane. 'Faeroes, north-west backing south-east three, increasing five or six,' was all she had to say. What a pro, I thought, but no sooner will she finish the forecast than she'll calmly take off her headphones, lay them down in front of her, gather her thoughts for a moment, then lunge across the desk for my throat.

Some golf news went through my right ear, while in my left I heard Jane announce that South-east Iceland should expect 'occasional rain, good becoming moderate with fog patches'. My mouth was increasingly dry, expecting violence later, dead by five or six, good. I tried to stand but felt as though my legs would buckle under me. I could have been imagining it but I'm sure I felt the cold, steely stare of the ghost of Lord Reith on the back of my neck. I was mortified.

There was a moment's pause before in perfect unison I heard the disembodied voice in my ear and Jane say, 'And now on Radio 4 it's time for *You and Yours.*'

Of course. I'd been so full of the fact that I was actually sitting there while the shipping forecast was read out I'd forgotten the warning that the FM broadcast would cut into Jane's rendition. I hadn't brought down one of the last bastions of broadcasting after all, and the cold sensation on the back of my neck wasn't the accusatory glare of a long-dead peer, it was just the air-conditioning.

The cold sweat disappeared, Jane shook my hand and I promised to send her a postcard from each area. My legs eventually stopped trembling. Getting to North Utsire would be a piece of cake after this.

VIKING, NORTH UTSIRE, SOUTH UTSIRE

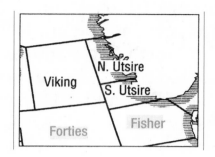

North Utsire and South Utsire are the smallest of the sea areas, and lie off the south-western coast of Norway. Formerly part of the Viking region, North and South Utsire are named after the island of Utsire and were added to the shipping forecast map in 1984, isolating Viking in the central northern part of the North Sea.

The North Sea. For me, the name itself conjures up swelling mounds of black water crested by foam and pockmarked by rain. It carries none of the attraction of the Caribbean Sea, with its clear, light-blue water scattered with shimmering sunlight, nor any of the mystery of, say, the Sargasso Sea. No. This is a sea, and it's in the north. No mucking about.

It's a stroppy old sod, the North Sea. Stormy and heavily tidal, it's also shallow. Only north of the Shetlands does the depth reach a hundred fathoms. Over Dogger Bank the depth subsides to as little as fifty feet, and by the time you get towards the Strait of Dover you couldn't sink St Paul's Cathedral, even in the unlikely event of you wanting to. The North Sea pounds the east coast of Britain, knocking great lumps out of it when and where it can. Two and a half miles of coast-line have disappeared since Roman times, accounting for some thirty towns and villages. Take Ravenser, a town that stood at the mouth of the Humber and was once so significant it returned two MPs. Gone. Claimed by the North Sea sometime in the early sixteenth century. Dunwich in Suffolk was once a thriving town and one of the most important ports in England, boasting six churches, a monastery and even a mint. All gone, a new village having sprung up further inland. Half a mile of Suffolk has been pilfered by the North Sea since the fourteenth century.

The North Sea surge of 1953 took three hundred lives from the east coast between Lincolnshire and Kent, flooding twenty-four thousand homes and making forty thousand people homeless as high tides and fierce storms combined on one of the North Sea's grumpiest ever nights. Even today, the North Sea eyes the British coastline and thinks, Hmm, I'll have some of that. In 2003 protesters against a coastal road in Sunderland pointed out that the sea would claim it in fifty years anyway. And in the first three years of the current millennium, the sea encroached upon Winterton-on-Sea in Norfolk by sixty yards, making the village's name more apposite than it might seem.

The North Sea also provided passage for the invaders who plundered the British Isles after the Romans left, most notably the Vikings, who would paddle enthusiastically across it in their longships and set about stealing, looting, raping, pillaging and burning anything or anyone in sight from the end of the eighth century until William the Conqueror put a stop to such shenanigans. Hence the first sea area of the shipping forecast bears the name of the people who were the first to cross it.

The North Sea has also produced good things, however. The fact that so many key European rivers empty into it has made it a vital trading pool. It's also been a fertile fishing ground, although that's something increasingly under threat, and provided key reserves of natural gas to benefit Britain and Norway in particular.

We get on better with the Norwegians these days, now they've stopped paddling across the North Sea, setting fire to our roofs and generally throwing their weight around. Indeed, Norway is now a highly civilised place, where fewer people live than live in London, yet Hammerfest in the north is as far north of its capital Oslo as London is of Rome. Norway also boasts one of the most beautiful (and

51

lengthy) coastlines in the world, and it was on a small island off that coastline that I began my journey into the shipping forecast.

I'd set myself a few rules for this odyssey. I determined to visit the areas in the order in which they are broadcast, but I knew I'd not be able physically to get to all of them so I would visit those in which there was somewhere to go. There is no landfall in Viking, Dogger, Forties, Rockall or Bailey, for example, meaning that the first destination on the list had already thwarted me. But I surmised that as I would cross these regions by boat or, more tenuously, by air at some point on my odyssey, then strictly speaking this meant that I would at least spend time in each area. Hence my first trip was to a small, bleak island off the south-western coast of Norway, one that few people could pinpoint on a map but one whose name is more familiar to most of us than some of the islands off our own coasts.

There aren't many places where you would pay £25 for a bowl of shrimps, the chance to see a comedian at whom you will laugh not once and a covers band with an unconventional take on the lyrics of popular songs and then leave feeling as though you've had a thoroughly good time. Particularly if as part of your twenty-five quid's worth of fun and frolics you'd had to take your own booze. But then there are probably not too many places in the world like Utsire. Stumbling through the fearsome wind and pitch darkness looking for my bed after the idiosyncratic night on the Norwegian tiles described above – adopting an unsteady arms-outstretched gait not dissimilar to that which served Frankenstein's monster so well – it suddenly dawned on me that I was on one of the most unintentionally famous islands in Europe. As soon as I thought this I cracked my shin against a rock and fell on a sheep. I was also on one of the darkest islands in Europe.

The only place to warrant more than one mention in the shipping forecast, Utsire is a tiny island roughly fifteen miles off Haugesund, populated by 240 hardy souls. Officially Norway's smallest community and just four square miles in size, this rocky outcrop in the North Sea is an unlikely candidate for broadcasting immortality. But after spending an eventful weekend on its rocky surface I can assert with some confidence that it deserves it, for Utsire is as fascinating as it is windy, and Utsire is very windy.

It's certainly more fascinating, not to say considerably more windy, than Haugesund, a coastal town roughly halfway between Bergen and Stavanger among Norway's south-western fjords. If I tell you that Norway's first ever death from a drug overdose occurred in Haugesund that might give you an idea of the ambience of the place. If you ever have cause to spend three hours there, as I did on my way to Utsire, you'll not be surprised to discover that the reason most people come to Haugesund is in order to leave again.

Having been transformed from sleepy fishing village to medium-sized town on the back of the nineteenth-century herring boom, Haugesund's harbour became the major departure point for Norwegian émigrés, most of whom headed for the United States in the early part of the twentieth century. I didn't know it at the time, but emigration would become a major theme of my journey around the forecast. Today Haugesund is a busy ferry port on the Stavanger-Bergen-Trondheim route, as well as serving both Newcastle and Utsire.

A local baker called Martin Mortensen was just one of many thousands who crossed the Atlantic via Haugesund in the 1920s. On arrival he changed his name to that of his profession in order to assimilate, married and had a daughter whom the Bakers named Norma Jean. She went on to become Marilyn Monroe and the rest, as they say, is conspiracy theory. Martin didn't see much of his daughter's rise to celluloid immortality, however, as he had been killed in a motorcycle accident when the fledgling film goddess was still a baby. The Haugesund baker's claim to paternity is still a fevered topic of debate among Marilyn fans (there was apparently another Martin Mortensen who may have also married Marilyn's mother, or something), but the story is good enough for the burghers of Haugesund. Good enough in fact to have them erecting a statue of Marilyn and painting her image on the front of the coastal ferry even though she never went anywhere near the place. Well, when your only other alumnus of note is Harald the Fair-haired who died at the end of the ninth century, you're going to latch on to any bit of reflected celebrity you can. I know I would. And frequently do.

Marilyn Monroe paternity pilgrimages aside, there are probably only two reasons why you would ever find yourself in Haugesund. Either you're travelling to Newcastle in a particularly roundabout way or you're heading for Utsire. Now, at this point I should point out a slight inconsistency between the shipping forecast and Utsire. Despite twenty years of BBC weather reports to the contrary, Utsire's inhabitants still labour under the misapprehension that the name of their island is spelled 'Utsira'. They can argue until they are blue in the face (which after an hour or so in Utsire's biting gales most people are), but centuries of documents, not to mention family trees dating back to the 1700s, wash with neither the BBC nor me. For the purposes of this narrative, Utsire it is. So I allowed myself an exasperated sigh and roll of the eyes when a small blue car ferry nosed around the headland bearing the name *Utsira*, docked in front of me and set down a ramp. Will these people not be told?

I have to confess to being a little wary of the crossing to the island. I had sought assistance in planning the trip from my friend Mike, whom I had asked one night whether he knew anyone who spoke Norwegian and might be able to help me with some research. Mike thought hard about this for a week or so before telling me shortly before departure that alas, no, he didn't know any Norwegian speakers. Which was a pity, he said, because being half Norwegian himself and thus fluent in the language, he would like to meet someone of similar linguistic ability to help keep his hand in. Mike read up about the crossing, and the news wasn't good – it appeared the waters between Haugesund and Utsire were among the roughest in the North Sea.

'If you are not used to boat trips then this could be a traumatic experience, but most of the time the passengers get by,' said one website with a shrug.

'The ferry trip is an adventure whether the weather's good or bad,' was the cheerful message on another. 'When storms toss the water, it's fascinating to watch the waves.'

Now even I could read between the lines here, and I take everything anyone ever tells me at face value. Gingerly I boarded the vessel, noting with some alarm the racks of sickbags in strategic places around the walls of the passenger lounge and the proudly framed newspaper account detailing a local shipwreck and dramatic rescue from 1937. Only impressive self-control stopped me from looping my arm and head through a lifebelt and lashing myself to a pillar with ropes.

I sat down nervously at a table and turned to the travelling companion I had brought with me to share this oddest of odysseys. Reaching into my inside pocket I pulled out a cracked, yellowing old photograph of a young man in military uniform that suggested First World War vintage. It was a head-and-shoulders portrait whose subject wore a thick army shirt a couple of sizes too big and a wide-brimmed hat, the left side of which was pinned up against the side of the crown. His large, mischievously twinkling eyes looked just past the camera and the slightest hint of a smile tugged at the corners of his mouth beneath a moustache that looked as if it was putting up a struggle but reluctantly staying just under control. This was Harry, my great-grandfather. No one is sure, but it seemed likely from his clothes that the photograph had been taken on his epic voyage, the one that ended with him hitchhiking back from the Falkland Islands. On the back, written in a firm, almost copperplate hand, presumably his own, are the words 'If you see this young chap wandering in London, treat him well.'

It seemed like a good motto for my journey if you substituted 'London' with 'windy places in the north Atlantic' and Harry, I felt, would make an appropriate travel mate. I thought about his hungover jaunt to the south Atlantic and realised that my own predicament was nothing by comparison. I vowed to pull myself together and returned Harry to my pocket.

As it turned out, the crossing was, by local standards, a gentle one. The odd downward lurch aside, no worse than driving over the brow of a hill, the gentle motion of the waves had a lulling effect that was more likely to send me to the Land of Nod than the Kingdom of Neptune.

As we prepared to disembark just over an hour later, a huge bearded man in blue overalls appeared. 'Are you English?' he ventured. This was Toralf, the man whose holiday cottage I would be renting. It turned out that Toralf was also the skipper of the *Utsira*. 'Are you a birdwatcher?' was, curiously, his next question. Birds, it seems, are the key attraction for visitors to Utsire. There are more species of bird on the island than there are people and the Utsire bird observatory is a thriving concern that brings in most of the community's visitors. The absence of binoculars, tripod, dandruff and beard probably made me quite a curiosity.

Utsire is a monument to hardiness. Its people live strung along the centre of the island, north to south, where there is a little shelter from the incessant wind thanks to hills to the east and west. There is evidence of settlement on the outcrop dating back to 2000 BC, and there has apparently been a permanent human presence on the island since the third century AD. Utsirans, or 'Sirabu' as they prefer to be known, presumably to make them sound less like bad guys from *Star Trek*, make up a proud, independent community. Such is their remoteness that people in Haugesund have trouble understanding their accent and even taunt them for being bumpkins (as if Haugesund is some kind of funky throbbing metropolis). Fishing and farming have been the island's major economic mainstays but the former has all but died off over the last half century or so. Whereas in the years following the Second World War Utsire boasted a community of nearly five hundred people and forty trawlers, today the population has halved and just two fishing boats are based at the island's man-made harbour to the north. Yet still the traditional families remain as they have since records began in the 1730s: the Klovnings, Kvalviks, Hovlands and Austrheims, the latter being the clan that produced the giant Toralf who now stood before me.

Toralf said that his son Tor would meet me at the harbour and drive me to Sjølyst, the cabin that would be my home for the weekend. And, sure enough, as I disembarked a huge cloud of dust followed a battered brown Toyota to the quayside at an impressive velocity. Tor had arrived. Square of jaw and late of teen, Tor unfurled his gangly arms and legs from the driver's seat and opened the boot of the car for my bag; through the rear window of which peered a football scarf reading 'Liverpool FC – Anfield'.

Tor set off at breakneck speed along the main road and before long we were at Sjølyst in the south-east of the island. He showed me into the cabin and advised me that tonight was party night at the Old Schoolhouse: Utsire Football Club was having its annual knees-up and I'd be very welcome. Oh, and I might want to bring along some drink if I was coming as there was no bar.

I heard the Toyota engine gun and was able to follow the cloud of dust across most of the island as it took off at supersonic speed. I felt a bit like Wile E Coyote watching Road Runner get away again and hence expected a delivery in a box marked 'Acme' at any moment. Darkness had begun to fall as I opened the fridge, which cast an apologetic puddle of weak light over my feet. The fridge was indignantly empty and it was clearly time to search for provisions. The cabin was self-catering and I had failed so far to cater for myself.

The sun sank beneath the horizon and the lights of Haugesund winked on in the far distance as I headed up the gravel track in search of the road. The roaring wind buffeted my progress and caused the sea to boil away to my left in huge fans of spume. The tarmac wound between enormous rocks and the wind whistled tunelessly through the coarse, flattened grass. Somewhere in the distance a rope clanged against a flagpole like the vigorous ringing of a church bell. A couple of lights in the distance betrayed the presence of houses and, hopefully, a shop. The island has just one, but I knew it was near here somewhere. It had to be: everything on Utsire is near here somewhere.

Naturally when I found the shop it was shut. It was around 4.30 on a Saturday afternoon, but the shop had closed barely half an hour earlier and would reopen promptly on Monday morning at 9 a.m. – when I would be on the ferry back to Haugesund. Faced with the prospect of nearly two days without food or drink I was remarkably calm, beating the shop windows with my fists in frustration for only a few minutes and sitting outside the door sobbing for little more than an hour. I decided to press on. Through his fine preparatory translation work, Mike had found several words for 'remote', 'weather' and 'windy' relating to Utsire, but none that roughly equated to 'bar', 'trattoria' or 'award-winning pizza'. Nevertheless I struck out northward into the wind in search of somewhere, anywhere, that might sell me stuff I could insert into myself to stay alive.

After twenty minutes of making slow progress into the wind and watching the darkness fall around me, I found a big, newish building that seemed to be some kind of civic office and community centre. There were no lights on but a sign in the window looked promising. I pulled out my small Norwegian phrasebook and leafed through its food pages with a feverishness only the imminently hungry can achieve. The wind taunted me by whipping the pages back in the opposite direction but I emerged victorious after a short struggle. There was a restaurant on the island, and it opened in two hours. My whoop of joy would have carried for miles on the easterly gale and had people all along the east coast of Scotland looking up from whatever they were doing and raising their eyebrows quizzically at each other. Unfortunately the notice didn't tell me where the restaurant was. However, the combination of my phrasebook and another notice told me that if I did go to the football club jolly-up, there would be shrimps.

I had passed the Old Schoolhouse earlier so had the advantage of knowing where it was. The restaurant, inviting though it sounded, could have been anywhere. Being Norwegian, its prices would also have been whoppingly expensive to an English pocket, whereas the shrimps were complimentary, or at least covered by my twenty-five smackers. I might even be able to stuff a few into my pockets for breakfast the next day. And lunch. And dinner. Oh, and breakfast on Monday morning too. The wind was deafening me, not to mention hindering my progress (in every direction I turned, somehow), and as it was now dark I decided to cut my losses and go for the shrimp option. It was now six hours since a startlingly priced hamburger at Bergen Airport had failed to satisfy my curmudgeonly stomach. It was also about five hours since I'd eaten the chocolate I was given on the connecting flight between Bergen and Haugesund – quite possibly the shortest flight I have ever taken. There was barely time for the stewardess to unbuckle herself after take-off and sprint up the aisle flinging chocolates around before we started descending and she had to throw herself back into her seat and buckle up again.

By the time I had returned to the cabin it was soon time to depart for the Old Schoolhouse and the evening's festivities. There being little in the way of streetlighting on Utsire it was stupidly, unnecessarily dark. There was really nothing to be gained from it being as dark as this, except possibly instant death by strolling off a cliff. Surely if we can put a man on the moon and a chicken in a microwave we can somehow set up satellite floodlights? After a few hundred yards of nervous groping in the wind I was alarmed by a tremendous commotion somewhere in the whistling darkness ahead. Suddenly a fiery-eyed beast came roaring and snorting over the brow of a hill towards me. I fled to the side of the road to let this hellhound pass but instead it shrieked to a halt beside me and sat there, growling menacingly.

'Jump in,' shouted a vaguely familiar voice. It was Tor in his Toyota, accompanied by an enormous bearded friend swigging from a bottle of clear liquid, kindly come to give me a lift to the Old Schoolhouse. I climbed into the back seat as Tor shot off into the night, and I swear the car was actually airborne for most of the journey.

'Did you bring some drinks?' he asked, turning alarmingly to face me from the driving seat as a succession of telegraph poles flashed past in the headlights. With uncharacteristic forethought I had, in the light of Norway's rumblingly huge alcohol prices, brought supplies with me from Gatwick.

'Yes I have, thanks for the tip-off,' I replied, before shrieking, 'Look out!'

Out of the darkness I had seen the pale, frightened face of a cyclist appear fleetingly in the headlights before flinging herself sideways into a ditch. Tor and his friend found this hilarious.

'He killed two on the way over to you,' laughed the man with the beard. I think he was joking.

At the Old Schoolhouse I cheerfully handed over the equivalent of £25 and wandered into the hall, a large wooden high-ceilinged building that seemed to sway in the fearsome wind. With hindsight, before that night I don't think I'd ever paid £25 to see anything. Just three days earlier I had shelled out less than half that amount to see Scotty Moore, Elvis's guitarist, and got to shake his hand afterwards – the hand that played the guitar break on 'Heartbreak Hotel'. All I'd be closing my hand around on this occasion would be freshly caught shrimp, but by now I was so hungry I'd have happily handed over the deeds to my house in order to get my pinkies on quivering crustaceous flesh.

The wooden hall was filled with tables and chairs, dimly lit by candles. There were football shirts, shorts and socks pinned up around the walls, there was a stage at one end of the room and a long table across the back clearly intended for Tor and his friends. On each table was a basket of bread and a bowl of shrimps so large you could have dived headlong into it and comfortably won a game of Olympic-standard hide and seek. Tor and his cronies were clearly the in-crowd so, ever keen to be a hanger-on, I sat at an adjoining table. I asked Tor, who it turns out plays in central midfield, if the island's football team is any good.

'We used to be,' he said. 'The advantage we had was that the crossing to get here is so rough that all the teams would arrive very seasick. We would always beat them and won lots of trophies. Then the other teams complained to the league and now we have to play all our matches on the mainland. These days we don't win anything.'

The place filled up quickly, but the best table at the front remained empty. I got to work on the shrimps, emptying flimsy shells faster than a fish-wife. The cold bits of pink flesh slid down my throat with machine-gun regularity. My hands must have been a blur. Just before I disappeared completely behind a pile of husks a hush fell over the room, and in strode a large bearded man in a suit, his long dark hair slicked back from his forehead. It was Toralf, who strode to the table at the front accompanied by various members of his family. Clearly, he's an important man in these parts. With Toralf safely ensconced in what is the closest you'll get to a royal box in Utsire's Old Schoolhouse, a lugubrious man with a hangdog expression took to the stage. This was the comedian. Naturally I understood not a word, but concerned as I was with inserting as many shrimp as possible into my frame in order that I might make it through to Monday morning, I wasn't too fussed. The pile of husks had now reached my chin. The comedian was going down well, but not half as well as the shrimps. I have to say, freshly caught shrimp washed down with an Australian chardonnay is a satisfying combination, and never more so than when you're on a windy rock in the middle of the North Sea and there are no other foodstuffs on your personal horizon for the next two days.

By the time the comedian had left the stage and the band had creaked into gear I was so full of shrimp you could have covered me in Thousand Island dressing, laid me on a bed of lettuce and used me as the opening course at a wedding reception. And then the fun really started. The wind whistled around the building, rattling at the window frames, while a rainstorm battered against the panes like gravel being thrown on to a tin tray. But inside the Old Schoolhouse the people of Utsire, this tiny exposed rock in the middle of the fiercest seas north of Biscay, rejoiced in the warmth. The band played for four hours, no less, and the room was filled with whirling figures, their rosy, shining faces caught in the candlelight, eyes flashing and laughter rising above the music. Gasping, frantic conversations came and went and a woman whisked me from my seat and whirled me around the floor for several minutes. Given that I dance about as well as a herring plays the harpsichord this was a selfless act on her part that seriously threatened the well-being of her toes. The band played 'Heartbreak Hotel' and I pointed out to anyone who would listen that my right hand, here, this one, had just three days earlier shaken the hand of a man who played on the original. They pretended to be impressed.

My shrimp-'n'-chardonnay-fuelled attempts at shaking my booty in a lithe and groovy way had not gone unnoticed. As I threw some impressive shapes, skidding occasionally on the odd bit of discarded seafood, Tor bopped towards me. 'You know what?' he shouted above 'Wake Up Little Suzie', 'I really admire people like you who can get up and dance so embarrassingly!'

The four hours passed in a flash, as if Tor had put them on the back seat of his car and driven them around the island for a bit. Eventually the band finished, the candles guttered and died in their holders and the lights came on. The floor was awash with spilled drinks and shrimp husks and the air swam with laughter and farewells. Then I was invited to a party and before I knew it was in somebody's house. Once we'd gone inside (having all taken off our shoes in the manner of the politest of housebreakers) I asked whose house it was but no one seemed to know; its occupant wasn't there. But how did we get in, I asked? Oh, no one locks their houses here, there's no crime on Utsire.

Somebody told me that there are no police on the island. Not one single officer of the law. Crime is almost non-existent, but should there be a misdemeanour the islanders take it in turns to sit on the culprit until the next available ferry. The rapscallion is then escorted on to the boat to be picked up by waiting police at Haugesund. The briefest thought of Toralf sitting on Jeffrey Archer flashed through my mind, but was gone before I could really enjoy it. A tall youth came over wanting to talk football. English football is hugely popular in Norway and this lad, a little the worse for drink by now, professed relentlessly that his heart belonged to Everton. Such was his devotion to the Toffees that the following weekend he was taking the ferry to Newcastle in order to have an Everton crest tattooed over his heart. How a Geordie tattooist might have reacted to this assignment I am keen to learn. I conjured up the image of a wincing Norwegian boarding a ferry at Newcastle the following weekend, gingerly protecting an Everton badge perfectly illustrated except for the motto 'Sir Bobby's Toon Army' in place of the Toffees' Latin inscription *'nil satis nisi optimum'*.

Everton pointed out a number of Liverpool fans around the room, expressing his contempt for them by referring to Liverpool as a 'cesspit'. 'I'm proud that in my heart I come from Everton,' he said. I couldn't bring myself to break it to him. His low opinion of Liverpool supporters and the labelling of their home town as a cesspit soon became his sole topic of conversation, and it took a while but I managed eventually to extricate myself. But not before I had learned the wonderful news that Everton's mum worked in the shop, and it would be opening for a short time at about noon the next day.

More shrimps came out, but I couldn't look any of them in their lifeless black eyes. Instead I fell into conversation with a schoolteacher from Stavanger called Wenche (which is pronounced 'venker' incidentally, not as if it should be preceded by the words 'comely' and 'serving'). Wenche was on the island for the weekend visiting a friend with whom she'd studied who was now teaching at the school on Utsire. As she had a twenty-four-hour advantage over me in terms of Utsire experience, I asked what she made of the place. Fortunately we were about the only two people in the room sober enough to hold a conversation that didn't involve labelling British cities repeatedly as cesspits or shouting slurred, spittle-flecked nonsense into each other's ears. Even more fortunate for me was that Wenche spoke perfect English, chiefly the legacy of having spent a year in suburban Surrey working as an au pair.

'Before I came to Utsire I had heard a few things about the place,' she told me. 'I think that the island is sometimes mentioned on the weather forecast. And my father, who's originally from Haugesund, has always told me that it's really beautiful here. I think this is what most Norwegians know about Utsire. Having been here for a day now I have to say that my father is right. The scenery is absolutely beautiful, with the ocean visible from almost any angle. And it's windy. You don't have to go far here to get the impression that you're completely alone in the world.'

Wenche told me that she found the people on the island to be very friendly; typical of a small Norwegian community.

'There's certainly less stress here than on the mainland,' she said. 'Everyone knows each other and they know everything about everyone. It's quite relaxing to go to the shop without having to consider what you're wearing or whether you remembered to brush your hair when you got out of bed. Comfort and warmth come before everything else, which, of course, is sensible.'

Could she live here on the island?

'I don't think I would be able to live here for a long period of time,' she mused. 'It's a beautiful, deceptively spacious place but I don't think it's for me. Maybe if I'd been born here I'd think differently. And if I didn't know the meaning of the word "variety". That's a joke, by the way.'

Before long it had become indecently late so I bade farewell to Wenche and ventured out into the night in search of Sjølyst. As the pool of light from the doorway diminished behind me and the darkness was cleaved only by the beam from the lighthouse sweeping above my head, the roaring wind seemed to carry two words to me from behind. I couldn't be too sure, but they appeared to be 'Liverpool' and 'cesspit'.

Back at Sjølyst I gazed out of the window at the choppy silver path that led across the water from beneath the cabin all the way to the moon. The lighthouse beam swept round from behind me and disappeared out to sea and by the time it returned I was asleep, dreaming of candles and dancing.

The next day I had an important appointment: high noon at the shop. I was there on the dot but the place was still locked. My knees almost gave way. Nothing so much as a cup of tea had passed my lips since draining the last of the wine the previous night. There was, however, a handwritten note stuck to the inside of the door that announced the shop would indeed be open today, but for half an hour from 2.30. Another note gave the opening time of Dalanaustet, the restaurant, as noon on Sundays. It also told me where it was, on the north side of the island, so off I set.

Walking along the road I passed nearly all of the island's amenities, the school, the cemetery and the civic centre, which also doubles as a sports hall and houses Utsire's swimming pool. The cemetery, reached from the road by a long path, is situated some distance from the church, presumably because the rocky nature of the island meant that this location was the only place where it was possible to dig deep enough for graves. The same names adorned the stones: the Klovnings, Hovlands, Kvalviks and Austrheims.

Before long I had found Dalanaustet, a pleasant wooden building on a man-made harbour next to where the *Utsira* docks. Brightly coloured boats bobbed gently on the water, the sunshine enhancing the blues and reds. I pushed open the door and was instantly encased in warmth. The smell was an intoxicating mixture of old wood, fresh coffee and hot meat, while my only fellow diners were an elderly group of four at a far table. Around the walls were pictures of old Utsire, including a photograph from the 1870s of the harbour under construction and a picture from the 1950s showing a fleet of fishing boats lashed together, some fifty in number.

On the menu was a plate of pork, potatoes, vegetables and gravy washed down with coffee. Perfect, and no matter that this combination set me back £16. Within seconds I had inhaled the contents of my plate and was lingering over the coffee watching the sun on the water. The woman who served me and who evidently ran the place was the woman who had whirled me around the dancefloor the previous night. She turned out to be Toralf's sister-in-law, and, to my relief, did not appear to be limping.

Which set me to thinking. There is one shop and one restaurant on the island, one community centre and one ferry, yet 240 people live here. Whatever did they do? Some perhaps commuted to Haugesund, but the fishing industry here is now, alas, nothing to speak of, the two boats and two small fish-processing plants aside. Clearly the islanders were not poor (I later discovered that many of them were away at their Spanish holiday homes that weekend), but there was surely not much for them to do here? At that moment the door opened and a bookish-looking man walked in whom I remembered from the party the previous night. He recognised me, waved, ordered his lunch and came to sit opposite me. Atle Grimsby works at the bird sanctuary, and although not a native Sirabu is a man clearly in love with the island and his job.

'Utsire is Norway's number one bird-site and I'm a birder,' he told me with pride. 'In 1992 when I finished my studies, there was a vacancy here on Utsire, and I got my dream job. People have been coming here to study the birds since 1921. In fact it was an Englishman named Chatsworth Musters who put Utsire on the birding map when he predicted and found six new species for Norway and Utsire. The young residents helped Musters collect the birds, so there has always been a strong link between the community and birdlife.'

Having paused briefly to wish that I had a name as tremendous as Chatsworth Musters, I wondered whether it was easy to adjust to living on the island compared to the mainland.

'Yeah, there was no problem at all. I came out here as a single man with no worries except perhaps keeping one eye on the clock and the other on the ferry timetable! Now I'm married to a local girl and we have three kids. You need to plan trips to the town, and make sure you have plenty of spare parts just in case something goes wrong, but otherwise it's easy living on Utsire. I love the birds, the Sirabu, it's a wonderful place for children and the landscape is beautiful.

'People do a variety of things here: fishing, maritime jobs offshore, administration, the school, care for the elderly and farming, so it's a busy community. The young people have sports, nature and fishing to keep them occupied, and they all seem to like it here. Some do get bored, but you find bored youths on the mainland too. There is a bit of gossiping behind people's backs. It's not a huge problem, I just try not to be a part of it.'

Typically, given that I only had to be somewhere at a certain time once during the entire weekend, I dallied so long in my post-lunch chat with Atle that I almost forgot about the shop. It took a forced march of considerable velocity to cover the island's length just before the shutters came down again, and provisions were secured from Leif Klovning, Norway's 1999 Shopkeeper of the Year. I'm not kidding. The islanders celebrated the accolade by gathering outside the shop en masse and serenading him with a version of an old Europop classic suitably amended to 'Leif is Life'.

I had to leave Utsire before dawn broke the next morning. I took my final walk across the island from North Utsire to South Utsire in darkness and silence. The moon was out and I could see stars behind stars behind stars. The light from the *fyr* swept overhead, as a light has done here for more than 150 years, silently, efficiently, keeping watch over the sleeping islanders.

The bright lights of the ferry shone in the distance.

FORTIES, CROMARTY, FORTH

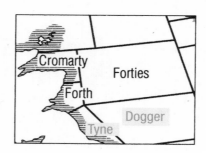

Area Forties is one of only seven names to survive from the original shipping forecast map of 1924. Originally it covered most of the northern North Sea. It reduced slightly in size in 1949, then further when Viking was introduced to the north in 1956. Like Viking it used to stretch as far as the Norwegian coast until the introduction of the Utsires, but now has no land boundaries at all. Area Cromarty stretches along the coastline of north-east Scotland from John O'Groats to Aberdeen, meeting Area Forties out at sea. Area Forth continues down the coast until it meets Area Tyne just south of Berwick-upon-Tweed and, like Cromarty, meets the western boundary of Forties.

There is probably a good reason why the words 'sexy' and 'oilrig' rarely appear together. There surely aren't many people who could find the thumping great legs of an oil platform, with its hotchpotch of cranes and charmless buildings topped by a skeletal tower, even remotely alluring. Wordsworth would not have eulogised them in verse. Constable would have taken one look at an oilrig and made a mental note to stick to haywains. Oilrigs are functional, designed purely to suck the fossilised remnants of ancient trees from below the sea bed with the minimum of fuss, not sit there up to their thighs in water looking all cute. Hence no one was more surprised than me to find my breath whipped from my lungs in admiration of one of the North Sea's finest as I stood on Cromarty waterfront one still and silent evening on the north-east coast of Scotland.

My shipping forecast mission had got off to a lively start: Utsire had set the bar high in terms of quirkiness, not to mention contributing significantly to the average wind speed of my forthcoming journeys. The wind was calmer in Scotland, variable three or four according to that morning's forecast, but it was a dark night on the Black Isle.

I had just arrived on a bus driven at such speed that I blinked and almost missed the picturesque village of Cromarty looming out of the gloaming of a wintry dusk. Given the velocity with which the bus had propelled a small group of shoppers and myself from Inverness, I half expected to be shot out of the doors as it took a sharp bend, straight through Cromarty and out to sea, skimming across the surface of the water like a pebble. Fortunately the driver managed to throw out the anchors and halt only a few hundred yards beyond the stop. Once the smoke from the tyres had dispersed and the sonic booms of the bus getting back up to speed had bounced around the hills in the distance, I was able to commence a haphazard amble in search of my hotel.

I wandered through the heart of the small town, a charming hotchpotch of tiny streets and ochre Georgian cottages, in search of a grand old harbourfront pile called the Royal Hotel. Although much of the coast further east had been battered by storms the previous night and the nearby town of Elgin submerged by floods, the weather was calm, with not a breath of wind to tease the musky woodsmoke easing from every chimney. It was very quiet and the streets were totally empty. Cromarty's position on the headland at the very tip of the Black Isle means it is surrounded on three sides by water; hence no through traffic and no noise beyond my own footsteps and the distant sound of the waves breaking gently on an unseen shore.

So far it was all very picturebook. The streets were dimly lit beneath the dark skies. Narrow lanes led down to the waterfront, soft light tipping out of cottage windows on to the pavement below. Inside, brass kettles hung over huge brick fireplaces and glinted softly in the firelight. There was an almost tangible air of contented benevolence. There didn't seem to be anyone around though – maybe this was all a front and the entire population of the isolated village was out in the woods stripped naked, torturing squirrels and smearing their torsos with squirrel blood while wearing crowns of twigs and chanting incantations in an incomprehensible ancient language.

Rounding a corner to the waterfront, however, I was greeted by one of the most startling sights I think I have ever seen. Out in the firth, barely six hundred yards from where I was standing, was a full-scale oil platform lit up with dazzling orange and white lights like an enormous floating birthday cake. A few hundred yards further on was another, identical construction. Having expected to have my breath taken away by rolling hills and snow-capped peaks I had been stopped dead in my tracks by an oilrig. There in the dark stillness, as I watched this brilliant display of technology and light, it struck me that these hulking behemoths picked out against the hills beyond were probably among the most beautiful things I have ever seen. A faint thrumming emanated from them, barely audible above the apologetic lapping of the waves on the pebbly shore beneath me, the tiniest vibration that I could only just feel deep in my chest. As a display of awesome beauty and power this was hard to beat. After this, Cromarty had a lot to live up to.

The Royal Hotel is an ancient sprawling building on the harbourfront, all beams and undulating floors, the sort of place where walking from your bed to the bathroom makes the wardrobe doors on the other side of the room rattle. Come to think of it, there may actually have been someone trapped inside. Maybe I should have checked. After a hearty meal of local Black Isle lamb, eaten alone by a roaring fire in the hotel restaurant, I returned to my room and pulled the curtains on the now strangely reassuring constructions in the harbour. The mouth of the Cromarty Firth is protected by the Sutors, two hills that are purported to be the slumbering forms of two giant shoemakers who had protected Cromarty from ancient pirates and Vikings in centuries past. But on that crisp, clear winter night it was the gentle throbbing of the twin giants a few hundred yards from my window that made me feel protected, alone in a strange bed hundreds of miles from home.

I left the hotel the following morning and watched as the sun came up from behind me, warming the autumnal reds and yellows from the dark hills opposite that blended with the leafy rust colours of the platforms. Cromarty, I would discover as I walked around the village, is a difficult place to pin down. A cursory examination of its history reveals an impressive propensity for reinvention; the town has been variously an important fishing port, the site of impressive proto-industrial factory work, a naval base, and now sits close to the heart of the oil-platform construction and maintenance industries. It has been in turns impressively rich and chronically poor. Yet despite this chameleon development, Cromarty retains a pleasant, welcoming demeanour and a strong sense of community. It's known good years and bad, prosperity and penury, yet every time this small town on a remote headland has come up against another existence-threatening economic challenge, it has bounced back stronger. You can almost feel the sense of pride and satisfaction in the air. The people you pass in the street or who sell you your newspaper have a tangible air of confidence. There's a stubbornness about Cromarty that runs through the generations.

Cromarty first came to prominence in medieval times when travellers progressed along the east coast on a series of ferries. Robert the Bruce and James IV of Scotland are just two regal Scottish figures who purportedly journeyed north on the Cromarty–Nigg ferry, which perhaps inevitably became known as the King's Ferry. Today two motorists at a time can make the crossing on Britain's smallest car ferry service.

It was in the late seventeenth and early eighteenth centuries that the town truly began to flourish as an important trading centre for fish and grain. By the end of the eighteenth century Cromarty, a royal burgh, had hit boom time. A successful businessman named George Ross bought the Cromarty estate, investing a huge amount of money into the town and turning it into one of the great economic successes of the Scottish Highlands. He built a handloom factory to work hemp brought to the town by ships from St Petersburg which would arrive with Russian snow still on the decks. A brewery, new harbour and courthouse were also constructed using Ross's money, not to mention the sumptuous Cromarty House built on the site of the old Cromarty Castle.

Before Ross built his pile, the most famous residents of the castle had been the Urquharts, several of whom were magnificently bonkers. One early Urquhart, for example, lived for several years convinced he was actually dead. Every night his bed would be wheeled into the courtyard and winched up to battlement level by a series of pulleys so that it might be easier for his maker to come and spirit him away in the night. Despite this apparently foolproof method of contraception – I can't imagine Mrs Urquhart was too enamoured of her husband's morbid alfresco nights – he and his wife reputedly produced thirty-six children, the poor woman. The best known Urquhart, however, was Thomas, who lived in the mid-seventeenth century. Thomas was the first man to translate Rabelais into English and indeed did it 'more Rabelais than Rabelais himself' according to Bernard Levin. He was also a total fruitcake. Among other things, Thomas claimed to have traced his family tree right back to Adam and Eve. Although his Rabelais translations remain in high regard, his other writings were so eccentric as to be practically impenetrable. Making up words on the spot didn't help. 'Amblygonosphericalls', 'extrinsecall', 'grediftal', 'bagrediffiu', 'pubkegdaxesh' and 'obliquangular', for example, all appeared in the space of one paragraph in his book *Trissoetras*, and none was ever heard of again. Flushed with etymological creativity he tried to start up his own language in his 1653 book *Logopandecteision*. It didn't catch on. Thomas, knighted by Charles I in 1641 – although no one seems to know why – was present at the Battle of Worcester and fled to Holland after the English Civil War where he is reputed to have died laughing on hearing of the restoration of Charles II. Alas the castle in which these terrific characters lived, slept and went cheerfully nuts is no more, demolished in the 1770s and replaced by Cromarty House.

One man who knows more about the culture of Cromarty than most is David Alston. The curator of the Cromarty Courthouse Museum, local historian, author and also a district councillor, few have a more encyclopaedic knowledge of Cromarty than he does. He is one of those most valuable of people: a historian committed to local history and the possessor of a startling intellect, most of which has been devoted to the town in which he arrived seventeen years ago. His enthusiasm for Cromarty fills the room as soon as he walks in, and he speaks briskly and urgently as if his mouth can only just keep up with the information his brain has to impart. He's a busy man, which meant he had a window of barely twenty minutes in which to see me, something I discovered via a mobile phone call while I was out walking on the Sutors. Hence I had to practically sprint to the courthouse, arriving sweating, panting, and with my shoes and jeans spattered with mud.

'Cromarty's heyday was probably between about 1770 and 1830,' he tells me, politely overlooking the muddy footprints I've left across the carpet in a room high up in the eighteenth-century courthouse, 'but for various reasons, including the fact that the herring-fishing industry collapsed and that the railway was built through Dingwall and Invergordon rather than Cromarty, it went into a period of fairly substantial decline after that. The town went from being an important centre of communication to being cut off from the development of the rest of the region fairly swiftly.

'That's partly why Cromarty has survived in such an unspoiled form; it's a tremendous example of a Georgian town and has avoided development. Really it wasn't until the coming of North Sea oil in the 1970s that there was any kind of development so we rather fortunately missed out on some of the architectural monstrosities of the 1960s, for example.

'Hugh Miller was born here in 1802. He was famous for many things but mostly as a journalist. It's his writing about life here in the nineteenth century that combines with the unspoiled architecture to make Cromarty a valuable place in which to reconstruct that period.'

Miller is Cromarty's most famous son. Fêted by

contemporary luminaries like Charles Dickens, Miller's star faded mysteriously in post-Victorian times. A remarkably versatile man, this son of a Cromarty sea captain was a pioneering geologist, church reformer, journalist and key chronicler of life on the Black Isle during the first half of the nineteenth century. He was almost entirely self-taught, certainly in terms of geology, and his giant frame topped with a shock of red hair was a common sight in the fields and on the shores of Cromarty as he carried out his research. His father had been a Cromarty sea captain who had drowned when Hugh was five, an event which saw the family sink into poverty. Hugh became a stone-mason and travelled widely in Scotland, but it was Cromarty that he held closest to his heart even when living in Edinburgh as editor of the Presbyterian newspaper the *Witness*. It was in Edinburgh that Miller shot himself in 1856 at the age of fifty-four. Some attribute his suicide to an inability to reconcile the growing evidence for evolution with his strong belief in the Book of Genesis, but most apportion the blame to some kind of brain disorder, possibly a tumour. Miller had complained that his 'brain was burning' in the months leading up to his death. As a tragic foot-note, the revolver Miller had put to his chest to kill himself was returned to the dealer whence it came, where it went off accidentally while being cleaned, killing the foreman gunsmith. Both funerals took place in the same cemetery on the same day.

Miller's influence is still strongly felt in Cromarty, and he is the key draw for visitors to the village. A month before I arrived, Cromarty had marked the bicentenary of Miller's birth with an international conference and a number of events designed to restore his name to its former prominence. A commemorative stone had been erected on the links in front of the town, and a specially commissioned children's opera staged. The National Trust-maintained cottage where he was born is one of Cromarty's key attractions, while his statue sits on top of an impressive column high up by the old Gaelic chapel, looking out to sea and providing seagulls with a startling vantage point which they probably don't appreciate.

That morning I'd sat on the links by the firth, close to Miller's stone. Erected to commemorate the thousands of people who emigrated from Cromarty – sixty-four ships left in 1831 alone – the inscription describes an emigrant ship passing the place where I sat. Written by Miller, it reads:

The *Cleopatra*, as she swept past the town of Cromarty, was greeted with three cheers by crowds of the inhabitants, and the emigrants returned the salute, but, mingled with the dash of the waves and the murmurs of the breeze, their faint huzzas seemed rather sounds of wailing and lamentation, than of a congratulatory farewell.

Much has been written about emigration over the centuries, but few can have captured the emotions of those leaving and those left behind so succinctly as Miller has here.

'In addition, the site next to the Royal Hotel is what they call a proto-factory, dating from the part of the industrial revolution before mechanisation,' David continued. 'Here hemp would arrive from St Petersburg and the Baltic ports and would be processed ready for transportation to London where it would be made into sacking. At the time, these were the biggest buildings of their type in the United Kingdom.

'When you look around modern Cromarty though, you have to say that although it's got this historic ambience, it's managed to avoid being twee; it's quite a gutsy place.'

I spent the afternoon back at the Royal, reading some of Miller's work in books lent to me by Neil Campbell, the hotel's amiable owner, who had suggested I speak to David in the first place. So engrossed did I become that darkness had already begun to fall when I remembered that there was still one thing I needed to see before I left Cromarty: the grave of Sandy Woods. For Sandy Woods, although he had lived an unremarkable life, epitomised for me the bloody-minded stubbornness that has maintained Cromarty through the centuries. Sandy had lived in Cromarty in the latter half of the seventeenth century, spending many years in a fearsome dispute with a neighbour over a boundary between their properties. The two men argued for decades, and so entrenched did the argument become that Sandy asked to be buried outside the cemetery, close to the road. That way, he surmised, when the Day of Judgement came he'd be able to get his side of the story in before his opponent. As a display of taking an argument to its furthest possible conclusion it could not be bettered.

The light was failing as I walked east, out of the town itself, in search of the now abandoned St Regulus' cemetery on the far side of Cromarty House. The lights on the oil platforms in the firth were picked out sharply as dusk fell. Before too long I found the old plot shrouded by low-hanging, melancholy trees and a rusty old iron fence. The graveyard was in a poor state of repair, with most of the tombs rendered illegible by moss and lichen. I passed through a gap in the fence and wandered in silence for a while among the long grass between the stones. Many of the plots were substantial family affairs containing several generations of noble Cromarty residents. Although they retained a certain dignity, the stones were lopsided and overgrown, with great-great-grandfathers leaning against mossy descendants for support.

At one end of the cemetery the iron fence was lying flat on the ground, bent over at the base as if it had given up trying to mark the boundary of the abandoned burial ground and fancied a long lie-down. I stepped over the ancient ironwork and began to examine the undergrowth. The grass was damp and slippery and I skated around the sloping earth in search of Sandy Woods. In the tangle of bracken and coarse grass there was little to go on but the hope of eventually tripping over a big slab in the undergrowth. And indeed, after a few minutes' scrabbling and shuffling, I stubbed my toe hard against something about six yards beyond the cemetery boundary near the road. Admirably restraining myself from swearing loudly and at length, by scraping back some undergrowth I found a six-by-three stone tablet almost perfectly camouflaged with moss and criss-crossed with coarse long grass. There was no hope of reading the inscription but this had to be it. Sandy's final resting place. Somewhere below my feet, deep in the cold Cromarty clay, lay the remains of a man biding his time until the day arrived when he could finally prove that he'd been right all along. It had been more than three hundred years now, but his old bones were still poised for the moment when he could finally say, 'I told you so.'

I entertained brief hopes of scraping away the moss so Sandy's inscription could greet the sky once again, but it had been centuries since anyone tended this tomb. Any significant restorative work was certainly beyond me, but I made the cursory gesture of pulling away some of the longer grass before leaving Sandy in peace. I stood at the base of his grave looking across to the gloomy silhouettes of the tombstones beyond and remained for a few minutes, quietly impressed by the strength of spirit, exemplified by Sandy Woods, that had kept Cromarty alive, frequently against substantial odds. As I turned to leave, for a split second I thought I could hear the impatient drumming of Sandy's fingers somewhere beneath my feet.

I left Cromarty the next morning and headed down the east coast for Arbroath, a coastal town in the Forth region. I knew little of the place beyond the fact that ever since I'd first shown an interest in football I'd been able to tell people that the world record football score was Arbroath 36 Bon Accord 0 in a Scottish Cup tie in 1886. If that wasn't enough to warrant a visit in itself, I was also going in search of lighthouses and smoked fish. I'd phoned ahead and booked into a guesthouse, in front of which I arrived in the early evening. It was a dark, freezing night and the wind whipped in from the North Sea as I rang the doorbell. Nothing happened. I rang it again. Still nothing happened. After a while I rang the bell for a third time and a man in a vest with a roll-up cigarette in his mouth answered the door.

'Hello,' I said, 'I've got a reservation here.'

'Doesn't bother me, pal,' came the reply. 'I'm a resident. I was just getting fed up of you ringing the bell.' And with that hearty welcome he was gone. I stood there in the hallway for a few minutes, still not time enough apparently for me to realise that Arbroath in winter was not a popular tourist destination and there were likely to be other beds available in the town, until a large woman appeared. 'Who are you?' she barked. I gave her my name and told her I'd made a reservation. She gave me a disbelieving look, as if I'd just claimed that W.C. Fields had appeared to me in a dream and told me to go to an Arbroath guesthouse and fill every room from floor to ceiling with Brussels sprouts. 'Really?' she asked, with unnecessary suspicion. 'Well, yes,' I replied. She moved sideways to a low table on which sat a large diary, not once averting her gaze from mine. She opened it, glanced down, ran her finger along the page, and slammed the diary shut.

'Hmm, okay,' she said. Phew, I thought, I'm in. She led me up a flight of stairs and along a narrow corridor thick with cigarette smoke and the blare of televisions from behind closed doors. She showed me to my room, which was just big enough for me, my bag and the bed to all fit in at once as long as the first two items were on top of the last. Stale cigarette smoke pervaded the air and the bedclothes, and it was a choice between leaving the window closed and choking to death or opening it and dying of hypothermia. The woman left me to it and I attempted to make myself at home, which was certainly a challenge. I'd arranged to meet a man about a lighthouse that night and so went across the corridor to the bathroom for a shower. I pulled the cord to switch on the light and discovered that the bathroom had clearly been the recent location of a murderous

91

brawl. A wooden chair lay on its side, filthy towels were scattered around and there was blood on two of them. I should have left there and then, but I'm British and don't like to make a fuss. And anyway, I'd booked.

One brief shower later, on the way back from which I noticed a paperback book lying on the dresser in the corridor titled *Well-Schooled in Murder*, ulp, I waited outside the guesthouse to meet David Taylor, a man who knows more about the Bell Rock Lighthouse than is probably good for him. Looking younger and sprightlier than his sixty-five years, David picked me up in his car and asked if I'd eaten. I hadn't. 'Well, Nessie and I have had something already,' he said, 'but I'll tell you what, we'll go back to my house via the fish and chip shop and you can pick up something there.'

Fifteen minutes later I was walking into the home of a couple I'd never met before carrying a greasy paper parcel of fish and chips. At the dining table David's wife Nessie had laid a single place complete with a huge plate loaded with bread and butter, a full range of condiments and a pot of tea replete with cosy. The warmth of their welcome matched the warmth of the house on this cold winter's night on the east coast of Scotland. After my bizarre introduction to Arbroath hospitality at the bed and breakfast, I could have hugged them both for the welcome they'd given this lonely stranger far from home. They repaired to the living room to allow me to eat a fantastic fish supper in peace before David returned to talk lighthouses with me.

Like David Alston in Cromarty, David Taylor performs a valuable service. His website dedicated to the Bell Rock Lighthouse, which stands repelling the sea and the weather eleven miles from the coast of Arbroath, contains every possible detail pertaining to the construction and maintenance of this remarkable feat of Scottish engineering. Now retired, David keeps a second home in Arbroath while living mainly in Edinburgh, devoting much of his time to chronicling the history of the Bell Rock light.

'I have a personal link to the Bell Rock, which is the oldest working lighthouse in the world, incidentally,' he told me. 'My great-great-great-grandfather, Captain David Taylor, was master of the *Sir Joseph Banks* tender during its construction, and later commanded the supply vessel the *Smeaton*. In later life he took up the post of lighthouse storekeeper in Leith, and I have a great affection for the light as a result.

'Of all the terrors known to mariners navigating the east coast of Scotland in olden days, the Inchcape Rock, better known as the Bell Rock, was probably the most notorious,' he told me. 'The fear of striking it was so great that probably more ships were wrecked on the neighbouring shores trying to avoid it than actually struck it. It's basically a treacherous submerged reef, situated in the northern reaches of the Firth of Forth, and lies directly in the way of shipping approaching the River Tay and Dundee. It was given the name Bell Rock because according to legend, the Abbot of Aberbrothock once placed a bell on the rock to warn nearby ships. Apparently a notorious pirate called Ralph the Rover cut down the bell, only to be wrecked himself there a year later. Southey wrote a poem about it.'

I was amazed to learn from David that the Bell Rock, like most other Scottish lighthouses, had a remarkable literary connection. The Northern Lighthouse board, which okayed the building of the Bell Rock light, was largely comprised of members of the Stevenson clan, one of whose number was Robert Louis Stevenson.

'It's hard to emphasise just how important the Stevensons were to the safety of mariners, and not just in Scotland,' said David. 'In the space of five generations they were responsible for the design and construction of ninety-seven lighthouses around Scotland. They were also responsible for supplying many of the world's greatest lights, for building harbours, roads, bridges and railways, deepening rivers and constructing canals, and in their heyday had an international reputation as consultants. It is a little incongruous that of all the members of this family, the one who should be best remembered is not one of its engineers but Robert Louis Stevenson.'

As someone who has trouble standing on a chair to change a lightbulb, I could appreciate the problems involved in building a lighthouse on a rock eleven miles out to sea. Particularly one covered by the tide twice a day. It took four long, grim years to build but despite the hardships and logistical problems, aside from a new light room in 1902 the structure standing today is the same as that constructed nearly two hundred years ago. It was almost eighty years before the light failed for the first time, and it's survived two fires, machine-gun and bomb attacks and being struck by an RAF helicopter in 1955, an accident that killed the crew of the aircraft. And that's before you even consider the storms and heavy seas it's had to contend with for nearly two centuries. You can't even possibly hazard a guess at the number of lives the light has saved.

We got back into David's car and headed off. 'I want to show you something,' he said. We drove to the outskirts of town and parked in a deserted car park facing the sea. The white tips of the waves showed faintly in the darkness and the wind gently rocked the car. 'Look out there,' said David, pointing across me to my left, 'and you'll see it in a moment.' I stared into the blackness. Seconds passed, then suddenly in the far distance a tiny pinprick of light appeared and then vanished. 'Did you see it?' asked David, his eyes flashing with excitement.

'Yes,' I said, 'is that . . . ?'

'That's the Bell Rock!' he told me with pride.

'There, after all the talk you've actually seen it now.'

We drove off again and parked outside the Foundry Bar. David had suggested we get there early as the famous Foundry Bar musicians were playing that night. We did so, and found ourselves to be the only customers. The elderly accordionists and fiddle players had got through a fair few tunes before others came in to join us. Around the bar were black and white photographs of various vintages, all of which showed the same musicians in their younger days sitting in exactly the same places:

The next morning dawned cold and dark. It was around ten thirty before Arbroath enjoyed anything close to being described as daylight, but fortunately it was light enough for me to find Scott's Fish in a narrow lane close to the harbourfront. I wanted to learn more about the famous Arbroath smokie, and Campbell Scott, a diminutive, bespectacled man in a David Coulthard baseball cap, knows more about the town and its smoked haddock than most.

Walk around the harbour in Arbroath, particularly in the late afternoon, and your nostrils will fill with the musky smell of smoking fish from the smokehouses. Arbroath's smokies are famous the world over and Scott's Fish is one of the prime exponents of this ancient art. Like Arbroath itself, however, the smokie business is feeling the pinch.

'Tourism's died off a bit here,' Campbell told

me when I asked about Arbroath. 'It used to be a popular spot, people would come here for their holidays. We used to get a lot from the west of Scotland, Glasgow and surrounding areas, because Arbroath is their main seaside resort – Billy Connolly lost his virginity in an Arbroath caravan park – but then the arrival of package holidays abroad meant that tourism declined from the seventies onwards. Also, the main bus routes don't pass through here any more. There is talk of doing the harbour up and turning it into a marina, but whether that'll come off we'll just have to wait and see.'

Scott's Fish was begun by Campbell's father in 1964, and Campbell has worked here since the age of ten, a career now spanning some thirty-five years. He runs the shop with his brothers and sister; a genuine family business.

We walked through a doorway draped with heavy strips of plastic and into a room at the centre of which was a giant table where the fish are prepared for smoking.

'The smokie originally came from Auchmithie, a wee village just outside Arbroath,' he told me, 'where it was the fishwives that did all the smoking and the working of the fish. They used to carry their husbands on their backs out to the boat so that they wouldn't get their feet wet for fishing. The wives would work the fish when they came back, so basically the husbands just went to sea and caught the fish and the women did the rest.'

We moved out to the back of the shop, where a large smokehouse stood. The remnants of a fire were glowing on the floor, the fire that had smoked that morning's catch, while long wooden slats lay across the top, over which the fish were hung.

'Originally, barrels would be sunk into the ground, and the smokies would be hung on wooden sticks after being headed and salted for curing. Then a hardwood fire would be lit in the barrel, and the fish would be smoked for an hour, or an hour and a half. A few years ago we had a bit of a problem with Europe; they were trying to get us to use metal sticks. That was totally impractical because the heat that's generated would make metal too hot to pick up – we won that battle, I'm pleased to say, so we can still use wood.

'At the moment we're trying to get a trademark registered, a bit like the French cheeses, to trademark the "Arbroath Smokie". If it's successful then you'll have to be within a thirty-mile radius of Arbroath to call them that. There are a couple of companies down south who sell smoked fish to supermarkets and call them Arbroath smokies but really it's just fillets, not the whole fish at all. Anybody who knows a smokie will know that it's not the real thing, but what worries us is that people might try it and think, So that's a smokie? What's all the fuss about?'

The decline in the fishing industry off the east coast has taken its toll on Arbroath, and Campbell's family firm is one of only a few still producing the traditional smokie. As recently as twenty years ago there were forty or fifty family merchants in Arbroath, and the majority would work from a smokehouse behind the family house. They'd smoke the fish, load it up in their cars and drive around areas that didn't get fresh fish and sell to the locals. A sort of 'creels on wheels' service, if you like.

'My father started that way,' said Campbell. 'He'd drive up to Aberdeen in a Volvo estate, load up with fresh fish, which we'd smoke then drive around the countryside selling. At weekends the car would go back to being a family vehicle.

'I go out two or three times a week in the van and sell to housewives in the area. Most people around here won't buy fish from the supermarket because it's just not the same quality. We can guarantee that if it's caught on, say, a Tuesday, it will be smoked and on your plate by Thursday. We've also started up a mail order service through our website and we're sending smokies all over the world. It's a different world altogether from selling fish out the back of a car.'

But for all the international expansion of Scott's Fish, the crisis sweeping Scottish fishing was looming over Campbell's business like a vast black shadow. He told me of a meeting coming up in the European Union to set the fishing quotas, the subject of the report I'd heard on the radio back in London.

'If Europe closes down the Scottish fishing industry

we might as well just close the door overnight,' he said. 'They work really hard on the boats with no guaranteed reward; they're a different breed. The problem they have now is finding young lads to crew the trawlers.

'As recently as fifteen years ago this was a busy port with twenty, thirty, maybe forty working fishing boats sailing out of the harbour here. Now I think there are three boats registered in Arbroath and they sail out of Aberdeen. The town's still quite busy, but they lost a lot of other industries, factories and so forth, as well. Unemployment's quite high in Arbroath at the moment.'

As I left the shop, with two large shrink-wrapped packets of smokies and two slabs of the most delicious smoked salmon under my arm, I walked back towards the harbour with a feeling of melancholy. There was a real sense of a town dying here, and with the European Union fisheries directive imminent, I could feel a disillusionment hanging over it, as if the people were just waiting for the axe to fall. For all Campbell Scott's terrific efforts at moving with the times, if there's no fish then there's nothing for him to send off to Canada by international courier. To stem such morose thoughts I went for a lunchtime pint in the Smuggler's, a cosy pub on the harbourfront, and waited to meet an old university friend.

It was quite a coincidence that Julie, whom I'd not seen for a good ten years, had moved to Arbroath just before I arrived. She and her Arbroath-born husband Clive and their two children had moved in temporarily with Clive's parents while they waited for a new house to be built in Glasgow. She burst through the doors of the pub and gushed greetings, but announced they couldn't come in as the pub didn't allow children. It was a long way from the days when a group of us would meet in the student union bar at around this time and spend the rest of the day skulling pints before descending to the bowels of the union dancehall and dancing spastically to the Stone Roses and Happy Mondays. Children, careers, responsibility; suddenly ten years seemed an awfully long time as Julie, Clive and I walked around the harbour with two occupied pushchairs. We passed dozens upon dozens of old lobsterpots piled up on the harbourfront in front of a huge abandoned shed.

'Ten years ago, this was a thriving fishing market, but look at it now,' said Clive. 'This harbour used to be packed with boats, and me and my mates would come down here and catch loads of fish. It's actually quite sad to see it like this.'

At the end of the harbour stood three men in survival suits, long fishing rods propped against the high sea wall that protected the little haven from the excesses of the North Sea beyond.

'Caught anything?' asked Clive.

'One,' came the reply.

'How long have you been here?'

'Seven hours.'

Later that evening we'd return to the harbour

and find the same men still there. In another eight hours they'd caught a further three fish.

After a raucous night in the Smuggler's spent reminiscing about old times and bemoaning the demise of Scottish fishing, I ventured out on a murky, dark Sunday morning for a final walk around the town. About a dozen boats of various sizes were moored, most painted bright colours, many with large 'For Sale' signs displayed prominently. It was an image that encapsulated the town. Arbroath puts on a positive front, but behind it lies a sense of melancholy, of a struggling town wondering where the next knockback is coming from. The tourists have gone and now fishing has all but disappeared, leaving very little behind except rising unemployment and hardship. Cromarty had taken knocks and come back stronger, but then the oil business rather fell into its lap. Arbroath has not had that stroke of good fortune. While it retains a strong and fiercely defended community spirit, Arbroath seems to be on the ropes and the trainer is ready to throw in the towel.

Yet if the town needs a symbol of defiance all it has to do is look up to the shell of the ancient abbey that overlooks it. Founded in 1178 by King William I, the Lion of Scotland who is buried there, Arbroath Abbey was the scene of the Declaration of Arbroath. This ancient document from 1320 asserted the independence of Scotland following Robert the Bruce's victory over the

English at Bannockburn in 1314. It was composed by the Scottish parliament in Arbroath Abbey and sent to the pope at Avignon.

> For as long as but a hundred of us remain alive, never will we on any conditions be brought under English rule. It is not for glory, nor riches, nor honours that we are fighting, but for freedom – for that alone, which no honest man gives up but with life itself.

Arbroath may be on its uppers, but deep within its people lies that defiance spelled out within the walls of its abbey seven hundred years ago, a resilience matched by the lighthouse eleven miles out to sea, a pinprick of hope in the darkness.

TYNE, DOGGER, FISHER

Area Tyne, introduced to the map in 1949, stretches along the north-eastern coast of England from a point just south of Berwick-upon-Tweed south to Flamborough Head. Its eastern border adjoins the seabound Area Dogger. Another of the original areas, Dogger once covered most of the North Sea with a land border from southern Norway to the Hook of Holland. Area Fisher, named after a local sandbank, was introduced in 1956.

I think I am allergic to Newcastle. I've been there four times and on each occasion have ended up snuffly, sneezy, rheumy of eye and my head has swelled to a considerable size, the latter something that usually only occurs when I see my name in print. No other town in the world has ever had this effect on me, but something about

Tyneside produces a reaction not even the strongest anti-histamines can reverse. Even watching reruns of *Whatever Happened To The Likely Lads?* brings on light sniffles and an itchiness in the roof of the mouth that I can't shift until the closing credits have rolled. My parents always used to tell me that I was allergic to hard work, which could be why Newcastle has me reaching for the tissues because Tyneside was once the engine room of the British at sea. In the late nineteenth and early twentieth centuries the North-east was a centre of hard graft and intense production. William Gladstone went to Newcastle in 1862 and was knocked out by the place.

'I do not know,' he said, once he'd picked himself up from the floor, 'where to seek even in this busy country of ours a spot or district in which we perceive so extraordinary and multifarious a combination of the various great branches of mining, manufacturing, trading and shipbuilding. I greatly doubt whether the like can be shown upon the whole surface of the globe.' Which as a spontaneous reaction is pretty erudite. You should have heard him when he'd had time to prepare something.

Collier ships from Newcastle buzzed up and down the east coast. New ships were churned out of the Tyne and Wear shipyards as fast as the rivets could be hammered, and bubbly would barely be bottled before it was being smashed against the bows by women in big hats. In the second half of the nineteenth century, every major development and innovation in ship-building occurred in the North-east. Then came the twentieth century and the call for battleships. The world's superpowers came knocking on the metallic doors of the Tyne and Wear shipyards for their frigates and destroyers, and vast passenger liners like the *Mauretania* started thundering down the north-eastern slipways.

It couldn't last. The 1930s saw an irreversible slump and, the odd blip aside, Newcastle and its ilk never hit those heights again. Long before all this, however, one man from the region had made his mark on world exploration. This was a man whose exploits opened up the globe for the ship-builders of the future, a man who focused my attention further down the coast, and I found myself heading over the North Yorkshire Moors to Whitby, once the home town of Captain James Cook.

Once you leave the motorway, for thirty miles of dark moorland you see barely another soul on the road to Whitby. It's a cracking drive. You go through just a couple of villages and pass the mysterious enclosure of the Fylingdales early warning system. When Whitby does finally come into view it could almost be alone in the world. The ruined abbey overlooking the town is the first thing you see, silhouetted against the grey sea beyond, before you descend into the maze of narrow streets and steep, dark passageways that tumble down the hillsides to end up at the harbour in a pile.

It had been raining all day when I arrived, just

as the noon shipping forecast had predicted, and Whitby glistened beneath a turbulent grey sky. The guesthouse was snug and warm and I was reluctant to venture out of my room into the drizzle until I really had to. I pulled Harry's picture out of my pocket and placed it on the bedside table. He eyed the room approvingly. I examined the chocolate-box still-life on the wall with a critic's eye. It wasn't very good. That just left the information folder next to the kettle, the perusal of which revealed a quite fearsome no-smoking policy.

> We are a strictly non-smoking establishment and guests are respectfully requested to comply with this policy. Any guests found to be or to have been smoking in the building will be required to pay a surcharge for additional cleaning and will be asked to leave immediately.

As someone who has never understood the appeal of setting fire to something and putting it in my mouth I knew I'd like it here.

It was getting late by the time I ventured out into the Whitby evening. Set in a cleft in the cliffs, the town has a hunched-shouldered appearance born of narrow streets and steep inclines. It sits astride the mouth of the River Esk with its two halves joined by a narrow swing bridge at the centre of town, and it was close to the bridge that I found an appealing pub.

Inside I found my only fellow drinkers were a young priest with a floppy fringe and a portly, grey-haired monk in a black robe who sat together in silence while the priest scowled, sucked on a cigarette and furrowed his brow in deep, troubled thought. The monk looked a little less as if he wanted somebody killed than the priest, but together they resembled a scene from some kind of *Father Ted* meets *The Godfather* production. Both had half-drunk pints of bitter in front of them, and bitter and half-drunk they both looked. Neither gave me so much as a glance as I walked past them from the bar and sat on a stool near by. The priest's steely gaze passed through the curling wisps of smoke into the middle distance, and he kept glancing at his watch. I'd never thought it would be possible for a priest to look really hard, especially one with a Hugh Grant haircut, but this one was truly unsettling. I got the feeling that confession with him would end in a hail of bullets rather than Hail Marys. Near where I live lie the ruins of an old abbey built by Richard de Lucy as penance for his role in the murder of Thomas à Becket. Was a modern equivalent taking place in Whitby, for which these ecclesiastical mobsters needed an alibi? Was there a 'turbulent priest' somewhere being rubbed out at that very moment?

At the end of the room a balding middle-aged man in a loud shirt was setting up a small PA system and meticulously tuning a Fender Stratocaster.

A sense of musical expectation was filling the air, intertwining with the effluent from the priest's Bensons. Suddenly a synthesised drum beat thundered from the speakers as the man crouched over a small mixing desk at the side of the tiny stage. Straightening himself up and facing front he launched into a lusty version of 'Forever in Blue Jeans' at ear-splitting volume. The priest and the monk continued their sulky, silent contemplation apparently undistracted by this, but then I guess that lifelong exposure to hymn singing would tend to create an innate resistance to bad music. After a couple of Shadows instrumentals the singer announced, 'Here's one you can all sing along to,' before crashing into 'Achy Breaky Heart'. Surprisingly, none of us sang along. In fact, by the time the second chorus had come around I was splashing through the puddles towards my bed, hoping that the residue from the priest's fierce smoking which had attached itself to my clothes wouldn't see me and my belongings turfed out on to the street. I wondered later how long my fellow music lovers had had to wait before they received the message that 'Reverend Cholmondeley-Pottlestone sleeps with the fishes', or some such.

I was up and about early the next morning hoping to catch the fish market open for business on the west quay. I am probably unique in loving the smell of wet fish, and can frequently be seen strolling back and forth in front of fishmongers' breathing deep lungfuls of lovely fishy whiff. There was a distinct lack of piscine tang in the air that morning, however, and the shutters of the fish market were living up to their name. Three small trawlers sat lashed together at the quayside, and a small group of weather-beaten men in wellies and waterproofs stood around a hot-dog stand in the drizzle sipping from steaming polystyrene cups.

From there I wandered the narrow streets watching Whitby wake up. Shops unshuttered, people emerged from houses, cafés began optimistically to place furniture outside on the pavement. I passed an hour with the local newspaper in a tea room, all pink plaster between brown beams, steamed-up windows and a mixture of bleach and cigarette smoke in my nostrils.

'That went to two editions a week recently,' an elderly woman in a headscarf and maroon quilted anorak told me when I unfurled the paper. 'God knows why. Not enough happens here to fill one newspaper a week, let alone two. Bloody waste of time and money if you ask me. Still, you have to buy it, don't you?'

And there, folks, is the English community spirit in a nutshell. She was right about the paper too. About the most interesting story was the theft of two fire extinguishers, one of which turned up later in somebody's greenhouse beneath a broken roof pane surrounded by shattered glass. 'What is Whitby's youth coming to?' asked a letter on page two from a man who had been walking his dog one morning and seen a teenager 'deliberately smash a bottle'. Anywhere else they would have given thanks that there wasn't a lighted rag and a pint of petrol involved.

Elsewhere I read that the European Union had set the fishing quota at 45 per cent of its previous level, enough to appease neither the environmentalists nor the fisherfolk. Still, at least it meant that back in Arbroath, Campbell Scott wouldn't necessarily be pulling down the shutters of the family business for the last time.

Once the town had woken, yawned, stretched and eased itself into the day, I made my way across the swing bridge, turned right into Grape Lane and entered the Captain Cook Memorial Museum. The museum is housed in the former home of John Walker, a Quaker ship owner to whom Cook was apprenticed at the age of eighteen in 1746. It was in this house that Cook studied, ate and slept while learning the elements of navigation and seamanship that would take him around the world to become arguably the most successful explorer in history. If you run your finger down the index of an atlas you can appreciate the extent of Cook's achievements. Assuming you have it open at the letter C, of course. The Cook Ice Shelf in Antarctica, Cook Bay in the Society Islands of the Pacific, Mounts Cook in both New Zealand and Alaska, Cooktown in Queensland, Cape Cook of Vancouver Island and Cook Inlet on the South Sandwich Islands. All visited by and named for the man who had come to this house as an ambitious teenager and learned from the fast-running treacherous waters of the east coast how to steer carefully through uncharted, unknown seas. Cook would spend three years in Whitby, studying and running colliers to London, where he would eventually join the Royal Navy and commence the remarkable maritime career that would see him circumnavigate the globe three times.

The house is a mixture of tastefully restored rooms and exhibitions, from the original kitchen floor to the attic where Cook and his fellow apprentices would have slept. The attic is whitewashed and subtly lit now, a far cry from the dark, draughty and creaky room where the future explorer and up to fifteen other teenagers would have sweltered in summer and frozen in winter. While his colleagues hit the taverns in the evenings, the studious Cook would often beg a candle from the housekeeper and spend the evenings up here alone, poring over charts and tide tables. Which probably explains why he was no good at pool and knew little of pop trivia.

It was hard to appreciate that this room, with its white walls, angular ceiling, polished floor and glass cases, was the cramped space where Cook slept, studied and banged his head on protruding beams for three years. I tried to imagine the attic in Cook's time, wondering whether the adventures he dreamed of at the dead of night on the very spot where I stood could have come anywhere near the ones he would actually experience before his untimely, unnecessary and grisly end on a Hawaiian beach in 1779. There is a small window at one end of the attic which faces the harbour, through which Cook must have gazed at the ships moored outside and tried to imagine how and where he would spend his maritime career. I peered through the glass at the harbour and thought I must have been seeing things. I could have sworn that out there facing me, its masts rocking gently from side to side, was Cook's most famous ship, the *Endeavour*, on which he undertook his first voyage and made the mythical Antarctica and Australia a reality.

Formidable though my subconscious mind undoubtedly is, I am not yet able to make historic ships appear by the power of thought. I do have some cracking dreams where I can move things about just by looking at them, from which it's always a great disappointment to wake up and note that all the cars parked in the street outside have not been mischievously moved around in the night after all. But tangible materialisation? No. At least not yet. The ship whose masts and rigging were rocking gently on the other side of the harbour was a replica, seen in the BBC series *The Ship* and now a mobile visitor attraction. Although it's not the original vessel, which was broken up by later owners in the nineteenth century, this didn't stop around a hundred thousand people converging on Whitby to see the replica sail in in 2002. It was an event billed as 'The Homecoming' by locals, the original *Endeavour* having been built in the town's shipyard, and demonstrated the strong pull of Cook even three hundred years after having his head stove in by angry Hawaiians. Cook had selected the *Endeavour* purely because it was a north-eastern barque with an almost flat-bottomed hull: not only was it a type of ship with which he was wholly familiar, it was also ideal for picking your way through hazardous straits and rocky shallows.

What strikes you when you board the *Endeavour* is just how small it is. Even the deck is claustro-phobic, being littered with masts, storage chests and so on. Barely one hundred feet long, when the *Endeavour* set out on her three-year voyage to Tahiti and Australia there were ninety-five people on board. It's astoundingly cramped and, once you go below, much of the mess deck is less than four and a half feet high. I had the raging hump, literally, after being bent double for ten minutes, let alone spending three years like this with ninety-four other grumpy, smelly sailors in stripy shirts and silly boaters with the odd landfall providing the only relief. Can you imagine being locked in, say, a medium-sized detached house with a hundred other people and told you could only come out briefly every three or four months or so? Not only that, you'd be locked in with little fresh food and water and absolutely no telly. I know I couldn't have done it, particularly if the only source of entertainment was a salty old sea dog with a concertina and a repertoire that didn't extend much beyond 'Heave Away, My Johnny'. Mind you, there's probably a television executive somewhere pitching that idea right now.

On the mess deck, an amiable, bearded man gave us the low-down on life on board. Each sailor would sling his hammock from the beams and was allocated a space fourteen inches wide to do so. I don't sleep that close to Katie, let alone a whiskery, snoring, flea-ridden, scabby, bronchial seaman with a digestive system betraying the effects of months of salted meat, bad beer and ship's biscuits. Cook tried to ensure that his crew washed daily, but I cast my mind back to my student bedroom and tried to imagine the smell of that multiplied ninety-odd times over. It didn't bear thinking about. Mind you, at least the mess-deck floor wasn't covered with Soup Dragons LPs, three-week-old takeaway cartons, underwear of dubious hygiene and ownership and mouldy coffee cups. A bloke I knew as a student was so unhygienic he actually contracted scabies. I think he might even be an MP now.

I learned from the guide that the cat o'nine tails was kept hanging in a cloth bag here as a deterrent against misbehaviour, hence the phrase 'letting the cat out of the bag' entered modern parlance, as did 'not enough room to swing a cat'. If ever there's an enduring legacy of maritime Britain it can be found in the English language, and you'd be surprised at how many common phrases have their origins on ships like this one. Did you know, for example, that three sheets to the wind, by and large, the whole nine yards, minding your Ps and Qs, to go by the board, in the offing, to be at loggerheads, crew cut, skyscraper, square meal, toe the line, pipe down, close quarters, dogsbody and shake a leg are all terms of nautical origin? The best place to hear nautical English is Pitcairn Island in the Pacific. You'd have to really want to hear it though as it takes weeks to get there and, unless you just want to stay for a couple of hours, you have to stay for about three months. The remote location has meant that the descendents of the *Bounty* mutineers have retained much of their ancestors' style of speech and they talk about 'all hands' when they mean 'everyone', which sounds like tremendous fun. Henceforth I intend to speak in eighteenth-century sailors' vernacular and nothing else. That should bamboozle the next Jehovah's Witness.

The *Bounty* was, of course, captained by William Bligh, who a decade before the mutiny had sailed with Cook on his final voyage of circumnavigation aboard the *Resolution*. Which was also built in Whitby, and was a ship of which Cook took command after a period of temporary retirement at the Royal Hospital in Greenwich. See? It all fits together.

As I finally managed to stand upright in Cook's

116

quarters at the rear of the ship, I couldn't help wondering how the crew, at sea for years at a time in cramped, crowded conditions, didn't return as lunatic hunchbacks. Even a stroll on the deck was fraught with hazards lurking to crown you on the head or crack your shinbones, let alone the hardships involved in actually working on the ship. Fortunately Cook was, by all accounts, ahead of his time as far as the welfare of his crew was concerned, and was one of the first to note the effects of fresh fruit in combating scurvy. Even so, when one of the few enjoyable aspects of life on board was getting to suck on a lime every now and again, it really is astounding how Cook managed to keep the crew alive, let alone happy.

I'd had quite enough of living the life of an eighteenth-century sailor, which I had now done for half an hour, and decided to ponder upon their lot further over a pint in the Duke of York, which overlooks the harbour from the eastern side. In the pub I examined my latest purchase, a print of the shipping forecast map which I'd bought from the Cook Museum gift shop. 'Ooh, I love the shipping forecast,' said the woman behind the counter as she placed it in a paper bag the size of a mainsail. 'We grow up with it here. Babies in Whitby, their first words aren't "Mummy and Daddy", they're "Dogger and Fisher".'

I looked up from the print to see out of the window that the west quay had completely vanished. A squally rainstorm had snuck in from the North Sea unnoticed and was lashing this pleasant, friendly, unspoiled harbour town. As the masts and rigging of the *Endeavour* loomed in and out of the murk, I thought about all the great seamen who had learned their trade here and departed for global adventures, of whom Cook is the best-known example. A map of the world in the museum plotted the courses of his circum-navigations of the globe, routes that went hither and thither, from the Antarctic Circle up to Nova Scotia, around the numerous Pacific islands and the coasts of Australia and New Zealand. The haphazard journeys represented by the different-coloured lines looked like what would appear if someone plotted my whimsical trolley-pushing around Safeway, but Cook wasn't making a two-minute detour back to the tinned fish aisle via the teabags; each deviation required careful navigation and weeks or months of hard work.

The Whitby in which I now sat awaiting a 'freshly caught crab sandwich' (wouldn't the sea make the bread all soggy?), that appeared and disappeared out of the squally rain outside, has barely changed since Cook's day. He'd still be able to find his way around. He might raise an eyebrow at the swanking up of his old attic and the difference in the price of a pint since he was last in the Duke of York, and people would probably point and laugh at his trousers, but apart from that he'd see virtually no difference. I was growing to like Whitby a great deal. It has the same air of calm surety that stays just the right side of smugness as Cromarty. Like Cromarty, Whitby doesn't rope off its history, it lives it. Late at night as you wobble out of the pub ready for the climb home (my host at the guesthouse had told me, 'Everywhere you go in Whitby it's downhill to get there and uphill to get home'), you half expect to turn the corner and find a press gang lying in wait to shanghai you into a life on the ocean wave. And believe me, after having been aboard the *Endeavour*, an eighteenth-century ship is no place to wake up with a raging hangover. Especially when you open your eyes to find the spittle-flecked, yellow-toothed grin of Jolly Jack Tar a foot away in the next hammock.

It seemed strange that over the years, most of Whitby's sea-faring sons and students had put as many nautical miles as possible between them and the town. I could quite happily have stayed for good. Where many of Britain's seaside towns can be garish and tacky, Whitby is almost too self-effacing. Most of the t-shirts and souvenirs in the visitor centre by the harbour just say 'Yorkshire', with barely a mention of Whitby. Having demolished a crustacean-filled baguette the size of a small submarine, eventually I emerged from a post-crab reverie in which Katie and I were living in a lovely cottage overlooking the harbour with a freezer full of crabs and baguettes, and noticed that the rain had stopped. The squall had washed the air clean and Cook's statue on the other side of the harbour was picked out sharply against the scudding grey clouds.

The Duke of York is the last watering hole before the 199 steps up to St Mary's church, made famous by Bram Stoker's novel *Dracula*. Stoker actually wrote some of it while staying around the corner from the guesthouse in which Harry and I were ensconced in a smoke-free environment, and it was from near where I stood that the evil count leaped from his ship in the guise of a black dog and scampered up the steps to await the nocturnal arrival of Lucy in the churchyard for a sanguine supper.

At the top of the muscle-twanging steps, beyond the church and its spooky gothic graveyard (Whitby now stages two goth festivals a year, when pasty-faced youths in top hats accompanied by girls with purple streaks in their hair roam the cobbled streets drunk on cider and cheap red wine) lie the ruins of Whitby Abbey. There's a new visitor centre next to the ruins, with glass lifts and interactive touch screens featuring some fantastically hammy performances by actors dressed as figures from Whitby's past. Most notable is a terrific Bram Stoker in a false beard played in full comedy stage-Irishman 'bejaysus' mode. He actually says 'the top of the morning to ye' when ye touch the screen.

Impressive though the visitor centre is, however, it can't come close to the atmosphere of the ruins themselves. There's been an abbey here since the mid-seventh century, and Caedmon, credited with inventing the hymn after God apparently came to him in a dream and commanded him to sing, lived, worked and died here. Having had to sing at least one hymn a day throughout my school career, Caedmon has, in my opinion, a lot to answer for as hymns are without exception rubbish. Caedmon has an obelisk memorial at the top of the 199 steps, and I was sure to shake my fist at it as I passed. The east side of the abbey is almost complete, with three storeys of arched windows rising to an immense height. Pigeons coo somewhere near where the roof used to be. The breeze carries in the cries of seagulls and gentle sound of the waves. A middle-aged couple stood reading an information board on the west side, which consists of little more than a few stunted pillars. 'Amazing, isn't it?' I said as I walked past them. 'Yes,' replied the male half of the duo, 'absolutely breathtaking.' 'It'll look great when it's finished,' I said, before setting off back to the town whistling to myself.

I walked back down the steps, through the cobbled streets, past the tea shops, gift shops and pubs, and crossed the bridge. There was a chill in the wind and the odd droplet of rain from the fast-moving grey clouds overhead. The *Endeavour* replica creaked loudly as it rocked at its moorings. I headed towards the western peninsula ready for the climb back to the guesthouse, the wind ruffling my hair. I sat on a bench at the top of the cliff to get my breath back and looked out to sea. In front of me was Cook's statue. He stood with his legs shoulder width apart, braced for action, looking out in the direction of the South Seas, a map in one hand and a pair of dividers in the other. Suddenly, directly behind him as I looked out to sea, the clouds parted slightly and a wide shaft of sunlight snuck through and shone down on Cook's statue. It was the only break in the cloud in the entire sky.

That evening I risked strong allergic reaction by driving to Newcastle to take a ferry to Norway. Fortunately I was late and ushered straight on to the ferry before my head could really start to fill with snot. The dull throb of the engines soon lulled me to sleep, and I passed blissfully unaware across Dogger. For an empty patch of sea, Dogger has an eventful history connected in the main to the fertile fishing grounds of Dogger Bank, sixty-odd miles off the coast of Northumberland. The bank is a shallow patch of sea that covers much of this shipping forecast area, where cod have traditionally appeared in great numbers. In addition it's been the scene of two major sea battles, a substantial earthquake and one of the most remarkable examples of a naval cock-up in maritime history.

The first Battle of Dogger Bank was a relatively minor skirmish between the British and the Dutch in 1781, a battle in which Captain Bligh saw service as it happens, but it was in 1915 that the biggest battle over the bank took place. In December 1914 the German fleet had launched a daredevil raid on the north-east coast, shelling

122

Scarborough, Hartlepool and Whitby. Eighteen civilians were killed. Buoyed by this, the Germans decided to have another crack a month later. This time the British were waiting and a fierce sea battle ensued that resulted in the deaths of 15 British and 954 German mariners.

By far the most controversial occurrence in the region, however, was the 'Dogger Bank Incident' of 1904. The Russian Baltic fleet had been instructed by the Tsar to sail for Japan, some eighteen thousand miles away, to participate in what would become the Russo-Japanese War. Signs that this wasn't the brightest of naval flotillas ever to weigh anchor emerged almost immediately when the fleet opened fire on a Swedish trawler believing it to be a Japanese ship. Now, bear in mind that the fleet had not even left the Skaggerak, the patch of sea east of Denmark, and then consider where Japan is. Meanwhile, a fleet of around forty British trawlers had left Hull and were working the fishing grounds on and around Dogger Bank. The Russians, under Admiral Rozhdestvensky, came to the obvious conclusion that this was a fleet of Japanese torpedo boats and opened fire accordingly.

Now, it was dark. Can any of us, hand on heart, say that if we'd been a Russian admiral two hundred yards from a fleet of trawlers in the North Sea, we wouldn't have assumed they were warships from a navy based several weeks' sail away and opened fire with all the restraint of Prince Philip let loose with a blunderbuss in Regent's Park zoo?

Especially when the decks were floodlit and the fishermen could be seen hauling in the nets and sorting the fish? Come on, we've all done it. Rozhdestvensky certainly did, which is why he ordered his ships to give these Japanese a demonstration of naval firepower they'd never forget. The Russians gave the Hull vessels everything they had for a good ten minutes, without once wondering why these, er, Japanese weren't firing back, and the trawler *Crane* was sunk, killing the captain and the boatswain in the process. The captain's fourteen-year-old son received a serious bullet wound to his arm; it was the first time he'd ever been to sea. A man was killed on another trawler, reportedly dying of shock, and several more were injured in an incident that caused major outrage and brought Britain and Russia to the brink of war. An international commission sat in Paris which heavily criticised Rozhdestvensky and instructed the Russian government to pay compensation to the families of the victims. A statue still stands in Hull to commemorate the tragedy.

In 1931 Dogger Bank again hit the headlines as the epicentre of the most violent earthquake ever to hit Britain, measuring 5.5 on the Richter Scale. The tremor was felt as far away as Northern Ireland and Germany, tossed people from their beds along the east coast and rotated a church spire at Filey. At Madame Tussaud's the head of the Dr Crippen effigy in the Chamber of Horrors fell off, landing at the feet of Arthur Deveney, the Kensal Rise murderer. Headless waxworks and trigger-happy Russian admirals were far from my mind, however, as I snoozed across the North Sea to Stavanger, passing among the wispy ghosts that still sail Dogger Bank in the night.

Obviously, when you're in a foreign country and have twenty-four hours to kill in a town you've never been to before, you're going to bump into someone you know. It stands to reason. So it was that as I wandered the chilly streets of Stavanger one brisk Thursday night and ventured into a randomly selected bar, I ended up bumping into a familiar face. I was en route to the Danish port of Hanstholm, north Jutland. The tapering of the Fisher region towards Denmark left me few options along the north-west Danish coast, and with a ferry service running from Egersund on the southern tip of Norway to Hanstholm as my only real option, Hanstholm it would have to be, reached from Whitby via Newcastle and Stavanger.

Which is why I found myself wandering around the centre of a Norwegian town one chilly night looking wistfully through the windows of bars to see if they contained friendly faces. I have a fear of entering establishments alone, particularly if I can't see inside them first. A terrifying scenario runs through my mind where I step through the door and the whole place falls silent. Everyone turns look at me, some wag makes a comment lampooning an unfortunate physical characteristic of mine and the place erupts in laughter. I dash back through the door, trying in vain to dodge a hail of beer-mats, peanuts and the odd potted plant. So it is that before entering somewhere new alone I can be seen walking backwards and forwards in front of it several times, staring through the window, the progress of this human pendulum interrupted only by collisions with passers-by and the occasional lamppost.

At length I settled upon a friendly looking bar called Newsman, an establishment dedicated to newspapers. I ordered a beer, handed over a sum of money large enough to make a significant deposit on a house in return for a stalked glass of frothy amber and settled on to a stool underneath a large framed photograph of Henry Kissinger. Looking around the place I noticed a woman in the corner who looked familiar but I couldn't fathom why. Not being someone inclined towards staring at women in bars, I began employing subtle tactics. Rubbing my chin, I angled my head upwards as if to look at the collection of framed newspaper front pages around the walls, at the same time swivelling my gaze across the bar to this strangely familiar face. This went on for some time, long enough in fact for the bar's other customers to assume that I'd ricked my neck and was in need of some form of medical attention. Eventually the woman in question caught sight of my lofty jawline and strange swivelly gaze, and frowned slightly as if she too was trying to place

126

the man in the corner with the neck problem. She came over. 'Charlie?' she said. And then the penny dropped with an audible clang. 'Wenche!' I cried. Here, sitting in the same Stavanger bar as me was the schoolteacher I'd met at the party on Utsire. She was, needless to say, surprised to see me. After all, when you meet someone briefly on a draughty island in the middle of the North Sea, you don't expect a few weeks later for the same person to amble through the door of your local. Let alone for them to sit down near by and start gurning in a most alarming manner.

Anyway, after I'd explained why I was there, Wenche, who had no particular plans for the weekend, shrugged and said, 'Sure, why not?' when I half-jokingly asked if she fancied coming along. Hence I found myself at eleven thirty the following night boarding a train at Stavanger station bound for the south-Norwegian port of Egersund with a fully fledged Norwegian. Being in a different country with a native speaker has the remarkable effect of striking me dumb for no reason. Give me someone to hide behind and I'll go missing for hours. Going to buy the train tickets, I whispered urgently to Wenche from the side of my mouth, 'You'd better do the talking,' as if we were hapless fraudsters about to be rumbled by the filth.

'Don't worry,' said Wenche, 'everyone here speaks English.'

Called to the window, I faced the ticket clerk

who said something to me in Norwegian and, predictably, I froze. 'Um, ah, erm . . .' was about all I could manage, when had I been alone or with another non-Norwegian speaker I would have calmly enquired as to whether the person spoke English. With a roll of the eyes Wenche elbowed me aside and booked the tickets. Once on the train we were soon joined by a group of drunken Norwegian men. We didn't know it at the time, but this would become the key theme of the next few hours. One of them held up a bottle of some kind of alcopop whose contents were bright green. A short discussion ensued about this bottle, which an incredulous Wenche translated as going something like this:

'You see this stuff?'

'Yeah. What does it taste like?'

'Well, it just tastes . . . green.'

'What, green like a pear you mean?'

'No, it just tastes green.'

'Green like a kiwi fruit?'

'No, it just tastes green.'

'Green like an apple?'

'No, it just tastes green.'

And so on, with the group members reeling off a number of green foodstuffs that might sum up the taste of this particular drink only for the owner of the bottle to rebuff them with the news that no, it just tasted green.

As an experienced traveller, I feel qualified to dish out the following piece of advice: if you're looking for fun and larks that don't involve stag-geringly drunk Norwegians, don't go to Egersund ferry terminal in the middle of the night. We had a good hour before the ferry departed at 1.45 a.m., and the waiting room at Egersund port was starting to resemble Valhalla in the aftermath of a particularly popular happy hour. As we looked out of the window into the night, drunk men in saggy jeans and cheap, imitation-leather jackets came lumbering and staggering across the vast car park from all directions, emerging from the dark-ness like a scene from a low-budget zombie film. The swing doors of the waiting room would bang open every few seconds and another bibulous Scandinavian would announce his arrival with a bellow, a belch, or simply by falling flat on his face.

You have to say it's an impressive way to round off a Friday night. In England we have a few beers and think we're being exotic and adventurous by going to the kebab shop. In Norway they get tanked up and go to Denmark. Wenche and I sat timidly at a table in the corner as the room filled with stumbling, sweaty men, all bonding in booze. Firm handshakes were exchanged, shoulders were clapped, bottles of spirits were offered around and slurred conversation was had at high volume. The smell of alcohol was so great that I prayed no one would light a match or we'd all go up. One man sported a huge shiner and cuts on his face, while everyone clearly betrayed the fact that given the choice between spending their money on clothes, haircuts or strong drink, it was the grog that triumphed every time. Now, I have a lot of time for Norwegians. It's a great country, full of wonderful people. But it appeared that an instruction had gone out this night for all the ugliest, worst-dressed and most chronically dipsomaniac men in the country to gather in the waiting room of the Egersund-Hanstholm ferry and make as much noise as possible. And, by crikey, they'd answered the call. These were, I have to say, quite easily the ugliest people I have ever seen in my life, and I've been to Selhurst Park when Crystal Palace are at home. Admittedly no one looks their best when they're in their cups, but, man alive, this was destined to be a Night on the Ferry of Freaks. I'm not exactly an oil painting myself, but even I was starting to feel a self-confidence about my physical characteristics that I had not previously experienced.

Eventually we were allowed to board, and this barely mobile audition for *Ripley's Believe It or Not* stumbled down the gangway. Two men were prevented from boarding on the grounds that they were drunk. Given that the entire passenger list, bar Wenche and I, was breathing enough proof to fuel the ferry itself, I can only assume that this was a token gesture. On board the place was heaving with even more drunks; the ferry had begun its journey further up the coast at Bergen, and those passengers had already been making hefty inroads into the ship's booze supplies. We made the mistake of popping into the bar before retiring to our chairs for the night, and, of course, accidentally seated ourselves next to the loudest, drunkest group on this entire ship of fools. A country-and-western duo were playing in the corner, the singer/guitarist mangling both chords and words at once (which is quite a feat of synchronicity) while his colleague made a pedal steel guitar sound exactly as if he was disembowelling an entire family of feral cats.

We sat nervously for a few minutes before the inevitable started. A peanut arced over from the next table and bounced off my ear. Another pinged off my forehead and a third struck me right on the hooter. I had to concede that this was impressive marksmanship. A sideways glance at Wenche indicated she too was under aerial bombardment from salted snacks. However, this wasn't aggression; it seemed it was some kind of Norwegian mating ritual. Wenche was about the only woman on the ship and this appeared to be the drunken Norwegian male's way of attracting her attention.

A man in his forties with a face full of burst blood vessels that congregated sociably around his proboscis suddenly pushed his chair back so he was sitting right in front of Wenche. He did this with a hilarious self-conscious nonchalance for which I almost felt obliged to shake his hand. He slurred a few words of Norwegian in the direction of where, in his stupor, he presumed Wenche would

131

be if only she'd stop spinning, and with a stroke of genius Wenche pretended to be English and not understand. This meant that her suitor, clad in a pair of jeans worse than I'd seen in pre-glasnost Russia, had to speak English, which, considering the swamp of inebriation in which he wallowed, was highly impressive. Hence I was able to understand that he and his mates had been to the pub that evening, had a few drinks and decided on a whim to go to Aalborg in Denmark for the weekend. Wenche asked him if he was married. He paused for a second to squint at her and consider whether telling the truth would harm his chances of forming a meaningful relationship with her. He belched impressively, and admitted that yes, he was married and had two children in their early teens.

'Didn't your wife mind you just heading off to Denmark like this?' asked Wenche over the sound of the pedal steel player now castrating the cats, while his colleague attempted 'Ruby Don't Take Your Love to Town' but made it sound more like 'Booby, Dint Turk Yer Fluff to Tom'.

The man paused, gazing vacantly down at his shoes and cocking his head to one side slightly as if there was a thought somewhere in there if only he could shake it loose. He moved his head around slowly, as if his mind was a maze and the thought was a marble he had to manoeuvre carefully to its centre.

'I don't know,' he said when it had finally arrived there, 'my wife doesn't know I'm here.'

His attention was snatched back, however, by the arrival of one of the bar staff bearing a huge tray containing around forty bottles of Smirnoff Ice which she placed on the table at the centre of the group. The man shot Wenche a 'sorry, love, but you know how it is' look and dived headlong towards the bottled booze bonanza in front of him. The band finished, and a young man in a sheepskin-lined suede jacket, whom I recognised as the owner of the bottle of 'green' from the train and who appeared to be the leader of this particular pack of prime Norwegian manhood, produced a large cassette player. He hit play and the room was filled with distorted synthesiser music and shouty Norwegian lyrics. Wenche said she'd be too embarrassed to translate the words, so let's just assume they were bawdy.

It was clearly time to go, and we headed for our sleeping chairs in a lounge at the rear of the ship. In the reception area three scruffy men lay comatose on the floor, as if there was an assassin from the fashion industry loose on the ship. I tried to push the door of the toilet open but it wouldn't move – there was somebody lying dead drunk behind it in a pool of urine. Further along the boat a man lay asleep on a small circular table, his arms, legs and head hanging over the sides as if he'd been lying on the ground and the table had risen beneath him. People were slumped against every available wallspace. Eventually we picked our way through the casualties to the sleeping lounge, where blankets had been left on rows of chairs in order to make you think they were designed for sleeping on when they clearly were not.

A restless, uncomfortable night disturbed by snoring, bodily emissions, some of which weren't mine, and a young Norwegian couple talking and giggling behind me all night, was ended at what seemed like an ungodly hour by an announcement that we were about to dock at Hanstholm. I peered through the porthole as Wenche's head emerged from beneath the chair next to me, she having decided that the floor offered a more comfortable sleep than the seats, while a port loomed up ahead that looked as charming and alluring as downtown Grozny.

The ship of fools prepared to disgorge its human cargo on to an unsuspecting Denmark. Snoring corpses still littered the walkways, but the bulk of the boozy brethren had gathered at reception ready for the door to open. The man asleep behind the toilet door had gone. The man in the sheepskin-lined suede coat pulled a bottle of Jägermeister from a pocket, drank deeply from it and passed it around his bleary, bloodshot friends. He tried to start a singsong, but no one was having any of it. Which wasn't surprising considering that he was honking away like a walrus in the throes of a violent death.

Eventually the doors opened and we left the ship. Despite the haphazard staggering by which most of the passengers made their way along the quayside, nobody fell into the harbour and the drinkers boarded the bus for Aalborg. This appeared to leave Wenche and me as the only people from the ship actually remaining in Hanstholm. As the buses left, most of which had the curious legend 'Hanstholm Touristfart' on the back, bleary faces looked at us with expressions that suggested we were clearly nuts. With good reason as it turned out, for Hanstholm is, without question, the most boring place in the world. We walked out of the harbour, took the road that wound up the hill and emerged into . . . nothing. Having expected some kind of throbbing port town I was startled to see miles and miles of coarse, flat, uninterrupted grassland. Over to the left, sunk among the scrubby dunes, there appeared to be a small shopping centre across the road from what could only be our hotel. And that was it. That appeared to be Hanstholm in its entirety.

'I actually talked to someone at work about Hanstholm recently,' said Wenche as we stood at the top of road, the whole of Denmark in front of us, feeling suddenly like the only two people in the world. 'She was with a group of friends who went on a sort of twenty-four-hour trip down here. They spent two hours in Hanstholm, and I don't think they were too impressed by the place.'

Great, I thought. We're here for two days. 'Bleak' didn't do it justice. Featureless, lifeless, character-less, and that was just my eyes within two minutes

135

of arriving here. The wind rustled the grass, which was long, coarse and blown flat against the ground.

'But what do they know?' Wenche continued. 'A place is what you make it, right?'

She looked hopefully at me. Bless her naïve Norwegian optimism, I thought. We booked into the hotel and set out to see the sights of Hanstholm. Something told me it wouldn't take long.

Until the 1960s Hanstholm was a small fishing community. As long ago as 1917 someone had had the bright idea of turning it into a modern port with a population of twenty thousand, but nothing happened for half a century and the new harbour wasn't completed until 1967. The population barely reached a tenth of its proposed figure, however, despite the proud boast that Hanstholm was home to Denmark's largest fish auction. Apparently, according to local legend, the name Hanstholm is a corruption of *handskeholm*, meaning 'the islet of the glove'. The story goes that a woman once lost a glove here. That's it. That's the story. Would you hold out much hope of fun and larks in a place where a woman losing a glove is an incident so worthy of note they named a town after it?

We reached the shopping centre, a single-storey characterless concoction of concrete. 'The largest roofed shopping centre in the region', boasted a tourist leaflet in English outside the empty, closed tourist office. Wow, I thought, I'm glad I didn't miss this then. The leaflet detailed some of the local shopping attractions: 'The largest selection of pipes of the region', claimed one advert proudly. That's mighty big talk, I thought; the north-west Jutland pipe market is well known for being a cut-throat one where few prisoners are taken. 'Come inside and have a nice chat about pipes and tobacco in the grocery shop', suggested the ad, which given the clear paucity of things to do in Hanstholm sounded quite tempting even to this non-smoker. Unfortunately the shop in question turned out to be in a completely different town, so the opportunity for me to have a nice chat about pipes and tobacco in the grocery shop would fail to knock.

We wandered around the shopping centre, which consists of a central square from which four small, covered avenues extend not very far. There was a supermarket, a bowling alley, a chemist, a post office, the empty tourist office, a pizzeria (hurrah!), two pubs (hurrah! Hurrah!) and two solariums (hurr . . . eh?). We strolled around for an hour or so, looking through shop windows and occasionally ambling in if we were feeling particularly daring. We needed to pace ourselves though, our senses couldn't cope with too much hedonism and excitement all at once. There was a men's clothes shop called 'Engelsk' ('English') full of clothes that I have never seen anyone wear in England in my life. For a start there were no Burberry baseball caps, Stone Island sweatshirts or a single sovereign ring. But most worryingly, we'd been here an hour and seen everything. More than once. We had run out of things to see and we'd not even got the noise of the ship's engines out of our ears yet. For want of anything better to do we went for something to eat. Choice was limited. Walking across the central square towards the pizza restaurant Ristorante La Pizza (they must have been up all night coming up with that name) where we would have lunch and every other meal during our time in Hanstholm, I slipped on something and went skidding forward, just about keeping my balance with all the grace and poise of Bernard Bresslaw on ice skates. Looking back to see what had caused this, there, almost perfectly flat, other than the slightly raised impression of the sole of my shoe, was a very small and very dead mouse.

After lunch we spent the afternoon in Sir Henry's Pub, sitting beneath a sign that read 'A wife and a steady job have ruined many a good biker'. We read it several times for something to do, taking it in turns. There were a few other patrons but in the two hours or so we were there, nobody left and nobody else came in. Nobody seemed to be saying much either. Having extracted every subtle nuance and hidden meaning we could from the biker sign, we went elsewhere in search of mental stimulation. We walked around the outside of the shopping centre by way of variation. Then we walked back in the other direction, which made it look a bit different. We tried to memorise the number plates on nearby cars and test each other on them. We looked at the bus timetable in the shelter outside to see if there was anywhere else to go. There wasn't. We went back inside. Perhaps there would be the opportunity for some more mice skating. There wasn't. Wenche bought some cosmetics from the chemist. 'They're cheaper here than in Norway,' she said, instantly producing the most interesting thing to happen all day. Except possibly for slipping on the mouse.

There was a photo booth tucked away in a corner, but this was no ordinary photo booth. Called 'Van Gogh's Studio', it took your picture and turned it into either a charcoal drawing or a pencil sketch. We decided to save that treat for tomorrow. There's only so much fun you can have in one day, after all. Darkness fell and we returned to the hotel. Well, it was a change of scene. We wandered along to the restaurant to find the place jumping. A band was playing and in full swing. The room was packed with people sitting at long tables, banging beer glasses and singing along while waitresses darted among them with plates of food. Must be a wedding or something, we said. Whatever it is, it's clearly a private party. We walked back to the shopping centre, which looked a bit different in the dark, and had another pizza. Just like at lunchtime we were the only diners. It got to as late as nine o'clock by the time we'd finished, so late in fact that the restaurant owner/chef/waiter had to phone up the night security guard to let us out of the shopping centre. No one appeared to suspect me of the mouse killing yet.

We went back to the hotel again, had a drink in reception and asked what the occasion in the restaurant was. Turned out there wasn't one. It was just the weekly night out for the locals. 'Do you know something?' asked Wenche as we made to return to our rooms. 'This is the first time I've ever had a hotel room to myself.' That's Hanstholm for you. A veritable horn of plenty when it comes to new experiences. I lay in bed and switched on the television. It wasn't tuned in. I flicked through all the channels but the little green number in the bottom right of the screen counted upwards to a background of silent static. I switched it off. I thought of the sign in the pub. 'A wife and a steady job have ruined many a good biker'. I still couldn't work out why it was supposed to be funny. Around the corner from where I live, there's a house with a little sign in the front window by the front door. 'Piss off!' it reads, 'I'm having a bad day'. Often when I've walked past it I've thought about the process that led to be it being there. Somebody came up with the phrase, thought it would make an amusing sign, designed it, manufactured it and sold it. The person who lives in this house saw it somewhere and thought it was funny. So funny in fact that they bought it. Not only did they find it funny enough to buy it, they took it home and stuck it in their front window, so everyone who approached the house would be greeted by the cheery message 'Piss off! I'm having a bad day'. Friends who dropped by must have commented on it and everyone would have had a good laugh. It used to be a vibrant yellow and black, but now the sun has faded it to grey letters on a beige background. They're probably wondering why they've had no post for three years. But even so, right now they were having a much, much better time than I was. Everybody was having a much better time than I was. In fact there was probably only one person not having a better time than me and that was Wenche. Not only was she in Hanstholm, but she was there with me for company.

I cursed the arbitrary nature of the shipping forecast map for forcing me to spend a weekend of my life here. Knowing my luck, just yards beyond the imaginary line separating Fisher from German Bight was a groovy town where groovy people were having a really fantastically groovy time. And here I was. In Hanstholm. With mouse blood on my hands.

At breakfast there were people drinking spirits with their cheese, jam and cold meats. They were probably teetotal when they arrived here. We ventured out to revisit the shopping centre. Perhaps people had bought stuff; we could play a game whereby we had to spot things missing from shelves and hangers since we last looked. The paper shop had different papers in it, but its huge stock of pornography remained undisturbed as far as I could see. Mouse Murder: Anglo-Norwegian Hit Squad Suspected, said one headline. It didn't really, but the boredom was causing my mind to play tricks on me. Every shop seemed to have crates of beer stacked in the corner, even the chemist. Was booze dished out on prescription here? Is that how people survived? Come to think of it, where did people live? Was Hanstholm really just a hotel and a shopping centre? There were a handful of houses but they didn't look inhabited. I'd read in the tourist brochure that people weren't allowed to have holiday homes here, something that made me guffaw out loud, but there really was little sign of human habitation. Once the sun had passed over the yardarm we popped into the pub, and it seemed that the same people were sitting in the same places wearing the same clothes as the day before. The thought crossed my mind that these were actually mannequins, but then someone sneezed. Nope, they were human all right. But where did they come from? Where did they go to?

We went for lunch. Pizza again. The owner didn't seem to recognise us despite the fact we'd apparently been the only customers all weekend. I must point out that we didn't have the same pizzas every time, we mixed it up a bit. The ferry was due to leave in a couple of hours, and we could contain ourselves no longer. The flashing lights of 'Van Gogh's Studio' winked at us, beckoning us forward. Wenche and I squeezed into the booth and nervously I inserted some coins. We sat grinning like idiots, waiting for the picture to be taken. Nothing happened. I leaned forward to press the coin reject button and, of course, the flash went off. There was a brief whirring sound and an A4 piece of paper curled into the cradle in front of us. Wenche had been captured in pencil quite nicely, while the top of my head looked very tidy.

Giddy with excitement and adventure we put some more coins in and selected charcoal this time. I managed to actually get my face in shot on this occasion, but unfortunately there was something wrong with the charcoal setting and we both looked as though we'd gone through a car windscreen just before entering the booth. Still, what terrific souvenirs we now had of a weekend of high jinks in Hanstholm.

We were at the harbour waiting for the ferry almost before it appeared over the horizon. Once the ship had docked, the Touristfart buses arrived and disgorged some horribly familiar figures on to the quayside. Sheepskin-suede walrus boy was still in boisterous mood, clutching a bottle of clear spirits and still trying to cajole his comrades into a singsong. They'd now all been wearing the same clothes for three days, and they still weren't singing along. I gave silent thanks that I couldn't understand the anecdotes of their weekend that they swapped with unbridled merriment. But hey, they'd still had more fun than us. Thankfully the crossing was quieter and less eventful than when we'd arrived as the revellers finally crashed out. Even sheepskinsuede walrus boy was asleep in a chair before we'd left port. When we disembarked at Egersund some seven hours later, his mum was there to collect him. She even licked a tissue and wiped something from his cheek. Wenche's gin-blossomed suitor didn't seem to recognise her, and looked thoughtful and pensive all the way across. I imagine he was trying to come up with an answer to the wifely enquiry 'And where the hell have you been?' pitched somewhere between the truth and alien abduction. I thought of suggesting the reply 'Piss off, I'm having a bad day' but then thought better of it.

Outside the window, it began to rain.

GERMAN BIGHT, HUMBER, THAMES

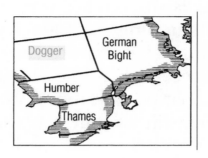

The area now known as German Bight was introduced in 1949 as Heligoland, with a coastline stretching from Den Helder on the tip of the Hook of Holland up to the west Jutland coast near Esbjerg. Renamed in 1956, it has seabound borders with Fisher, Dogger and Humber. Area Humber appears on the original 1924 map, stretching along the east coast from Berwick to just south of Great Yarmouth. The introduction of Area Tyne in 1949 halved the size of Area Humber, the border between the two being at Flamborough Head. Area Thames, whose coastline runs from the border with Humber to North Foreland on the tip of Kent, has remained unchanged since 1924.

It may sound a bit like a theme park constructed from little coloured bricks, but mention Heligoland to a shipping forecast enthusiast of a certain age and you can soon watch them drift off into nostalgic reverie. It's half a century since German Bight replaced Heligoland as the name of the shipping forecast region covering the north German coast up to Denmark, and the question remains – why? The official explanation for the 1956 change was that it brought us into line with the continent, but was there more to it than that?

One thing I didn't realise, which is a bit daft when you consider the last syllable of the word, was that Heligoland is a place; it exists, and during the summer months you can go and visit it. It's an island roughly thirty miles off the northern beaches of Germany, which is now owned by the Germans but used to be ours. It was ours for a long time, in fact, until a bizarre Victorian land swap that not only sold the islanders totally down the river, if you'll excuse the watery pun, but also turned out to be an almighty own goal of near-catastrophic proportions. Some dubious post-war shenanigans on our part also added to the list of unfortunate British connections with Heligoland. All of which might explain why the name of the sea area was changed not long afterwards and why few people know the island even exists, let alone that it used to be the closest territory of the British Empire to Britain itself. The British authorities might feasibly have been a teensy bit embarrassed. These days, however, it's a popular day-trip and holiday destination for Germans, not least because of its tax-free shopping. It's also subsumed in German consciousness because the old German national anthem 'Deutschland Über Alles' was written there – while the place was owned by the British.

Things were looking good as I flew out of Heathrow one sunny morning heading for Hamburg. I'd read up on the story of Heligoland, over which the plane must have passed, and thought it was a tremendous yarn. Not only that, I'd managed to find myself a startlingly cheap travel deal that had landed me in a five-star hotel for not much more than I'd paid for that doss house in Arbroath. 'Some people say that Hamburg's Hotel Vier Jahreszeiten is the best in Europe,' chirruped one reviewer, 'others that it's the best in the world.' It was handy for the train station and handy for Hamburg port, from whence the hydrofoil to Heligoland, or Helgoland to give it its proper German name, departed. Where some trips were hard to organise, this one was running itself. Perfect.

An old schoolfriend of mine known affectionately as Sleazy Tim was joining me on this particular leg of the trip. It's probably best not to go into how he got the nickname; suffice to say he's had an eventful love life. His New Year's resolution one year was 'not to be so sleazy' – note the clever insertion of the word 'so' to still allow a certain amount of sleaze to take place with a clear conscience. When you consider that Hamburg's Reeperbahn is one of the best-known places in the world for strip clubs and peep-shows, Sleazy's presence on the trip isn't particularly mysterious. We arrived at the hotel in jeans, trainers and t-shirts, with holdalls slung over our shoulders. Sleazy's holdall was bright yellow, and he looked as if he had just stepped off the rigs. Despite this, an immaculately dressed man in a top hat pushed the revolving door for us and in we went. Surprisingly we weren't directed straight to the boiler room on the assumption we'd come to repair a dodgy pilot light, but were allowed to pass unmolested across the polished floor to the vast reception desk.

'Hello,' I said chirpily to a young bespectacled man behind the counter. 'Good afternoon, sir,' he said with a welcoming smile that betrayed not the slightest hint of 'what are you doing in my hotel, you oik?' and then spotted Sleazy, which wasn't hard seeing as he appeared to have an enormous banana over his shoulder. 'Gentlemen,' he expanded, 'welcome to our hotel. You have a reservation, Mr Connelly, I believe?'

By jiminy, this was a classy joint. I could get very used to this, I thought.

'Now,' he continued, 'the reservation is for one room but with separate beds, is that correct, gentlemen?'

Mumble, shuffle, oh yes, absolutely correct, cough, mumble. He gave us our key and a man with tassels on the shoulders of his jacket wrestled our bags from us and carried them the ten feet to the lift. At the lift, a fresh-faced young man in a suit appeared from nowhere to press the button just so we didn't have to. The room was magnificent. The kind of furniture you see on the *Antiques Roadshow* accompanied by the phrase 'I think you should consider insuring this for around, ooh, £15,000' was scattered nonchalantly around the place. The bathroom was the size of Slovenia. The room itself was so big I had to call Sleazy on his mobile to find out where he was. He was inside the giant walk-in wardrobe in which we could conceivably have staged golf buggy races. Indeed, so keen to please had our new friend at reception been that if we'd phoned down to request two golf buggies I'm sure he would have had them sent up straight away with a complimentary bottle of champagne on the seat.

By the door was a framed piece of paper with the regular tariff for the room. I read it, fell over, stood up and read it again. Once I'd picked myself up from the floor for a second time I began to wonder whether I'd read the deal wrong. I could suddenly envisage the words 'Thank you for your deposit, the balance is payable on departure' printed on the receipt in my bag. Nervously, I checked again. Nope, the entire package, with flights, really had cost significantly less than half the daily rate for the room. I never get this lucky normally; what on earth was going on?

Sleazy and I followed the ball of wool we'd been unfurling in order that we could find our way to the door again and ventured out to explore Hamburg. The hydrofoil to Heligoland left early the next morning, which left us with an evening in Hamburg to kill.

Although it sits to the north of the East Friesian chain in the Deutsche Bucht, or German Bight, and is closer to Germany than any other country, the island of Heligoland has had strong links with Britain for as long as written records exist. In fact, the island's very name may be essentially British in origin. According to legend, an English missionary from Lindisfarne by the frankly splendid name of St Willibrod was washed up on the island after a shipwreck in 699 and stayed for a while. It seems that it was then that the island acquired the name Heligoland, which means Holy Island. The records are hazy, but in the ensuing centuries various Norse chieftains laid claim to the island until King Cnut of Denmark became King Cnut of England too in 1017, and the island passed officially into English control. The inhabitants seem to have been Friesian sheep farmers and fishermen. However, very few people beyond the fish merchants of Billingsgate, who traded with the Heligolanders, knew the place even existed. After the death of Cnut the island remained nominally under Danish rule but, surprisingly given the strategic advantage of an island so close to the mouths of the Elbe and the Weser, the islanders were left largely to govern themselves.

It was during the Napoleonic wars that Britain first began to take note of Heligoland. Although the place was less than three hundred miles from the east coast of England, and had once been under English jurisdiction, it took until 1807 for Britain to twig just how useful Heligoland could be to its naval ambitions. Having compromised Denmark's neutrality by the subtle means of sailing up to Copenhagen and blowing it to pieces, the Admiralty turned its attention to possibly useful Danish possessions that would help the campaign against Napoleon.

So unknown was Heligoland at the time that the only written reference anyone in Britain could find to the place was in the journal of an English merchant who'd been blown close to the island by a storm – in 1553. Yet the advantages were obvious. Its craggy terrain and steep cliffs made invasion difficult and it provided important shelter for ships, an anchorage that could be defended by batteries on the island itself. Heligoland was ideal. Not only did it provide shelter for the British fleet, it was a good base to mastermind blockades of Napoleon's ports. 'Clang' went the penny as it dropped, echoing around the corridors of the Admiralty, and before long the small garrison of Danish soldiers on the island gave in to a large and intimidating British fleet without bloodshed.

In the years that followed the British adopted a distinctly laissez-faire attitude to their only north-European colonial possession. Despite advertisements in the London press that boasted you could reach the island from London in thirty hours, few people visited, certainly not from the government. In the meantime the island became a popular health and bathing resort for Germans. Writers and composers found the place inspiring: Mahler, Liszt and Kafka all visited, while Bruckner even wrote an orchestral suite about this British-owned island in the choppy waters of the North Sea. In 1841 Heinrich Hoffmann sat down and wrote 'Deutschland Über Alles' one evening after a day walking on Heligoland.

In fact, Heligoland seemed German in all but name, the place was booming, Britain didn't seem in the slightest bit bothered and Bismarck's bristly moustache was starting to twitch with interest. The British, however, were more concerned with Germany's acquisitions in East Africa, notably Zanzibar and Uganda, which they had rather fancied for themselves. This was the issue that would drive Heligoland into the Victorian headlines, and one over which the Brits would not so much shoot themselves in the foot as blow off an entire leg. Not only that, they would then practically go on to deny the existence of the leg in the first place.

By 1890 the prime minister, Lord Salisbury, had come up with a bit of a brainwave. Why didn't they just swap the island for German East Africa? The Germans were in favour, Salisbury certainly was. So there we go. No problem. The only thing was that no one had asked the Heligolanders, who were quite happy under British jurisdiction, thanks very much. This didn't bother Salisbury, however. Indeed, he even fibbed to Queen Victoria about it. 'I am anxious,' said Victoria in June 1890, 'not to give my consent unless I hear that the people's feelings are being consulted and their rights respected.' 'Of course they are,' said Salisbury, his nose growing longer with every word. He even told Victoria that the islanders were keen to become part of the German empire, a porky pie of gargantuan proportions.

Nevertheless Salisbury managed to persuade the Queen to give her consent, although she did so with the caveat 'I think you might find difficulties in the future. Giving up what one has is always a bad thing.' These would be highly prescient words when reviewed in the decades that followed, not to mention words that Gibraltarians might be keen to display on big banners across the rock.

Appallingly, the Heligolanders only found out that their homeland had been traded for Zanzibar after the event and that was via the newspapers. The formalities were completed in a simple ceremony on August 8, 1890, when the British flag was lowered over Heligoland at exactly the same time as the German flag came down in East Africa.

Not surprisingly, when war broke out in 1914

newly fortified Heligoland was right in the firing line and the Battle of Heligoland Bight of August 1914 was the first significant military skirmish of the First World War. The islanders had been evacuated days earlier, to German internment camps.

After the Armistice, despite their previous treatment by London, the islanders held out hopes that they would return to British ownership. It didn't happen. Indeed, Heligoland was the only piece of territory the Germans were allowed to keep under the Treaty of Versailles, on condition that the fortifications were dismantled. The British clearly had no interest in the place. Which when you think about it is rather extraordinary. Would we have treated any of the Channel Islands with such disregard? Or the Isles of Scilly? Or Gibraltar?

Fortunately for the islanders the tourists began to return once the German economy started to get back on its feet, and then Hitler came to power. Again, the Führer knew the significance of the island and even visited it himself, something no British head of state had ever done. So aware was Hitler of the island's strategic importance that he billeted much of his navy there.

Important though the island was, the way the British attacked the place in the final weeks of the war suggested that they rather fancied blowing it completely out of the water in an effort to expunge it from the history books. In one raid during April 1945 more than a thousand bombers flew out over the North Sea and attempted to obliterate the place.

After the war the British got really carried away in their desire to see the end of Heligoland. 'Operation Big Bang' was commissioned, a 1947 assault even greater than the thousand-bomber raid at the end of the actual conflict. Ostensibly designed to demolish Hitler's fortifications, the exercise seemed rather excessive for an island now uninhabited. Indeed, a senior naval source was quoted at the time as saying that when they'd finished with it, the island would 'never again be fit for human habitation'. Just what did the British have against Heligoland? Clearly something was bugging them, because on April 18, 1947 seven thousand tons of explosives were detonated there. But, presumably to British chagrin, barely one tenth of the stubborn old lump of rock had been destroyed. Instead, the government contented itself with using Heligoland for bombing practice for a while and, apparently, chemical weapons testing.

It would take until 1952 but finally Britain would return Heligoland to Germany and the clean-up and rebuilding could commence. The surface was scarred with craters that can still be detected today, but the stubborn old island had refused to be beaten, a grim determination that had over the centuries been instilled in its people. Once again, Heligoland is a thriving destination. Virtually nothing is left of the pre-war island, but apparently in the wall of the rebuilt Church of St Nicolai there is an old plaque dedicated to Queen Victoria, still legible despite extensive shrapnel scarring. I wanted to see it. I also wanted to see the direction sign whose arrows point to England, Denmark, Schleswig-Holstein and Zanzibar. It was making points in more ways than one.

All this was in store the next day, and as we made to leave the hotel I thought I'd better check with the world's most helpful man the best way to find the Heligoland ferry in the morning.

'You will be travelling to Helgoland, gentlemen?' he said, as if it genuinely was the best idea he had ever heard in his life, even if it did come from two scruffy Englishmen who were making his nice hotel look untidy. 'Would you like me to book your tickets now for you?'

Sleazy and I looked at each other, very impressed. Oh, why not? It was then I noticed that a computer screen hooked up to the Internet had been built into the desk itself. By crikey, this was amazing stuff. They didn't have this in Arbroath. Within seconds he'd called up the relevant website and tapped in the date, which is when the plan that had been going so ridiculously smoothly was suddenly and consummately blown apart as if it were a rocky island bombed by a thousand planes. Even with my sketchy schoolboy German, I knew that the word 'Ausverkauft' which smothered the date of the crossing meant that the ferry to Heligoland was sold out. Oh, sodding hell. Sodding, buggering, sodding, buggering, sodding hell. I descended immediately into a gargantuan slough of despond, in the lower reaches of which I became aware of a muffled thumping noise and presumed there was some building work going on in the hotel somewhere.

'Sir, I don't think it's a very good idea for you to repeatedly bang your head against the desk like this,' said the world's most helpful man. He was right of course. He always is. I stopped.

The ferry was booked out for the entire week. The whole of Germany was clearly decamping to Heligoland purely in order to prevent me from looking at a battered old plaque and stocking up on duty-free whisky. Things had been going too well. I mean, what were the chances of the world's greatest ever flight and hotel deal being thrown in my direction, and then the point of the trip, the whole reason for going, actually coming off? I should have known better. Damn. Damn damn damn. We mooted several alternative plans. Or rather the receptionist did, while I shrugged grumpily, pursed my lips and gazed into the middle distance. So helpful was he that I half expected him to offer to row us out to Heligoland and back, but he stopped just short of that. It was when he suggested chartering a private helicopter that I remembered exactly what kind of a hotel I was staying in, and truly realised that I wasn't going to get out to this flipping island.

'Is it only Helgoland you are interested in, sir?' he asked, lifting my sobbing head from the counter by the hair in order that I might hear him.

'Yes,' I sighed. 'Just Heligoland. Sorry, Helgoland.'

'Have you considered Sylt?' he asked, with genuine sympathy.

Sylt? Sylt? What on earth was Sylt? Some kind of strong German drink? A particular German method of suicide?

'It's another very popular island for Germans, up in the North Friesian Islands. You can take the train from here in Hamburg, it's no problem.'

I looked up and stood straight, cleverly wiping up the accumulated dribble I'd left on the desk with one swish of my sleeve.

'It's an island? And you can get there by train?'

'Yes, sir, it's no problem at all. Here.' From beneath the desk he handed me the relevant train timetable he'd just printed from the Internet as well as a leaflet about the island of Sylt, even though the idea had only just occurred to him. This man, this wonderful, immaculately dressed, perfectly mannered man had saved my bacon. He had become Jeeves to my Wooster. This wasn't a situation quite as bad as when I persuaded a magazine to pay for me to go to Italy to cover a football match only for me to arrive and discover that it had taken place the night before, but it was close. With his diplomacy, forward thinking, level head and unfailing politeness, the man behind the reception desk at Hamburg's Hotel Vier Jahreszeiten should be appointed head of the United Nations forthwith. The Middle East, Sierra Leone, third world debt, he'd have an answer for it all, an answer delivered calmly and without fuss while calling taxis and summoning bellhops all at the same time. Here was an extraordinary man. A brilliant man. A handsome tip was surely his only reward.

'Nice one, thanks, mate,' I said, whipping the documents from his hand and skipping lightly towards the revolving door, which a man with tassels on his shoulders was already setting in motion for the convenience of Sleazy and me. Heligoland. Pshaw, who'd ever want to go to Heligoland? Sylt. Now there was the place to be.

Sleazy and I gravitated towards the Reeperbahn with a stoop-shouldered inevitability. We'd been at school together, and while I'd been the runty little kid with thick glasses, Sleazy was a good-looking sod who had always been a hit with the ladies; something he had exploited to the full over the years. The Reeperbahn could have been made for him, and to go there was probably his destiny. I'd been there a few years earlier when I toured Germany with a friend's band as chief t-shirt seller and equipment carrier. It was an enjoyable jaunt, notable for the fact that hardly any pre-publicity had been circulated before we arrived, and although the band played in venues capable of holding crowds of up to two thousand, there were precisely twenty-seven people at every gig, every night for two weeks. I recalled that when the tour reached Hamburg we'd gone on a late-night excursion to the Reeperbahn. So excited were they about visiting the famous street of iniquity that in their encore version of Jonathan Richman's 'Road

Runner' that night the band had changed the hook line 'radio on' to 'Reeperbahn'. I'm sure I remembered going into a back-street bar through double doors, on either side of which had been painted a woman's leg. Heavy rubber curtains inside the doorway served only to heighten the illusion that you were entering some kind of gynaecological ghost train. This had been a number of years earlier, and I was starting to wonder whether it had been an illusion. In fact, I was beginning to hope it had.

But no, as we progressed down the street fending off men with large moustaches and sleeveless denim waistcoats over leather jackets who were keen that we should go into their establishments to see 'live girls' (as opposed to dead ones, obviously), down a sidestreet was a familiar leggy mural. There it was! It was starting to rain so Sleazy took little convincing to enter. Which has always been a characteristic of his, as it happens. Inside it's a normal bar, just as I remembered. Rather than pole dancers and guys who would make Sleazy's lifestyle look like Cliff Richard's, there was a respectable post-work crowd much as you'd find in many a high-street pub in England. The barmaid chatted amiably to us in English while she poured our drinks, and we went and sat at a table underneath a television showing a live Borussia Moenchengladbach football match. It was all very relaxed, apart from the thuds and grunts of someone getting a right good kicking downstairs, which no one in the bar appeared to be acknowledging. Fortunately, a trip down the stairs to the toilet revealed that there was in fact a perfectly legitimate explanation. Either that or the full-size boxing ring in the basement was a very effective cover for gangland beatings.

After a pleasant evening spent wandering among the bars of Hamburg and keeping Sleazy out of the strip clubs, we returned to the hotel, where a man in a top hat emerged and opened the door of the battered minicab we'd flagged down on the Reeperbahn. I'm always uncomfortable when people do things like this. I really wish they wouldn't bother. At the risk of sounding like Uriah Heep I know my place, and it's not having taxi doors opened for me with a tip of the top hat. When I'm in a restaurant I sometimes feel I'd have an easier time if I volunteered to go and collect my meal from the kitchen myself, just to save anyone the trouble. I gave the doorman a strange kind of shrug-cum-nod, designed to say Look, I'm grateful and everything, but I don't think I'm anything special, you know, so there's really no need. To prove it, can I offer you a piggy-back up the steps? He probably just thought I had a nervous tic.

We repaired to the hotel's cosy bar for a nightcap, looking out on the Binnenalster lake across the road. I wouldn't have been surprised if chummy from reception had gone out and dug it himself that afternoon, just so we might have some silvery moonlit water to look at on the off chance we popped into the bar on the way up to our room. We had a beer and a whisky, and headed for bed. I signed off the bar bill against the room, and collapsed in the lift when the figures under which I'd scribbled my name with a hefty tip actually sank in. Two small beers and two whiskies? That's £35 to you, squire, thank you very much indeed.

Sylt is an extraordinary place. As well as having a name that sounds like someone accidentally swallowing a peach stone, it is little more than a giant sandbar just before the Danish border. Indeed, the Hindenburgdamm causeway out to this anchor-shaped island is practically adjacent to the border with Denmark: if you look east from List, Sylt's northernmost settlement, that's the Danish coast you can see. Major Danish towns like Tønder and Naestved are closer to the equator than the German town of List. Sylt borders the North Sea roughly on the same latitude as Middlesbrough, but the two couldn't be more different. Sylt styles itself as the 'St Tropez of the North', a playground for Germany's filthy rich. If you've got cash to burn in Germany, a holiday home here is practically mandatory. Luminaries from Thomas Mann to Brigitte Bardot have spent time on Sylt, whose climate is believed to be one of the healthiest in northern Europe.

Few people outside Germany seem to know

about the place, but over a million Germans head there for holidays or daytrips every year. Many of them minus clothes; Sylt is one of Germany's most popular destinations for naturists, hence you can often see the wobbly flesh panniers of ageing Germans darting between some of the most expensive cars in the world.

Sylt is apparently a little less snobby these days, and given the amount of tabloid scandal that's been uncovered there, where barely a summer week would go by without some German celebrity being caught *in flagrante* with someone they shouldn't have been, this isn't a surprise. However, when a few years back German Railways introduced a cheap-day ticket for families, Sylt objected. The only way on or off the island is by train across the causeway (the Ferraris, Audis and BMWs have to be loaded on to the train too), and the island authorities were terrified they would be overrun by riff-raff.

After the green-and-yellow patchwork fields of northern Germany, not to mention the hundreds upon hundreds of white electricity-generating windmills turning slowly and soothingly in the wind, the vast expanses of grey, featureless mud either side of the causeway were something of an anticlimax. The mudflats extended to the horizon on both sides beneath fluffy clouds – so low I could have leaned out of the train and dragged them along with us – and a deep-blue sky.

Suddenly the vista turned green and we were

on the island. Fields of shiny black horses flashed past, as did picturebook thatched cottages, and before long we pulled into the station at Westerland, the island's main town. Outside the station, giant green statues leaned at impossible angles, their hair straight out behind them. I think the message is that it's windy here. Which it is – the World Windsurfing Championships are held on Sylt and as recently as 1999 as storms lashed northern Europe the wind on Sylt got up to 115mph.

As we walked up the main street towards the beach, a street packed with daytrippers like Sleazy and me, Westerland certainly didn't look like the beating heart of German swankery. Souvenir shops sold the usual stuff, and there were amusement arcades and a couple of expensive-looking jewellery shops, but that was about it. I'd expected Nice and got Neasden. There was even a McDonald's.

We ventured on to the beach, a seemingly endless expanse of fine white sand. The sun was out but the wind was barrelling along at immense speed, blowing sand in our faces. The beach was crowded with *Strandkörbe*, literally 'beach baskets'. These are two-seater wicker chairs with backs and sides that rise up and over the occupants, sheltering them from the fierce wind. They were all white with huge numbers painted on them in black, which combined with the sand to make the beach look like some kind of lunar dump for space debris. Huge breakers crashed on the shore with tremendous force, while the *Strandkörbe* occupants looked out to sea, huddled together against the wind. It was almost the classic British seaside scene except the men wore expensive watches instead of vests and braces. It was so windy that we couldn't hear ourselves think, and given that all the *Strandkörbe* appeared to be occupied by elderly Germans wearing ostentatious jewellery, Sleazy and I decided to head north for List.

List is the northernmost community in Germany, right at the tip of Sylt. There's not much to say for it beyond the novelty value of being this far north and still in Germany: a fish market, a couple of tired-looking souvenir shops, an ice-cream parlour, a sausage stand and a bar were all we could find to look at. And flags, lots and lots of flags. It appeared that if you give someone in List a square yard of ground, within minutes he'll have stuck a pole in it and be running up a flag of some description. They can't seem to help themselves. List is also the docking point for the ferry to Romø, a Danish island just to the north of Sylt, which had just departed as we stepped off the bus after a journey through russet-coloured fields and past candystriped lighthouses. Again it was ridiculously windy and there was a distinct nip in the air. We ducked into the Alte Bootshalle bar, the northernmost in Germany, and ordered Germany's two northernmost beers while sitting on the nation's northernmost bar stools. Opposite the bar stood Germany's northernmost fish counter. The northernmost tape of German sea shanties came out of the country's northernmost speakers, which we took as the northernmost hint in Germany that it was time to go back to Hamburg.

As the train passed along the seven-mile Hindenburgdamm over the mudflats, the sun set blood red on the horizon while ribbed clouds glowed pink above us. Our faces stung from the constant battering of the salty wind, but that was nothing to how stung we'd feel in the morning when presented with a £44 bill for a breakfast we'd thought was included. If we'd known, we might have had more than a ham roll and two fried eggs.

My next place of residence, a bed and breakfast in Cromer, was not quite as swanky as the last, but then the room itself cost considerably less than my German breakfast. Where I'd been greeted in Hamburg by being addressed as 'sir', the first words spoken to me when I rang the doorbell in Cromer were 'sorry about the smell of boiled cabbage', a phrase I'll wager has never passed the lips of my dapper friend at the Vier Jahreszeiten.

Cromer might not be the most obvious place to visit in the shipping forecast's Humber region. Given their fishing heritage Hull and Grimsby would have been more logical choices, particularly given the former's connection with the Dogger Bank incident, but my reason for choosing the north Norfolk coast was to go in search of one of the most extraordinary people Britain has ever produced. In the summer of 2002 the BBC commissioned a poll to find the hundred greatest Britons who ever lived. Robbie Williams was on the list, so were David Beckham and Michael Crawford. But the name of the man who would probably come top of my list was nowhere to be found. Admittedly, until recently the former Charlton Athletic striker Clive Mendonca would have figured highly in my reckoning, but for me, the greatest of Britons was unquestionably Henry Blogg.

It's not exactly a name to conjure with, and it's pretty unlikely that you've ever heard of him. Most people won't have heard of him but he wouldn't have minded. In fact, he'd have preferred it that way. That's probably why he never got himself sent off against Argentina, or wore a beret, pulled camp faces and reported donkeys doing whoopsies in corridors. He kept himself to himself did Henry Blogg, and rarely left Cromer other than when the town's football team played local cup finals at Norwich City's ground, or he was receiving the latest of his large collection of decorations in London. But Henry Blogg was a hero in every sense of the word. He was modest, self-effacing, unassuming and brave, quite startlingly brave, and he was probably the greatest lifeboatman who ever lived.

I have a great deal of time for the Royal National Lifeboat Institution, given that it's feasible that were it not for lifeboats and their repeated rescuing of my grandfather, I wouldn't be here. Every crew member who ever put to sea in a distinctive orange-and-blue boat deserves a tip of our collective hat at the very least, but Henry Blogg was a giant among greatness. He was a member of the Cromer lifeboat crew for fifty-three years, thirty-seven of them as coxswain. He retired at the age of seventy-one, having been awarded the George Cross, the British Empire Medal, the RNLI gold medal for gallantry three times and the silver medal four times. But most importantly, he helped to save 873 lives at sea, which isn't a bad record for someone who couldn't swim.

It was cold, wet and rainy when I arrived in Cromer. Katie had joined me on this leg of the journey (she gets to see all the glamorous places: on our first Valentine's Day together I took her to see Brighton play Doncaster Rovers at Gillingham's ground, and she paid), and having eaten the picnic we'd planned for a sunny seafront in a rainy car park and checked into our cabbage-whiffy bed and breakfast, we took a walk in the drizzle towards the pier. The sea off the Norfolk coast is notoriously treacherous for shipping, and the stretch off Cromer is not known as the Devil's Throat for nothing. Thirteen miles out to sea lie the notorious Haisborough Sands, which have combined with the strong currents around them to create an historic graveyard for ships plying the coastal route between the Thames and the Tyne.

From the esplanade on a drizzly Friday late afternoon, however, there was nothing but grey murk out to sea; no hint of the perils to shipping that lay not far from this pleasant seaside town. We strolled on to the pier as the wind whipped in from the sea and speckled us with either rain, sea spray or a mixture of the two. The planks we walked on were dark, wet and shiny, with the choppy sea visible between them. At the end of the pier is the Pavilion Theatre, and beyond that the lifeboat station with its slipway dipping into the churning waves. A couple of miserable-looking anglers in full-scale luminous survival suits lolled against the theatre looking bored, while the only other occupants of the pier were two pasty-faced teenage boys with their hoods pulled over Burberry caps sitting in one of the shelters, smoking self-consciously.

The present pier celebrated its centenary in 2001. It's the only pier in the country that still puts on a 'Seaside Special' show, although a perusal of the posters of forthcoming attractions revealed the next big-name star to tread the boards over the waves would be Bobby Davro with a show called *Not in Front of The Children!*. 'Adults Only!' it affirmed over a picture of the Bobster with his hand over his mouth. The cheeky scamp. Another poster announced that the previous week the pier had hosted a music festival at which my mate Sid performed, the head honcho of the band with whom I'd first experienced the genitalia-festooned bar off the Reeperbahn. The Seaside Special poster revealed that the show this year would star 'Tucker', Melissa Merran, Leo Shavers, Vicki Carr and David Lawrence. I was none the wiser.

We spent a drizzly evening wandering the narrow, mazy streets of Cromer. There didn't appear to be anyone around, and in the end we spent the best part of the evening in a pleasant pub called the Wellington Inn, which, I learned the next day, stands on the site of the birthplace of Henry Blogg.

Lifeboats in Cromer date back to 1804, when locals, sick of watching helplessly as sailors perished in stormy seas often a matter of yards from the shore, subscribed £500 to commission a boat. Tragedy was a common theme along the Devil's Throat: one particularly stormy night in 1693 saw two hundred ships lost off Cromer, along with more than a thousand lives. It was this sort of tale which reminded me why I was here; how important the shipping forecast is. Practically every mile of our coastline has similar tales to tell. Until FitzRoy began assembling his weather reports, lives were being needlessly lost for want of information. Cromer, and particularly the story of Henry Blogg, reminded me that behind all the talk of poetry, romance and quirky notions of Britishness, the shipping forecast is all about the thin line between life and death.

Blogg, the man destined to become the greatest

lifeboatman of them all, was born into a fishing family in a cottage on the site of the Wellington Inn on February 6, 1876. His stepfather, J.J. Davies, was second coxswain of the lifeboat; J.J.'s father was the coxswain. Henry left school at eleven years old – despite having shown academic promise – to join his father's crab boat and soon became an accomplished longshore fisherman. It was during his teens that Henry learned the seamanship and intimate knowledge of Cromer's complicated, unpredictable waters that would help save so many lives in the following decades. He became a lifeboatman at the age of eighteen in January 1894 but had to wait a year for his first active service, a lengthy attendance to the *Fair City of Gloucester* four miles off the coast. The lifeboat then was an open, rowed affair and Henry, under J.J. Davies's command, was out at sea all night. That evening he got roaring drunk for the first and last time in his life, never touching another drop as long as he lived.

During the long Cromer summers Henry would supplement his fishing income by working the bathing machines on the beach, where he met his wife Ann. They were married in 1901 in Cromer's enormous parish church, which now houses a stained-glass window featuring his image, and a year later had a son, Henry, who died at two months. A daughter, Queenie, followed in 1907, by which time Henry had become second coxswain of the lifeboat. Two years later he became coxswain, voted unanimously by the crew. To list Blogg's great rescues would be time-consuming and probably serve only to numb admiration of his and his loyal crew's bravery. Instead let's stick to the tale of the *Fernebo*, which got into difficulties off Cromer one stormy night during the particularly harsh winter of 1917.

January 9 was a day of weather so filthy that when a rocket went up around lunchtime from a ship two miles off the coast of Cromer, it was picked out against a raging sky as black as night. Front doors flew open all over the town as the crew hit the streets running and made for the thirty-eight-foot *Louisa Heartwell* in the old lifeboat house on the shore near the pier. Within minutes of the distress signal the boat had been rolled out to the edge of the boiling surf and the crew began to row her into the crashing breakers. Now, bear in mind that this is during the First World War and most of the nation's young men were either dead or embedded in swampy trenches across Europe. The youngest member of the fourteen-man lifeboat crew that night was Blogg at forty-one, the rest ranged in age from fifties to the odd septuagenarian, and they were putting to sea in an open rowing boat on the stormiest night for years. Every ounce of strength they possessed was heaved into the oars but the *Louisa Heartwell* was pulled towards the pier and seemed set for certain disaster. She missed by a matter of yards. It took two hours of energy-sapping hardship but eventually the lifeboat reached the distressed *Pyrin*, rescuing the sixteen Greek sailors on board and rowing them back to shore.

Before the tired crew had even stripped off their drenched oilskins, however, the *Fernebo* sent up distress signals four miles out to sea. She was twice as far out as the *Pyrin* had been and now, with the tide higher, the conditions were twice as bad. The rain and wind continued to batter the coast but Blogg rallied his ageing crew, the *Louisa Heartwell* was dragged back into the thunderous waves and the Cromer lifeboat struck out once again. The *Fernebo* had struck a mine and the explosion had broken her back. It was only her cargo of timber that was keeping the stricken ship afloat. Six of the crew had decided to risk putting to sea in a small boat and fifty yards from shore it capsized. A human chain of onlookers ensured that every man was saved.

There were still men on board the ship, however, and Blogg and his crew represented their only hope. Fortunately the storm had blown the *Fernebo*, now broken in two, closer to the shore but the conditions were so bad that it took half an hour even to launch the *Louisa Heartwell*. When the lifeboat was halfway out to the stricken ship, a vast wave washed over her, smashing five oars and washing three more overboard. Blogg had no choice but to return to the beach, locate new oars and start out yet again. Eventually the *Louisa*

Heartwell reached the *Fernebo*, rescued eleven men and returned to shore at one o'clock in the morning. Blogg and his motley crew of near-pensioners had battled the roughest seas and worst conditions in living memory for fourteen hours and saved twenty-seven lives.

It was typical of Blogg's bravery and determination that he refused to accede to the elements and insisted on putting to sea when he and his men were already exhausted. It also says everything about him that the crew was prepared to follow him out to the *Fernebo*, knowing that they risked death by doing so. That was the kind of trust and loyalty the man inspired. Blogg led countless similar rescues, encompassing two world wars. By 1946 he was still coxswain at the age of seventy, ten years beyond the statutory retirement age for the RNLI. Even then he asked, and was allowed, to continue for another year before retiring in 1947 after fifty-three years' service.

After his retirement, whenever the maroons sounded and the lifeboat, a new vessel that bore his name, plunged down the slipway into the surf, Blogg would be on the pier, staring after it out to sea. Ann Blogg died in 1950, and in 1953 Henry watched helpless from the shore as a fishing boat containing two of his nephews capsized. The old man helped to launch a crab boat from the shore, but it was in vain and the men were drowned. On top of that the exertion caused him to collapse, and the grief combined with a weakening heart conspired to kill him the following year. Despite a life spent cheating death and snatching others from its clutches in the most dangerous of circumstances, he had outlived his wife, his son and his daughter.

Blogg was a quiet man. While the crew would often unwind in the pub after a rescue, the coxswain would just go home, change and park himself in his armchair. His modesty was legendary; he would rarely talk of his rescues, with one local dignitary once complaining that Blogg had spoken about a particularly dangerous shout 'as if he had merely crossed the road for a bottle of milk'. The numerous medals he received were kept in a drawer and never displayed.

The next morning I visited the lifeboat museum in the old lifeboat house near the pier. It was from here that Blogg would have launched on his first rescue, to the *Fair City of Gloucester* in 1895. From there it was a short walk to Blogg's old house, Swallow Cottage. It looks surprisingly modern from the outside, and sits in a tiny cul-de-sac a stone's throw from Mary-Jane's Fish Restaurant. What surprised me most was that you couldn't see the sea. When bad weather arose Blogg would be up on the cliffs that flank Cromer, pacing up and down as the clouds boiled and the waves crashed below, squinting against the rain looking for the slightest sign of a ship in trouble.

Swallow Cottage has now been renamed, unsurprisingly, Blogg Cottage. It's in a narrow, quiet street, the only noise being the roar of the wind and the crashing of the sea.

I headed east along the upper path, climbing the steps up the cliff and through a small public garden to find the bust erected in Blogg's memory. From here, on the top of the cliffs, Blogg looks out to sea just as he did for most of his life, straining his eyes for the faintest hint of humanity in peril. Just as at Whitby when I'd sat beneath Cook's statue, as I stood with Blogg looking out to sea, the sun burst through the clouds for the first time since I'd arrived in Norfolk. The tide was way out and the wet sand twinkled in the sunlight. In the distance, protruding just above the waves was a black lump of old timber: the keel of the *Fernebo*, still visible more than eighty years after the *Louisa Heartwell* brought its crew to safety.

The plaque beneath the bust details his awards and the bare statistics of his lifeboat career, but at the bottom it proclaims simply in large letters 'One of the bravest men who ever lived'. From the deceptively calm waters below me, Henry Blogg and his crew had plucked 873 people; 873 husbands, wives, sets of parents and children had Blogg to thank that their loved ones were able to return home after their respective calamities. But every time he returned from the stormy seas the old sailor would simply hang up his oilskins, walk along the pier, up the steps of the sea wall, past the Hotel de Paris and turn right to his cottage where Ann would be waiting with hot soup. A rescued Dutch sailor once tried to slip the coxswain a few quid in thanks for his safe deliverance. 'That's not what I'm here for,' Blogg replied, 'spend it on letting your wife know you're safely ashore.'

As the sun warmed my face the church bells began to peal. The sun began to pick out the pinks and yellows of the seafront buildings for the first time. People began to walk along the pier below, couples arm in arm. If it had been a century earlier the men would have been wearing frock coats and top hats and the women would have twirled parasols above their ringlets and crinolines. It was a scene of the most pleasant calm: out at sea, the tiny black stump was the only clue that terrible events had met with incredibly brave deeds off the beaches of Cromer.

The following day I walked along the pier in the sunshine, heading for the lifeboat house where I'd arranged to meet Richard Lees, the new honorary secretary of the Cromer lifeboat.

I was escorted into the inner sanctum – the lifeboat sat raised on its platform ready to plunge down the slipway – and through to the mess room where I sat with Richard at the end of a long table. Photographs adorned the walls; I recognised both Henry Blogg and his nephew and successor as coxswain, Henry 'Shrimp' Davies. 'Shrimp', who died in July 2002 at the age of eighty-eight, also had a remarkable career on the Cromer lifeboat between 1931 and 1976, saving more than five hundred lives. Like Blogg he received the British Empire Medal and also the Maritime Medal, France's highest award for bravery at sea. On retiring he featured on *This Is Your Life*, and his nephew Bill Davies is now the Cromer coxswain. Indeed, the Davieses have a long and proud tradition in Cromer lifeboat history. When the Cromer boat attended Clipper gas field helicopter crash in the summer of 2002, it was the first time in 130 years that a Cromer lifeboat had launched without a Davies aboard.

'We work on a range of around fifty miles,' said Richard over a cup of strong coffee. 'We have a Tyne-class lifeboat, which is the one you can see out there, but also an inshore lifeboat, an inflatable twin-hulled speedboat. When a person first joins the RNLI they start on the ILB [inflatable life boat], which is tougher than it sounds. Because it's so thin it's a bumpy ride; you're smacking into the waves at around twenty miles an hour, feeling every impact under your backside. You know you've been out on one of those things. The RNLI retirement age is fifty-five, but it's forty-five on the ILB because of the demanding physical conditions.

'The crew's a mixed bunch. Up until the seventies it was all fishermen but that's changed now. There are about thirty in the Cromer crew, and we've got a butcher, a thatcher, a fisheries officer, taxi driver, builder, chef, even a newspaper photographer. Most of the lads are self-employed, but those that aren't generally have understanding employers. When you sign up you go to the RNLI headquarters at Poole for an intensive four-day course. You're on the water eight hours a day, working with helicopters, winching people on and off, all that sort of thing. They even capsize you, so your head comes up in a small air pocket under the boat, and you can smell the leaking fuel, which is quite scary. They used to make you walk the keel of the boat underwater, but not any more.

'There's no shortage of volunteers; we've got four training with us at the moment. It's not really a glamorous business – the boats are pretty spartan. Space is at a premium, even on the big boat, so the facilities are fairly basic, especially when you consider you could be out there for a day or more. The toilet facilities, for example, are best described as rudimentary. We have cans of food that are heated chemically, and you get scrambled egg and sausage in them. They're pretty disgusting, really, but if you're out there, cold and starving hungry, they can be the best thing you've ever tasted.

'One disadvantage about Cromer is that we don't have a harbour here, only the boathouse. Where most lifeboats can moor, here we have to get back up the slipway. If the weather's bad that can be tricky. It can take hours, and sometimes we have to give up and go to Yarmouth or wherever and wait for the conditions to improve.

'The RNLI receives no money from the government; it's all funded by donations. There's a full-time mechanic in each station who maintains the lifeboats and keeps the place ticking over, doing odd jobs and whatever. The coxswain gets a small monthly retainer, and the second coxswain gets a nominal amount, but that's about it. It costs around £100,000 a year to run the Cromer lifeboat and we rely totally on donations. Legacies are an important source of income – one local man left us £97,000 recently, practically enough to run the place for a year, while about five years ago a lady left us £500,000 in her will.'

It's a quiet afternoon in the boathouse, and there are few people around. For a service that runs with no state funding, it's extraordinary what these men achieve. Once their pager goes off they drop everything, whatever they're doing, wherever they are, and sprint up the pier to the boathouse. Generally it's whoever gets there first who goes. If there's a big group, the coxswain can choose the most experienced, but these are selfless people. Like Henry Blogg they are modest, likeable and unassuming, carrying on the legacy of Cromer's biggest hero. As we sit chatting with a calm sea visible through the windows, Blogg's photograph smiles down on the men in overall trousers and RNLI t-shirts lounging around with styrofoam cups of coffee, exchanging local gossip.

The words of Henry Blogg's only recorded speech came to mind. It was the occasion of his retirement more than half a century ago, and is believed to be the only time he addressed a mass gathering. 'Cromer has always had good boats and good crews,' he said into an enormous lollipop microphone on the seafront, before adding, 'and it always will.' He knew that the eternal love-hate relationship between Cromer and the sea would ensure a never-ending supply of future Henry Bloggs.

A few days later, I knew exactly what Richard had meant about feeling every wave when you're travelling on the inshore lifeboat. I wasn't aboard an ILB though; I was on probably the most bizarre royal yacht in the world, piloted by a crown prince. The prince was clad in jeans, a checked shirt and a bomber jacket and he was at the wheel of a large, black, twin-engined inflatable speedboat, on which I and a select handful of fellow travellers were hanging on grimly as we battered into wave after wave of grey-brown North Sea. Between facefuls of briny spray our destination became gradually more visible out of the haze on the horizon, a hotchpotch of buildings on a platform atop two giant concrete legs. As we drew nearer, the prince eased off the throttle, turned to us and said, 'Well, folks, welcome to Sealand.' It had taken a while, but I'd got here.

The Principality of Sealand was founded and

declared independent in 1967 on Roughs Tower, a Second World War fortress constructed and subsequently abandoned by Britain a few miles off the east coast in Area Thames. Sealand is a place shrouded in mystery and rumour, with tales of gun battles, court cases, invasions, pirate radio stations, princes held hostage, even renegade lawyers forging passports linked to the murder of Gianni Versace. It's a remarkable story for a nation whose history barely covers a generation and whose surface area is roughly the size of a football pitch.

I had to go. The prospects for a visit didn't look good though. 'Due to the current international situation and other factors, visits to the Principality of Sealand are not normally permitted,' read an official notice on the website. 'Emergency or other special circumstances suggesting that a visit might be appropriate require prior approval from the Bureau of Internal Affairs and may be considered by making a written application. It is highly unlikely that permission to submit a visa application would be granted.'

It had to be worth a try though. I sent an e-mail explaining my shipping forecast mission and asked to be considered for a visa. Days became weeks and nothing happened. I'd almost forgotten about Sealand when an e-mail popped into my inbox in the name of 'Chief of Bureau'.

It informed me that the principality thanked me for my request and found my suggestion particularly interesting, therefore, in principle, they had no objection to my proposal.

It was signed 'Chief of Bureau, Bureau of Internal Affairs, Sealand'. It was a promising start at any rate, inasmuch as it wasn't a 'no'. I replied assuring the Chief of Bureau of my best intentions and set about learning more about Sealand.

The principality started life as one of four Maunsell forts around the Thames estuary, constructed and sited during the Second World War. A gun platform sat atop two giant hollow legs that provided the accommodation and storage facilities for soldiers stationed there. The forts prevented the Germans from laying mines in the estuary and between them shot down twenty-two aircraft and thirty doodlebugs. The forts were maintained during the immediate post-war years with the advent of the Cold War, but by 1956 all had been abandoned and no one appeared to give Roughs Tower and its three sisters a thought. By the mid-sixties, however, Radio Caroline had begun broadcasting from a ship in international waters off the Essex coast. Soon afterwards Screaming Lord Sutch took over a sea fort off Herne Bay and began broadcasting Radio Sutch, while before long most of the disused forts off the south-east coast of England had been occupied by shaggy-haired youths with turntables, boxes of records and a desire to bring music to the masses. One of the people behind these stations was Roy Bates from Westcliff-on-Sea.

Bates's life would make a cracking Ealing film. A born adventurer, at the age of sixteen he made his way to Spain because he fancied having a look at the civil war. During the Second World War he saw action in the Middle East and Sicily and was wounded several times, five of which were on the same night. After the war he met his future wife, Joan, at Southend's famous Kursaal ballroom and dabbled in a number of different business ventures. He became aware of the abandoned sea forts while running an inshore fishing fleet, and capitalised on the pirate radio boom by setting up Radio Essex on the Knock John fort, Britain's first twenty-four-hour local radio station.

Bates was charged with illegal broadcasting in 1966, and despite being fined £100 by Essex magistrates continued with his radio projects. When the government moved the goalposts on what constituted territorial waters and Knock John was no longer viable, he moved his operation to Roughs Tower eight miles from Harwich. Roughs Tower was outside UK limits, and after a brief disagreement with Radio Caroline over who should occupy the place, Bates moved his family on to the fort and began renovations. On September 2, 1967 he declared the fort independent, appointed himself Prince Roy and raised the flag of the Principality of Sealand for the first time. Passports were produced, with Sealand coins and stamps not far behind.

The British government, of course, took a dim

view. A naval cruiser sailed close to Sealand raising a thoughtful eyebrow at the prince but was warned off by shots fired from the platform, an incident that saw Roy Bates in court again. A year after the creation of Sealand, Mr Justice Chapman at Essex Assizes ruled that as it was outside the three-mile limit of British territorial waters, the United Kingdom could not claim sovereignty over the former Roughs Tower. British law did not appear to extend to Sealand, and, on the face of it, the royal Bates family seemed perfectly entitled to their sovereignty.

Prince Roy was no mere eccentric, however. He was shrewd enough to recognise the commercial possibilities of the fledgling nation and looked into creating a tax haven, replete with hotel and casino complex. It was in 1978, while Prince Roy was off Sealand engaged in discussions about this very idea, that Sealand was invaded by a German lawyer named Gernot Putz, who turned up with a bunch of German and Dutch raiders when Prince Regent Michael was there alone. Michael, then fifteen, was locked up, and it took a daring helicopter raid by Prince Roy to wrest back control of his nation. Putz had been a business associate of Sealand and had been granted that rare thing, a Sealand passport, for his services to the country. While the other invaders were permitted to leave, Putz, as a Sealand citizen, was charged with treason and imprisoned in the brig, deep inside one of the platform's towers. He was fined £20,000 by a specially convened Sealand court and told he couldn't leave until the sum was paid. The German government prevailed upon their British counterparts to intervene, but as the British did not recognise Sealand there was nothing they could do. In the end, after forty-nine days in captivity and a visit from a German consular official, Putz was given a royal pardon and released.

The next couple of decades passed relatively uneventfully, with Prince Roy and Princess Joan eventually retiring to Spain and leaving Michael in charge of Sealand affairs. In 1997, however, Sealand's name became embroiled in a remarkable catalogue of fraud and international terrorism, none of which actually had anything to do with the Bateses' mini-state in the North Sea.

On July 15, 1997, the designer Gianni Versace returned home from a trip to the paper shop and was shot dead by Andrew Cunanan. Cunanan had convinced himself that he was HIV positive – he wasn't – and had already killed three people when he turned up at Versace's house. The story goes that the designer apparently blanked him once at a party, triggering a festering murderous hatred. A few days later, Cunanan's body was found on a Miami houseboat where he had shot himself in the head. A search of the boat turned up a Sealand passport – a fake one. The Bateses are very particular about the people to whom they grant passports, particularly after the failed Putz putsch, and only around three hundred have ever been issued. Certainly they have never been sold as commodities. The owner of the houseboat, a German, had also been driving a car displaying what purported to be Sealand diplomatic licence plates, a discovery that went on to open a substantial can of worms.

Fake Sealand passports started showing up all over the place. Four thousand had been sold in Hong Kong prior to the British handover of the territory to the Chinese at £1,000 a time. A website appeared claiming to be that of the official Sealand government and boasting of 160,000 passport holders and several overseas embassies. The operation was traced to Madrid, where a fake Sealand 'embassy' was discovered to have been selling false passports to a range of ne'er-do-wells from Moroccan drug smugglers to Russian gangsters. Rather than the genuine North Sea principality, this was no more than a chancer knocking out dodgy gear from a cyber suitcase by the side of the information superhighway. Sealand driving licences and even university degrees were banged out at up to £40,000 a time. People involved in illegal eastern-European pyramid selling operations were found to hold bogus Sealand passports. Heading up this international operation was a disgraced former Spanish policeman and failed businessman named Francisco Trujillo Ruiz, the self-styled and wholly false 'regent' of Sealand. Of his ten-strong 'cabinet', nine had previous convictions for, among other things, fraud. Most alarmingly, however, the Sealand gang were implicated in a £35 million plot to sell fifty Russian tanks and ten MiG fighter planes to Sudan, in contravention of an international trade embargo on the African state. It was big-league stuff, none of which had anything to do with Roy Bates and his family on their rusting old platform with a distant view of Harwich.

Meanwhile, another e-mail had arrived in my inbox from the Chief of Bureau, thanking me for my interest, and telling me that my visa application had been passed on to the office of the Head of State for consideration. They would get back to me soon with further comment.

Six months passed until I received another e-mail informing me my request had been 'favourably received', but was 'still under discussion'. However, an application form for a visa had been attached. I was a little bit closer. A few weeks after carefully filling in and dispatching my visa application I received a letter on Principality of Sealand headed paper. My visa had been approved.

It was official: I was going to Sealand. The letter went on to detail how I should arrive at a hotel in Harwich early on a specified Sunday morning where I would be met and, on production of my visa and passport, escorted by boat to the principality.

I set out from home at dawn one Sunday morning and headed up the A12 for Harwich feeling slightly nervous. My research had thrown up a website claiming that Sealand was an 'armed terrorist base' and describing the Bates royal family as 'terrorist thugs'. Another site claimed to have seen 'armed goons' brandishing automatic weapons on the platform. Yet here I was meeting someone for whom I didn't even have a name in a hotel lobby in a strange town, to whom I would hand over my passport. An hour or so later I arrived at a deserted quayside and parked in front of the hotel. I took a couple of deep breaths. Harry's picture was on the passenger seat beside me – was I also about to disappear off to sea for several months? I didn't even have the excuse of being blind drunk. I picked up the picture and levelled my gaze at my great-grandfather. Where Harry was looking slightly to the right of the camera, he now looked as though he was deliberately avoiding my eye. I left him on the seat. Well, he didn't have a visa. Picking up my passport and documentation, I climbed out of the car, walked edgily through the doors of the hotel and up to the reception desk.

'Hello,' I said, 'I'm, er, supposed to be meeting someone here.'

The girl smiled and gestured to my left. 'I think that might be the gentleman through there, sir,' she said. I looked into the bar. All I could see was a wisp of cigarette smoke curling upwards from behind a tall-backed leather armchair, and a cup of strong black coffee on the table beside it. A hand emerged from behind the armchair and lifted the cup from its saucer; it disappeared and emerged again a second later to replace the cup on the table.

Gulp.

I walked into the bar, breathing heavily, and rounded the partition. A tough-looking man with a lined face sat there alone, his piercing, ice-blue eyes staring straight ahead without registering my presence. He wore a black sweatshirt with the words 'Sealand Security' emblazoned across the front in large letters. I cleared my throat. Nothing happened. 'Er . . .' I ventured, eloquently. 'Hi. My name's Charlie, I, er, was told to meet somebody from Sealand here?'

Without shifting his gaze, the man put out his right hand. I shook it. 'Sit down,' he said levelly, still staring straight ahead. I sat down. 'Do you have your passport and visa?' he asked, still not having actually looked at me. I handed them over. He scrutinised them for an agonisingly long time, finally snapping his gaze to my face to compare me to the photograph in my passport. I gave a weak little wave.

As it turned out, my fears were unfounded. The man was, I deduced, the Chief of Bureau of Internal Affairs of the Principality of Sealand with whom I had been corresponding and his name, I would find out later, was Lew. In football parlance Lew could probably be described as Sealand's midfield engine room. He deals with

190

the principality's official correspondence and sees to it that the constitution and Sealand law are upheld to the letter. Once he'd satisfied himself that I was who I purported to be, he relaxed a little. There'd be a small group of us going out to Sealand, he told me. A documentary filmmaker was producing an official DVD on behalf of the Sealand government and he was coming out with a photographer to take some stills of Prince Michael. Michael would be driving what Lew called the 'service ferry' out to Sealand. A local historian, Frank Turner, was also coming, a man who was an expert on the Thames estuary forts.

Finally Prince Michael himself arrived, a huge bear of a man with a deep, resonant laugh emitting from beneath close-cropped hair whose appearance alone, despite a surprisingly refined accent, caused me to make a mental note never to get on the wrong side of him. Not ever.

Once our motley crew was accounted for and their visas approved, we headed for the quayside and boarded the speedboat. It's a serious machine, the sort of thing you see the US Navy Seals bombing around on. Lifejackets were distributed, crash helmets given out and the journey to Sealand began with a roar of engines, a swirl of seawater and the whiff of expended diesel. The swell was substantial. As I have a larger-than-average bonce that isn't even a conventional shape, helmets are always a problem for me. The one I'd been given perched tightly on the back of my head at an angle that could have been described as 'jaunty' if it hadn't folded my ears over against the side of my head so I couldn't have heard it described as anything. It was a bumpy crossing. Michael stood at the controls opening out the throttle, every bump of every wave impacting my vertebrae and taking another fraction of an inch off my height, stature I could ill afford to lose. Strafed by salty spray we thundered and crashed through the waves at whiplash velocity. There were six of us huddled together in two rows of three behind Michael, and in our white helmets we must have looked from a distance like a box of eggs being thrown around the sea.

After half an hour or so of pounding through the waves, Sealand appeared on the horizon looking like a bizarre maritime Stonehenge. A further half hour saw us draw near enough to see the word 'Sealand' picked out on the side of the buildings and the red, white and black national flag fluttering above it. We slowed to a halt as we drew near to the base of one of the legs, looking up a good sixty or seventy feet to where two figures waited with what looked horribly like a winch to lift us one by one from the boat. This is the only way in and out of Sealand, the most bizarre border crossing I've ever made. Down came the winch, which was grabbed by Michael, hooked on to a harness in front of my breastbone and suddenly my feet were dangling in the air. Up and up I went, hanging on grimly to the cable as the boat shrank below me and the bottom of the platform drew nearer and nearer while the North Sea crashed against the concrete legs below. After what seemed like an age, the arm of the winch swung me over the platform and dropped me on to Sealand territory with a metallic 'bong'. For some reason the whole place appeared to be vibrating. Then I realised it was just my legs shaking with fright.

One by one the others were hoisted on to Sealand before the boat itself was winched up with Michael aboard, the Crown Prince arriving in his domain. We removed our lifejackets and helmets, which meant I could hear again, and walked into the building that made up much of Sealand's business district, seat of government and housing. We gathered in the kitchen and cups of tea were handed out as Lew took my passport and stamped it with the official Sealand immigration seal.

Although it consists of just a corridor and two concrete legs that each contain seven floors of rooms, Sealand has road names. Three to be precise. The corridor along the principality's upper level, the building in which we sat sipping tea and looking out of the brine-spattered windows, is The Row, while the towers are respectively North Deep and South Deep. Above The Row, on the roof, was a helipad.

When we'd drained our tea and our spines had finally stopped jarring from the crossing, Michael led us along the corridor and down the stairs to the first level of South Deep, a circular, white-washed room full of swanky-looking computer equipment. These racks of sleek technology were Internet servers, the latest method Michael has found to utilise Sealand's national status. Sealand leases the space to a US-based company called HavenCo, which offers its secure servers to organisations and websites away from more conventional government control. Child pornography, hacking, terrorism and racism are not tolerated, indeed Prince Michael has said that if he discovers the servers being used to house any such websites he will personally chuck the equipment into the sea, but anything else goes. Frank Turner, the historian, meanwhile turned out to be a walking, talking encyclopaedia of Sealand. Even though he'd never actually been here before, he told Michael about what the various rooms and cupboards were used for, things even Michael didn't know despite having practically grown up here. You got the impression that Frank could walk around the place with his eyes closed and not actually bump into anything.

We returned to The Row and passed along the corridor. On a cork noticeboard was a pizza delivery menu from Harwich, which must produce some interesting responses when the Sealanders start giving them directions. Further along The Row is the principality's sitting room, from whose windows you can't fault the sea view. Books and videos line the shelves, among which I note are *The Perfect Storm, Ice Station Zebra* and *The Cruel Sea*. It's actually surprisingly cosy; the double-glazing keeps out the noise of the sea crashing around below while the wall-to-wall carpet and heater keep out the chill of the icy North Sea winds.

North Deep is a little more accessible. Here is the main accommodation space for the Sealanders, with one room containing a double bed and the tiniest snooker table I've ever seen. The lower we went the darker it became, and when I heard the sloshing and glooping of water outside the metre-thick walls I realised that we were actually beneath the sea.

'Bear in mind,' said Frank, 'that there were often as many as two hundred soldiers stationed here during the war, and if you weren't on duty on the guns then you had to stay inside. You could be here for weeks at a time and rarely see daylight. Add to that the constant threat of being bombed, shot or mined and the permanent sloshing of the sea and it's no wonder that many of the soldiers went a bit loopy. There was even one suicide: an eighteen-year-old lad who got up one morning, calmly made his bunk, walked up on top and just jumped into the sea.'

As I stood in this dark, circular room with the sound of the sea echoing around the walls, it wasn't too hard a stretch of the imagination to guess how he felt. On the furthest level down, before a sheer drop to the base of the leg, was the brig, a dark, cavernous room with a thick steel door where Gernot Putz spent his six weeks in captivity. Not a barrel of laughs, I'd imagine. I made a note to be careful what I wrote about Sealand. I didn't fancy ending up down here as a result of a bad joke going very wrong.

It was a relief to emerge again into the hazy sunshine of the upper deck. I sat on a crate, squinting in the sunlight, and chatted to Prince Michael. I'd met a crown prince before, but he was a multi-millionaire holding a giant reception in the gardens of his thirteenth-century castle in the Alps. This was a little bit different.

'I've known this place for almost as long as I can remember,' said Michael. 'I've been coming for periods of between six weeks and six months ever since my mother and father first came here, sometimes by myself. We've been through good years and bad though. The British government have tried it on a few times. The Navy came and the Admiralty turned up with a couple of military policemen claiming that my father had sold the fort. Which he hadn't, obviously. I was about fifteen at the time, here on my own. They tried very hard to convince me but I just said fine, if that's the case, bring him out here so I can hear him tell me himself. A couple of Royal Marines started climbing the ladder; I produced a pistol, showed it to them and they backed down. They were unarmed, and I didn't point the gun at them or anything. In fact it was all quite civilised. Very British, you might say.

'Another time, a couple of officials came out to service the buoys that mark the fort. My sister was here at the time, sun-bathing. They passed a couple of, shall we say, lascivious comments about her which resulted in us firing a couple of warning shots over them, and off they went. That's all it took – the advantage of this territory is that it's so inaccessible. I like the fact that you have to be winched on and off – if it's hard for people who are supposed to be here to arrive, then it's even harder for unwelcome visitors. We've even got a pole stuck in the middle of the helipad to stop helicopters landing without permission.'

I asked him about the 1978 incident, and he breathed deeply, looking out to sea.

'Well, I was out here on my own at the time, when a helicopter showed up. I wouldn't let it land, but this German man I knew came down on a winch wire. He showed me a telex purporting to be from my father saying he'd handed over Sealand to him. I went into the lounge to talk about it, only to find the door closed behind me and a camera tripod stuck through the handle so I couldn't get out. This was before we had the double-glazed windows put in, so there were only little portholes and just no way I could get out. Three or four days they kept me in there, before giving me the choice of going to England or the Netherlands, or staying put. I said, "I'll stay here please." Despite that they put me on a trawler and sent me to Holland. I landed illegally, of course, no passport or anything.'

I asked if he was scared, having been a teenage boy alone, locked in a room while men with guns clumped around his father's principality.

'Scared? No, I definitely wasn't scared. I was more infuriated. In fact, I was absolutely wild. By the time I got back to my father we'd learned they were apparently planning to put ten Belgian ex-paratroopers on here the next day, so we had to move quickly. My father phoned a friend of his who was a stunt pilot – he'd flown helicopters in Bond films – and we surprised them by flying in low over the sea and suddenly coming up from underneath with my father and me on the skids of the chopper with coiled ropes in our hands. It was very, very close to becoming a firefight, but eventually we, let's say, persuaded them to stick their hands in the air. We took the German prisoner and charged him with treason. Eventually a German diplomat came out and my father pardoned the guy. Since then we've always made sure there are at least two people here at all times.'

Michael and his father have made every effort to have Sealand recognised as a sovereign state. In 1987 Britain passed a law extending its territorial waters from three miles to twelve, but the day before the law came into being, Sealand announced its own territorial waters to be twelve miles. Sealand and the UK appear to have reached a silent impasse. The British refuse to comment on Sealand, let alone attempt to take it back by force, as this would necessitate their admitting its existence. Sealand is reasonably happy with that, but still campaigns for active recognition.

Michael: 'Lew's working away at the UN, submitting our imports and exports, and our balance of payments. The fact that we've been involved in court cases in the UK, and the visit of the German in 1978, I consider to be *de facto* acknowledgement of Sealand's sovereignty. After all, for years America didn't recognise China, and you can't say China didn't exist. My ultimate hope is to see a small island built here. It's always been my dream to step off the platform on to terra firma.'

Some people have speculated that the British are hoping Sealand will go away once the elderly Roy Bates dies and they can chug smugly out to sea and blow it to pieces as they tried to do with Heligoland. But with Prince Regent Michael still around, and Lew beavering away at the legalese, it's unlikely Sealand will just disappear quietly. Unlike his father, Michael has known Sealand for almost as long as he can remember. He grew up here, was once imprisoned here, had the sort of *Boy's Own* adventures here that his childhood peers could only dream of. He's not going to just give all that up. Time and money have been invested into Sealand, and its commercial potential is yet to be exploited fully. But beyond that Sealand has developed a tangible sense of national identity, one that I detected even in the few hours I spent there. As I parked my backside on the bosun's chair and was hoisted out over the North Sea, aiming for the quite startlingly small boat below, I felt a genuine pang of regret at leaving one of the most remarkable nations I'd ever visited. The fort's designer, Guy Maunsell, claimed that, barring accidents, Roughs Tower could stand for two hundred years. Prince Michael will be long gone by then, but I wouldn't mind betting that Sealand will still be around.

Michael wheeled the boat around, opened the throttle and shot us between the legs of his domain back towards Harwich. I twisted round to look at Sealand for the last time. It's rusty, battered and certainly not beautiful in the conventional sense. There are no mountains, meadows, cathedrals or lakes. In fact there's only one toilet. But Sealand has a history, a culture, a flag, even an anthem. Like Heligoland, it stands defiant. But most of all, Sealand's greatest claim to nationhood is its place in the hearts of the Bates family. 'The song of Sealand rings across the sea,' says the Sealand anthem, 'the island of hope, of freedom and liberty.'

Back at Harwich, our little band of Sealand-ophiles dispersed. Michael heaved himself into his four-wheel-drive and departed for his UK residence in deepest Essex, while Lew folded himself into an old Trabant and chugged away up the street. I looked out to sea in the direction from whence we'd come. There were a few spots of rain in the wind blowing inland, but the sun was setting behind me. I bet it looked great from Sealand.

DOVER, WIGHT, PORTLAND

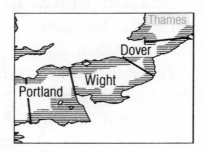

Area Dover is another product of the 1956 changes to the forecast. Its eastern border with Thames extends from the tip of Kent to the mouth of the Westerschelde River north-east of Bruges. The border with Area Wight runs from Beachy Head across the Channel to Dieppe. On the 1924 map Area Wight occupied its present position as well as the modern Dover and Portland. Since 1956 its western boundary has stretched from Hengistbury Head off Christchurch across to Cherbourg. Portland encompasses the Channel Islands, extending west to a line approximately between Salcombe in Devon and Roscoff.

I have to confess that as I drove down the A2 towards Dover I wasn't expecting a great deal from the place. I could conjure up only two previous occasions on which I'd had cause to visit, neither of which was particularly inspiring for me or for Dover.

Just over a decade earlier I had passed through on my way home from inter-railing with a student friend called Paul. And believe me, Dover probably knew about it. Nearly all our money had gone on the tickets, so we slept on overnight trains for a month. On two occasions we scraped together what money we could and spent a night in a hostel, which meant that in an entire month we had a grand total of two showers.

Our final major rail journey was an eighteen-hour clickety-clack-a-thon from Rome to Paris, from where we were heading for home. We turned up at the very last moment for the train and found nearly all the seats taken. Remarkably, however, despite the fact that people were hanging from luggage racks all the way along the carriages, we found a compartment occupied solely by a kindly looking old Italian woman who smiled encouragingly at us through the glass door. We yanked the door open, threw our holdalls on to the overhead racks and sat down. And then we noticed it. The smell. The old woman was giving off an odour the like of which had never assaulted my nostrils before or since. Even now, more than a decade on, I can still smell it: a potent mixture of cheese, old cabbage and about a million used nappies. But given that a) there was no way we were going to travel for eighteen hours standing up, b) we probably smelled just as bad and c) we were British and therefore more likely to nod and smile politely than shout 'Jesus Christ, woman, you need hosing down with disinfectant and a bonfire made of your clothes' before hauling open every door and window in the carriage, we had little option but to stay put.

Six hours of biological warfare later, in which even we were hopelessly outgunned, the old woman departed victorious. At the next stop a young woman entered the carriage and sat down. Within seconds, she had stood up again and begun addressing us in Italian, a language neither of us understood. I did however detect the phrase *a Roma*, in reference to the train's point of embarkation. She repeated this several times. '*A Roma*,' she said, rising to her feet, smiling, '*a Roma*.' 'Oh yes,' I gushed, nodding and giving her the thumbs up, 'Roma, we've come from Roma.' The woman nodded and smiled and left the compartment while Paul and I grinned at each other. This was our first vaguely meaningful encounter of the entire month with a member of the opposite sex, contrary to the shagathon we'd confidently expected courtesy of those relaxed, obliging and supple European gals across the continent.

Then it dawned on me. Joining together the *a* and the *Roma*, of course, produced the word *aroma*. She'd left the carriage with the fleetness of foot of a cat escaping a garden sprinkler because Paul and I stank to high heaven. At least by the time we reached Calais we were guaranteed plenty of space around us on the ferry, and by the time the White Cliffs hove into view you could practically hear us humming above the dull throb of the ship's engines. It's a wonder that we weren't stuck straight into quarantine at Dover or even turned away from the UK altogether on the grounds that we contravened United Nations directives on germ warfare.

The second time I had cause to be in Dover was a couple of years later when an old schoolfriend who had moved to Germany to work for a haulage company arranged for me to visit him. He had secured free passage for me on a couple of trucks, the first from his company's UK office in Essex to Dover, where I was due to rendezvous with a Dutchman called Jack who would drive me to Düsseldorf. The snag was that my free passage came as a 'second driver', ready to take over if the main driver became incapacitated. Given that I had barely mastered a Fiat Panda at this point, the arrangement was fraught with potential disaster.

Suffice to say that some imbecilic behaviour on my part combined with some really terrible luck to ensure that at around two o'clock one freezing November morning I was running around Dover's eastern docks looking for a Dutch lorry while soaked from head to toe in diesel. As the trucks began to load on to the ferry there was a loud parp of an aerosol horn and the driver at the front of the queue waved frantically at me. He was not eating cheese, did not appear to have his finger in a dyke nor was he executing a gravity-defying turn with a football, but I deduced that he was Dutch nonetheless and leaped aboard the moving lorry as it disappeared into the bowels of the ship. My ordeal was more or less over save for the terrifying – and thankfully unfulfilled – prospect of my taking the wheel somewhere between Calais and the Ruhr. My impressions of Dover, however, would henceforth be tinged with personal hygiene concerns and the musky tang of diesel.

This time I was smelling like neither a petrol station nor a municipal rubbish tip, but I still did not hold out great hopes for the Dover experience. I knew little of the place beyond its cliffs and its recent focus as the centre of attention for the Great Asylum-seeker Debate, and to be honest wasn't particularly relishing the prospect of spending any more time there than was absolutely necessary.

Having checked into a pleasant guesthouse I sauntered into the early Dover evening. Passing through the town's market square I spied water and headed for it, ending up on Dover beach. Now, you'd be forgiven for unleashing a derisive snort at the thought of Dover having a beach. Yet here, despite being squeezed between the western and eastern docks where oily ferries to-ed and fro-ed at all hours, was a clean, tidy and pleasant expanse of shingle sloping towards the gently lapping waves of the English Channel.

The sun was out and preparing to set. Away to my left, two P&O funnels peeped above the cranes and parapets of the harbour while the white cliffs glowed in the haze beyond. The impressive battlements of Dover Castle loomed from the top of the hill behind me. The shingle was neatly stacked and gently shelving, the waterline was notably lacking in the usually required plastic bottles and blue-and-white striped carrier bags, and there were even two little girls in pink fleeces with pink ribbons in their hair running away from the waves with delighted giggles while their mum sat watching from the rear of the beach.

I parked my behind on the pebbles and looked out to sea. Towards the horizon silhouettes of several tankers, transporters and ferries moved slowly through some of the world's busiest shipping lanes. More than 150 years earlier Matthew Arnold had sat here, maybe on this very spot, and written his poem 'Dover Beach'. As a teenager I had read quite a lot of Arnold; his 'I'm all alone and nobody understands me' stanzas were manna from heaven for a lonely post-pubescent seeking a meaning to life and at the same time hoping to appear interesting to girls. A book of his poems sat well next to my Marillion LPs.

Arnold's poem mused upon the pointlessness of life and how we'd never really know true peace nor joy. Love was about the best we could do and that wasn't really up to much, so we'd better make the most of it. Given that Arnold was on his honeymoon when he wrote this, one can only wonder at why his new wife had agreed to marry such a grumpy, self-obsessed gawd-help-us with a ridiculous moustache. Indeed, she may well have used that very phrase when he returned to the bridal suite from the beach clutching his new stanzas and still brushing the sand from his posterior. As I watched the two girls fail narrowly to win a foot race with the incoming waves, I thought of Arnold's 'eternal note of sadness' and his 'ebb and flow of human misery' and wondered what on earth I'd seen in the work of such a sulky-trousers.

At breakfast the next morning the talk in the dining room was of the weather in St Petersburg. An elderly British couple and a middle-aged American pairing – the male half of which had a terrific soup-strainer moustache – had just discovered that they were booked on the same cruise and were comparing notes. I had a slightly less glamorous destination that day. Mention the word 'Dover' and 'Calais' usually won't be far behind. The two towns are barely twenty miles apart across the sea and the cross-Channel ferry service is one of the most popular routes in Europe. They have much in common, and on the back page of the local newspaper that week was a story about how Dover Athletic had arranged two friendlies with their footballing counterparts from Calais. 'We've been travelling miles up through Kent for games,' a club official mused, 'yet our closest team is just across the water.'

I learned two things about Calais while I was in Dover. One, it's actually a island, and two, it was English for more than two hundred years. After the Battle of Crécy in 1346, Calais withstood an English siege for more than a year before being starved out. It wasn't until 1558 that the French got it back, and England's last foothold in France was gone. 'When I am dead and opened, you shall find "Calais" lying in my heart,' said Queen Mary, who died a few months later a broken woman. These days, Calais means cheap fags and booze to most people, and the port buzzes with cars and vans loaded with crates of stubbies and long, rectangular packages of cigarettes. The clink of wine bottles is a constant accompaniment to the disembarkation of vehicles down the ferry ramps.

'All the ferry services can trace their roots to ships that used to carry the odd parcel or packet across the water,' P&O's Brian Rees had told me. 'You can trace them back for centuries. There's the wreck of a small Bronze Age trading ship just off Dover Harbour. What we usually term the "packet ships" grew up out of the postal services, and moved from sail to the steam-packets – paddle steamers – and on to ferries that operate as extensions of the railway services.

'An awful lot of those railway-company ferry services became nationalised under British Rail in 1948. People started to travel more, arriving at stations like the old Dover Marine which drew up right in the docks – alas, no more, it's now the cruise terminal. Cars were craned on and off one at a time, believe it or not. Then as car ownership grew, roll-on roll-off ferries were developed.

'Margaret Thatcher's first privatisation was of the nationalised ferry company Sealink in 1984, which was a division of British Rail. Various private ferry companies also existed, including Townsend Thoresen. P&O operated from Dover to Boulogne in a modest way in the late seventies but sold out to Townsend. P&O came back to Dover in force in 1987 by acquiring Townsend Thoresen itself. Meanwhile the previously state-owned Sealink at Dover had been acquired by Stena Line of Sweden. In the mid-nineties P&O and Stena Line merged their Dover to become P&O Stena Line. P&O acquired the Stena Line interests at Dover last year, resulting in what we have today: P&O Ferries operating seven passenger ships and one freight ship from Dover to Calais, plus routes from Hull and Portsmouth.'

Got that?

I walked along the main road to the ferry terminal. So short is the crossing between Dover and Calais that I fully intended to be back in Dover by lunchtime. I quite fancied the idea of being able to answer an afternoon enquiry of 'Busy morning?' with 'Oh, you know, went to France.' Cross-Channel ferries never cease to impress me. I know that by using Eurostar you can be in France in next to no time, but for me you can't beat crossing above the water rather than beneath it. Going under the Channel doesn't feel right somehow; there's no real sense of leaving the country if you don't surround yourself with the sea at some point in the journey. Plus, as Brian pointed out, Dover–Calais sea crossings go back thousands of years. Take the Bronze Age boat for example.

It was 1992 when workmen digging the foundations for a pedestrian subway some two hundred yards from the beach came across some curious pieces of old wood deep in the ground. It turned out to be most of a boat dating from the Bronze Age so well preserved that the twine lashing the timbers together was still in place. Now housed in the Dover Museum, the boat is the oldest seagoing vessel in the world. At around 3,500 years old, Dover's Bronze Age boat is older than Tutenkhamen and Moses. As you look at the dark, freeze-dried wood in its dimly lit glass case, it's difficult to appreciate how long ago it was that somebody cut the timbers with such precision, made the twine to bind them together, poured wax over the joins to seal them and then, with a mixture of apprehension and confidence, placed it in the water and paddled out into the Channel. It may have been used to trade with the people whose distant land could be glimpsed across the water on a clear day, it could have been used for coastal fishing. Either way, it is the direct ancestor of the giant vessels that now cross the shipping lanes several times daily.

The first cross-Channel paddle steamer was the *Rob Roy*, which entered service in 1821, but it was the coming of the railways in the mid-nineteenth century that saw the Dover ferry service take off. Various vessels were tried, of which my favourite was probably the *Bessemer*. Launched amid a great hullabaloo in 1875, the *Bessemer* was a revolutionary craft in that its passenger lounge was suspended by ropes from the superstructure in order to prevent motion sickness, a major deterrent to potential Channel crossers. While the ship pitched and tossed on the Channel's racing tides, the passengers could safely walk on tippytoes in a straight line, enjoy a game of snooker or build houses out of playing cards. Or at least that was the plan. Alas, the *Bessemer* was destined to make just three crossings, crashing into the harbour on each occasion before being taken out of service.

Brian had offered me a ticket on P&O's newest ship, where the club-class lounge was apparently out of this world. Naturally I eschewed such swankery, preferring instead the regular proletarian crossing. This, of course, had nothing to do with the new ship sailing at an ungodly hour at which I had no intention of doing anything other than snore. However, the trickle of grim-faced people leaving the ticket office as I entered gave me a hint of what was to follow. Calais was closed, the French port workers having gone on strike over pension conditions.

'We're hoping it'll be open again this afternoon,' said the woman behind the glass, 'but it means we can't sell any day trips today, I'm afraid.'

I walked back into town past the shabby row of bed and breakfasts along the front. Men of Middle-Eastern and Balkan appearance stood outside them, smoking cigarettes, making desultory conversation with each other and looking plain bored as they waited for the better life they sought to creak into action.

Later that day, when a drizzly overcast morning had become a hot, sunny afternoon, I was walking along the White Cliffs when a text message arrived on my phone. It was from my service provider. 'Welcome to France!' it said, before telling me I could access my voicemail 'just the same as at home'. I looked out to sea and could just make out the French coast on the horizon. It might have taken twentieth-century communications technology to achieve it, but finally I realised just how close Dover is to the rest of Europe.

That text message also made me realise why Dover has a mentality of its own. For thousands of years, since before that Bronze Age shipwright gingerly pushed his boat into the water for the first time and checked frantically for leaks, Dover's inhabitants have lived under the constant threat of invasion. Since before Julius Caesar first landed a few miles from where I stood on top of the cliffs, Doverites had been looking over their shoulders. Caesar had arrived first at the foot of the White

Cliffs in 55 BC, but dismissed it as a landing point when the locals massed on top of the cliffs ready to drop rocks on anyone seeking to come ashore. He later chose a more genteel landing at Deal, further up the coast, where the inhabitants wore cravats and blazers and waited patiently for music hall to be invented.

After the Battle of Hastings the first thing William the Conqueror did was head for Dover, sack the castle and burn down the town. A hundred and fifty years later the French successfully laid siege to the castle and at the end of the thirteenth century burnt the town down again. Throughout history invading forces have had Dover in their sights, most recently in the wars of the twentieth century. The first bomb ever to land in Britain fell on Dover on Christmas Eve 1914, before the town became 'Fortress Dover'. As it was an important embarkation point for British forces, even the local residents needed passes to go about their business.

Dover suffered more than most places during the Second World War. The Battle of Britain was fought in the skies above the town, earning this part of the Kent coast the nickname Hellfire Corner. With Hitler's forces lined up almost visibly on the French coast, it's no surprise that the locals feared invasion daily. During the conflict 2,226 shells fell on Dover launched from across the Channel, with barely a single building left undamaged by enemy artillery.

Such conflicts seemed hard to believe as I sat in a field at the top of the cliff. It was a peaceful, sunny day, the water was a deep shade of blue and the only noise came from the muted workings of the port below. I'd never really given much credence to the symbolism of the White Cliffs, dismissing them as just the subject of a syrupy wartime song. But since I had spent time on their peaks and in the town they overlook, my appreciation had been much improved. I wasn't on the point of rushing out to buy a Vera Lynn CD, but the cliffs' historical significance was much, much clearer to me. From Caesar approaching them out of the Channel mist to find hostile Britons massed along them to the hundreds of thousands of terrified men rescued from Dunkirk whose first glimpse of them would have confirmed that they were home and home safely, the White Cliffs of Dover deserve a special place in our consciousness. Pollution may have taken the edge from their whiteness, but the cliffs are still an imposing sight.

I made my way back down the chalky path along the cliff edge, stopping to examine the generations of graffiti carved into the face. There were enough initials across the chalk to create the world's largest wordsearch, and I felt sure that somewhere among the jumble of letters there was probably a complete script of *Hamlet*. Some of the dates revealed just how stubbornly hard-wearing the cliffs are. If D.W. is reading this, for example, the initials you carved into the chalk in 1973 are still there, looking as sharp and as spruce as if you'd done it yesterday.

It was while examining these that I became aware of a faint buzz growing louder over my shoulder. I turned around to see a twin-engined aircraft heading straight for me. I froze, at the same time attempting to adopt a nonchalant 'he'll turn away in a second' gait. It was a similar feeling to when you're sitting in a car-wash and the drier is heading for your windscreen. Although you know that it won't come crashing through the glass to scalp you, there's always that fraction of a second of doubt between when you expect the twin-fanned metal bar to scoot gracefully upwards and out of sight and when it actually does. As I was less used to having planes flying straight at me on cliff faces, however, that fraction of a second was a lot longer in this case. Just when the plane was close enough that I could not only see the whites of the pilot's eyes, I could tell that he was wearing contact lenses, the nose lifted and its white belly passed over my head and banked round in a semi-circle and back out to sea. A few feet away from me stood a wood-pigeon. We exchanged embarrassed glances, clearly having both been just on the point of throwing ourselves to the ground and covering our heads.

The plane buzzed me twice more on my walk back along the cliffs, but on both occasions I loftily ignored it despite the fact it was passing close enough to part my hair. It was so low that had I needed to get rid of any incriminating documents I could have held them up above my head and had them shredded by the propeller.

Despite having spent the afternoon being picked on by a propliner I still went in search of the Blériot monument. As I had grown up in an era when enormous aircraft transport people to every part of the world in a matter of hours, it's easy to forget that it's less than a century since powered flight was still a risky, dangerous business attempted mainly by unhinged maniacs with more money than sense. One of these was Louis Blériot, a Frenchman who had made a small fortune manufacturing spare parts for cars. Most of Blériot's wealth went on building – and usually crashing – aircraft, and despite numerous mishaps he was not deterred from his dangerous hobby. When in the summer of 1909 Lord Northcliffe, the proprietor of the *Daily Mail*, offered a £1,000 prize for the first person to fly across the English Channel, Blériot put his eleventh monoplane, most of the previous ten having been wrecked in various fields across France, on to a train for a village just outside Calais determined to claim the cash. I shall pause for a moment here and allow the thought of the *Daily Mail* offering money to foreigners to make their way to Britain from Sangatte to truly sink in.

When Blériot arrived at Sangatte there was only one other competitor, Hubert Latham, an Anglo-American playboy. Latham had made one attempt already, but his engine cut out almost as soon as he'd left the French coast. Blériot did not exactly look like a man capable of making aerial history when he arrived, not least because he was on crutches, having tipped hot oil over his foot a few days earlier and suffered serious burns. In the pre-dawn mist of July 25, 1909, however, Blériot pointed his machine at where he thought Dover might be and took off. Sporting a wool-lined khaki jacket over his tweeds, a cap and a considerable moustache that would surely have hindered his aerodynamics, Bleriot flew over the choppy waters at a speed of just 40mph. He had neither map nor compass which, when halfway across and able to see neither France nor England in the mist, probably became a bit of a problem. However, half an hour after take-off the mist cleared and there were the White Cliffs. Sixty feet above ground over a field close to Dover Castle, Blériot cut his engine and crash-landed. There to meet him was a French journalist waving a tricolour, while puffing across the field towards him were two customs officials with a raft of forms for the pioneering pilot to fill in. When Blériot pointed out that the 'mode of transport' section didn't have an entry for 'monoplane', the customs men looked at each other, scratched their heads for a few seconds and told him to just tick the box marked 'yacht'.

It might not have seemed it at the time, but the crash-landing of an accident-prone French car-spares salesman marked the end of several millennia of British history. The Channel had been a crucial factor in preventing invasion. The moment Blériot's wheels touched Dover soil, followed very closely by a wrenching of metal, splintering of timbers and possibly the odd *'Zut alors!'*, Britain's impregnability vanished. Within barely thirty years hundreds of aircraft would be crossing the choppy waters depositing their explosive payloads on Dover and most other British towns and cities, while British planes did likewise in the other direction. Above the cloth-capped heads of the awed crowd that soon gathered around Blériot's machine some of history's fiercest airborne dogfights would take place, well within the lifetimes of those who had assembled to gawp at the French adventurer.

A wood has grown up around the site of Blériot's landing since that hazy summer morning in 1909. The monument takes some finding: a bent direction sign from the road is the only clue, which leads you along a cobwebby footpath between trees until you come to a small clearing. On the floor of the clearing are concrete paving stones arranged in the shape of Blériot's aircraft with a plaque at its centre informing visitors that Blériot landed 'on this spot'. For the moment that started it all, it seems an insufficient memorial somehow. After all, here was the catalyst for air travel today. As if scripted, at that moment a large passenger jet flew overhead with a mournful roar. I stood respectfully for a moment trying to appreciate the significance of what Blériot achieved that day. Then I remembered that he'd triggered the process by which that smug tosser could swoop over me on the cliffs, and stomped out of the clearing.

The night before I left Dover I went for a pint in the pub next door to my guesthouse and was glad I did, for I can pronounce with some authority that the White Horse is one of the finest inns in the land. Said to have been first established in 1365, it is steeped in history and one of the few buildings to have survived what fate has thrown at Dover in the intervening 640 years. In more recent times it became the haunt of actors from the nearby Dover Theatre, and renovation work in the fifties unearthed an 1809 playbill for a production of *Mother Goose*. In the nineteenth century the White Horse was used as a place of inquest for bodies washed up on the beach, a rare case of people being carried *into* a pub. What really makes the White Horse stand out is the felt-tip scrawl on its walls. For all the ways in which modes of transport have shaped Dover over the centuries, it's only in the last hundred years or so that people have crossed the Channel with no other support than their own limbs. Ever since Matthew Webb became the first person to swim across in 1875, the busy shipping lanes have been criss-crossed by grease-smeared, bathing-capped human amphibians. And most, it seems, have sloshed straight out of the water and headed for the White Horse in order to sup a restorative pint. Covering one wall are the signatures of those who have conquered the fast-running waters between Dover and Calais, alongside the date of their success and the time it took them to do it. 'Pain is temporary, glory is forever,' wrote Anne Cleveland who had swum the Channel in fifteen hours during the summer of 2002. These were people at the peak of their physical powers, coming as close as anyone to conquering nature unaided. As I drained my pint and wondered whether to dine on pizza, Chinese or curry, my twenty-five-metres swimming certificate suddenly didn't seem quite so impressive. I resolved to remove it from the wall over my desk when I got home.

Before I left the next morning I wandered into the ruins of St James's church, next to the White Horse. Founded in Saxon times and mentioned in the Domesday Book, St James's is derelict, its interior open to the elements. The church was badly damaged by German bombing in the Second World War and left half ruined as a monument. Most of the walls above the ground floor are gone, and the floor is turfed and paved with old tombstones. In the corner is the gravestone of Thomas Bradley, who died in 1720 aged twenty-one months. The inscription was easy to read given that it had recently been soaked in human urine. Brightly coloured wild flowers burst from the masonry and a butterfly fluttered haphazardly where the choir used to sit. Some lighter brick-work at the base of where the tower used to be surrounded a concrete plaque. 'The tower of this church from the roof upwards was repaired in AD 19 . . .' it reads, the actual date of the restoration obliterated by a shrapnel scar.

'Pain is temporary, glory is forever,' I repeated to myself as I headed out of Dover and mused that that could almost be a motto for the town itself. Dover has fought off marauders for as long as it has existed and it's a shame that most people pass through without stopping. There's a hardy bunch of people living down there on the corner of Britain, a town of resilience that has always been at the front line of any conflict. Maybe that's why asylum seekers have become such an issue there. In 2002 seventeen thousand asylum seekers, almost one fifth of the entire UK influx for that year, passed through Dover, and the town has become a focus for protests by neo-fascist organisations. Such was the hysteria that at one point local police had to read the riot act to some of the local press for its irresponsible xenophobia.

Perhaps to Doverites this was just another form of invasion. It's the same defensive, stubborn attitude that produced the Second World War sign in the town's museum that read:

In the event of a shell warning this dance will close immediately. No money will be refunded on tickets issued for another

222

dance. Dances will not close for air raids unless instructed to do so.

Even further back, the words of an old port workers' song about the Cinque Ports also demonstrated this parochial defensiveness. Now, I've always used the French pronunciation for 'cinque' – evidently I would have been run out of town if this ditty is anything to go by:

Who names us SANK and not our SINK is a foreigner and a foe. His ship to be engaged and after bloody battles SUNK, no prisoners to be taken.

It's a pity that the term 'asylum seeker' has become interchangeable with 'illegal immigrant' in recent times. Seeking political asylum used to be seen as an heroic act; today, depending on which newspapers you read, it's often viewed as a thinly disguised route to a life of dole-scrounging and benefit fraud. The people I passed in Dover had nervous, frightened eyes. They suffered the humiliation of using vouchers instead of money, and were not even allowed to cook for themselves in their accommodation. They certainly didn't strike me as benefit-system entrepreneurs; a life of eighteen-hour shifts washing up in restaurants, or endless days spent gazing out to sea from a shabby room with stained sheets and cracked plaster doesn't seem to be a cushy existence. All

most of them want is a better life and the opportunity to send some money home to their families.
It's easy to forget what these people have left
behind, the wars, the torture, the persecution, especially for put-upon Dover. But after all, just over
three hundred years ago forty thousand French
Huguenots arrived in town and arguably set Dover
on the road to prosperity.

The drive along the south coast was vaguely
depressing, but then seaside towns never look their
best in drizzle. Nothing in the depression stakes,
however, can compare to Beachy Head, where I
decided on a whim to stop en route to the Isle of
Wight. As soon as I'd left the A259 I was swallowed up in a thick cloud of fog that had
descended from nowhere and I drove hesitantly
along the windy road as the odd blasted tree, bent
almost double by the wind, loomed out of the
murk. I parked the car and walked to the cliff edge
in total silence, no birdsong or traffic noise, just
the crash of the waves far below. I stood for a
while as entrails of fog wound around me and
realised why Beachy Head is such a popular
suicide spot. The place has a pall of depression
hanging over it. In fact I'd almost venture to
suggest that most of the people who've leaped to
meet their maker from this spot were as happy as
an entire charabanc outing of sandboys when
they'd left home that morning. A large crow landed
a few feet away, looked at me, and barked in that
throaty way that crows do before heaving itself

into the air again and disappearing into the mist. I edged nervously closer to the precipice, hoping to catch a glimpse of the rocks and the sea far below. When I'd got to within five feet of the drop, a seagull suddenly swept upwards in front of me from below the cliff edge, a flapping, squawking mass of feathers that was as surprised to see me as I was to see it.

This trip was the first outing for the new traveller's hat that I'd purchased in Australia. It was a great hat of which I'd already grown very fond, a wide-brimmed, brown suede thing of the sort made popular by alleged celebrities who want to get out of the jungle in order to revive flagging careers by presenting television programmes. I knew it would serve me well when before I'd even taken it out of the house the cat had been sick on it. I thought it gave me the appearance and bearing of a mysterious man-of-the-world with a tale to tell as I swanked around beneath it, although it might just make me look a bit of an arse. Today I had taken the precaution of removing it from my head in case the wind should whip it from my bonce and send it barrelling out to sea, and I was gripping it firmly in my right hand. However, the sudden appearance of the seagull from below rather than, as is usual, above caused me to throw up my hands in fright. As I staggered away from the edge, the hat arced towards the misty abyss. I sprawled on my knees, the seagull flew off and I looked around to see my hat had landed right on the edge of the cliff. The wind wasn't strong, but it teased the brim playfully. The slightest hint of a gust could have sent it after the generations of suicides dashed on the rocks below. I crawled forward, but even this wasn't enough. Despite my attachment to my natty headgear, I was still going to get no nearer the edge than was absolutely necessary. Which is why I ended up flat on my stomach on the damp grass stretching every sinew before my fingers closed around the edge of the brim and the hat was saved.

After a brief stop in rainy Bognor Regis to pay £5.95 for half a dozen chips and what appeared from its size to be a domestic goldfish in batter, Portsmouth soon hove out of the drizzly mist. The ferry to the Isle of Wight was packed with people aged over sixty from north of Watford, and me. It's a short hop across the Solent, no more than half an hour, but my journey was accompanied by the soundtrack of half a mobile phone conversation from the seat behind. Imagine, if you will, the low thrumming and vibration of a ferry's engines providing the bass accompaniment to the following monologue.

Hullerr? Hullerr? It's Nana. Aye, Nana. Aim on a boowert. A boowert. Aye, a boowert. I'm on a boowert to the Ale of Wait. Aye. Nana loovs yer. Yes she does. Nana's on a boowert, and she loovs yer. A big boowert.

226

A big boowert to the Ale of Wait. Hullerr? Are you there? It's Nana here on a boowert, she loovs yer, yer knaa, even though Nana's on boowert to the Ale of Wait.

For a full thirty minutes. As soon as the announcement was made inviting drivers to rejoin their vehicles I was out of my seat like a bullet from a gun. Nana, so engrossed in her expressions of love, might conceivably have gone back and forth between Portsmouth and Fishbourne for a full two days unless someone gave her a nudge.

With an uncharacteristic slice of luck I was at the front of the ferry as she docked, and hence first off the boowert. Er, boat. I pulled in on Ryde seafront, startled by just how close the mainland was on the other side of the Solent. You couldn't just see buildings, you could practically see through the windows. A cross-Solent game of badminton seemed entirely possible. The Isle of Wight is diamond shaped and larger than you might think. Its spine runs east to west, a huge chalk hill rising in the centre and culminating at the western tip of the island at the notorious Needles. I was booked into a hotel in Shanklin on the south-east coast, and presented myself at reception whereupon I was handed a receipt. When I'd given them my debit card number over the phone I'd presumed, as was normal practice, that this was security against my not showing up. But no, the hotel had put through the full amount of my stay as soon as I'd put the phone down. Two days before I was due to arrive. It was a concept that would become entirely familiar during my stay on the Isle of Wight, which displays an energetic and vigorous determination to relieve you of your cash. This isn't necessarily a problem in itself as tourism is a key aspect of the island's economy, but it's the fresh-faced enthusiasm with which they do it that can take you aback.

'Do you have a car?' asked the man behind the desk. 'Yes,' I replied, 'it's parked outside.' 'Ah,' he said, reaching down for a cash tin, 'in that case you'll need a parking permit; that's £7.80 for three days, please.' Meekly I handed over a ten-pound note. 'It's valid for every council car park on the island,' he beamed, with as much pride as if he was announcing his daughter had just gained a first from Oxford University. He handed me the parking pass and a key (for which I half expected to be charged rental), and I set out to discover this oft-overlooked part of Britain.

The Isle of Wight has a long and undervalued literary history. Running a finger down the index of any Wight history book turns up names like Charles Dickens, Lewis Carroll, Henry Fielding, Christopher Isherwood, Thomas Hardy, John Keats, Elizabeth Sewell, William Makepeace Thackeray and Alfred, Lord Tennyson. Swinburne was born near Shanklin. Charles Darwin commenced writing *The Origin of Species* in Sandown, a mile or so east of Shanklin, yards from the place where Lewis Carroll wrote *The Hunting of the Snark*. Dickens, who wrote some of *David Copperfield* in Ventnor, set the honeymoon of Mr and Mrs Lemmle from *Our Mutual Friend* in Shanklin, writing of their footsteps visible in the sand.

I set out in the early evening along the same stretch of beach in search of Shanklin Chine, a deep ravine cut into the cliff by thousands of years of water that runs from the old village on the clifftop down to the end of the esplanade. It trickles and tumbles in waterfalls of varying magnitude, banked by ferns, plants and green pools. A path criss-crosses the water and, with its fern canopy providing a roof and keeping the noise of the world at bay, it's little wonder that the chine has been imbued with magical properties. Keats was a confirmed admirer as far back as 1817 when he stayed in Shanklin in poor health, writing to his friend John Reynolds:

Shanklin is a most beautiful place – sloping wood and meadow ground reaches round the Chine, which is a cleft between the Cliffs of the depth of nearly three hundred feet at least. This cleft is filled with trees and bushes in the narrow parts; and as it widens becomes bare, if it were not for primroses on one side, which spread to the very verge of the Sea, and some fishermen's huts on the other, perched midway in the

Balustrades of beautiful green Hedges along their steps down to the sands.

It was a warm evening and the sun was going down when I arrived at the bottom of the chine to discover that it would cost me £3.50 to walk up it. Avaricious this may have seemed (although there has been an admission charge since the footpath was built in Keats' time), but nothing could detract from the charm of the place. A confirmed traditionalist, even I had to admit that the subtle-coloured floodlights and strings of fairy lights actually enhanced rather than detracted from its magic. I emerged at the top calmer and more at peace with the world than I'd been at the bottom, and celebrated this fact with a couple of leisurely pints at the Crab Inn. The top of the chine represents Shanklin's pride and joy, a higgledy-piggledy collection of immaculate thatched cottages, pubs and shops, and arguably the most attractive building of them all is the Crab, a sprawling, thatched inn that dates back to the seventeenth century. It was here in July 1868 that Henry Wadsworth Longfellow stayed, and on the fountain outside is an inscription written by him:

O traveller, stay thy weary feet; drink of this fountain, pure and sweet; it flows for rich and poor the same.

Having so far forked out more than a hundred pounds just to get out of the car and walk up a hill, the concept of being anything but poor on the Isle of Wight was quickly becoming alien to me. At this rate of expenditure the Isle of Wight would own my house by breakfast.

Inside, the Crab is a bit of a disappointment. Any old nooks, snugs or crannies had been demolished in favour of a split-level open-plan pub completely devoid of character but designed to cram as many people as possible into the dining rooms. Just before I'd got to the chine I'd noticed an interesting-looking establishment called the Fisherman's Hut and endeavoured to return there instead. Baulking at handing over another £3.50 to walk downhill, instead I walked along Shanklin's main street to the lift that serves the village and the undercliff. Naturally, you have to pay to use it.

Darkness had fallen by now, and the lights of the esplanade hotels shone brightly to my right, in contrast to the dark blues and blacks of the channel to my left. The tide was out, and I walked along the ribbed, puddly sand among the tiny coils left by burrowing amphibians waiting for the return of the sea. I reached the end of the esplanade, passed the public conveniences and the beach huts and found entirely on its own the Fisherman's Hut, possibly Britain's most secluded hostelry. It used to be a cottage, built in the early nineteenth century by William Colenutt, the man who had constructed the footpath up the chine and charged sixpence for the journey in 1817. The admission fee had remained the same until around 1960, which is when the last of the Colenutts was flooded out of the cottage and the place was turned into a hostelry.

The pub was quiet and I appeared to be the only customer. I left the bar with a pint and went around the corner to the seating area, where I discovered a middle-aged couple sitting together. Just from their sheepish body language I could tell that this was a secret liaison, and there were significant others somewhere on the island thinking that one or the other was at an evening class or working late. Feeling like one great big gooseberry I sat down and stared pointedly at the pages of the book I'd brought with me. Given that they had been deep in conversation when I walked in, the staccato smalltalk they indulged in between long pauses suggested that I really had messed up their evening. Eventually they drank up and left, leaving me as the only customer. The David Gray CD that had been playing in the background finished, and the only sound was the subdued electronic jingles of the fruit machine as the barman whacked the buttons and the metallic tambourine clatter of his pound coins landing in its bowels. It was around ten thirty now. I finished my drink and left, passing the barman as I made for the door. He bade me a hearty goodnight and I ventured into the darkness. No sooner had I taken two steps than I heard a key turn in the lock and bolts being shot across the jamb.

I had Shanklin beach and esplanade to myself. The chains of lights strung between lampposts shone brightly but couldn't obfuscate the stars in the sky above. The sea lapped gently away to my right and I heard a clink of cutlery to my left. On a balcony, silhouetted by the dim lights within, a couple sat at a table in post-dinner contentment. The man lifted a bottle of wine, held it up to the light and poured a measure into each glass. The woman's giggle carried to me on the breeze, mixing with the gentle sloshing of the tiny waves. Out at sea the lights of a ship anchored for the night twinkled on the horizon. I paused and took out Harry's photograph. More than eighty years ago Harry's ship would have passed along exactly the same horizon. If it had been a quiet night, seafront promenaders might have heard 'She's going to bloody kill me' and 'I swear, I'll never touch another drop as long as I live' carried in on the breeze.

The next morning I headed south for Ventnor and parked the car opposite one of the most astonishing shops I've ever seen. Its ancient wooden frontage was warped and buckled, and the windows were so ancient and dusty you could barely see through them. There was no name above the door and signs advertised a 'closing down sale', but these looked as though they were put up half a century ago. A jumbled row of old pewter drinking tankards lined the windowsill. Not only did they look three hundred years old, so did the price labels. I half expected them to be in ducats. Inside the dingy shop there was total silence and the damp musty smell of old books. It was very spooky. There were books stacked everywhere, most of them old cloth-bound hardbacks. I edged between the piles: it was impossible to get to most of the rambling, disorganised stock of bric-à-brac, but I did unearth a couple of H.V. Morton first editions. Suddenly a woman dressed from head to foot in black appeared next to me. And I mean appeared. I have no idea where she came from as it was practically impossible to move in the place, let alone sneak up on someone without them noticing. I paid her for the books and concluded one of the most curious shopping experiences of my life. I felt sure that if I'd mentioned this to somebody in the village, they would have said, 'Where did you say this shop was? No, love, there's no shop there. There used to be, but the woman who owned it died of a broken heart when her husband never came back from the Somme. It burned down soon afterwards.'

I didn't spend long in Ventnor, but felt a definite sense of sadness there. My first impression was the melancholy atmosphere of that curiosity shop, which might not have helped, but I couldn't put my finger on why this charming seaside town sent me into a bit of a decline. It could have been the oppressiveness of St Boniface's Down, the eight-hundred-foot drop at whose base Ventnor sits, backing up against the cliffs as if to escape the sea. The beach is one of the cleanest in Britain, and Ventnor's temperate climate made it a popular destination in the nineteenth century, particularly for the infirm. Karl Marx came to Ventnor towards the end of his life, at the suggestion of Engels, to escape the fog and dirt of London that clogged his lungs. Twice he wintered in Ventnor, and was staying in the village in 1882 when he learned of the death of his daughter, Jenny. Marx set off for London immediately, and was dead himself within two months.

The six-year-old Winston Churchill stayed in Ventnor with his nanny in 1880. The young future prime minister was thrilled to see a large troop ship less than a mile off the coast, but within hours the ship had sunk with all three hundred on board lost. Churchill was horrified to hear tales of the fish feasting on the corpses.

The atmosphere was subdued, and I felt that Ventnor was a tired old place, longing for its Victorian heyday. Facing the beach was the impressive Hotel Metropole. At least it probably was impressive when it was open. Now its doors and windows are boarded up, its pink paint flaking and fading, its balconies rusting. On the hardboard that covered the main doors, behind which a grand staircase probably swept up into the dusty darkness beyond, someone had scrawled 'fuck me Jon', an unrequited, anguished cry of frustrated passion which seemed somehow fitting here. I walked back up the hill, to the main part of town, which had built its way upwards as its fortunes went in the other direction, and resumed my journey hoping that something, anything would cheer me up.

Once you pass St Catherine's Point, the southern tip of the Wight diamond, the scenery changes almost immediately. Where the south-east coast has the golden beaches of Sandown, Shanklin and Ventnor, the south-west is bleak; wind-blasted trees bowing their heads away from the gales. Even the weather obliged by turning from breezy sunshine to scudding clouds and the odd pregnant droplet of rain.

I arrived at Freshwater Bay, just before the Needles, to find the sea pounding the shore and the wind whipping salty spray at the small cluster of buildings near by. To the right as you look out to sea, the Albion Hotel, whose bar W.H. Auden and Christopher Isherwood once frequented, had optimistically put out plastic garden furniture. There was nobody around except an elderly couple drinking soup from a flask in their car and peering out to sea through a rainy windscreen.

It was nearly noon, so I switched on the car radio to catch the shipping forecast. 'Dover, Wight, Portland,' it said, 'southerly veering south-westerly five to seven, rain or showers, moderate or good,' which didn't sound too promising. I went out into the gale, rounded the Albion and started to walk across Tennyson Down. The poet Alfred, Lord Tennyson had moved to Wight in 1853, eventually buying Farringford, an impressive pile close to Freshwater Bay, which is now a hotel. A private man, he stayed for many years before being effectively driven out by the sightseers and wellwishers who blighted his summers. At the high point of the down that bears his name, where the poet walked for hour upon hour, stands a memorial, a twenty-foot-high Celtic cross towards which I struck out as the wind tried to blow me inland. As I crested the first hill, striding across the soft downy grass while the sea crashed against the base of the cliffs below, I caught sight of the monument in the distance. But the more I walked, the further away it seemed. Halfway there, the rain started. A few droplets in the wind at first but then a steady drizzle. After an hour of trudging in a heavy coat with nothing but seagulls and the sound of my own breathing for company, I arrived at the memorial just as the rain really began to get into its stride. It absolutely threw it down. If I looked out to sea, and given that as doing so would have rewarded me with a faceful of stinging rain it wasn't something I intended to do, the first landfall would have been not France, not even Spain, but Brazil. No wonder then that when the local weather turns inclement, Tennyson Down knows all about it. The wind came at me in huge gusts, thumping against the enormous coat I was wearing, which was busily soaking up every drop of rain. I walked around the monument hoping to find an angle whereby it might shelter me, but the stone cross is fenced off and there was no chance of hiding from the elements. So fierce was the rain that I couldn't see anything beyond a radius of about fifteen yards. Occasionally when the wind dropped to a howl rather than a scream, the dark outlines of nearby trees would loom briefly out of the murk, but that was about it. I was alone, on an exposed headland in filthy weather with nothing but a twenty-foot Celtic cross for company. No one knew I was here, and yards away the land disappeared in a sheer drop on to the rocks below. It was then that I noticed the box chained to the fence, on which a notice asked for contributions towards the upkeep of the memorial. At the very moment I was feeling about as remote as it was possible to feel in Britain, someone was after my cash. Only on the Isle of Wight.

I set off back the way I came, which fortunately meant the elements were attacking me from behind. My coat was a thick, padded, denim number which kept me dry not by deflecting the water, but by absorbing every drop. It weighed a ton. The hood was now so heavy my head was bowed and, with the coat coming down to below my knees, I must have looked like some kind of spectral monk gliding out of the mist. Mind you, I imagine that monks, even spectral ones, don't use language like I was employing as I sloshed across the down. I turned to take one last look at the monument, and as the huge gusts of rain blew inland, its dark-grey silhouette against a lighter grey background appeared and disappeared out of the mist. It was almost gothic. It was certainly eerie.

The journey back was long, squelchy and sweary. My coat was now so heavy I might as well have been carrying a rucksack full of bricks and a papoose of assorted rubble, topped off with a granite sombrero. Not only that, my jeans below coat level were also soaked, clinging heavily to my calves. I won't even begin to describe the state of my shoes. Back at Freshwater Bay I found a tearoom and blundered inside like a mobile mini-monsoon. I shook off the coat, which practically cracked the floorboards when it landed, and headed for the counter, my soaking trainers squeaking on the floor as if I'd just skated in on a pair of Marigolds. I was very, very grumpy and very, very soggy. I was also ill-disposed towards humankind in the way that only a man who has been persistently rained on for a significant period of time can be. However, the woman behind the counter was so lovely that my curmudgeonly outlook evaporated as quickly as I hoped the small lake forming on the floor beneath and around my coat would before she noticed it. Dark of hair, wearing a mauve jumper, a green apron and a shy smile, she was a beacon of niceness in a tempestuous world. So happy was I to find such a human being I barely noticed that the cheese roll and cup of tea she sold me cost £6.

Once I'd showered the table with grated cheese, spilled milk and rainwater, I heaved on my ridiculous coat, left my personal dairy-disaster area behind, headed back to the car and drove on in search of the Needles. Wight's most westerly point, a jagged row of chalk teeth that have seen off countless ships over the centuries, is arguably its most recognisable landmark. It could be a place of dignity, a place where visitors can wonder at nature and the power of the sea and lose themselves in the solitude of their surroundings. It could be that. But it isn't. It isn't, thanks to whoever decided to put a cheap, tacky fairground-cum-pleasure park there. Now admittedly the weather wasn't great and, still soaking wet from my Tennyson Down excursion, I wasn't in the best of moods. But the only rollercoaster ride the Needles pleasure (ha!) park sent me on was from grumpiness to outright depression.

The merry-go-round was going round but there was nothing remotely merry about it. Boarded-up booths marked Hollywood Bowl and Tin Can Alley rocked gently in the wind. A hot-dog stand was open; inside a radio blared so loudly that whatever was playing was totally unrecognisable. Over a century earlier, in 1897, Marconi had sent some of the first ever radio signals from this spot to a post office in Poole Harbour. I was glad that he wasn't here now; a few seconds' exposure to the wall of distortion coming over the sausages and bread rolls would have had him heaving his equipment into the sea. And the Needles themselves? All but obscured by mist.

As I drove back across the island to Shanklin I felt frustrated by the Isle of Wight. It had clearly been an astonishing source of creativity. As well as the poets that came a-calling. Turner spent time here and produced some of his best sketches. And when bass-slapping Mark King went to the top of the charts with Level 42 he was the second former Wight milkman to do so; Craig Douglas had led the way in 1959 with a song called 'Only Sixteen'. When Anthony Minghella picked up his Oscar for *The English Patient*, he leaned into the microphone and said, 'This is a great day for the Isle of Wight.' The American audience might have responded with 'The Isle of What?', but Minghella had been born and raised on the island, selling ice-creams for the family business (every seafront has a Minghella's ice-cream stall). Even Turgenev conceived his greatest novel, *Fathers and Sons*, while staying in Ventnor in 1860.

But instead of capitalising on this stunning record of creativity, the island seems instead to rely on a tacky seaside culture. The place has a lot going for it, don't get me wrong, but the breathtaking awe that inspired the likes of Tennyson, Keats and, er, Level 42 to creative heights is hard to find. Nowhere is this better demonstrated than at the Needles. What was once undoubtedly a sublime, inspiring spot has been thoroughly ruined by this shabby shantytown of pretend pleasure. It's an extreme example, but a clear indication of Wight's missed opportunities. What gibbering, half-mad buffoon looked at the Needles and thought, Wow, tell you what, what this place really needs is a ghost train, the chance to buy miniature plastic lighthouses and a candyfloss emporium? Such was my frustration that I knocked my plastic lighthouse off the dashboard and dropped candyfloss all over my lap.

The following day I called in briefly at Cowes at the northern tip of the island, stopping for lunch among the nautical-clothing boutiques and chandlers. West Cowes is where it's at, the yachties' playground to which the forest of masts in the bay is testament. I didn't stay long, feeling out of place as the only person in town not wearing a rugby shirt, shorts and espadrilles (there's probably a joke about exposed calves and Cowes there somewhere, but I'm not going in to look for it). Instead I drove haphazardly on through Ryde, passing Osborne House whither Queen Victoria and Prince Albert would decamp at the slightest opportunity. Victoria died at her beloved Osborne in 1901, continuing an unfortunate Wight theme of seeing off royalty: Charles I had fled there hoping to find refuge, only to be imprisoned in Carisbrooke Castle and dispatched back to London for execution.

Just outside Ryde I spotted a sign for Quarr

Abbey. 'Visitors welcome' it said, so I turned off into the tree-lined avenue. There's been an abbey here since 1132, although the original building fell into disrepair after the dissolution of the monasteries in 1536. The name comes from the ancient quarry near by, and Quarr stone was used to build the White Tower at the Tower of London. The modern monastery dates from around 1900 and is home to an order of Benedictine monks.

Now, I am not a religious person and will argue till the cows come home that the gospels are clearly nothing more than a foretelling of the coming of Elvis Presley. In fact the closest I have ever come to a religious experience, other than Clive Mendonca's play-off final hat-trick at Wembley in 1998, occurred in Florence on my inter-railing excursion. Paul and I were in a large, ornate church and I was getting on to my high horse about how scandalous it is that these places occupy prime real estate, and how if you flogged off all the gold and knocked the place down you could build decent homes for poor people. Humour me, I was a student. I was getting stuck into an impressive rant that was starting to attract attention when I was suddenly struck by an attack of barely controllable diarrhoea, necessitating a sprint out of the church, down the steps, across the piazza and into the nearest bar before there was a terrible accident. Call it divine retribution, call it a dodgy pizza the night before, I'm open to interpretation. But I've never been quite so forthright with any ill-informed religious opinions since.

Given my committed secularism, I wasn't really sure how you went about visiting a monastery even if, as the sign proclaimed, I was a visitor and therefore welcome. I took a hesitant stroll towards the immaculately tended gardens, at the end of which I saw a tearoom. There was a woman behind the counter and at a table an elderly, jowly nun, looking remarkably like Margaret Rutherford in a habit.

'Are you on retreat, sister?' asked the woman as she poured me a cup of tea.

'Yes,' replied the nun through a mouthful of cake. Then she paused. 'Well, no, it's more of a holiday actually.'

With that she turned and gave me an elaborate theatrical wink. The conversation then turned into a discussion of the benefits of dishwashers. They were, according to my new ecclesiastical friend, a marvel at cleaning oil holders for candles. We finished our tea and walked back through the gardens together, discussing other domestic appliances, house prices in London and the great nuns versus monks singing debate (Sister Joanna favoured men's voices, I came down firmly on the female side). With that, she bade me farewell and disappeared through a vast oak doorway.

After a few minutes wandering around the ruins of the original abbey a few hundred yards from the current building, I was walking back to the car when a bell began to toll. It was just before five o'clock and I knew from the discussion in the tearoom that this was for vespers. The image of monks riding around the abbey on noisy scooters flashed briefly through my mind, and I considered going inside. A young couple in matching trousers and nylon jackets walked past me, and I watched them open a big door and disappear into the darkness beyond. I followed.

I emerged into a huge vaulted church, simple in construction but still jaw-droppingly beautiful as the late-afternoon sun streamed through the high, arched windows. I took a pew at the very back; my only fellow attendees were the couple I'd seen walk in before me, Sister Joanna near the front, a young man in a fleece and combat trousers, and a puffing middle-aged man supporting himself on two walking sticks. A door opened to my left and around twenty monks in black cassocks filed in and took up places in the pews facing each other at the altar end of the church. An older monk with grey hair and glasses followed, and I saw him making straight for me. Uh-oh, I thought, they've sussed the unbeliever. I could almost hear the rack being cranked up in readiness on the other side of the wall. The monk put his head close to mine and whispered, 'Are you Brother Justin?' I goggled. He was asking probably the most un-monkish person on the Isle of Wight. Before I could open my mouth he said, 'Ah, no, you're not, are you?'

I shook the noggin, he nodded politely and took up a position in the pew in front.

There followed around forty minutes of the most soothing chanting, sometimes solo, sometimes in unison, sometimes with a simple organ accompaniment. But it was all beautiful, just beautiful. Occasionally the monks would bend forward at the waist, sometimes they would kneel, and from the way the young man in the fleece was keeping up with this ecclesiastical choreography, I deduced that he must be Brother Justin. The monks themselves were of all ages and sizes, and they seemed incredibly content. Standing in that abbey, listening to the wonderful music and seeing the looks of beatific calmness on everyone in a black robe, monastic life seemed suddenly quite appealing. If it wasn't for the sandals . . .

It's probably not often that Weymouth gets compared to southern Spain, but I imagine approaching Portland must be a little like approaching Gibraltar. On the face of it, Portland doesn't look promising. A bleak, treeless, windblasted lump of rock the shape of South America hanging off the bottom of Britain that looms up menacingly at you as you approach the causeway from Weymouth, it's home to a prison, a borstal and a prison hulk is moored in its harbour. The wall of scree and rock that faces you as you leave the mainland is a forbidding prospect. Slate roofs atop grey houses are jumbled up on the hillside, homes built by the people who hewed the rock to create such buildings as St Paul's Cathedral, the London Law Courts, Tower Bridge and the Cenotaph at Whitehall. In fact, once Sir Christopher Wren got started using Portland stone there was no stopping him. When you wander around Portland, which has an area of just four and a half by one and a half miles, it's amazing to think that a significant part of London came from here. I'd passed Portland stone every time I'd walked along the Thames past the old Royal Naval College at Greenwich, the Admiralty in Whitehall is clad in Portland stone and so is the United Nations building in New York. Some of history's most momentous decisions have echoed around walls that originated here, on this curious peninsula off the coast of Dorset. When I'd been in the studio at Broadcasting House listening to Jane read the shipping forecast, the building in which we sat was encased in Portland stone. Perhaps most movingly, the British war graves that can be found across Europe and beyond are all made from Portland stone: half a million after the First World War, and a further eight hundred thousand after the Second.

Driving across the causeway and up the steep, winding street that runs through Fortuneswell, the town at the end of the causeway, I headed south for Portland Bill where the gentle slope of island reaches the sea. I stopped off at Wakeham for a quick visit to the informative local museum and found the tablet that commemorates where the stone used to make the Cenotaph was quarried. A small quarry was opened specifically for this purpose and closed immediately afterwards, but nearby Perryfields Quarry is still in operation, grinding away at giant white chunks that dazzle the eyes on a sunny day.

The road to Portland Bill is long and featureless, running alongside abandoned quarries, but at the Bill the red-and-white lighthouse provides a rare splash of colour. The unobtrusive visitor centre and carefully thought-out amenities were in stark contrast to my last coastal extremity at the Needles. Portland Bill is a place where you want to spend time, and there's not even that much to see. It was a calm sunny day, but just a couple of hundred yards or so out to sea white foam tips betrayed the clash of currents that make the Bill such a dangerous place for shipping. Portland's churchyards are full of shipwreck victims, and the walls of the museum are covered in pictures of boats of various vintages lying at curious angles in the surf. The churning sea over treacherous rocks is known as Portland Race, labelled by Hilaire Belloc as 'The master terror of our world'.

Fourteen ships were lost here in one stormy night in 1901 (just ten years before the prototype shipping forecast would be broadcast); nearly a century earlier the *Earl of Abergavenny* had run aground and broken up costing 260 lives, among them the ship's captain John Wordsworth, William's brother. I'd wondered how so many could perish when a ship is so close to land, but dropping on to the shelving rocks below the lighthouse you see at close hand the power of the waves that hurl themselves at the shore even on a calm day. Combine these waves, sharp half-submerged rocks, gale-force winds, driving rain and bits of ship flying about the place and it's not hard to understand how the sea has claimed its victims here.

From Utsire onwards I'd seen so many lighthouses that I hardly noticed them any more, but without them we'd still be filling coastal churchyards with bloated, soggy corpses. Churchyards like St George's in the north-west of Portland. St George's is a classic Georgian construction that no longer serves a congregation. Placed on a hilltop above the craggy western coast, the churchyard is an overgrown hotchpotch of higgledy-piggledy tombstones and opulent memorials, though the weather has rendered some of the more elaborate statues limbless. Tramping through the coarse grass, every now and then you come across a cluster of graves that bear the same date, often with foreign-sounding names. On the way out I greeted the discovery of the final resting place of an Edward Stone from Lymington, who departed this life in 1909, with disrespectful glee. I had gone into a graveyard and found an Ed Stone.

North of St George's is an abandoned quarry slowly being reclaimed by nature. It's also been claimed by artists, and Tout Quarry is littered with superb sculptures and carvings in the rock-face. At Tout you can gain a real sense of what life must have been like working in one of Portland's quarries. As I walked through ravines and fissures, the sheer whiteness reflected by the sun forced me to screw up my eyes. It was almost like a moon-scape. Tout fell into disuse between the wars, but it was worked by the convicts who spent twenty-three years quarrying and building the breakwater that created the harbour on the eastern side of the causeway between the mainland and Portland, and who changed the nature of Portland for ever.

The convicts began arriving in 1848, the first time Portland had been seriously infiltrated by outsiders. Portlanders had always been a close-knit community, suspicious of mainlanders, and the causeway wasn't established until the 1830s. Many spent their whole lives on the island without once going 'to England'. Mainlanders were regarded with suspicion and given the derogatory nickname 'kimberlins'. People attempting to reach Portland were often sent back under a hail of rocks and stones, a reputation which prompted Thomas Hardy to name Portland the 'Isle of Slingers' in his Wessex novels. 'A curious and almost distinctive people cherishing strange beliefs and singular customs' was how he described the Portlanders, whose customs included not marrying until the female half of the coupling was pregnant.

The arrival of the convicts and the construction of the causeway practically ended the existence of Portland as an entity separate from the mainland, and many of them would have worked here in Tout Quarry. I wandered among the footpaths and gullies, the only sound the crunching of chalky gravel beneath my feet. Sculptures appeared hither and thither: a crouching figure here, a boat there. I passed beneath a bridge, over which the railway would have passed to take the stone to the ships waiting in the harbour to transport it around the south coast and up the Thames to London. A keystone in the white bridge was engraved with 'J.C. Lano 1853', but such is the resilience of Portland stone that it could have been built a week earlier. I passed beneath the bridge into a ravine that looked as though it had been constructed in layers by craftsmen, so defined were the strata. I rounded a corner and the ground fell away steeply in front of me, revealing a startling panorama. I must have been a good three hundred feet up. Beneath me was Fortuneswell, while the causeway led over to Weymouth and the long strand of Chesil Beach stretched off into the distance as far as I could see. The sky and sea were both a deep blue, and the sound of the waves breaking on the pebbles far below carried faintly on the breeze. I sat and waited for my eyes to adjust to the technicolour vista in front of me, having spent so long among the whiteness of the quarry.

I tried to imagine what it must have been like for a convict to emerge here on to the same scene, a vision of the freedom denied to him by whatever misdemeanour had led to him hacking away at bits of rock on a godforsaken island off the south coast. As he rested, wiping the white dust from his eyes, he would have seen children playing on the beach far below, people on Weymouth seafront and the Portlanders going about their business in Fortuneswell. Drinking in the panoramic view would have been the closest he'd get to a feeling of genuine liberty, and he might imagine himself stepping off the ledge and flying like the circling sea birds on the breeze, before a shout from behind would bring him back to reality, the clanking, chipping and blasting impinging on his consciousness once again. Down below, people on the streets of Fortuneswell would look up and point at the ghostly white figures high up on the cliffs, the poor wretches whose hard labour was the starting point for some of the finest and most important buildings in the land. The next time I passed along the Thames path in front of the Royal Naval College, I promised myself I would stop and look at the stone. I would try to imagine the plight of the dusty, half-starved man who puffed and sweated to separate the fossil-strengthened limestone from the ground in which it had lain for millions of years, before watching the ship that carried the fruit of his hard labour steam into the Channel with a freedom he could barely remember.

PLYMOUTH, BISCAY, FITZROY

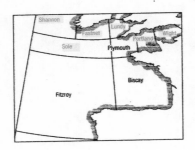

Areas Plymouth, Biscay and Finisterre first appeared on the shipping forecast map in 1949. A line stretching north–south between approximately Puerto de Vega on the northern Spanish coast to Rosslare on the south-west coast of Ireland provides the western boundaries of Areas Biscay, Plymouth and Lundy. Plymouth's southern border with Biscay emerges westward from France, roughly on the same latitude as Brest. Finisterre was renamed FitzRoy in February 2002, and its coastline stretches from Puerto de Vega around to a point just south of Porto.

Plymouth was nothing like I had expected. Given its association with British maritime history where it's up there with Portsmouth and Greenwich at the top of the briny hit parade,

I had visions of ancient, narrow cobbled streets where the rickety Tudor buildings were so tightly packed you couldn't see the sky. Old crones would emerge from alleyways with a 'Hello, my pretty' and a flutter of the eyelids, tavern doors would swing open and a waft of gin fumes and concertina music would drift from within while men in tights and ruffs would caper through the streets, skipping around the raw sewage to avoid soiling their big-buckled shoes. Well, okay, maybe that's a bit of an exaggeration, but I was certainly looking forward to walking in the footsteps of Sir Francis Drake and maybe even uttering the odd 'zounds' and 'verily' myself.

Unfortunately for these plans there is practically nothing left of Plymouth as it was in Drake's time, which is a great pity because Plymouth has a maritime heritage that's hard to rival. From its early provision of ships for the Hundred Years War in the fourteenth century to Sir Francis Chichester's arrival after sailing around the world single-handedly in 1968, Plymouth has played a crucial role in Britain's maritime affairs. Bligh, Cook, Ralegh and Hawkins are just some of the great seafaring names who passed through the Devon port in their time, and the Pilgrim Fathers left Plymouth on the Mayflower in 1620. But the town's most famous resident was Sir Francis Drake, and it was this famous old sea dog whom I sought.

Few British historical figures have been revered, revised and reviled as much as Drake. To the

255

reverent he was a great seaman and naval tactician, a man to whom most credit is due for the impending millennium milestone since Britain was last successfully invaded. To the revisers he was a glorified pirate who should have been clapped in irons and thrown in chokey with the key presented on a cushion to the King of Spain for His Highness to swallow with a good rioja. Either way he is one of maritime history's greatest figures, and it's a shame that so little remains of Drake beyond a few old pictures that make him look like James Robertson Justice in a ruff.

There is some debate as to exactly when he was born, with historians pinning their research tails on to the Drake birth donkey anywhere between 1539 and 1543. What's certain is that Drake was born on a farm at Crowndale on the outskirts of Tavistock in Devon. The house in which he entered the world was demolished a couple of centuries back, but I passed through Tavistock en route to Plymouth hoping there would be something there. There's a statue at the town's main roundabout, but Crowndale today appears to be little more than a sewage works and the local municipal rubbish dump. The young Francis was a cousin of the noted explorer John Hawkins and it wasn't long before he moved to Plymouth to learn the ways of the sea. With Hawkins he sailed slave-trading ships to the West Indies, and on his first major voyage in 1567 the fleet was attacked in the Gulf of Mexico by the Spanish. Only

Drake's and Hawkins' ships made it back to England after the attack, an incident that left the fiercely Protestant Drake with a lifelong hatred of the Spanish and their Catholic ways. Indeed, he spent the ensuing years getting his own back by leading successful privateering raids on the Spanish Main.

In 1577 came the commission that would truly establish Drake's reputation when he was asked by Queen Elizabeth to lead the first circumnavigation of the world by an Englishman. Officially the mission was to discover the then mythical *Terra Australis Incognita* and find the North-west Passage, but the unspoken and genuine reason for sending Drake to sea was plunder. The Treasury's coffers were sparse and echoing, and Drake was identified as the man to fill them. The nature of the mission was known only to the queen, Drake and the shadowy sponsors, but Drake took a trusted sailor he'd selected for the voyage named Thomas Doughty into his confidence a few days before the fleet left Plymouth. Doughty blabbed the whole caper to the queen's adviser, Lord Burleigh, who was appalled at the potential damage that setting about Spanish ships and settlements around the world would do to already frosty relations with Spain. Clearly unable to prevent the mission, Burleigh urged Doughty to disrupt it as much as he could. As soon as the fleet of five ships had left Plymouth, Doughty began sowing discord and mutinous talk among the crew. Arriving in the Magellan Straits for the voyage's first landfall Drake, who had rumbled Doughty and even accused him of sorcery in conjuring adverse winds, found the gallows where Magellan had hung mutinous members of his crew and drew great inspiration from them: he charged Doughty with mutiny and had him beheaded.

Shortly after they passed beneath South America a series of storms separated Drake's *Golden Hind* permanently from the rest of the fleet. Despite this, Drake successfully sacked a number of unsuspecting Spanish settlements in the South Seas and set off for Plymouth with booty worth £500,000. Arriving back in Plymouth in 1580 Drake had to tentatively enquire whether the queen was still alive – her passing would have left him defenceless against Spanish charges of piracy. Fortunately Elizabeth was still alive and well and, six months later, knighted Drake at Deptford. The *Golden Hind* stayed there in dry dock until she fell apart. Until the ship fell apart, that is, not the queen.

In 1585 Drake led successful attacks on Spanish ships in the West Indies, and returned to learn of the preparation of the Armada. Never one to turn down the opportunity of having a crack at the Spanish, Drake led a fleet to Cadiz and destroyed a number of ships, famously 'singeing the King of Spain's beard'. Probably as a direct result of this daring raid, Drake was appointed vice-admiral of the English fleet at

Plymouth specifically to deal with the threat of the Armada. When the Spanish fleet was sighted off the Lizard and the news was relayed to Drake, he was playing bowls on Plymouth Hoe. Once the breathless messenger had panted up the hill and imparted his news he might have been forgiven for expecting Drake to cry, 'Odd's bodkins! To the docks, we shall have tapas for tea!' and hotfoot it to the harbour. Instead he calmly picked up his next wood and said, 'There's time to finish the game and finish the Spaniards too.' The cocky sod.

At least, that's what I was always taught at school. Spoilsport revisionists have pointed out that this story did not emerge until more than a century later, and that Plymouth Hoe was a public space and bowls was not allowed on public spaces. Whether he was the David Bryant of his day or nor, Drake proved to be a crucial factor in the defeat of the Armada, leading skirmishes in the Channel and co-ordinating the fireship raid on Calais that scattered the Armada into total disarray. If he hadn't been a national hero before, he was now. A year later, however, in 1589, he was sent to northern Spain with instructions to set about the bedraggled remnants of the Armada. It wasn't a successful mission and Drake's star lost a little of its lustre, to such an extent, in fact, that it would be more than five years before he was asked to put to sea again. In the meantime he became mayor of, and eventually MP for, Plymouth. His final mission in 1595 was another plunder campaign on the Spanish Main with Hawkins, but this time the Spanish were better prepared and the English ships were given a thorough twatting. Hawkins died of dysentery and, as 1595 became 1596, Drake caught yellow fever and died, being buried at sea in a lead coffin off Porto Bello.

Intrigued by these tales of adventure I had hoped to follow in the footsteps of Drake around the streets he had frequented, represented and, in many cases, owned. I went to visit his house at Buckland Abbey, where the famous Drake's Drum is still kept. Believed to have accompanied him on most of his voyages, the drum will supposedly beat of its own accord whenever England is in danger of invasion. Having been disappointed by Crowndale I followed the signs for Buckland Abbey, passing through the village of, heh, Crapstone along beautiful tree-fringed roads, being eyed all the while by quizzical sheep. Finally I pulled up at the gates of Buckland Abbey itself. Which were padlocked shut. Owned by the National Trust, Buckland Abbey is open to the public every day except Thursday. Guess what day it was.

So having been thwarted by Drake's birthplace and his house, my last chance was the town in which he'd worked when not setting about the Spanish. Plymouth has a proud record. Despite being one of the most important maritime and naval towns in the country, it was never attacked successfully, let alone invaded. Until, that is, the coming of air warfare. In a nine-month period from November 1940, when more than a hundred German bombers attacked the town, Plymouth was practically flattened by the Luftwaffe. There was barely anything left of the place, with more than half its 220,000 population either leaving voluntarily or being evacuated. Hundreds of civilians were killed, while nearly fifty churches, twenty-four schools, eight cinemas and more than a hundred pubs were destroyed. In the town centre virtually nothing was left standing. Plymouth had, in the language of the time, copped it.

If any good came out of the destruction, however, it was the solving of a major town-planning headache. Before the war Plymouth was practically eating itself. The growth of the naval dockyard meant an influx of people with whom the labyrinthine streets of the town simply couldn't cope. The town's traffic congestion problem was second only to London's and, short of knocking the whole place down and starting again, there wasn't an obvious solution. Then Hitler came along and pulverised the place. The task of rebuilding the shattered city fell to the architect Patrick Abercrombie, who designed a spacious, airy town centre – most of it clad in Portland stone – in sharp contrast to its claustrophobic forebear. A wide, sweeping boulevard was driven through the heart of Plymouth right up to the Hoe and named Armada Way, with gardens in its centre and shopping streets leading off it. It was that rare thing: a triumph of town planning.

I learned all this thanks to a film show in the informative Plymouth Dome, an equally well-planned tourist centre dedicated to the town and its history which overlooks the harbour. On entering I'd been rather startled to find Sir Francis Drake standing there, lolling against the reception desk discussing Britain's possible entry to the Euro with the girl behind the till. Predictably perhaps, Sir Francis was against the idea, even if he was only a lookalike.

From the Dome I climbed up to the Hoe. It was a beautiful hot day and the sun twinkled back from the deep blue of the water. The Hoe is a vast expanse of well-manicured grass on which the good burghers of Plymouth were prostrating themselves in the sunshine. Despite the several football pitches' worth of grass, however, space must have been at a premium as many of them seemed to be prostrating themselves on each other. If Plymouth left one impression on me, it was as the canoodling capital of Britain. All across the Hoe there were couples in clinches sucking each other's faces in a display of synchronised snogging the like of which I had never witnessed before. Everyone was at it, on the Hoe and later when I ventured up through the gardens of the main street. Concluding that there must be something in the Plymouth water, I made sure to bottle some and take it home. When I picked up the local paper later that day the front-page story was of the rocketing levels of sexually transmitted diseases in the town: 16,500 people had visited the town's STD clinic over the previous twelve months compared to 12,000 the year before. I poured the water away.

Plymouth Hoe on a fine day is a truly uplifting place. Such is the camber that from most of the Hoe you can't see Plymouth at all, and with a huge sky all around you can feel as though you're actually among the clouds. The grassy area where Drake was meant to have rolled his woods is dominated by a vast memorial to RAF personnel killed in both wars. The memorial, a huge obelisk, is in effect the focus of the entire town, situated as it is at the end of the sweeping main street. To the left as you look out to sea is a memorial commemorating the repulsion of the Armada, inscribed with the phrase 'He blew with his winds and they were scattered', proof, apparently, that God was not only an Englishman but a Protestant too. Drake also has a statue, identical to the one that I'd seen in Tavistock, and one that survived the devastation of the blitz unscathed.

Another construction that survived the bombs and worse is Smeaton's Tower, the fourth Eddystone lighthouse and the precursor to the one that stands fourteen miles south-west of Plymouth today. Like the Bell Rock off Arbroath, the Eddystone is a dreadful hazard to shipping, lurking just beneath the surface of a busy stretch of water. As it is too far from land to be seen in poor weather, the number of ships lost on its rocky teeth is incalculable. It was when a rich London merchant named Henry Winstanley lost two ships on the reef in 1695 that the story of what is arguably the world's most famous lighthouse began. Winstanley was already known as a bit of an eccentric. He'd built a remarkable house in Essex with a full-scale windmill in the front and a giant lantern on the roof, which was lit every night. Inside he had distorting mirrors, chairs that moved around on rails and artificial 'ghosts' that appeared at opportune moments. So bizarre was his residence that Winstanley erected a turnstile at the gate and charged admission to see 'Winstanley's Wonders'. Even Charles II showed up. He then built a water theatre in Piccadilly, an intricate display of fountains and spouts that was the wonder of its day. When he heard of the loss of two of the five ships he owned, however, Winstanley set about building a light on Eddystone. Everyone thought he was nuts, but his mind was made up with a mixture of altruism and an unshakeable desire to be noticed. It took three years, during which time French privateers showed up, ransacked the place, stripped the workmen naked, cast them adrift in a boat and took Winstanley back to France and threw him in prison. It took the intervention of Louis XIV himself to get Winstanley out of chokey, but finally, in November 1698, the architect himself lit the first beacon ever to be seen on Eddystone.

After a year Winstanley realised that his largely wooden construction was having trouble standing up to the rigours of life in the English Channel, so he renovated it to such an extent that it was in effect a new lighthouse. In true Winstanley style it was a flamboyant affair, all pulleys, weather vanes and Latin inscriptions wherever there was space, but it worked. Four years passed with no wrecks on Eddystone: Winstanley's lighthouse was working. In November 1703 its designer went out to visit Eddystone himself, despite local seamen warning him a storm was brewing. If anything their weather forecast made Winstanley more determined, as he had expressed a desire to be out there in the 'greatest storm that ever blew under God's heaven'. He got that all right: on the night of November 24, 1703 the worst storms ever recorded lashed the whole of Britain. As dawn broke the following day and the people of Plymouth emerged nervously from their houses to inspect the damage, all that was left of Winstanley, his lighthouse and the other three men who had been inside it was some twisted metal sticking out of the rock. Nothing was ever found. Two nights later a freight ship struck the reef and went down with all hands – the first accident on Eddystone since Winstanley had lit the beacon five years previously.

Its replacement was completed six years later, also a wooden construction. It stood for forty-six years until one night when Henry Hall, a ninety-four-year-old lighthouse keeper, noticed flames coming from near the top. Despite the efforts of

Hall and his fellow keepers to put out the fire, the lighthouse gradually burned down around them, and they were found the next afternoon clinging to the rocks among a few smoking stumps. Hall died a few days later after suffering horrific convulsions: when he'd looked up at the fire a big dollop of molten lead had dropped into his mouth, which he swallowed. The lead solidified in his stomach and killed him – the first documented incident of lead poisoning.

The fourth tower was built by John Smeaton, who realised that the only way to ensure the Eddystone lighthouse would stay up was to build it out of stone. Not only that, he would carefully cut each stone to make a dovetail construction for extra strength, taking as his inspiration the oak tree, with its thicker base smoothly slimming towards the top. Smeaton also carried out scientific experiments to come up with a cement that would not erode at sea. It was all revolutionary stuff, and it worked. Smeaton's Tower stood for 130 years, and was only replaced when the rock itself began to erode faster than the lighthouse. It was dismantled piece by piece, leaving only the bottom quarter or so on the rocks, and re-erected on Plymouth Hoe, where I strolled out of the sun and into the coolness of its dark interior.

Inside it was tiny. It was remarkable to think that three lighthouse keepers used to live in this claustrophobic tube fourteen miles out into the English Channel. Ever since David Taylor had told me about the Bell Rock light, I had rather fancied the idea of being a lighthouse keeper. There was no way of doing so, of course, as these days they're all automated, but I could certainly see myself in a chunky jumper, blue blazer and smart peaked cap, with a pipe clenched between my teeth. I would even have noted on my application form my willingness to grow a beard, which would hopefully have swung it for me. I could quite comfortably have polished the glass of the lens while indulging in a merry song and dance like Mickey Rooney in *Pete's Dragon*, or sat cosily in a chair with a good book and dog called Sprocket at my feet like Fulton Mackay in *Fraggle Rock*. The solitude appealed to me; it would be quite cosy inside the thick walls of a lighthouse while the elements did their worst outside. Give me a pizza oven, a well-stocked drinks cabinet, satellite television and the complete works of P.G. Wodehouse and you could have left me for months. I climbed through the different levels, to the kitchen with its sink and stove, then up to the bedroom, barely ten feet in diameter with a hole in the middle where the stepladder came up. The sleeping quarters were just beneath the lantern itself, and I knew that if I'd actually been a lighthouse keeper I would have absent-mindedly switched the light off before going to sleep at least once a week. But it was when I climbed up into the lantern room itself that I remembered why I could never have been a lighthouse keeper in a million years.

I have absolutely no head for heights. It's something I forget with astonishing regularity, despite coming over all giddy reaching into a top cupboard in the kitchen, going all wobbly when climbing a stepladder to hack away at our unruly front hedge and especially after a terrifying experience in the mountains of Liechtenstein a couple of years ago. Hence when I emerged from the dark, cool, windowless interior of Smeaton's Tower into the bright, dazzling dome of glass that crowns the tapering construction I reacted as only a true coward can. I panicked like buggery. As already established, Plymouth Hoe is already quite high up. Smeaton's Tower is on the highest point of the Hoe and I was at the highest point of Smeaton's Tower in a room of floor-to-ceiling glass. To my right was Plymouth itself, spread below me like a map and giving way to the Devon countryside beyond. To my left was the harbour, beyond it the Channel, and if I'd had any inclination whatsoever to enjoy the view I could probably have seen France and the curvature of the earth beyond that. In front of me was the yawning chasm of the ladder hole that went all the way to the bottom. I tried to get a grip on myself, but first I needed to get a grip on something solid. I reached out to the railing, which wasn't a railing at all – it was part of a rope cradle hanging from the ceiling to show

how the original lights were suspended. My momentum, which blind panic was doing nothing to slow, caused me to stumble forward slightly still clutching the cradle. There was no way I could fall, the real railing prevented that, hence I remained completely composed in order to retain every scrap of my dignity.

'Hyaaaaarrrrrrggghhhhhffffffffffuuuuuuckinellllll-llll!'

That's what I said. Loudly. Well, what do you expect? I thought I was a goner. Smeaton's Tower had for 130 years reverberated with the crash of the sea and the roar of the wind. Now it resonated with the panicky cry of a yellow-bellied scaredy-cat. I heard the echo escaping down the stairwells. I stood upright again, swaying alarmingly in an effort to get my balance back. Below me I noticed that several of the canoodling couples had broken from their clinches and were staring up at the top of the tower, shielding their eyes from the sunlight. At the foot of the tower was a small marquee in which a corporate presentation of some kind was taking place. Only right now it wasn't, as everyone was outside the marquee and looking up to where I was cowering. I'm sure that even Drake's statue twisted its head towards me.

I needed absolutely no further encouragement to put less distance between me and the ground, but I scampered down the ladder like an experienced stevedore descending into a container ship anyway, before anyone could get a fix on me. I was the only person in the tower at the time and I was aware that people would be watching the door to see the Plymouth Yodeller emerge. There was only one thing for it: I had to sit tight until someone else had come in and left again before I could escape. Forty minutes later a man finally entered the lighthouse, finding me examining the blank cement walls with studied interest. Actually the walls weren't completely bare; I found the initials WHG and FAH carved together inside a heart with the date August 22, 1910 – sixty years to the day before I was born. Well, fancy that.

Finally I could escape and put my feet back on the ground, my toes grinding down through the soles of my shoes just to make sure I was actually on the floor properly this time and not mucking them about. I sat for a while on the grass in an effort to recover from my high-altitude trauma. I wasn't cut out to be a lighthouse keeper after all. I'd turned into a big quivering jelly just visiting an old lighthouse stuck on dry land on a beautiful clear day. Imagine if I'd had to go up and change a bulb in the middle of a storm, miles out to sea with the top of the tower swaying in the gale and the sea crashing over the top of it. Somehow, I realised, the performances of Messrs Rooney and Mackay, fine though they were in their own ways, hadn't really captured the true essence of lighthouse keeping. They could, nay, should have played it a bit grittier, if you ask me.

Once I'd recovered, and had a t-shirt made that read 'If you see me heading towards something that's very high up please wrestle me to the ground', I headed south from Plymouth to Biscay, a circuitous journey involving Stansted Airport and Biarritz. As it is one of the most notorious of the shipping forecast areas, even the most relentless landlubber is aware of Biscay's tempestuous reputation. It's the kind of place the forecast was devised for, but it's also home to one of the world's pioneering maritime communities.

Biscay is a region that takes its name from the people who inhabit its south-eastern corner. The Basques are a mysterious lot, their history as distinctive as their characteristic long noses and dark features. Mention the word 'Basque' to most people and 'separatist' won't be far behind, as ETA's armed insurgence against the central Spanish government is the only aspect of Basque life that flits across most people's radars outside the Iberian peninsula. In fact the Basques are a noble, historic people, genuine pioneers, particularly at sea. The Basques are fiercely proud of their culture, something that doesn't come as a surprise considering that regimes from the Romans to Franco have done their best to stamp it out without success. Hence everything Basque is highly praised by its people. I was at a football match at Athletic Bilbao once, a club that fields only players born in the region, and my neighbour in the stadium nudged me and said, 'See that pitch out there? That's Basque grass. Basque grass is the best grass in the world.'

There are seven provinces in the ancient Basque lands, most of them mountainous and verdant. Four lie in Spain, the rest in France, hence the popular nationalist graffiti slogan '4+3=1', and it was to the French Basque lands that I went first. When I learned French at school, it was at a time when textbooks were becoming more accessible. Groovy people started to get involved with them, groovy people with the crazy idea that education could be fun. When I was at school, even Latin had progressed from the dusty likes of *Kennedy's Shorter Latin Primer* to a series of pamphlets featuring the comic-book adventures of a Roman family under the benevolent eye of the father, Caecilius, and his streetwise, fashion-conscious children. The writers must have cursed (*vituperare*) the fact that advanced though the Romans were they hadn't invented glam rock, hot pants and discothèques, but they struggled manfully to make this ancient, dead language hip to us kids. Their masterstroke was having the family live in Pompeii, so we kept reading purely in order not to miss the grisly, volcanic end that was inevitably heading their way.

The great minds behind our French textbook did a similar thing, although they clearly weren't the same groovy cats as the Latin dudes. Most of our French textbooks were based around a series of stories set in the Basque country under the umbrella title *Aventure an Pays Basque* and revolved around Captain Louyat, a fishing-boat skipper operating out of St-Jean-de-Luz. Two extraordinarily irritating children would hang around with him, their chief task in life being the apprehension of smugglers. They did this quite successfully with the help of the obliging Louyat, who never actually seemed to do any fishing. St-Jean-de-Luz customs officials had it easy. They could just stay in their office with their feet up listening to Johnny Hallyday records while a beardy fisherman and a pair of brats did all the work, regularly hauling in nautical miscreants for questioning. Hence the only French phrase I can really remember with any confidence is *Estce-que vous avez quelque-chose á declarer?* Do you have something to declare?

For terms on end we would read these stories of smuggler after swarthy smuggler being apprehended by a couple of smug kids and their captain, all of whom, thankfully for us, seemed to converse in only the most rudimentary French. Beyond this the writers had only one plot device, which involved the inadvertent consumption of poisonous mushrooms. Every story would feature them. The kids' parents would go to the theatre and halfway through the performance there'd be a cry of '*Aieee! Les champignons sont vénéneux!*' and the house lights would go up to reveal one or other of the parents being consumed by convulsions in the stalls. The simple task of buying a baguette from the bakers would see either baker or customer hit the deck with a cry of '*Aieee! Les champignons sont vénéneux!*' Tourists would turn up at the tourist office asking about hotels, and within seconds would be rolling around the floor hollering, '*Aieee! Les champignons sont vénéneux!*' I mean, they'd only just arrived, what was going on in St-Jean-de-Luz? Were they force-feeding people mushrooms as soon as they got off the bus? Several gangs of smugglers came unstuck this way, and I recall even the castiron constitution of Captain Louyat fell victim on at least one occasion. The kids, instead of floating out into the Bay of Biscay and suffering a lingering death from starvation as we all hoped they would, managed to sail the boat back to port, no doubt lassooing a couple of *contrabandiers* on the way. Hard as we hoped though, the smug little gits never succumbed to the tainted fungus themselves.

I called in at St-Jean-de-Luz on my way around the Basque coast to Bilbao. It's a beautiful little town clustered around a picturesque harbour and backed up against the Pyrenees, all red-and-white timbered buildings. St-Jean-de-Luz is just six miles from the Spanish border, and was a key centre for Basque resistance during the Franco years. We never learned this at school, of course. To us, the Basques were little more than a bunch of swarthy smugglers inept enough to be foiled by a couple of kids and unable to distinguish between a mushroom and a toadstool.

I took a pleasant early-evening stroll around the centre of the town. As I loitered down by the harbour (there was no sign of Captain Louyat, alas; hopefully he was out drowning the children) a man in a red cagoule, skimpy blue shorts and a pair of sandals so terrible I presumed they'd been proper shoes before he'd got too close to the lawnmower, came rushing up to me, clearly agitated. He babbled something in French and I asked if he spoke English. He shook his head in irritation, but kept babbling. When he'd finished he looked at me waiting for a response so I asked him if he had anything to declare. His eyebrows registered surprise briefly, but then he started babbling again. It dawned on me, from the way people were stopping on the other side of the street and grinning, that he was a fruitcake who had accosted others in this way in the recent past. I looked around in vain for a man in a white coat rushing towards us with a giant butterfly net, shrugged my shoulders apologetically and walked away, telling him that the mushrooms were poisonous. He made to follow but had decided, given the nature of my two contributions to the conversation, that I was further away with the fairies than even he was, and scampered up a side-street.

I walked through the Place Louis XIV, named

after the Sun King who had released Winstanley from his French incarceration and who in 1660 married Maria Teresa, the Infanta de Castile, here in the church of St-Jean-Baptiste (St-Jean-de-Luz was, I decided, the hyphen capital of the world. Discarded hyphens must make their way here from all over the globe to find a warm welcome between local words). On the day I was there, Place Louis XIV was a relaxed place; café tables spilled on to the pavement and on the bandstand a group of musicians was gathering, plonking their battered instrument cases on the ground and shaking hands with each other.

I found a pleasant restaurant on Rue-de-la-République and was delighted to find that it had a dish of fresh local mushrooms as a starter. Once I'd cleared up the issue of whether the waiter had anything to declare, I ordered the mushrooms and a dish of locally caught tuna with more mushrooms as a main course. I was playing Russian roulette with my constitution, not to mention the rest of my Basque odyssey, but if events progressed in the proverbial textbook fashion, at least between convulsions I'd be able to tell local paramedics precisely what was wrong with me. On the way to the hospital I could also verify whether they had any illegal contraband on board. Fortunately the mushrooms were fine, not to say delicious. Any imperfections would anyway have been neutralised by the garlic. Luckily for the man at the bus station the next morning, there was a pane of glass between him and me, and I was able to buy my ticket to Bilbao without sending him reeling backwards on a tsunami of garlic breath.

Any city down on its luck and hoping to regenerate should go and see Bilbao. The Basque port in the eighties was on the uppers of its uppers following the decline of its twin economic mainstays, steel and shipbuilding. The city was filthy and depressed, unemployment was nudging 25 per cent and the clouds that scudded in from the Bay of Biscay were notable for their lack of a silver lining.

The city's big cheeses sat around the table chewing their biros and furrowing their brows at Bilbao's plight. Ideas for urban salvation would be put forward hopefully, discussed wearily and rejected glumly. So it must have been the end of a particularly long and late night with the councillors totally strung out on caffeine when somebody suggested knocking down some of the shipyards and building a great big art gallery. Now, my reaction would probably have been something along the sarcastic lines of 'Oh, great idea. Never mind that a quarter of the people here are out of work, they'll have plenty of time to go and look at the pretty pictures'. Fortunately I would have been shouted down. Someone might even have blown little balls of screwed up paper through the shell of their biro at me. Either way, my opinion would have been disregarded, and rightly so. The result of that decision, the Guggenheim Museum on the banks of the River Nervion, is now the centrepiece of what is arguably Europe's most successful regeneration. The Guggenheim brought in tourists. Budget airlines began to fly into the city's airport. A state-of-the-art metro system was built, boarded-up squares and plazas were cleaned up and planted with flowers, and today Bilbao is almost perceptibly humming with life. The Guggenheim is an extraordinary-looking building, and that's before you get to the art inside. Designed by Frank Gehry, it is a jumble of smooth curves covered in thousands upon thousands of titanium plates. It was only when I'd walked around the place by the water-side and then looked down upon it from the road bridge behind that I realised the theme of the building was fish. The carefully laid out titanium domes and arches looked like a pile of fish, their heads and tails chopped off ready for filleting. Frank Gehry had done his research, for fish is what made Bilbao and the Basques great.

I went deep into Casco Viejo, the old part of town with its dark, cobbled, narrow streets, perched myself on a stool in a cool and cavernous café, ordered a coffee so strong and hot that I thought they must have a well out the back from which they drew up molten lava from the earth's core, and read up on Basque history.

The Basques are an ancient people with a long tradition of seafaring. Indeed paleolithic cave drawings in Vizcaya, the Basque region that gave its name to the Bay of Biscay (ancient maps mark the bay as El Mar de Los Vascos, the Sea of the Basques), are of fish, while everywhere else contemporary cave drawings show deer or bison. What truly established the Basques' maritime reputation, however, was the discovery that whales and dolphins wintered in the Bay of Biscay. From the seventh century, the Basques began hunting the whales in particular. Not only were the meat and bone valuable commodities, but whale blubber could be boiled down to make a highly effective and economic heating oil. The Basques also caught cod in large quantities, which they soon learned could be preserved with salt. This meant that when the whales moved north after the winter, the Basque fishermen now had enough provisions to follow them. The Basques chased the whales as far north as Norway, the Faeroes and Iceland, their ships well stocked with salted cod for a long voyage.

Long journeys such as these needed sturdy, reliable ships and it wasn't long before the Basques were established among the finest and most innovative shipbuilders in the world. Indeed, as far back as the mid-seventeenth century a Basque engineer named Blasco do Garay approached the king with a revolutionary brainwave: a ship propelled not by sail and oar, but by a wheel turned by the vapour produced by boiling water. It'll never work, said Carlos I. It would be another two hundred years before somebody else invented the steamship and revolutionised the maritime world. So proficient were the Basques on the sea that there are fairly substantial claims they were visiting North America up to two hundred years before Columbus (whose ship the *Santa Maria* was Basque-built and crewed largely by Basques). The European fishing communities were awash with rumours that the Basques had discovered a land across the sea as early as the fourteenth century – certainly the Basques were returning from immensely long voyages with massive catches, hauls far beyond anything within immediate striking range of Europe. When asked where they'd been, the Basques would tap a metaphorical nose; they wanted these fertile fishing grounds for themselves. Within only a few years of John Cabot discovering Newfoundland for the Europeans in 1497 it was well known that the fishing grounds in the vicinity were being tirelessly worked by Basque boats. There were even stories that when Cabot landed at Newfoundland he met native Americans speaking Basque, an almost impenetrable tongue full of Ks and Xs. Indeed, several North American languages bore traces of Basque.

As I swallowed my coffee, removing most of the skin from the back of my throat and resigning myself to being awake for about a week, I understood why the Basques are such a fiercely proud people. Their language, music, indeed their whole culture was outlawed during the Franco years:

speaking a few words of Basque was enough to land you in prison. Indeed, the only place where Basque could be spoken freely was at Athletic Bilbao football matches where it would have been impossible to arrest forty thousand people at once. Somehow, though, the Basques kept their culture alive for the forty-odd years under Franco, and now the language is widely spoken. In parts of Bilbao it's best to ask someone if they speak Spanish if you're looking for the railway station, have something to declare or have consumed some mushrooms you suspect might be poisonous.

Today Basque culture is everywhere. The Basque flag, a red, white and green creation similar in design to the British Union flag, is prominent, usually bigger and in a more raised position than the Spanish flag on public buildings. Road signs are in Basque and Spanish. Pelota courts are everywhere, often tucked away in dingy sidestreets, the only clue they are there being the thwack of the hand slapping the ball and the grunts of the players. Peer into what appears to be an anonymous gateway and you'll see men of all ages whacking a ball around the court with the palms of their leathery hands. Most men wear the Basque beret, a larger piece of headgear than its French counterpart. A Basque national football team even plays an annual 'international' friendly at Athletic Bilbao's San Mames stadium. If a Basque team was ever ratified by the game's governing body they'd make a tremendous dark horse for the World

Cup – some of the better players from the Spanish and French national teams would be eligible to play for Euskadi.

One advantage of drinking the volcanic coffee was that it stripped my mouth and throat of any trace of the St-Jean-de-Luz garlic. In fact it stripped my mouth and throat of any sense of feeling or taste for the next couple of days, hence I wasn't really able to enjoy the locally caught fish in a restaurant on the fringes of the old town later that evening. Afterwards I took the funicular railway up one of the hillsides that surrounds this compact, busy city. From the top of the hill at sunset my gaze was drawn inextricably to the curious curves and shapes of the Guggenheim. The cars crossing the bridge seemed to disappear into the complex. The dark silvery waters of the Nervion passed lazily by. A car pulled up next to where I stood and the young couple inside commenced some energetic heavy petting. I checked, but the car didn't have Plymouth plates.

From Biscay I travelled on around the northern Spanish coast to FitzRoy. In a brief moment of laziness I had toyed with the idea of just visiting the grave of Robert FitzRoy, a short jaunt across south London to Upper Norwood, but I decided I rather fancied going to Finisterre. Telling people that I was going to see the end of the world would give me an air of mystique for a start, and given the controversy that surrounded the renaming of

Finisterre as FitzRoy in February 2002 it seemed a good idea to go and see what all the fuss was about.

The wringing of hands that greeted the renaming of Finisterre was quintessentially British. The trouble began when it became clear that Britain's Finisterre region differed in size from the sea area of the same name used by the Spanish. Quite reasonably the Spanish argued that as it was their coast and their waters, it ought to be Britain who renamed our area. The Met Office was all for it; after all, it gave them the chance to commemorate their founder and the man directly responsible for the birth of the shipping forecast itself. Everything appeared to be hunky-dory.

But no. This is Britain, where we don't do change, especially when it means kowtowing to Johnny Foreigner. There were letters to *The Times* and the *Telegraph*. Mrs Stephanie Waring of Tyneside, who with her sister had named three of their daughters Shannon, Bailey and Tyne, told the *Today* programme, 'FitzRoy sounds more like a Doberman dog than a sea area.' It represented the further emasculation of Britishness for the sake of political correctness. We were being sold down the river. It struck at the very heart of what had made this country great. Drake would be spinning in his watery grave; we might as well have just let the Armada win. What was next, the ceding of Gibraltar to the Spanish with a big pink bow around it, for heaven's sake?

Nearly all of this was a blustering load of old cobblers, of course, because if anything it was a confirmation of Britishness rather than another chip off the White Cliffs of Dover by swarthy continentals. The area was given a British subject's name after all, despite the fact that the region in question hung off the north-western tip of Spain. Like Martin Rowley back in Bracknell, another place that could be suitably described as the end of the earth, I was all for the change. The forecast would lose a little of its poetry, but it represented a more fitting memorial for a pioneering meteorologist than an austere, leaf-strewn tomb in Upper bloody Norwood. Which is why I found myself in the bus station at Santiago de Compostela one muggy afternoon buying a ticket to the end of the world via the coast of death. The westernmost tip of mainland Europe, Cape Finisterre sits on the Costa da Morte – names that give the local tourist board a marketing challenge, I'd imagine. It was the Romans who named my destination *finis terrae*, the end of the earth, because back then that's exactly what it was: the westernmost point of the known world.

There were a number of people milling about in the bus station who looked a bit odd. This perhaps shouldn't have come as a big surprise as every bus station I've ever been to has served as a tractor beam for weirdos. These people were not weirdos, however, at least not in the conventional sense. Most of them wore cagoules and shorts, in the manner of my friend from St-Jean-de-Luz. Unlike him though, there appeared to be a certain amount of planning in the outfits, not to mention rather less insanity in the demeanour, as rather than sandals these people were wearing sturdy walking boots, carrying staffs whittled by hand and sporting hefty-looking rucksacks. Most of them were sinewy, weathered and all bore the same expression: a kind of relaxed, healthy satisfaction. These were pilgrims heading for home after completing the Way of St James, the ancient pilgrimage to the reputed bones of the saint housed in the elaborate cathedral of Santiago de Compostela. As it turned out I had followed a large section of one of the pilgrim routes myself through the Basque lands, Asturias and into the holy town itself. Except instead of walking the well-trodden pilgrim routes, sleeping in special pilgrims' hostels and cleansing my spirit, I'd done it sitting on my backside and eating crisps in an air-conditioned bus that smothered the pilgrims in a cloud of carbon monoxide as it swished past.

The real hardcore pilgrims press on for Finisterre, several days' walk beyond Santiago. It must be like crossing the finishing line of the London Marathon, eschewing the Mars bar and Bacofoil cloak with a contemptuous flick of the hand and jogging straight off for a couple of circuits around Hyde Park. Finisterre was for serious pilgrims only. As I threw my holdall into the belly of the Finisterre bus, it was followed by a couple of rucksacks and a pair of pilgrims' staffs. A German couple, who would be my only fellow travellers on the two-and-a-half-hour journey, were taking the easy option. I'd read in a guidebook that pilgrims who walk into Finisterre town, or Fisterra to give it its Galician name, are given a certificate to show that they've made it that far. I bet myself that the Germans were going to hop out of the bus at the stop before and saunter into the pilgrims' refuge waggling their staffs wearily and claiming their certificates, the cheats. Just like I was planning to do.

The journey to Finisterre winds its way around the Galician hills. Galicia is one of Spain's poorest regions and many of the ancient villages through which we passed seemed to have slipped back in time around a century. Horses and carts clopped through the streets, and everywhere you looked there were old stone grain stores, raised from the rats and the damp by what appeared to be stone toadstools at each corner. The sleekness of the bus was entirely out of place, not least when the driver would rush up behind a hay cart and toot impatiently.

It had got dark by the time we arrived in Finisterre itself, which turned out to be a relief on two counts. First, the late-afternoon sun streaming through the bus windows had been more dazzling than any I'd ever experienced, a searing white light that had my eyes screwed up for most of the journey. Second, the harbourfront on which we were deposited looked singularly unattractive. Bright neon light spilled out from a couple of unappealing bars, rubbish blew around in the wind and dogs trotted aimless and ownerless among the scrubby grass and cracked tarmac. The buildings appeared to have been sited by a town planner afflicted with blindness and a twitch while working on the plans; they were scattered randomly and mostly facing out into the harbour. Some looked as though they were only there to fill a gap between two other buildings, while with one in particular I couldn't tell whether it was half built or half demolished. Within ten seconds I'd trodden with an audible 'spludge' into a mountainous cloying dog turd, which meant I had to spend my first minutes in Finisterre scraping my foot in a small patch of gravel, doing circles that must have suggested to onlookers that someone had nailed my left foot to the ground.

The Germans, incidentally, had not cheated and had alighted at the final stop. Which was a pity because I'd been relying on them to know where to get off in order that we might secure our certificates. So instead of a crisp new certificate to go over my desk, I now had a training shoe covered in poo instead, something I wasn't quite as keen on seeing mounted and affixed to my office wall.

I'd booked into the Hotel Finisterre because I relished the idea of staying in the 'hotel at the end of the world'. It looked suitably soulless, a modern block with a neon sign outside where the 'o' in 'hotel' flicks on and off randomly as it prepares to give up the ghost altogether. I'd booked a room via the Internet before I'd left but messed up the dates – the first reservation I'd made was for a stay of three months. I'd tried again, with a note to say sorry, I'm an imbecile, ignore the last one, this is the real thing, honest. Just to be sure I'd sent them a fax too. I'm nothing if not a cautious traveller who prepares thoroughly. It did strike me that they might have thought they'd been selected as the venue for a get together of lots of people called Charlie Connelly, but when I presented myself at reception it turned out they weren't expecting me at all. They'd never heard of me in fact, let alone my nomenclaturally twinned chums. It didn't matter though, because there was only one other guest booked into the forty-eight-room hotel that night so it's not as if there was a shortage of space. I was, however, put into the room next to the other guest, whose foghorn snoring coming through the wall would keep me awake for most of the night.

I rose early the next morning and had a stroll around town before heading out to the Faro de Finisterre, the lighthouse at the end of the finger of land that is continental Europe's westernmost landfall. There was a curious atmosphere, a sort of resigned, stoop-shouldered gait to the place. Clearly it wasn't a rich town, after all we were at the furthest reach of one of Spain's poorest regions, but my first impressions were of a semi-broken spirit, a little like Arbroath only without the musky smell of smoking haddock. Even the morning itself emerged almost reluctantly from the night: it was nearly ten before it got light to reveal a scruffy-looking town. I'd woken many times during the night, but on one occasion I hadn't been roused by the Olympic snoring champion next door. I was roused instead by a bright white light that shone through my eyelids and into a dream I was having about being chased up a lighthouse by a giant poisonous mushroom. I opened my eyes slightly and it took a moment to realise what this intense white glare was. I'd pulled the curtains across too hard and there was a gap of around two feet between the end of the fabric and the end of the window. I was facing this gap and there, fitting perfectly into that space, was the full moon. It was enormous and it was startlingly bright, as if someone had hung it directly outside my window. Following the fierceness of the sunlight earlier in the day, I began to realise why Finisterre was said to hold magical properties related to the sun and moon's diurnal rotations.

I wondered whether the sun, shining from the east on to the harbour in the morning, would make the jumbled harbourfront look any more attractive and was faintly startled to realise just how much it didn't. Avoiding the giant cone of doggie doo-doo that still bore my footprint from the previous evening, I plunged into the jumbly maze of streets behind the harbour; dark, narrow lanes of flaking paintwork and cracked plaster, and emerged into the main square of the town. This being Finisterre it wasn't actually a square, more a lopsided rhombus. I sat on a decrepit bench in the shade. Even though the sun hadn't been up long it was already a hot day, and several elderly Galicians paused to drink the water gushing from beneath a large and incredibly ancient-looking stone cross that was the focus of the square. Beyond the harbour, I discovered once I'd moved on, was a slightly more appealing vista. There was a small sandy beach overlooked on one side by palm trees and on the other by an ancient little fortress. A clothes market was setting up on the road that skirted the beach, a sudden multi-coloured splash that the harsh Finisterre light picked out vividly. As I walked through the market the town clock prepared to chime the hour with a slow, mournful, strangely apologetic tune. It was almost as if it were saying, Well, there you go, folks, that's another hour gone and another hour you're closer to death. Twelve doleful clangs followed to denote midday. The chatter of the women exam-ining the stalls mingled with the slow, gentle lapping of the waves on the beach and a solitary seagull let out a tired-sounding squawk.

I set out on the walk to the end of the world. As I progressed along the headland the Atlantic shone a deep blue, the fierce sun reflecting off the water in a million shifting silver shards that were never still. After a while the lighthouse came into view for the first time, a sturdy, almost Georgian-looking building with a light tower on top. I made a mental note not to go up it even if I could. At length I passed a couple of boarded-up wooden cafés with faded posters of ice-creams next to long-closed serving hatches. It was very quiet and I was the only walker on the road. There was hardly a breath of wind and the Atlantic was calm. A couple of hundred yards in front of the lighthouse was a small stone pillar with a shell logo – the last marker post of the pilgrimage. I approached the lighthouse, an immaculate white building with green shutters and the words 'Faro da Finisterre' above the doorway, and walked past it to the rocks that mark the end of the world. I was at the point where the first Roman legion to march this far saw there was nowhere to go but back the way they came and presumably uttered a collective '*Eheu, testes**'. Here I was, at the very place that had caused those letters to the *Telegraph*, the Finisterre that had come out of British radios for more than half a century. I was also now the westernmost person on the European mainland.

I looked back and tried to imagine the whole of Europe spread before me and Asia beyond. I tried to imagine what it would be like to not know that America was out there somewhere behind me on the other side of the shimmering blue, tried to

---

* 'Ahhh, bollocks.'

believe that this really was the *finis terrae* of the Romans, but the discarded Coca-Cola can on the ground near by put paid to that. I began to understand why this was such a spiritual place going back thousands of years beyond Christianity to the Celts. Before me was all the land in the world as it was then: life, cities, traders, empires. Behind me was the unknown, the end of the world and the end of life itself. Out there was the Celtic Tir-na-Nóg, the Land of Eternal Youth. This headland was where the physical world met the spiritual world. There is probably no better place in the world to earn a sense of your own mortality than the headland at Finisterre.

I rummaged in my bag and pulled out a photocopied sheet. I'd come prepared. It was portrait of a noble-looking early-Victorian man wearing a double-breasted dark-blue naval tunic with gold trim and tasseled epaulettes. There was an assertive air about him, but a discernible melancholy in his eyes. I placed the picture on the ground and secured it there with a stone and the transition of Finisterre to FitzRoy was now complete.

From the erstwhile tip of the known world I headed uphill rather than back around the headland, along a winding road so steep I thought I was going to scrape my nose on the tarmac. Gorse bushes and pine trees lined the route (the Galician 'national' anthem is called 'Os Pinos', 'Pine Trees': 'Listen to the voices of the murmuring pines, they are the voices of the Galician people'). Breathing hard beneath the fearsome sun, I walked around a hairpin bend and the road gave way to a track leading more directly to the top of the hill. Passing between forests of shady pines, after about twenty minutes I found a tiny pathway of trodden grass. This was what I was looking for. As I crested the hill, facing east, I saw a giant boulder ahead of me. Rounding the boulder I found that it served as one wall of a tiny ruined building, no more than twenty feet long to the base of the overhanging boulder and six wide. Stunted walls emerged from the undergrowth, rising three feet from the ground with pink flowers growing from between the stones. At the far end was a rock whose top had long ago been chiselled into a bowl shape, allowing rainwater to collect. By the right-hand wall as you looked out across the bay to Monte Pindo, the Mount Olympus of the Celtic gods, was a long, flat stone slab into which long lines had been scored and a dip cut at one end in the vague shape of a very small person. This was the ancient hermitage of San Guillermo.

Guillermo is believed to have lived here alone for many years in the sixth century. St James himself is also rumoured to have spent time here. San Guillermo's bed, the flat slab with the slight hollow to lay his head, is believed to have magical fertility properties and for centuries couples having trouble conceiving have come here to do the business. Considering it had taken me a good sweaty two hours to walk here, not to mention the fact that it looked decidedly uncomfortable, you'd have to have a fairly determined libido to succeed in performing the necessaries, let alone have a chance to spawn life. But clearly it must work: laid carefully on the bed, presumably in thanks for the recent birth of a local child that had been conceived here, was a white lace handkerchief on which someone had placed a small bunch of wild red flowers, weighed down with a couple of stones.

The 'bed' was placed end-on to a gap in the wall, facing east. Hence Guillermo would have been woken every morning by the first rays of the sun streaming over the peak of Monte Pindo, sent up into the sky by the Celtic gods themselves from their lofty peak to disappear over Monte Facho and on to Tir-na-Nóg in the evening. I sat down on a rock within the walls and time stopped. The shadow from the huge boulder that protected Guillermo from the westerly winds spread slowly across my feet just as the mournful sound of the Finisterre town clock reluctantly chiming the hour floated up faintly on the breeze from far below. Otherwise the only noise came from the odd fly and a chirruping cricket somewhere near by.

I honestly don't know where the hours went. I wasn't doing anything to pass the time, I just sat on my rock with my chin on my cupped hand not even thinking about anything in particular. It felt like I'd been there for ten minutes, and it was only when the shadow of the boulder covered the entire ruin and the temperature fell accordingly that I realised I'd been there for nearly three hours. Shivering slightly in the cool shade, I left the old hermitage and walked over the top of the hill again where the late-afternoon sun was continuing its relentless crawl towards the Atlantic horizon beyond. I stayed up there for the rest of the day, parking myself on a big rock that I learned later was part of the ancient Ara Solis, a temple to the sun that pre-dates Stonehenge. In front of me was the long, uninterrupted horizon and above it the sun, sinking towards its repose in the Land of Eternal Youth. I watched it set, and when the silvery yellow path on the water that stretched from the horizon to the coastal rocks below me glinted on the surface of the sea I understood why the ancients saw this place as the gateway to Tir-na-Nog. It was almost as if the Celtic gods had rolled out a golden carpet to show you the way.

Eventually the sun set, leaving only pinky-purple fringes on the wispy clouds. Away to my left the lighthouse at the tip of the headland flickered into life and swung its beam around. The wind was turning chilly as the sky darkened, but the rocks of the temple were still warm to the touch from the day's sunshine, as if it was storing up energy from the flaming star whose worship it facilitated.

I walked back along the road around the headland to the town, and where in the morning the journey had been hot beneath the fearsome Finisterre sun, now it was dark and cold, the moon large, round and bright over Monte Pindo. A solitary fishing boat crossed the moonbeam spread on the surface of the water on its way back to harbour.

The town looked and felt different as I returned to the hotel. I realised as I left the headland and descended into the narrow streets that the tightly packed higgledy-piggledyness of the streets had a purpose: providing shelter from the elements that lash this remote peninsula in winter, and storing the day's heat for summer evenings. From the chilly night air, the dimly lit streets were warm and cosy. Front doors stood open to reveal families sitting inside. It was after nine yet all the shops were still serving; I saw an old-fashioned hardware shop, little cardboard boxes of nails, hooks and screws stacked to the ceiling in racks with a man in a brown coat behind the counter. The town square was lit by large, round orange lamps, the spindly trees casting shadows and the dim light bringing warmth to the cracked plasterwork that had looked so austere that morning.

The amazing snoring man had checked out so I spent a night disturbed only by the moonlight before departing under darkness the next morning. As the bus rounded the Coast of Death to leave Finisterre behind, a slight brightening in the eastern sky denoted that the sun was on its way back from the Land of Eternal Youth to the End of the World. Somewhere up on a dark hill, some drying flowers on a slab of rock rustled slightly in the breeze. Even on the Coast of Death new life begins.

SOLE, LUNDY, FASTNET

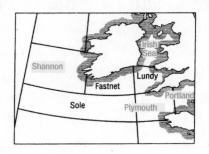

The area now covered by Areas Sole, Lundy and Fastnet was originally known as Area Severn. The divisions we know today came about during the 1949 changes. Sole, Lundy and Fastnet have a common nodal point just north-east of the Isles of Scilly. Area Sole has no land boundary. Area Lundy encompasses the entire north Devon coast, and the southern Welsh coast as far around as St David's Head, from where its northern boundary stretches across the Irish Sea to Rosslare. Area Fastnet's land boundary stretches from Rosslare around southern Ireland to Valentia Island just south of Dingle Bay.

Hanging around in airports has become a speciality of mine whereby a ridiculous amount of my life has been spent sitting in or wandering aimlessly around terminal buildings of various shapes, sizes and humidities. I dread to think how many months I've wasted walking polished floors with a boarding pass flapping around in my hand but it's probably even more than the time I've spent watching Charlton Athletic, with roughly the same quantities of boredom and disillusionment.

When I worked in the music industry, the motto of every touring band was 'Don't be late for the hanging about'. Touring with bands is supposed to be glamorous; in actuality it's an endless procession of hotel room to bus to venue to bus to next hotel room with a whole load of bored listlessness thrown in. It's the same with travelling, especially if, like me, you're paranoid about missing planes and so turn up at airports ridiculously early. Hence I spend much more time hanging around them than I really need to. This isn't necessarily a problem as I quite like airports. They're all different, yet most seem to be completely detached from the city they serve. In fact airports seem to be detached from everywhere; little self-contained towns and cities in which days, nights, seasons and climates don't exist. Their populations are entirely transient, save for the check-in staff, baggage handlers, security people and cleaners who watch everyone come and go with varying levels of disinterest and misanthropy. Most of the shops are useless; Boots, W.H. Smith and Waterstone's aside, the others sell useless things to people who are so transfixed with nerves at the thought of flying they just hand over cash willingly to anyone with a till, only discovering their purchases days later ('Where on earth did I get this tin of shortbread and these curling tongs?').

The aeroplanes themselves don't fascinate me greatly. I leave that to my dad, who has had a life-long passion for them. In fact, if it wasn't for this fascination then he wouldn't have met my mum when they both worked for an airline in London and I wouldn't be here. Only recently he flew from Bournemouth to Belfast and back in a day simply because the return leg was on a type of plane he'd never flown on before. Alas for Pops, the plane in question developed a technical fault while still on the ground and had to be taken out of service, meaning he'd given up a day and an airfare purely to sit in Belfast Airport for four hours.

But while most airports blend in the memory into one generic, neon-lit, shiny-floored terminal of snaking queues and expensive coffee, Land's End Aerodrome is a place I shan't forget in a hurry. For a start it was my first aerodrome, a word that immediately transports you to a world of handlebar moustaches, leather goggles and a time when Croydon was significant. Land's End Aerodrome is, not surprisingly, a small affair. It's so low-key, in fact, that it doesn't even have a runway, at least not in the conventional sense – the planes take off and land on grass. Checking-in has great humiliation potential: once you've handed over your bag they make you stand on the scales with your hand luggage. Now, I have to admit that the sedentary lifestyle of working from home means that I have, ah, let myself go a little from the svelte man-about-town figure I cut only a couple of years ago. While I wasn't quite in 'one at a time please' speak-your-weight-machine gag territory, I was still a little nervous that I'd have to have some kind of 'gutbucket express' plane all to myself. I stepped nervously on to the scales, already preparing unconvincing excuses about heavy shoes and hardback books. In a cartoon, the needle would have spun around like propeller, causing the entire dial to pop out to a twanging soundtrack of flying springs. Fortunately this wasn't a cartoon and the needle shot part of the way around the dial and came to a quivering halt. The woman checking me in nodded to herself and made a note on a piece of paper. I craned my neck; whatever she'd written didn't seem to correspond with 'piggy porker' or somesuch and I appeared to have passed the weight test.

After that trauma I needed sustenance and repaired to the Choxaway Café, which is a terrific name for an airport eaterie. There's even a fish-pond in the middle of it. The café that is, not the name. I waited patiently at the counter and after a short while a woman's head popped through the doorway behind the cake display unit.

'Ooh,' she said with surprise, still just a head in a doorway. 'Hello.'

'Hello.' I responded, and drew breath in order to request the sausage sandwich and mug of tea I had selected from the board of fare at the end of the counter. Before I could do so, the head in the doorway interjected.

'Do you want a waffle?' it asked.

'Pardon?' I responded.

'Do. You. Want. A. Waffle?' said the head, pausing between the words for full 'I am clearly addressing a buffoon' effect. Guessing that she was offering me a latticed batter cake rather than suggesting we draw up a couple of chairs and have a conversation, I responded, 'Er, I was actually hoping for something hot.'

'To eat?'

'Yes.'

'Or drink?'

'Yes.'

'Well which?'

'Oh, er, both.'

'Right,' said the head in the doorway, 'well, Lil will have to sort you out then.' The head rotated slightly and addressed the darkness behind. 'Lil!' It turned back to me. 'Sure you don't want a waffle?' it asked.

'No, really, I'm fine thanks.'

'Lil!' shouted the head again.

'Yeah, I'm coming,' came the response. 'Don't shout at me when I'm in the freezer.'

The head disappeared, Lil eventually emerged and my sandwich and tea were ordered. Before they arrived an elderly couple walked in, the man bald with a valance of snow-white hair at ear level and his wife in a cotton print dress and sun hat. 'Good afternoon,' they said with big smiles. They sat down at an adjacent table and we chatted for a while. They were two of the loveliest people I've ever met, the type of people you wish really hard that nothing bad would happen to, not ever. Eventually, the head in the doorway appeared behind the counter, attached, as it turned out, to a body. The old man went to the counter and ordered two cream teas.

'Now,' said the woman, placing both hands on the counter, 'wouldn't you rather have a waffle?'

The obvious answer here would, of course, have been no, clearly not, if I'd rather have a waffle why would I be ordering something else? That would plainly be highly irrational, not to say faintly masochistic behaviour. But these were nice people. Very nice people indeed who didn't want to be any trouble.

'Oh, well, yes, okay then, waffles it is. Thank you,' said the man. As he turned away with an encouraging smile at his wife, the former head in a doorway, whom I had decided was called Carol, all but punched the air with delight. Once the waffles arrived and were set about with appreciative nods and 'mmm' noises, Carol sat at an adjacent table and enquired after them.

'Do they taste all right?'

'Mmm.'

'Consistency okay?'

'Mmm.'

'Not too doughy?'

'Mmm.' This was accompanied by a furrowing of the brow and a shake of the head.

'Warm enough?'

'Mmm.'

And so the questioning continued before Carol played her joker.

'Yeah, we went to a catering fair the other day and got loads of them. They're really good. I mean, I'm an Anglophile, right, and these are French, but they're still really nice.'

'They're Belgian,' came Lil's voice from the doorway whence Carol's head had originally appeared.

'Ooh, are they?' replied Carol. 'Well, there you go. Even better if they're not French. They must be all right.'

The conversation continued. It turned out that they were short of pilots that day as two of them were marrying each other.

'They met here at the aerodrome,' said Carol, 'it's lovely really.'

'Love is in the air, you might say,' I ventured.

'Ooh, that's good that,' said Carol. 'Very good. Love is in the air. I like that. Yeah, we're going round to their house later, to leave champagne and flowers for when they get home.'

'And waffles?' I asked. There was a thoughtful silence.

'That's not a bad idea, you know,' said Carol.

Eventually the flight was called (with each of the eight passengers being notified by name) and we were ushered through to the departure lounge – a small extension to the terminal building with some office chairs in rows and patio doors at the end. A man in a high-visibility jacket switched on a television set in the corner and pressed play on a video recorder to start the safety demonstration and left the room. It ran through twice. Near the end of the second screening, he popped back in and asked, 'Is this the second time now?' Yes, we replied, bloody repeats. On the way back, at St Mary's Airport, when the girl pressed play for the safety demonstration and left the room, a documentary about dinosaurs came on.

He walked us to the plane and called us forward one by one. I was at the front, behind the empty co-pilot seat, which meant I had the best view. Once the man in the high-visibility jacket had shown us how to use the emergency doors he slammed them shut and was away across the field. At this point the pilot turned around in his seat and introduced himself, told us the flight would take about fifteen minutes and that we'd be flying at fifteen hundred feet. The Skybus service is brilliantly efficient and the staff are friendly and professional, but it's a strange experience when you're used to far bigger aircraft and airports. This is going to sound horrifically patronising and it's certainly not meant to be, but it was all a bit like people playing airports.

If Bergen to Haugesund had previously been the shortest flight I'd ever taken, this cut that flight time almost in half. There was no cabin crew because there was no aisle. If we'd had an in-flight movie there would barely have been time for an episode of *Willo The Wisp*. The plane roared along the grass runway and eased into the air, the tips of the right-hand propeller spinning barely two feet from my flushed rosy cheek behind the perspex. I had a panoramic view. We passed over Land's End itself, low enough to see people walking about below but high enough to recognise the headland from every map of Britain I'd ever seen.

The disadvantage of my seat was that I could also see the plane's dashboard instruments. Now I'm not a nervous flyer by any means, but this was far too much detail for my liking. I prefer just to hear the reassuring voice of the captain over the intercom while I peruse the in-flight magazine over a plastic glass of red wine. If there are cockpit fisticuffs over a disputed piece of sporting trivia, or debates as to whether we really should be this close to that mountain, I don't want to know about them. Observing the cockpit instruments I considered to be a step too far and every time a light flashed or a needle fluctuated in front of me I was tempted to tug the pilot's sleeve and ask, 'Er, should it really be doing that?'

Within minutes, however, my attention was distracted by the Isles of Scilly looming out of the wrinkled blue carpet of sea below us. It was a bright, sunny day and the dark green islands' golden beaches were clearly visible. There are fifty-five Isles of Scilly (don't call them the Scilly Isles or even the Scillies, the Scillonians hate it), of which five are inhabited. They are roughly twenty-eight miles from Land's End and are all very small. Even St Mary's, the largest, is only three miles wide at its fattest point and only ten miles around the coastline. Its position right in the firing line of the Gulf Stream means Scilly has an extraordinarily mild climate. Flowers are harvested here earlier than anywhere in Britain, palm trees abound and the water is so clear that the sea bed is visible even to depths of several feet. Scilly is also relatively free of air pollution, and the pure air makes it easier for ultra-violet rays to batter through the atmosphere; sunburn is harsher on Scilly than just about anywhere else.

Barely had we left the ground than we were swooping in low over coastal rocks and touching down at St Mary's Airport. It was then that I began to regret slightly opting to fly. The short hop from Land's End, all of fifteen minutes, had given me practically no sense of how remote these islands are; sailing on the *Scillonian III* takes up to three hours from Penzance depending on the weather. At least that way you know you've travelled.

I was staying in Hugh Town, Scilly's largest settlement, and once I'd checked in to my hotel, I went for a quick walk around the place, which, as it turns out, is the only kind of walk you can have in Hugh Town. It's so small that the map in the tourist guidebook has a fish and chip van marked on it. Much of this tiny town is clustered around the harbour and strung out on the narrow spar between two beaches at the south-western end of the island. I took a stroll along the harbourfront and sat in the Coronation Shelter for a while, looking out at the boats and the island of Tresco beyond. There's a small plaque on the shelter, announcing that it was 'Erected in 1954 to commemorate the Coronation of Queen Elizabeth II by the Isles of Scilly Council'. Now, I've only seen grainy footage, but I could have sworn that it was the Archbishop of Canterbury who was lowering the crown on to the royal bouffant. But hey, I could be wrong.

As the sun set I popped into the Atlantic Inn, which overlooks the harbour in the heart of Hugh Town, for a couple of leisurely pints. Inside, the local newsagent was announcing proudly to all who'd listen that he'd have Sunday papers available the following day. Given that he was imparting this information on a Saturday, this may not on the face of it seem like earth-shattering news. Indeed, non-islanders could have been forgiven for assuming he'd gone cheerfully nuts. However, the Isles, of course, rely on the

Scillonian for supplies, and the *Scillonian* doesn't run on a Sunday. On this occasion though, a local radio station in the south-west had arranged a one-off day trip for this Sunday, hence the newsagent's excitement at the prospect of the following day's papers. I'd seen him outside his shop soon after I'd arrived, calling out to passers-by to get their orders in. Handwritten posters either side of the shop doorway announced SUNDAY PAPERS – AVAILABLE TOMORROW which may seem to us like putting up a sign saying NEWS AT TEN – TONIGHT AT TEN O'CLOCK, but then most of us don't live on a small island. In cities especially, rampant consumer culture means that days of the week take on less and less significance and we become used to supermarket shelves being fully stocked – even in the middle of the night, for heaven's sake. The seasons have become almost redundant, with what used to be seasonal produce available just about all year round. On the Isles of Scilly and their ilk, however, the products and services we take for granted are so variable that reading the Sunday papers on a Sunday is a rare pleasure to be savoured. Which I think is a pleasantly sobering thought in this ridiculously fast-paced world. As I lay in bed that night I actually felt a sense of excited anticipation at the prospect of reading a Sunday newspaper on the day it was meant to be read, and I'd only been on Scilly for eight hours.

When I'd checked in to my hotel I was told that the clientele would be summoned for breakfast by the striking of a gong at 8.30, which I found a tremendous prospect as I had never been summoned for a meal by gong before. To me this was an experience akin to a fully tuxed butler tapping on the door and announcing that 'Dinner is served'. I was up and dressed early, ready for the off long before 8.30. I sat on my bed, ears cocked for the sound of the gong. Eventually, after what seemed an age, an energetic clanging rang up and down the corridors and I was out of the door like a shot. While disappointed that the gong was the size of a 45rpm record rather than the one walloped at the start of Rank films, I was determined to be the first to answer its call. My room was only at the top of the stairs and given my relatively nimble gait compared to my fellow guests, none of whom appeared to be under sixty, I was confident of having first choice of the fun-size cereal boxes. When I skidded to a halt in the doorway of the dining room, however, the place was already three quarters full. I was stunned. Either the Scillonian air had had remarkably restorative effects on the ageing occupants or they'd been out of the blocks before the starting gun, the dirty, low-down, no-good cheats.

The waitress headed me off at the pass. 'We've put you here,' she said, indicating a tiny wobbly table set for one placed behind the door just close enough to thump against it every time someone walked through. Such is the lot of the single traveller. I had become aware of the pitying smiles of fellow guests almost as soon as I started travelling alone in earnest. We lone travellers are frequently a curiosity and sometimes a nuisance to hotels, not least when the last room they have is a triple, they lease it to us at a single rate and then have to turn away a family of three ten minutes later. It's got to the stage now that when I walk into a hotel and announce that I'd like a room for one, I wouldn't be surprised if the owner produced a blunderbuss from under the counter and chased me into the street, emptying volleys of grapeshot into my posterior.

As I was the only one in the room not to qualify for a free bus pass, as well as being the only unaccompanied guest, there were plenty of sideways glances as I drained the orange juice jug. The waitress approached gingerly to take my breakfast order, as if lone travellers were bound by reputation either to pull her on to their lap panting 'My, but you're a pretty one', or request something outlandish, like a lightly buttered vole on toast. I did neither. Silence descended as I gave my order, and I could sense the thoughts of my spellbound fellow diners. 'Oooh, he's having a fried egg. Just like normal people.' 'Yes, he looks the sort who'd like black pudding.'

Once I'd begun to eat I found that every time I looked up a different old lady would be looking at me with a mixture of curiosity and suspicion. I started to guess which one would be next, a kind of Russian roulette of cauliflower-heads. When I finished my breakfast and stood up to leave, the clinking of cutlery and murmur of conversation stopped and every pair of eyes swivelled towards me expectantly. I felt as if I should have donned a pair of spats and danced my way out of the room, waggling a top hat behind my head and twirling an ivory-tipped cane.

I'd decided to take a walk around the coastline to Porth Hellick, whose little bay had been the scene of two of Scilly's most significant moments. This meant rounding Peninnis Head, which is a just couple of letters shy of causing a startling amount of mirth among schoolboys, particularly as at the end of Peninnis Head there is a local landmark called Blow Hole. Now now, stop sniggering. The map I was following cheerfully marks the major shipwrecks off the coasts of the Isles, of which there have been a large number. Peninnis Head is where *Minnehaha* went down (oh for goodness' sake, pull yourself together) in 1874, for example, so close to the shore that half the crew were able to save themselves by shinning along the bowsprit and dropping on to the rocks. Shipwrecks have become part of Scillonian culture over the centuries, and with tragedy have come benefits. Like many other island communities the Scillonians have always looked upon wrecks as blessings in disguise, for with wrecks come spilled cargoes, and from spilled cargoes comes useful stuff. Wrecking was a key, if not essential, part of island life, particularly before the twentieth century when communications and economics were not what they are today. Indeed, the Scillonians even used to offer up an ambiguous prayer:

We pray, O Lord, not that wrecks should happen,
But that should they happen,
Thou wilt guide them to these islands
For the benefit of the poor inhabitants.

Old Town cemetery, set on a bay just beyond Peninnis Head, bears witness to this history. Now a tiny settlement, until the development of Hugh Town, Old Town was the islands' commercial centre. Its medieval quay is still in use and, according to the information sign posted outside the Old Town church, there is a 'thirteenth-century castle near by that once stood here; the ruins are now covered in vegetation'. I found this strangely refreshing; in most places a visitor centre would have gone up dedicated to the 'Thirteenth-century Castle Experience' complete with interactive touch-screen technology and souvenir tea-towels. With nearly all of our cultural landmarks roped off and surrounded by gift shops and ice-cream stands, any sense of exploration and discovery has been entirely removed. Even Land's End, which I had visited before heading to the aerodrome, has a small 'theme village', with interactive shows and souvenir shops. While this was nowhere near as tacky as the Needles, it did seem to contradict the essence of Land's End: its sense of remoteness, almost loneliness. I'd naïvely assumed that Land's End would be just that, a road that came to an end by the famous direction sign, just like at Finisterre. But no. A series of hi-tech, multi-sensory 'experiences' had been devised when surely the appeal of Land's End is that nothing happens here. It's isolated. You stand and look out to sea and sense that the whole of Britain is now behind you. Towns, cities, villages, fields, your tax return, the bloke you once slapped around the back of the head because you'd mistakenly thought he was someone you knew, everyone and everything is behind your back as you look out to sea. It's enough to make you paranoid in fact.

Land's End could be a lot, lot worse, but the people in charge who think we all have an attention span and emotional shallowness similar to their own, diminish rather than enhance the effects of these places and it's getting out of hand. Expensively so for the humble sightseer. Even the Land's End direction sign is fenced off so they can charge you eight quid to have your picture taken beneath it. One day we'll have visitor centres dedicated to visitor centres, you mark my words.

Anyway, harrumph, in the Old Town cemetery

are a number of graves bearing the same date, May 7, 1875. On that foggy night the *Schiller*, a German liner en route from New York to Hamburg, hit rocks off Scilly and sank, drowning 335 of the 372 passengers and crew. Around a third of that number are buried here in a mass grave, the funerals taking place while yet more bodies were washed up on the shore. At the top of the cemetery overlooking the bay, a huge obelisk dominates the quiet churchyard, erected in memory of twenty-three-year-old Louise Holzmaister who was on the *Schiller* travelling home to Germany to be reunited with her husband of a few weeks. Her body was never found. I poked around in the cemetery for a while, conscious of the peace that surrounds it despite the stormy and violent ends met by many of its inhabitants. As I picked my way along this timeline of Scilly mortality I was startled to find, in a plot some way from the church, the grave of Harold Wilson. Wilson and his wife Mary used to spend a great deal of time on Scilly, enjoying the peace and the fact that the islanders would leave them be. Indeed, Mary Wilson still has a cottage not far from Old Town.

I carried on around the coast, passing the end of the runway on which I had arrived the previous day, and eventually came across the quiet, sheltered bay of Porth Hellick. The crescent beach was fringed with seaweed, beyond which the tide had withdrawn to its lowest point. Shallow pools and ribbed sand were interspersed with weed-covered rocks, rising to a peak at the Loaded Camel, a rock formation that looks, believe it or not, like a loaded camel.

Halfway around the bay where the beach meets the scrubby grass is a small cairn, the only evidence of one of Scilly's most famous tales; one that led almost directly to Greenwich's establishment as the maritime centre of Britain and arguably the world. The cairn, almost hidden among the gorse, marks what turned out to be the penultimate resting place of the splendidly named Admiral Sir Cloudesley Shovell. A brilliant naval commander who had seen action against Dutch, Irish and Barbary pirates, and played a key role in the capture of Gibraltar from the Spanish in 1704, Shovell became commander-in-chief of the Mediterranean fleet. In October 1707 he was sailing home after an inconclusive battle with the French at Toulon. Thick fog closed in as he approached the English Channel and there was some debate as to the fleet's position. One of his crew thought the ships were too far north and were heading towards the Bristol Channel rather than Plymouth, and made a strong argument in support of his case. After some discussion with his senior officers, however, Shovell concluded that the fleet was sailing steadily for Plymouth and had the sailor hanged for his dashed impudence. A couple of hours later, the dead sailor was proved utterly correct as, with a terrible wrenching of timbers, Shovell's ship the *Association*, as well as the *Eagle* and the *Romney*, smashed into Scilly's western rocks.

More than sixteen hundred lost their lives, and from those ships only one man survived. According to legend, despite being fifty-seven years old and of a build that suggested he had possession of the keys to the pie shop, Sir Cloudesley almost survived. Some say he made off in a rowing boat with his treasure chest and pet greyhound only to be wrecked a second time. Either way, the story goes that he was washed up on Porth Hellick beach half-drowned where a local woman found him, finished him off with a rock, wrenched an emerald ring from his finger and hotfooted it from the scene. His body was discovered soon afterwards and buried where it lay, the spot where I now stood looking at the small, modest memorial set up by his descendants. Sir Cloudesley is not down there now, however, the Admiralty having come to Scilly shortly afterwards, dug him up and laid him to rest in Westminster Abbey.

It was this terrible tragedy that underlined to the Admiralty the importance of determining the correct longitude at sea. Shovell had thought he was somewhere off Plymouth; instead he was charging towards the Bristol Channel and disaster on the rocks of Scilly, a miscalculation of many, many miles and a mistake that cost hundreds of lives. Within seven years of Shovell's demise the Board of Longitude had been set up at Greenwich and John Harrison went on to produce his chronometers; Greenwich became firmly established at the centre of time and large-scale disasters like that which befell such an experienced seaman as Sir Cloudesley Shovell became a thing of the past. The weather was one thing that couldn't really be helped, but such navigational own goals were soon minimised thanks to John Harrison and, arguably, the Isles of Scilly.

Sitting by the cairn on this warm, sunny, peaceful Sunday morning it was almost impossible to imagine the death, destruction and murderous theft which had occurred here nearly three hundred years earlier. I had the bay to myself – the islanders would be immersed in their Sunday newspapers – and there was barely a cloud in the sky. A feeling of warm, relaxed contentment developed that would stay with me throughout my entire stay on Scilly. Right on cue a white butterfly flew haphazardly past my nose, and everything seemed right with the world.

Sir Cloudesley Shovell was not the only reason I'd come to Porth Hellick, however. Despite the efforts of people like John Harrison and Robert FitzRoy, ships of all shapes and sizes continued to smack into the Isles of Scilly, albeit not as often as they used to. As the twentieth century progressed, the number of major shipwrecks became fewer and fewer, until March 1997 when the Scillonian wreckers' prayer was answered in the most spectacular fashion.

The third week of March 1997 saw Scilly shrouded in a fog so bad that the airport was closed for two days. During this time the German-registered container ship *Cita* was chugging along the Channel destined for Belfast with 145 forty-foot containers on board. It was the middle of the night and the watch on the bridge set the ship's course on automatic for Land's End, where he would alter it slightly and prepare to head north for Belfast. The unseemly hour, the thick fog and the hypnotic throb of the engines had a predictable effect. He nodded off. This left the *Cita* thundering through some of the world's busiest shipping lanes in heavy fog with nobody in control. Two and a half hours later, at just after three thirty in the morning, the Polish sailor was awakened by an unseemly grinding and wrenching of metal. The *Cita*, having remarkably missed every other ship in the channel in the pitch darkness, had run aground on Newfoundland Point just by Porth Hellick. The sailor awoke with a start and an ominously cold feeling that something had gone really terribly wrong and it was all his fault. He checked the ship's radar alarm system. They couldn't have hit anything, he thought, the radar alarm would have gone off. Or at least it would have if somebody had switched it on. He radioed for help and the eight-man crew was taken off the stricken ship, which was now sinking, by helicopter and the St Mary's lifeboat.

The Scillonians' immediate concern was an oil spill – thirty years earlier in 1967 the oil tanker *Torrey Canyon* had gone down seven miles from St Mary's, discharging eighty thousand tons of oil into the sea. Somehow Scilly escaped the spill, most of which ended up on the beaches of Cornwall, but it left the islanders aware of how vulnerable their ecologically fragile archipelago could be to environmental disaster. Fortunately this oil spillage was minimal and easily contained and the islanders turned their attention to the containers that were now bobbing about in the sea and turning up on the beaches, particularly at Porth Hellick. By the morning after the accident, the metal containers were already coming up on the rocky coast, and the Scillonian air was filled with the sound of screeching, wrenching metal. The first container to burst open on the shore of Porth Hellick contained more than a million carrier bags destined for Ireland's Quinnsworth supermarkets, all of which advised reuse to help protect the environment. By the afternoon the islanders had begun to break open some of the containers. A fishing boat had already towed two ashore, which contained trainers and PVC tubing. Cars, vans and even wheel-barrows were loaded with shoes and, as the cardboard packaging had quickly perished in the water, the islanders set about matching up pairs.

The *Cita* had been carrying an extraordinarily

varied cargo. On opening the containers the islanders found £3 million worth of baled tobacco, all useless because of seawater contamination. There were car tyres, computer mice, hardwood doors, toilet seats, tinned water chestnuts, golf bags, granite headstones, fork-lift trucks, toys, fridge magnets and, most usefully for the islanders, thousands upon thousands of items of clothing, from women's shorts to Ben Sherman shirts. Souvenir leprechaun keyrings were washed up on the beach with the message 'May the luck of the Irish find you'. It certainly seemed to have found the Scillonians.

No one was entirely sure of the legal implications of this *Whisky Galore!* situation. The islands' customs officer had retired five days earlier and the coastguard shortly before that. This left only the police sergeant and two constables to oversee the situation. All they could do was hand out salvage forms and advise people to declare what they were taking and file the forms with the receiver of wrecks at Southampton. Many of the goods recovered were useless, although the clothes and shoes were fine after a run through Scillonian washing machines. Technically, anyone removing items from the wreck or the beach was not looting or stealing provided they didn't attempt to sell the goods. For many Scilly families struggling to make ends meet, the clothing was an absolute godsend.

There's nothing left to see now. You might catch

sight of the odd Ben Sherman shirt on a Scillonian as you walk down the street and there's a display case of recovered goods in the Scilly Museum, but Porth Hellick has returned to normal. The *Cita* was broken in half by the sea and the superstructure now lies on the sea bed. The beach was littered with miles of shredded PVC film from one of the containers for weeks after the wreck, but it's remarkable to reflect on the benignity of the wreck. The *Cita* ran aground on the most populated of the islands. When you consider how small the islands are in comparison to the miles upon miles of ocean around them, it's extraordinary that the ship struck Scilly at all, let alone in such a convenient location. If the Isles of Scilly hadn't been there, the *Cita* would have kept going until either the mate woke up or the ship clonked into the Statue of Liberty. All in all the chances of it ending up here were pretty slim. So, not only did the ship run aground on St Mary's, a couple of miles from the main settlement, not only was nobody killed (one of the ship's crew suffered a broken leg, but that was it), not only was a pollution disaster averted, but the ship's cargo was largely of great benefit to the islanders themselves.

I picked my way around the rocks in the bay looking for something, anything that might betray the presence of the *Cita* today. A scrap of plastic bag poking out of the sand perhaps, a tell-tale tyre tread, or a flash of Ben Sherman beneath a rock. I was being ridiculously optimistic, of course, there was nothing there. I had been excited to see some packets of disposable nappies bobbing about on the shoreline on my way around the coast, but these later turned out to be from a German ship that had lost ten containers near the Channel Islands a few days earlier. Instead I contented myself with sitting on a barnacle-encrusted rock enjoying the sunshine and quiet, the only sounds the odd squawk from a sea bird and the gentle popping of the seaweed as it dried in the sun.

Back in Hugh Town the *Scillonian* had docked, disgorging a couple of hundred daytrippers into the town and, most importantly, the Sunday papers. I made for the shop, my breathing laboured with anticipation. I could almost see the newsprint on my fingers and hear the sound of the advertising inserts hitting the bottom of the waste paper basket. Yet the paper shop was curiously quiet and there were no triumphant posters outside. I walked through the door and, blinking a couple of times to adjust my eyes from the bright sunlight to the darker coolness of the shop, saw nothing but several teetering piles of the *Sunday Times*. The woman behind the counter looked at me and shrugged. 'The distributor messed up,' she said. 'All we got were a load of *Sunday Times*.' The newsagent himself was nowhere to be seen, presumably upstairs crying into his pillow.

That evening I took a boat to St Agnes, another

of the inhabited islands, whose population of around three hundred is Britain's most south-westerly community. In the evening there is the option of taking a vigorous tramp around the island or holing up in the Turk's Head, Britain's south-westernmost public house, for a couple of hours before the boat returns to St Mary's. Fortunately for me the vigorous tramp was busy, so the Turk's Head it was and I was the first through the door. Like most of the pubs I was frequenting around the shipping forecast, the Turk's Head is decorated with shipwreck flotsam and nautical prints. It's almost as if someone has set up a chain of theme pubs, only these are all genuine. What makes the Turk's Head different is the row upon row of nautical headgear displayed behind and above the bar. From a captain's peaked brim to the humble fisherman's cap, it's an impressive collection of nautical scalps. I hoped that their original owners were not buried in shallow graves around the island. I've seen *The Wicker Man*.

After a short while the door opened and five men walked in, all rust-coloured, weather-lashed faces and grubby oilskins. They were, it turned out, Breton fishermen. They addressed the barman in French; as they were Breton, French was almost a second language to them. It was certainly one the barman didn't understand. My schoolboy French deduced that they wanted some chicken, a strange request in a pub at the best of times. But this was not chicken in a basket or chicken in breadcrumbs, or anything involving chips and salad. They wanted *a* chicken. To pluck and cook for their dinner. A conversation in bad French from behind the bar and heavily accented English in front of it ensued, the upshot of which was that in exchange for a hat for the pub's collection, the pub would come up with a chicken. There was much nodding and shaking of hands and the Bretons departed.

After they had gone, three different Breton fishermen walked in, ordered drinks and sat down at a table in the corner, talking together in hushed tones without once attempting to instigate any headgear-poultry barter. Eventually the original crew returned brandishing an elaborate peaked cap with ornate gold braiding. In return they were given not a freshly slaughtered Foghorn Leghorn, but a tupperware container of diced pink chicken. Both parties seemed pleased with this and there was more handshaking. The three Bretons in the corner looked up, hailed the chicken bearers and a whole new round of handshaking commenced accompanied by a tirade of '*bon soirs*'. All eight hunkered down at the table and examined the diced chicken approvingly. Wondering whether I had inadvertently stumbled across some kind of smuggling ring ('Ask him for a chicken. Say you'll swap it for a hat and leave, promising to return. If, when you go back, he gives you a Tupperware box of diced chicken, then the coast is clear and you can move the merchandise') on which I have now blown the whistle, I set off for a walk around at least some of the island.

At the southern end of St Agnes is a tiny church. Inside there is a real sense of calm, which must be very welcome when the wind and rain hurtle in off the Atlantic. Indeed, the perilous location of the island is illustrated by the inscription on the stained-glass window above the altar, which reads 'To those who sailed from St Agnes to save those in peril at sea'. Plaques list the names of the St Agnes lifeboat coxswains, a list that terminates in the 1920s when the motorised St Mary's lifeboat took over sole responsibility for Scilly. The old lifeboat house still stands next door to the church, and is now used as a private boatyard.

The sun was preparing to set as I walked back around the western coast towards the quay. There was still a short while before the boat returned so I stood on the shore looking out to sea and reflected that at that moment I was the south-westernmost Briton in Britain. The sky was turning a rich yellow, and the rocks against which countless ships had been dashed over the centuries loomed black out of the silvery sea. One of the major ones is called Hellweathers and it was not hard to understand why, even as I stood there on a beautifully calm and clear summer evening. So treacherous are these waters that there has been a lighthouse on St Agnes since 1680, one of the first in Britain.

In the direction I was looking the next significant landmass would be South America, or even possibly

Antarctica. It was warm, it was peaceful, the Scillonians are tremendous. Sitting there on that rock, on that little island with the immaculate white lighthouse at its centre, its tiny seafarers' church and its frankly marvellous pub, I could have stayed. I could have gone home, sold the house, bought a place here and decamped for the rest of my natural. And then, as I lay on the beach watching the sun go down, I would have sat up with a start as I remembered Katie, suddenly homeless and not a little bemused at my sudden absence.

Many people love Scilly. You could say it's one of Britain's best-kept secrets, known only to a select few of us who've been there and been captivated by its magic. Most people return. Many return again and again. While out walking I bumped into more than one elderly couple who cheerfully informed me how many years they'd been coming here, a range from thirty-six right down to a pair of johnny-come-latelies who'd only been making an annual trip for the past fifteen years. The trouble is, some people fall in love with Scilly so deeply they decide to buy a house there. A few move permanently, but most buy up properties as second homes, which pushes up houses prices to astronomical levels (a quick glance in an estate agent's window in Hugh Town had me staggering backwards under the weight of the noughts on the end of the prices), creates a shortage of housing for Scillonians and leaves properties unoccupied save for a few weeks every year.

'The second-home thing is a problem,' one Scillonian had told me on the boat over to St Agnes. 'Young people are being priced out of the market. It's hard enough buying a first home anywhere, but when you have such a limited amount of space and houses to start with and you've got mainlanders buying up houses as holiday homes, there's just no chance for the locals. Most youngsters now have the choice of living with their parents until the parents pop their clogs and they inherit the house, or leaving for the mainland.

'What the second homers don't realise is that they're spoiling the very place they profess to love. They do nothing for the community; how can they when they're not here for ten months of the year? Scilly has always been a close-knit community but that's being undermined. If it carries on like this, the place could become one big ghost town outside the summer months.'

While certainly not a problem confined to Scilly, the islands' limited resources and space make it more acute. My sunset-induced relocation plans were mentally shelved. I had certainly lost myself in the captivating magic of Scilly, and St Agnes in particular. My heart sank when I saw the boat chugging around the Gugh, the neighbouring island reachable by sandbar at low tide, to take me back to St Mary's on a journey which saw us race the sun along the horizon as the fiery orange ball sank gradually out of sight. Three seagulls flew alongside us for a while, just a couple of feet above the waves, silhouetted black against the silvery ripples of the sea. I'd lost my heart to the Isles of Scilly. I knew I had when Hugh Town hove into view, the sight of its now-familiar harbourfront buildings provoking the same reaction as when you see your house for the first time after returning home from a long trip.

I climbed the steps from the boat up to the quay, and walked through the deserted, darkened streets of Hugh Town back to my hotel. All was quiet, the only sound my own footsteps as I walked past the houses in Hugh Street. A sudden chesty cough from one of the open upper windows was such an intrusion on the peace that instinctively I looked up to see where it had come from. A pigeon-chested teenager stripped to the waist was framed in the window. We looked at each other, Scillonian and mainlander, and I prepared a cheery greeting.

'What are you looking at, you fucking knob?' he said before I could draw breath. His mate, equally teen, equally skeletal, appeared beside him. 'Yeah, fuck off, you wanker,' he suggested. I said nothing, took the latter's advice and walked on, still lost in Scilly bonhomie. However, I did spend the rest of my waking hours thinking up really nasty things I could have said back to them. I can still remember which house it was. One day I'll go back, stand under the window and read out a selection of my best retorts from the piece of paper I wrote them all down on before switching off the light.

Each island has its own distinct character, and I visited two more before leaving Scilly. Tresco, the snootiest of the islands, was uninspiring, over-rated and outrageously expensive. Bryher mean-while, the island with the smallest population, was refreshingly wild and smeared with bracken and heather. The westernmost of the inhabited islands, it's the sort of place where the Romantic poets would have run around the clifftops at night during thunderstorms wearing nothing but their nightshirts and gone off to write odes about it afterwards. The western part of the island, where the Atlantic crashes against the rocks for its first landfall since America, is the most dramatic, and has intriguing names like Hell Bay, Badthings Hill and Port Stink. There's also a small inlet called Great Pottlestones, a name I blurted out as an admirable swearword-substitute when I learned the price of a pint on Tresco.

I was sorry to leave Scilly, a special part of the United Kingdom. Sit on the front at Hugh Town and look out beyond the palm trees across the clear azure water to the white sandy beaches of Tresco beyond and it's hard to believe that you're less than thirty miles from the English mainland. To call it an island idyll would be wrong; the Scillonians have suffered over the years like many other island communities, sometimes more so, and contemporary Scilly still has its social issues like anywhere else. But when I think of that Hugh Town vista and then look out of my window at my south-east London Victorian terraced beehive of a street as I write this, I know where I'd rather be.

If I'd regretted flying to Scilly rather than going by sea, the reverse was certainly true when I visited Lundy. As the ship pitched, tossed and corkscrewed through giant waves and sickbags everywhere were filled to overflowing, through my own crashing, heaving nausea I threatened Lundy Island that there would be serious consequences for it if this journey from hell wasn't worth every last moment of suffering.

Lying twelve miles from the north Devon coast, the long, narrow island of Lundy sits in the water like a half-submerged crocodile. It's an appropriately predatory analogy, given its long history as a base for pirates and smugglers; the island's remoteness and steep cliffs making it an ideal centre for wrongdoing and general piratical royster-doystering. In fact, for a seemingly insignificant lump of granite in the Bristol Channel, Lundy has an extraordinary history of international piracy, pillage, shipwrecks, attempted royal assassinations, crashing aircraft, ill-considered card games and ancient burial grounds. These days, however, the island is a much calmer place and since the 1960s has been owned by a trust which has restored the buildings and opened them as holiday cottages, built a shop and a pub, carried out ongoing conservation work and generally gone around the place being nice to animals and stuff. They also operate daytrips to the island, hence my arrival outside a Portakabin in a Bideford car park early one gusty morning waiting to join fellow daytrippers on a pleasant jaunt out into the Bristol Channel.

When you book your passage they advise you to ring a recorded message giving you the prognosis for the following day's crossing. When I did this on the way back from Scilly I was surprised to hear the crossing was in doubt due to an iffy weather forecast. I was up so early the following morning that I'd caught the early-morning shipping forecast, which had revealed nothing untoward for Lundy, so I had set off confident that by mid-morning I would have ticked off another area. Around a dozen of us were gathered outside the Portakabin. Eventually a man in black trousers and a white shirt complete with epaulettes arrived and inscribed 'no decision yet, expected in ten minutes' on a board outside the cabin, and with a jangle of keys disappeared wordlessly inside.

This didn't look good. My fellow travellers appeared in the main to be foghorn-voiced middle-aged women in fleeces, shorts and hiking boots, their knees glowing as pink as their cheeks in the early-morning chill. Every gust of wind caused us to pull faces at each other designed to convey the message, 'Brrr, eh? Not looking too good, is it?' As the gusts intensified, sending grey clouds scudding over Bideford and out to sea, the face-pulling grew more elaborate until I felt like the judge at a Women's Institute gurning competition. The minutes ticked by. The ferry, the MS *Oldenburg*, was moored a few hundred yards away with coloured bunting fluttering along its length. Its Lundy flag, a puffin in a white circle on a red background (the name Lundy comes from *lunde*, the Norse word for puffin), flapped vigorously. A bit of a stiff breeze wouldn't stop us sailing, surely?

It got to ten minutes before we were due to go. Suddenly the door of the Portakabin opened and the man with the epaulettes emerged, carrying one of those two-stepped stools that old ladies have in their houses so they can reach things in high cupboards. Having set it up, dramatically he climbed the steps, raising himself to a commanding position of at least two feet. 'Could I have your attention please, everybody?' he called out, relishing his moment on the centre stage. It was for moments like this that he ironed his short-sleeved white shirts so meticulously that you could slice ham on the creases. We stopped pulling faces and looked at him expectantly.

'The captain has still not made a final decision as to whether we will be sailing today,' said Mr Epaulettes. A murmur rippled through the crowd. 'In the light of this,' he continued, 'the captain has taken the first mate to the bar.'

Oh great, I thought, he can't make up his mind so he uncorks a bottle of the good stuff. It's not even as if the sun's over the yardarm. It was later that I learned 'the bar' is in fact the point where two rivers empty into the sea, creating shifting currents and often a considerable swell.

'When he returns, if he decides to sail we will be sailing immediately, so please be ready to hurry to the ship.' With that he stepped back down to ground level, folded up his stool, put his chin in the air and strode back into the Portakabin. Within five minutes the captain had evidently returned and given Mr Epaulettes the nautical equivalent of the thumbs-up, for he was soon marching out of the cabin and setting up his stool again. We'd barely had time to get back into our face-pulling stride. He cleared his throat.

'The captain has decided that we will sail today,' he said triumphantly, at which point we heeded his earlier advice and hotfooted it for the *Oldenburg* with a mass scraping of anoraks and clumping of hiking boots. This left Mr Epaulettes standing on his stool alone in the car park, watching a shifting mass of waterproof nylon in many colours disappearing into the distance.

As we queued to board, the purser passed along the line announcing that the crossing today would be very rough, and that anyone who didn't fancy it and didn't have a strong stomach would be given a full refund. Pschaw, I thought, cocky as hell for no good reason, I'd survived the Haugesund to Utsire crossing, not to mention Egersund to Hanstholm and back. I was now the saltiest of sea dogs and it would take more than a bit of a splash on the portholes to have me crying off and claiming my coward's penance from the booking office.

'The rougher the better,' I found myself saying out loud, 'bring it on!'

A man in front of me clad in a bright-red cagoule turned around. 'It won't sink, will it?' he asked meekly. 'Well,' I replied, so full of my own blustering bravado that I failed to notice the look of genuine fright about his features, 'they did say that about the *Titanic*.' The fear in his eyes melted away and was immediately replaced by hatred. So I suppose I did some good.

As soon as we'd left the quay and chugged out into the harbour I was first in the queue for a bacon sandwich and a cup of tea. In fact I was the only one in the queue. I claimed my place in the lounge at the front, pulled out the ancient book I'd found in a second-hand shop on the history of Lundy, and munched my sandwich defiantly.

'Ooh,' said an old lady at the next table, 'he's brave having a bacon sandwich.'

Pah, I thought, brave nothing. Flipping daytrippers, the Sunday drivers of the ocean wave. On the other side of the lounge the man in the red anorak clung to his wife, occasionally throwing looks of pure hate in the direction of my ketchup-smeared face. My bacon buttie had just hit the spot and my cup of tea was just sloshing around on top of it when it started getting a bit choppy.

Then it started to get very choppy, and within in a few minutes it was choppier than a convention of woodcutters. We had clearly reached the bar. And how. Through the portholes the prow of the ship would rise up to point at the sky before crashing down into the water, flinging salty brine at the panes and juddering the entire vessel from bow to stern. Flasks, books, pens, everything went flying off tables. Passengers exchanged worried glances. A couple of people retrieved sickbags from the rack on the wall and sat down again, nervously. This seasoned sailor, of course, was absolutely fine, and I pulled my book from my bag to commence nonchalant reading. After a few minutes, however, I became aware of rumblings in my digestive system. A sheen of cold sweat began to form on my face. The *Oldenburg* continued to corkscrew through giant waves, the prow thumping down into water combining with a constant swaying from side to side. This was the roughest crossing I'd ever known, and judging by the glances the crew were throwing at each other, it was the roughest they'd known for a while too. Even Harry's face in his photograph was looking paler than I remembered. I, meanwhile, was increasingly of the opinion that I'd inadvertently lodged my sea legs in the Portakabin with Mr Epaulettes.

After a good half an hour of being thrown about as if the Bristol Channel had mistaken the *Oldenburg* for a cocktail shaker and was mixing itself a quick pina colada, a crew member decided to dispense with etiquette and went around handing out sickbags to everybody. A few minutes earlier and I'd have dismissed him with a snooty wave of the hand, but instead I meekly accepted the glue-lined paper bag. 'You're looking a bit green about the gills, sir,' he said. I glanced at the man in the red anorak – he was looking at me with contempt as the traces of a faint smirk tugged gently at the corners of his mouth.

Finally I had to admit to myself that I was feeling really, dreadfully ill. I lumbered towards the toilet, bouncing off the walls, and stood over the bowl, the ship listing so spectacularly that the water from the toilet was sloshing over the side and on to my shoes. A good ten minutes passed and I kidded myself I'd be all right. I went back to my seat, and within five minutes had filled my sickbag in spectacular style. When I looked up, I saw through watery eyes that the woman who'd said I was brave to eat a bacon sandwich was grinning at me. The man in the red anorak was doing likewise, and I congratulated myself on being so selfless as to take their minds off the treacherous journey.

I spent the remaining hour of the voyage with my head on the table and my arms crossed over it. The ship was filled with the sounds of retching while outside the waves thundered against the hull and superstructure of this hardy little boat. Eventually I became aware that the engines had gone into reverse. We'd arrived at Lundy.

The weather had the nerve to be calm and sunny as we wobbled off the ship and on to the quayside. Everyone looked traumatised, like news footage of passengers who've just jumped out of a burning aircraft or walked away from a tall building that's been flattened by an earthquake. I'd been looking forward to visiting Lundy, but my current queasiness was not causing me to greet the place with a hey-nonny-nonny and a skip around the maypole. It's a long, steep winding path from the jetty up through the cliffs and on to the plateau, and not many of us were up to it. Lundy is a rugged island, and as you gingerly pick your way along the path after a rough crossing it's easy to understand how its earlier inhabitants ran startlingly successful piracy rackets from this practically impregnable location. Indeed, after the Norman conquest it took around 150 years to evict the de Marisco clan who had ensconced themselves in a castle here, living off the ill-gotten gains of boarding ships and raiding the north Devon coast.

In 1238 a spectacularly rubbish attempt to assassinate Henry III was traced back to William de Marisco of Lundy (the assassin climbed through the wrong window at the dead of night, causing the female occupant of the room to scream the place down. When the guards arrived he just pretended to be nuts. It didn't work). Henry ordered William's capture, which was effected by sailing in under cover of fog one evening, scaling

338

the cliffs and storming the castle. The element of surprise combined with the fact that the de Mariscos were roaring drunk at the time meant a fairly straightforward apprehension. William was hauled off to the Tower, found guilty of high treason and dragged through the streets to Whitehall where he was hanged, disembowelled, had his bowels burned and was then chopped into four quarters, each of which was sent to a corner of the realm. I'd certainly think twice about reoffending after that, I can tell you.

The castle looked down on me with tangible disdain as I climbed the steep pathway, my insides as turbulent and unpredictable as the history of Lundy itself. Once the de Mariscos had been usurped, the island endured a good few hundred years of dubious occupation, its windy plateau ringing out with piratical incantations in several tongues. In the sixteenth century French pirates occupied the island, cheerfully sailing out into the Bristol Channel and purloining any cargoes that took their fancy before returning to Lundy to celebrate with a good claret and a pungent Roquefort. It took a feisty expedition of Clovelly fishermen to finally wrest the island from its Gallic occupants, a disgruntled raiding party successfully capturing the cheeky French rapscallions before they'd even had time to set fire to any sheep. As soon as the French had gone, English pirates took up residence, prompting the authorities in Barnstaple to clear the place of 'divers rovers and pirates'. It wasn't long before the seafaring ne'er-do-wells returned, with one pirate named Salkeld attempting to declare himself Pirate King of Lundy. This was too much for his fellow exponents of cutlass diplomacy, however, and Salkeld was soon sent packing.

By the seventeenth century the local lads had been usurped in turn by some Turkish pirates, who made it known that they intended to burn down Ilfracombe. Fortunately for the Devon town they were kicked off the island by Spanish pirates before they could carry out their threat. In 1700 a boatload of Dutch pirates captured the island by means of the most tremendous subterfuge. They anchored in the bay and sent a couple of sailors to ask that they be allowed to come ashore as their captain was ill. The islanders refused, but allowed the Dutchmen to take back vegetables and milk. A few days later the Dutch announced with great solemnity that the captain had died, and asked whether they could come ashore and bury him. The Lundy islanders agreed and within hours a morose procession appeared from the ship carrying the coffin. Once inside the church the Dutch asked that they be left alone to say goodbye to their captain and the islanders did so, only for the Dutch to come charging out of the church armed to the teeth. The captain wasn't dead, on the contrary he was alive and well and leading the charge from the nave. His coffin had been packed full of guns, swords and knives, and the island was comprehensively looted. This Piracy World Cup appeared to have finished by the eighteenth century, at the end of which Lundy was put up for auction in an attempt to resolve its ownership once and for all. Part of the reason that Captain Pugwash and his ilk had found Lundy such an agreeable place to procure and store their stolen booty was that the succession of families who came into ownership treated the place like the last kid to be picked for football in the playground.

An aristocratic businessman named Sir Henry de Vere Hunt happened to be passing the auction house and, attracted by the noise, ventured inside. Within minutes he had bought Lundy, and to this day nobody is really sure why. As an impulse buy it certainly topped my purchase of a Captain Beefheart album a couple of years ago (I had not previously shown any interest in Captain Beefheart, and indeed haven't since the CD's one spin on my turntable). Some say he was attracted by the tax implications, others that it was a safer bet than the properties he owned in Ireland. I like to think that he just chose the wrong moment to assess the extent of his nostril hair with a forefinger. After almost selling the island to the UK government for double what he paid for it Sir Henry died in 1818 and left Lundy to his son, who promptly lost it in a game of cards.

It wasn't until 1834 that Lundy finally came into

the possession of somebody who actually gave a toss. William Hudson Heaven decided he would make Lundy his home and set about creating his own little island kingdom, to become known inevitably as the Kingdom of Heaven. Heaven built the impressive mansion Millcombe House above the landing place, past which I made my way on the seemingly interminable route to the top of the island. It's a large construction, made all the more remarkable by the fact that every brick, stone, tile, fixture and fitting had to come across from the mainland and be dragged up from boats in days before anything like the modern road-cum-footpath had been constructed. I'd had enough trouble dragging myself up from sea level, let alone a whole load of masonry. I stood and looked across the house down to the quay below, where the *Oldenburg* lay at anchor looking faintly traumatised. Finally I crested the hill and the plateau of Lundy opened up in front of me. Most of the island's buildings and amenities are clustered at this, the south end of the island, and the gathering of cottages, buildings and a not-insignificant church looked a little incongruous on the bleak, blasted, treeless vista of the island's surface. I crossed a field, passed between a couple of buildings and found a sheep to my right and a pub to my left.

Now, normally the sight of a welcoming-looking hostelry in an out-of-the-way place would be something akin to a mirage. But given the churning state of my guts and an inner ear that had apparently curled up into a little ball and was refusing to believe that the world had stopped rocking from side to side, the last thing I wanted was a pint. This was my first experience of sea-sickness; I wanted it to end as quickly as possible and I never wanted it to be repeated ever again. A sit down and a nice glass of cold mineral water were all I required. Given the choice between pub and sheep I soon surmised that the former would be most likely to fulfil my sedentary and bibulous demands and pushed open the door of the Marisco Tavern.

The pub, which bears the name of the island's most famous inhabitants, is the social centre of the island. Although the number of full-time Lundy residents barely tops twenty (and they are employees or volunteers of the Landmark Trust which administers the island on behalf of the National Trust rather than a genuine indigenous population), the amount and popularity of the island's holiday accommodation means that there are usually a good couple of hundred people here at any one time during the summer months. Apart from the island shop, the Marisco is the only place you can get food on Lundy, although at that stage food was something that lay over my still-undulating horizon. I felt pale, sick and dehydrated. I had a headache playing around my temples that was threatening to become a real humdinger. Yes, a pint was the last thing on my mind, it was iced mineral water for me.

I went to the bar, ordered my drink and settled

at a table by a big window with my brimming pint of Lundy Old Light bitter. The Marisco bar is a high-ceilinged room with a gallery. Around the walls are scattered the accumulated flotsam and jetsam of the numerous shipwrecks that have befallen Lundy. The *Maria Kyriakides*, the *Amstelstroom*, the *Ethel*, countless lifebelts, bits of driftwood and even the odd ship's bell served to remind me that the poor old *Oldenburg*, still at anchor three hundred feet below us, had actually done pretty darn well to get here without an unscheduled diversion to Davy Jones's locker. Looking at the accumulated memorials to fallen ships, I raised the glass to my lips and drank a silent but heartfelt toast to the captain of the *Oldenburg*.

My original plan had been to walk the length of the island and back, but the traumatic crossing had put paid to that. My headache was now really getting into its stride as I finished my drink and contented myself with the fact that at least I wouldn't be stupid enough to have another one, let alone a giant pasty with chips and beans.

An hour later I left the Marisco Tavern, wiping pasty crumbs from my chin. Whether my stomach found it as agreeable as my tastebuds is something both were arguing about. My stomach was winning convincingly and was determined to celebrate in a noisy and uncharitably curmudgeonly manner as I headed further towards the heart of the island. I picked my still-queasy way towards

Lundy's highest point where the old lighthouse stood, a construction whose folly was soon realised when it became clear that its central location meant that no one could see it in thick fog, the very time when it was needed most, and smaller lighthouses were built at the northern and southern tips of the island as well. At the time of its construction in 1819, the Old Light was the tallest of its kind and on a clear day, if you climb to the top you can see as far as the Cornish coast and the mountains of Dyfed. Given my Plymouth experience and the state of my insides, however, there was no way I was going anywhere near it.

Close to the lighthouse is the island cemetery in which many of the Heaven family are buried. When one of these graves was being dug in 1905, ancient inscribed Christian burial stones were discovered, believed to date back to the fifth century. Now propped against the cemetery wall, they looked as rough as I felt.

Much as I would have loved to roam across the whole of the island my legs were still too weak and shaky, and the ill-considered lunch had done nothing to settle a stomach that was now almost audibly whimpering to itself. I found myself incapable of straying too far from the south of the island where the *Oldenburg* had disgorged its wobbly passengers. I wandered down the western coast, the wilder side that the Atlantic hits with full force, passing Goat Island and the place where in June 1942 a British Whitley aircraft had misjudged its altitude in heavy fog and crashed into the cliffs at Pilot's Quay killing all five men on board. Two German Heinkels had already crashed on the island during the conflict. The crew of the first survived, two of the five German airmen on the second were killed and rusting pieces of aircraft still litter the plateau.

I was aiming for the landmark of St Helen's church, a surprisingly large-scale Victorian gothic construction completed and consecrated under the patronage of the Heavens in 1897 and capable of seating 165 worshippers. A rector and choir from the mainland had endured a rough crossing from which the rector extracted a rather fine religious gag that it just showed what purgatory one had to pass through to reach the Kingdom of Heaven. It's a quiet church; at the business end, behind the altar, there is a beautifully intricate marble relief of three panels, representing the Passover, the Scapegoat in the Wilderness and the Last Supper.

By now I was suffering quite badly from the combined effects of the traumatic crossing and my ill-advised choice of food and drink to replace that jettisoned aboard the *Oldenburg*. I could do little else but prop myself up against a wall near the church and wait until it was time to descend to the ship again. The crossing back to the mainland was mirror smooth, allowing my put-upon system to recover its dignity somewhat. As the *Oldenburg* steamed away from the island, I looked back and saw the South Light behind the ship's Lundy flag. My queasiness meant that I felt I hadn't really got a grip on Lundy, a quirky curiosity of the shipping forecast; its history an intriguing blend of piracy and piety. When I got back to Bideford, darkness was falling, the wind was rushing about in hefty gusts and it started to rain. I switched on the shipping forecast. 'There are warnings of gales in Sole, Lundy and Fastnet,' it said. The windowpanes of the Marisco Tavern would be rattling tonight. I turned the car towards Swansea. I was going home. Kind of.

Cork, the 'capital city' of the Fastnet area, should have represented some kind of homecoming for me. The Connellys were a Cork family, although the history is a little hazy. In fact there's even some doubt over the name itself: according to family legend, many moons ago a man was drowning in a bog (the Gaelic for Cork is Corcaigh, meaning 'boggy ground', so at least we can be fairly certain we're in the right place) and all efforts to save him had proved fruitless. The would-be rescuers asked the man's name just before he went under for the last time. The spluttered reply sounded a bit like Connelly, so that's what went down in the records – the sort of half-understood, poorly expressed approximation of the truth that by coincidence has characterised my own journalistic career.

Cork people have a reputation for having an independent, rebellious streak (it's not known as the 'rebel county' for nothing) and I've always been a bit of a rebel, but in a completely crap way. When everyone at school was listening to Madonna, for example, I was buying records by the Screaming Blue Messiahs. While most of my friends were glory-hunting Manchester United and Liverpool supporters, that would just strengthen my allegiance to the near-bankrupt and fanless Charlton Athletic. In my late teens, when most of my peers were wearing Farahs and Tacchini and sporting the 'wedge' haircut, I bought blue and green spray-on hair dye, donned a pair of old workman's boots, slashed the knees of my jeans and decided I was a punk. Even today I've never read a word of Harry Potter, have never seen an episode of *The Sopranos* and don't own a single album by Coldplay or the Stereophonics. Pretty rebellious, huh? It's the Corkman in me, see. It's in the genes.

But sometimes the people of Cork can seem as though they're being deliberately contrary. Cork supported Perkin Warbeck, the ill-fated pretender to the British crown in the 1490s, and revolted in favour of Oliver Cromwell in 1649 even though to the rest of Ireland he was, and remains, the devil incarnate. In the early part of the twentieth century Cork was a centre of staunch opposition to British rule, and parts of Cork city were burned down by the British in 1920 in retaliation for an attack on a British military convoy. Cork people were fierce opponents of the Anglo-Irish treaty of 1921 that divided Ireland into the country we know today and one of its signatories, Michael Collins, was assassinated there having mistakenly assumed that 'my fellow Corkmen will not harm me'. Collins' assumption, erroneous on this occasion, that Cork blood ran thicker than Irish blood, is still prevalent today; walking around the streets of Cork city itself I passed several people wearing t-shirts displaying the legend 'People's Republic of Cork' and 'Cork Republica'. Roy Keane, arguably the most famous Corkman since Collins himself, is a fine example.

'Like most Cork people I am inordinately proud of my roots,' he has said. 'I'm Irish by birth, Cork by the grace of God: a superiority complex is the mark of a sound Corkman.'

When Keane stormed out of the 2002 World Cup, winning himself few friends in the process, it was to his native county that he returned rather than his Cheshire home. He knew the people would understand, and they did. T-shirts appeared in the county bearing the legend 'Michael Collins and Roy Keane: two Cork heroes shot in the back'.

'Roy's like a protected species when he comes back here,' Tony Leen, sports editor of the Cork-based *Irish Examiner*, told me at the time. 'There's an almost telepathic rapport between him and the locals; everybody knows to give him breathing space. He can go for a couple of pints in his local, the Templeacre Tavern, and nobody will hassle him. It's a relatively small community so everyone knows the score.'

Cork city is a lively place. Ireland's second city and a centre of Irish industry, it's always bustling, busy and noisy, not least on my visit when they had decided to dig up and re-lay most of the roads in the centre, all at the same time. The whole town seemed to be decked out in red and white; the county's hurling team had reached the All-Ireland final and the place was suffering from a heavy dose of cup fever. Hurling is Ireland's national sport and Cork is traditionally one of the best counties at the game. They've won the All-Ireland title twenty-eight times, more often than anyone else. Their opponents in the final, Kilkenny, lay one victory behind in the all-time table and the talk in the pubs of Cork was of retaining their position at the top. Every other person I passed had a red-and-white replica Cork shirt on, and the newspapers were filled with previews and punditry even though the final was still more than a fortnight away.

Hurling is a terrific sport to watch. It's probably best described to the layman as a cross between hockey and lacrosse, requiring a combination of lightning reflexes, physical strength and speed. It's probably the fastest team game in the world, and the excitement and breathtaking skill on display will make you wonder what you ever saw in football. Hurling is also as Irish as Guinness. Its roots reach right back to pre-Christian times; its first reference coming around the Battle of Moytura in 1272 BC when the Firbolg defeated the invading Tuatha de Danaan first on the hurling field and then on the battlefield. Even the ancient Brehon Laws, a legal code dating from pre-Christian Ireland, prescribed compensation for those suffering injury through 'playing at hurling'.

It wasn't Cork city or hurling that I'd come to see, however. The morning after I had arrived, when the woman who owned the guesthouse had spent the whole of breakfast calling me James, I caught a train to Cobh, a harbour town along the coast of Cork that has possibly the saddest history of any place on the shipping forecast map.

In Cromarty I'd seen the emigration memorial carved with Hugh Miller's evocative description of an emigrant ship leaving the Cromarty Firth for Canada and in Haugesund I'd learned of how Marilyn Monroe's father had joined those emigrating from Norway. In Dover I'd seen for myself the victims of forced emigration. The shipping forecast map is littered with the embarkation points of the desperate; people driven out of their own countries by hardship and the dream that somewhere, anywhere, had to give them a better or at least a bearable life. Quaysides across the sea areas have been splashed with the tears of those left behind; mothers and fathers watched ships take their offspring away, before returning home to a house all the emptier for the absence of a loved one.

For a pretty little harbour town Cobh had seen

more than its fair share of heartbreaking partings in its time. Between 1848 and 1950 more than six million people emigrated from Ireland, nearly half of them travelling from Cobh, or Queenstown as it was known in the period between Queen Victoria's visit in 1849 and partition in 1921. The great famine of the 1840s was the true catalyst for emigration from Ireland. The potato crop, on which Ireland depended for its subsistence, failed in 1845 and 1846 and partially failed for the next three years. An estimated three quarters of a million people starved to death while a further one and a half million left the country out of a total population of around only eight million. In the 1850s, 291,300 people emigrated from Cobh: in the first decade of the nineteenth century that figure had been 1,100. By 1901 Ireland's population had practically halved in the space of fifty years to four and a half million. They went to Australia, America, Canada, England; anywhere, in fact, that wasn't Ireland. It wasn't all beer and skittles either. Passage was cheap, but that was because the conditions on board were often horrific. Accommodation and sanitation were rudimentary at best, and the vessels didn't become known as 'coffin ships' for nothing. In 1801, for example, the convict ship *Atlas* sailed from Cobh for Sydney with 153 passengers on board, mostly people found guilty on dubious evidence of involvement in the 1798 rebellion against the English. Conditions were so cramped that below decks there wasn't even enough oxygen to burn a candle. Dysentery and typhus were commonplace, and during the seven-month voyage seventy people died, nearly half the total number on board. The only censure the captain of the vessel received was being required to hand over the money he'd made from goods he'd brought to sell in Australia.

Cobh's railway station is the original building through which the emigrants passed and were processed prior to departure from the deep-water terminal outside. Between the station and the water stands a statue of Annie Moore and her two young brothers. Annie and her siblings set sail from Queenstown on December 20, 1891, arriving in New York twelve days later. What made Annie particularly notable was that she was first off the ship and hence the first person ever to be processed at New York's immigration centre at Ellis Island, which opened on New Year's Day, 1892. Today Annie and her brothers look out to sea towards the US, where there is an identical statue on Ellis Island looking back at them. The Americans have tried to claim Annie, who turned fifteen on the day she stepped off the ship, as the personification of the 'American dream', as if the young Cork girl had gone to America out of choice and a desire to experience this wonderful land of opportunity. This version of the Annie Moore story is, of course, utter bollocks. Annie and her two younger brothers travelled to New York in the cramped, oppressive surroundings of steerage class to join their parents who had emigrated with their eldest child, Tom, two years earlier, after their father couldn't find work in Ireland. Things didn't go too well in the States either. Unsettled and unable to get work in their new homeland, the Moores moved around, from Brooklyn to Indiana and then on to Texas, where in Waco Annie met Patrick, a fellow Irish émigré, and married him. They had eight children, of whom three died in infancy before Patrick himself died during an influenza epidemic in 1919. Four years later Annie was hit by a train and died a slow, painful death at the age of forty-six. Rather than the personification of the American dream, Annie's story is just one of millions like it; desperate people seeking escape from the insufferable hardships of home and finding something only marginally, if at all, better.

Annie's statue stands at the corner of the station looking out over Deepwater Quay from where the emigrant ships departed. The station building itself has been converted into a café and a museum devoted to the Queenstown story, grabbing you as you step off the train and arrive in the town, anxious to impart the tragic history of the place.

Inside it's a bright and airy building strewn with tables and chairs, trellises and pot plants. It must be a far cry from when the place was overcrowded with the anxious, fetid, crammed mass of people preparing to bid farewell to loved ones and leave behind everything they knew for the unknown. Standing among the potted shrubs and lattes it was hard to appreciate the sheer scale of this haemorrhage of humanity that shuffled through here in its Sunday suit, best shoes and flat cap. The piped music was a far cry from the hubbub of noise, the wailing of relatives, the hissing of the ship's boilers and the steam trains and the cries of the stevedores loading cargo. But credit to the people who redeveloped this place, there is no attempt to brush the historic truth under the carpet. Beyond the coffee shop the truth is here in all its cramped, tear-stained, scrofulous glory, as if any exhibition called the Queenstown Story could ever be anything other than tragic. Inside, sad, sallow faces peer out from grainy old photographs, groups of young men with their hands in their pockets, watch chains strung across waistcoats. Even in the blurry old pictures, you can see in the spaces between flat cap and moustache the unifying look of fear mixed with all but extinguished hope in every pair of eyes.

As if Cobh's association with the vast human tragedy of Irish emigration wasn't enough, this brightly coloured, pleasant fishing town on the southern coast of Ireland is also linked with two of the greatest maritime disasters of modern times: the *Titanic* and the *Lusitania*. Queenstown was the last port of call for the *Titanic* before New York, and on April 11, 1912, two tenders, appropriately the *Ireland* and the *America*, took 1,400 sacks of mail and the ship's last 123 passengers out to the vast liner moored in deep water just outside the harbour. The impecunious nature of Irish emigration is exemplified in the fact that of those 123 people, 3 were first-class passengers, 7 second and the rest destined for steerage. Of those 123, only 44 would survive.

One of them, Dannie Buckley from Ballydesmond, County Cork, made it to America and eventually joined the US Army only to be killed on the very last day of the First World War at the age of twenty-eight. I wondered what effect that night on the *Titanic* could have had on him. Would he have spent six years wondering why he'd lived and so many others hadn't? Had this influenced his decision to join the army, a sense that he was on borrowed time anyway? Did he feel as though he was living with ghosts on his back? The statistics of the disaster can often inoculate us against the stories of those involved. Fifteen hundred dead is obviously a huge figure, but it's easy to forget under the weight of numbers that these were individuals, people with loved ones, hopes, dreams and plans. Dannie Buckley and others like him had to cope with the aftermath of winning a macabre lottery that would leave them with dreadful memories, the cries of the drowning haunting their nights for the rest of their lives.

The exhibition shows some of the last pictures taken of the ship before disaster struck. On the wall is a list of all those who had joined the *Titanic* at Queenstown, most of whom have a cross by their name to indicate they hadn't survived the disaster. The list ran from floor to ceiling, and that was just those who had left from here; in all there had been 2,224 people on board.

The *Lusitania* was a more immediate disaster for the people of Queenstown just three years after the *Titanic*. One of the world's finest and most luxurious liners, the *Lusitania* left New York on May 1, 1915 carrying 1,959 people destined for Southampton despite the knowledge that German U-boats were operating off the south coast of Ireland and targeting shipping of all kinds. On May 7, around fifteen miles off Queenstown, the *Lusitania* was struck amidships by a single torpedo. It hit the engine room, the Achilles heel of the ship, and she sank in barely twenty minutes. The list of the ship made launching lifeboats on both sides almost impossible, meaning that 1,198 people drowned in the freezing water. Nearly all of the 761 survivors came ashore at Queenstown, most of the town's boats having gone to the liner's assistance once the *Lusitania*'s radio room had sent out distress signals. The bedraggled masses gathered on the quayside – now a picturesque park dedicated to John F. Kennedy whose own ancestors had departed for the US from Cobh – then were transferred to hospital or into local people's own homes. The bodies that were recovered were laid out on Cunard's Quay, in the town hall and in a shed on the quayside, all quickly converted into temporary mortuaries. One hundred and fifty of the *Lusitania* victims are buried in a mass grave in Cobh's Old Town cemetery, more than half of them unidentified.

The exhibition is crammed with simple yet poignant relics. There's a telegram from a survivor to his family in Scotland that reads simply: 'Transference to Lusitania, ship torpedoed, me safe in General Hospital, Queenstown, home Monday or Tuesday, lost everything, Johnnie.' Elsewhere is a letter from Winifred Hall of Cheshire to Mrs Swanton of Queenstown who had taken her into her home after the disaster.

> Will any of us ever forget, I wonder. I think not. But neither I am sure shall we ever forget the wondrous kindness shown to us who survived that awful experience by the people of Queenstown. Perhaps I may meet you again. Perhaps then I'll be able to say all that I wish but cannot write. I'm so very proud just to know you.

Of all the tragic tales and pictures in the museum, it was that last line that sent a tear down my cheek. Again, the scale of the disaster obfuscates the hundreds of tales like that of Winifred Hall and Mrs Swanton; this was a time of greater stress and heroism than most of us will ever know. For me at any rate, Mrs Hall's pride in simply having met Mrs Swanton in such desperate circumstances brought home the impact of the disaster more than any bare statistic.

As I left the exhibition and returned to the hall, I realised that my own unknown ancestor would have left Ireland through this building, trodden these same flagstones to set in motion the chain of events which had led to me being here now. I didn't know when, but a Connelly had stepped off a train on this very same platform, nervously clutching a suitcase and feeling completely alone and anonymous among the huge, noisy mass of humanity leaving their homeland behind. If family traits are handed down through the generations, that suitcase would have been packed frantically at the last possible moment and contain nothing useful. Thus unsuitably equipped, he would have passed into this building, presented his boarding card at a window on Deepwater Quay, taken one last look at his native Cork and stepped on to a ship bound for England. Me? I was booked on a Ryanair flight to London the next day, which I guess is the modern equivalent of steerage, only without the dysentery.

My time in Cork hadn't felt like a homecoming; too many years had passed since my ancestor had left here and somehow ended up in north-west London. I did, however, take home with me a genuine sense of the rebel county. Back in London a couple of weeks later I watched the All-Ireland hurling final that had gripped the county while I was there.

Cork, the underdogs, lost narrowly to mighty Kilkenny. Despite the gallant defeat, one moment in the second half served to illustrate for me the spirit of Cork. Late in the game their giant defender Diarmuid O'Sullivan thwarted a Kilkenny attack, but lost his hurley in the process. He was left stickless with the ball in his hand barely twelve yards from his own goal. You can't throw a hurling ball; without your hurley the only option is to slap a pass to a teammate with your open palm, but there was no teammate near enough for this to be viable. A Kilkenny forward charged, hurley in hand, intent on dislodging the ball. He literally bounced off O'Sullivan and landed on his backside. A second Kilkenny player charged at him from the other side; again O'Sullivan stood his ground and again the forward was sent sprawling. It happened a third time, leaving a trio of flattened Kilkenny players around the giant Corkman. O'Sullivan clenched both fists and bellowed, a roar that all but drowned out the eighty thousand people screaming from the stands, and played a hand pass to a teammate now within passing distance. Sitting in south London, I understood what it means to be a Corkman; it's just like Roy Keane said, you're Irish by birth and a Corkman by the grace of God.

IRISH SEA, SHANNON, ROCKALL

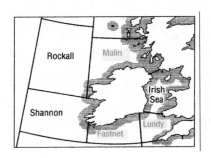

Area Irish Sea began life in 1924 as Area Mersey. Renamed in 1949, it was split into two sections, north and south, becoming one in 1956. It borders Area Lundy to the south, while its northern border runs roughly from Portpatrick in Scotland to Belfast. Area Shannon is a survivor from the original 1924 regions, although it used to cover sea now in Areas Rockall and Malin. Shannon's coastal boundary runs from the southern tip of Dingle Bay to Slyne Head on the western tip of Galway. Area Rockall, directly north of Shannon, was introduced in 1949 and has no land boundaries.

Looking back, there were two clues on the ferry crossing from Liverpool that the Isle of Man would be a little bit different from what I'm used to. First, there was the announcement that asked, 'Would any passenger missing a left shoe please contact a member of the crew.' Then there was the response to my query as to whether they had any of the day's newspapers on board. 'No, I'm sorry, we haven't,' came the reply. 'I think there might be a *Telegraph* from last week somewhere, if that's any good?'

These, as it turned out, would be two of the less surreal incidents on my short jaunt across the Irish Sea. They were knocked into a hat suitably cocked by, among others, Norman Wisdom, some fairies, a couple of rocks that spoke to me, a genuine all-singing, all-dancing pop superstar and a talking mongoose called Geoff. But such run-of-the-mill occurrences were still in the future when I nosed the car off the ferry at Douglas and headed for a swanky hotel on the seafront into which Jo the photographer and I had been booked by the marvellous Daphne at the tourist office.

The Isle of Man is almost exactly at the centre point between England, Wales, Scotland and Ireland. It's also the halfway point on a line drawn between Land's End and John O'Groats, a location that has not dimmed its Manx heritage one iota. Quite the opposite, in fact: it's claimed that the advantage of the Manx three-legged symbol is that it 'never kneels to England'. At thirty-one miles long and thirteen wide, Man was certainly the largest of the islands I'd be visiting on this journey. Okay, Ireland and Britain are islands, not to mention Iceland, but you know what I mean.

Most of the rocky outcrops I'd been exploring could be circumnavigated comfortably between breakfast and a hearty lunch. As I would discover, the Isle of Man presented a far hardier challenge, to my physical well-being, my sanity and even my liver.

My bizarre Manx experiences wouldn't have been possible at all if it hadn't been for Finn MacCool. According to legend the giant MacCool acquired his Celtic nous through cooking the Salmon of Knowledge caught for him by a well-meaning druid. MacCool, being a bloke, messed up the cooking completely and burned his thumb, the sucking of which transferred the inherent wisdom from fins to Finn. He must have been disappointed when *Star Wars* came out: on the way to his spiritual destiny, Luke Skywalker got to play with light sabres, meet Alec Guinness and snog Natalie Portman; Finn MacCool, his Celtic counterpart, was handed a dead fish by an old man, accidentally set fire to his thumb and probably ended up with a takeaway pizza. No wonder he was a stroppy so and so; if you believe the legend, MacCool was clumping around the north of Ireland in huff about some Scottish giant who was throwing his weight around, so he ripped up a clod of earth and hurled it out to sea. The clod became the Isle of Man, and the hole it left filled up with water and became Lough Neagh (in another tantrum, MacCool flung a pebble over Malin Head and into the Atlantic which became Rockall).

St Patrick is said to have visited the island in the fifth century, but it was the Vikings and Scots who had the strongest influence on Manx history. The island boasts arguably the oldest democratic parliament in the world, the Viking-influenced Tynwald, which first sat in 979. To this day new laws are handed down once a year from a special Tynwald mound, said to be made from the earth of all seventeen districts of the island. Until 1919 Manx common law was recited atop Tynwald by two judges known as Deemsters, from where we derive the verb 'to deem', as in 'his position was deemed untenable'. It's this sense of autonomy that helps the islanders feel independent: Manx first, British or Irish second. Man boasts its own banknotes and coins, it has its own laws and its own language. It even has a national anthem.

Although the island gave the vote to women, albeit a select few, as far back as 1881, homosexuality was only made legal in 1992. There was even a death penalty on the statute books until the following year, and there are relatively young Manx who will wince at the memories of when the birch was still permissible. Fortunately, I no longer risked visiting Man and being hanged, drawn and quartered and having my bowels removed and burned in front of me as a result of a bit of absent-minded jaywalking. Relaxed in this knowledge I switched on the car radio just as the local station began its hourly news bulletin.

The top story was that Douglas's golf course had flooded overnight, relegating George Bush's latest pronouncements about the 'war on turr' to second place. This Manx-centric eye on the world had been exemplified in a Manx newspaper I'd found on the Tube a few months earlier. BALI BOMB – MANX FAMILY SAFE said a headline. Examination of the story revealed that they were safe because they were in Fiji at the time. On the same page there was a contender for my all-time favourite newspaper headline: MAN BROKE INTO HOTEL ROOM, DONNED WOMEN'S TROUSERS AND WATCHED TV. Somehow, reading the story itself would have spoiled it.

Jo and I were staying at the Sefton, a fine hotel next to the Gaiety Theatre (a name that surprisingly pre-dates the 1992 legislation) on the seafront at Douglas. The wonderful Daphne had left us a pair of tickets for a production of Gilbert and Sullivan's *Pirates of Penzance* at the Gaiety, which exposed me to the Manx national anthem for the first time. There was practically a full house in the beautifully ornate and compact theatre which dates back over a century, when the orchestra suddenly struck up a lusty tune. The entire audience rose as one to sing:

Land of our birth, gem of God's earth,
O island so strong and so fair;
Built firm as Barool, thy throne of home rule
Makes us free as thy sweet mountain air.

Well I don't know about you, but for me that tops 'Send her victorious, happy and glorious' and that's without even knowing what a Barool is, let alone being able to pass judgement on its firmness. It was an impressive display of Manx pride, one that Gilbert and Sullivan found hard to follow. 'I Am the Very Model of a Modern Major General' could only be an anticlimax after that.

'Home rule' isn't strictly true, even if the island does enjoy a significant degree of autonomy. In fact, Man could almost be a microcosm of Britain itself. It's got the seaside towns complete with Victorian esplanades, the rolling hills, the chain stores and banks, but where it possibly scores over the rest of Britain is in its licensing hours (there aren't any) and its speed limits (ditto on many parts of the island). While I was unlikely to trouble the latter greatly, the former meant that, even after *Pirates*, Jo and I could get thoroughly stuck into a good few drinks.

The absence of licensing laws is for me a most civilised state of affairs. Not because I particularly want to throw booze down my neck all hours of the night until the stuff's sloshing up against the back of my front teeth, but because I think I'm responsible enough to decide when it's time to go home. The social disorder implications also win the argument for me. Many, if not most, pubs in London stop only just short of driving a bulldozer through the bars to get you out as soon after eleven o'clock as possible. Put a load of hassled drunks on to crowded pavements all at the same time and is it any surprise that town centres across the land get smashed up on a regular basis? On this occasion, however, Jo and I made the mistake of returning to the hotel bar and attacking first its bottle of Jameson's Irish whiskey and then, for some reason, its Cointreau supplies. I've no idea how we kicked off on the Cointreau as it's not a drink that has ever passed my lips before. All it meant to me was those cheesy ads from the seventies where a French smoothie would pronounce Catherine as 'Casserin' and then indulge in some highly suggestive innuendo purporting to describe the contents of the little square-shaped bottle.

It was still early in the proceedings when a diminutive but confident young woman in a baseball cap breezed in, asked the barman for a pen and joined a small group at a table just along from us. Jo's eyes narrowed slightly in thought. 'I'm sure that was Scary Spice,' she said. 'Don't be daft,' I replied, 'what on earth would Scary Spice be doing in a hotel bar on the Isle of Man? On a Tuesday?' I looked again. Okay, I thought, she would look like Scary Spice only she's about six inches too short. But as it turned out, Scary Spice is about six inches too short and we were, after all, sharing a bar with a former member of the recently rent-asunder Spice Girls. The bar was fairly small and its clientele fairly sparse and there was no mistaking this was Mel B, tentative enquiries revealing that she was here acting in a film about animal-rights campaigners. To be honest, Scary was anything but. In fact she was actually quite nice even if she's smaller than you think she'd be. Either that or I'm taller than I think I am.

The surreal nature of the trip was heightened by the fact that when someone in the bar was recognised, it was Jo. Jo has been a bit of a radio celebrity in the North-west in her time, and a couple of Scouse businessmen in the corner had recognised her voice as the decibel level increased in line with her alcohol consumption. Hence Scary Spice had to watch as the two blokes passed her by to get the autograph of the woman in the big black coat on the other side of the room sitting with the scruffy big girl's blouse drinking a girl's drink.

I have to confess that the proceedings get a bit hazy after this. A friend of mine told me later that he received a text message from me sent at about 2.30 a.m. that night which read 'I'm in a hotel on the Isle of Man and Scary Spice is behind the bar pouring me a pint of lager', before adding rather uncharitably, 'Her talents as a barmaid make her singing look good'. I don't drink lager. Then again I don't drink Cointreau either, but by the state of me the next morning I'd clearly lifted my personal lager and liqueur embargo for a fair few hours and that's before even considering the whiskey. My responsible attitude towards liberal licensing laws appeared to have taken the night off. I woke up on top of my bed, my clothes adhering to me all over thanks to a sheen of clammy, cold sweat. I was minus my shoes. I had a raging headache and a thirst so great that I could have stood up, marched out of the hotel on to the beach, put my lips to the salty brine and drained the Irish Sea. I reached gingerly for the phone and dialled Jo's room number.

'Uuurrrghh,' she groaned down the line.

'Uuurrrghh,' I concurred. 'Meet you in fifteen minutes for breakfast?'

'Can't we make it half an hour?' she whimpered.

'Well,' I said, 'don't forget you've agreed to be the celebrity speaker at those blokes' business convention this morning. You'd better get a move on.'

Silence.

'Oh God, I haven't, have I?'

'It's one of the last things I remember. Just after you'd challenged them to a game of strip arm wrestling and lost.'

'What?'

'Okay, I made that last bit up. But you did say you'd deliver them a blistering speech.'

'Oh no. Okay, fifteen minutes, maybe twenty. I'll bring your shoes. They're on my dressing table for some reason.'

'Okay, I'll bring your coat. I'm wearing it, for some reason.'

Fortunately for Jo's fledgling career as a corporate

motivational speaker, there was no sign of her two fans as we groped our way along the walls to breakfast. Hopefully they'd been too squiffy to remember as well.

'Bloody hell,' I said as we sat down, 'your eyes look terrible.'

'You should see them from this side,' said Jo weakly.

Later that day, long past lunchtime, we felt almost well enough to head for Castletown. In the morning, in an effort to blow away the cobwebs and escape the fug of fetid sweat and stale alcohol that hung around stubbornly in my room like a sea mist, I'd ventured into Douglas for a wander around. I climbed the steep slope up to the Manx Museum, which I wanted to visit in order to get a grip on the history of the island, and because museums are generally quiet and hence might assuage the chain gang that was setting about the inside of my head with mattocks. Outside the museum, however, the silence was suddenly shattered by bickering voices. A heated argument was developing although for the life of me I couldn't work out from where as there was nobody else around. For a brief moment I thought it must be my put-upon liver and pickled brain enjoying a good slanging match about the night before, but no. It turned out to be two lumps of rock. Outside the Manx Museum there are two rocks with faces on them who, whenever an unsuspecting punter with a raging hangover staggers past, break out

370

into an argument over who's the oldest and who's the most important and make them jump out of their clammy skin. I really could have done without it, to be honest.

I knew little of the Isle of Man before visiting, other than that it staged the TT races every year and had been the birthplace of a girl on whom I'd had an enormous crush when I was at school. Hence I learned a great deal from the museum, despite my not being in the rudest of health at the time. Early maps name Man as 'Mania', and I was beginning to understand why. Like most island and seafaring communities, the Manx are inherently superstitious. Man is brimming with legends about the fairies that are said to inhabit the place, and even today islanders go out of their way so as not to upset the 'little folk'. In the old days abandoned houses would be left untouched as residences for the fairies, and derelict cottages would have food and drink left on the doorstep by obliging neighbours.

At sea, Manx sailors and fishermen were not allowed to whistle as that 'aggravated the wind'. Fishermen were particularly superstitious about the third boat leaving port, as it was supposed to be unlucky. So much so that after the first two boats had left they'd lash the next couple together in order that there wouldn't actually be a third boat sailing out of port. Less esoterically I learned of the island's remarkable war years. During the Second World War Man was used as an internment camp for Jewish refugees, Germans living in Britain and people seen to have potential as Nazi spies. They were all sent to the Isle of Man and probably didn't have an enjoyable time of it. Recovering a little, and sobered in more ways than one by the thought of the thousands of people of different races, creeds and backgrounds who came here during the war as a result of a unifying persecution, I ventured further into Douglas. It began to rain so I ducked into a small bookshop and blundered straight into a table at which Norman Wisdom was sitting.

He smiled at me, a kind smile, but didn't seem to recognise me from our one previous meeting. A few years ago I shared a flat with a friend who was a breakfast television producer. This meant that when she'd been let down by someone, or was just short of stuff, I'd get a call from my flat-mate begging me to fill in on the show the following morning or else she'd lose her job. Hence I spent several freezing, wintry pre-dawns in east London hamming it up for the camera live to the nation. I'd written and performed comedic songs, I'd done a skit with some angry peacocks and I'd been a lovesick Valentine pining away with unrequited passion (after which I was interviewed by *Just Seventeen* because they thought I was 'you know, really sweet'). One morning I had to be a burglar, and was sitting in the Portakabin that served as a waiting room for people like me making arses of themselves for the amusement of breakfasting Britain, dressed in a stripy shirt with a mask over my eyes and a bag at my feet marked 'swag'. On one side of me sat a woman who had walked alone to the North Pole, on the other a couple from Yorkshire whose dog had eaten a pair of pants and later had to have them surgically removed from its intestine. They had the pants with them in a paper bag. Then Norman Wisdom walked in, dressed as a milkman. We chatted for a while about how tea never tastes right out of styrofoam cups, the vagaries of being picked up by a taxi at 4.30 in the morning, and how popular Norman was in Albania. He was a lovely, lovely man with the kindest, most sparkling eyes I think I've ever seen on a man's face. But here, in a little bookshop on the Isle of Man, the island where he now spends most of his days, our friendship wouldn't be rekindled. A polite queue of people were waiting to have their copies of his autobiography signed, and I was dripping rainwater on to the table. My eyes were also bloodshot and I was probably leaking Cointreau from every pore. Norman still smiled at me but I left nonetheless, waving wanly.

And so to Castletown, the island's ancient former capital. It's a lovely place, Castletown, clustered around a picturesque harbour of bobbing boats and overlooked by an ancient castle. Entering the castle I was confronted with a sign advertising tickets for Hop-Tu-Naa, a Celtic

Christmas Eve. Once you'd bought your ticket you were apparently entitled to a 'free turnip and candle', something I'd never been offered as part of a ticket deal before, not even when Charlton were really struggling to attract people through the turnstiles. This being the Isle of Man, the contents of the castle were appropriately quirky. No sooner were you through the door than you were beneath a 'murder hole', a space between two portcullises where unwelcome visitors could be set upon through holes in the ceiling. Now, I'm no military strategist, but it seemed to me that if you were going to invade a castle the last thing you'd do would be go and knock on the front door. Maybe medieval Jehovah's Witnesses were more persistent than they are now. Either way, I'm glad I wasn't Castletown's postman when the time came to deliver the gas bill.

Inside you progress through a network of low corridors and winding spiral staircases into various rooms, most of which were apparently designed to house female prisoners. No wonder it was called the Isle of Man, boom boom. My favourite exhibit was in a reconstructed medieval bedroom. In the corner was a closet in which sat a waxwork of a man, erm, about his business in the littlest room. From within came a soundtrack of pained grunting interspersed with bouts of drunken singing. Downstairs there was a table spread in the style of a medieval banquet, among which were several different types of bird on platters. No wonder this ancient Castletonian was having audible digestion problems; the food he was trying to expel from his system probably still had feathers on.

We didn't dally long in Castletown as we were heading for Dalby in search of a talking mongoose. Most of the places on the shipping forecast map have intriguing stories to tell, part myth, part folklore, and sometimes part wind-up-the-gullible-townie-with-a-load-of-old-cobblers. The Isle of Man is a miscellany of curious mythology all wrapped up and dropped in the middle of the Irish Sea, and of all Man's strange tales the Dalby Spook is my favourite.

The story dates back to 1931 when the Irving family occupied a remote farmhouse at Doarlish Cashen, near Dalby on the west coast of the island. Times were hard for James and Margaret. James had travelled the world in his time, selling pianos to Canadians among other things, but although their two eldest children had flown the nest they still struggled to support themselves and their thirteen-year-old daughter, Voirrey.

The cottage had been in disrepair when they moved in and James had made his own improvements, adding panelling to the cold stone internal walls. After a while, James became aware of a scuffling noise behind the panelling and, thinking it was a mouse, started to imitate a cat in order to scare off the intruder. To his surprise, whatever it was behind the panel started imitating James's imitations. When he told the rest of the family, Voirrey had an explanation. It was a mongoose called Geoff, and he had spoken to her many times. In fact they'd been having conversations for some weeks, during which Geoff had told Voirrey he'd been born in Delhi on June 7, 1852, spoke French, German and Spanish, and once commented modestly, 'I am the fifth dimension, the eighth wonder of the world.'

Geoff would announce his presence by singing the Manx national anthem – I wonder if he knew what a Barool was – and would depart with the word 'vanished'. Voirrey was the only member of the family to whom Geoff actually appeared regularly, although he did once allow James to touch his fur and teeth, the latter drawing blood from the farmer's finger. 'You'll want to put some ointment on that,' said Geoff, helpfully. Geoff would also scurry around the locality, earwigging in other houses and reporting back to the Irvings with all the local gossip and, if he was in a particularly good mood, he'd even bring in the odd rabbit for the pot. He was mischievous and clumsy. He'd break things in the night, and one day had the entire family concerned for his health when he writhed on the floor complaining of stomach cramps. When Geoff revealed that he was just kidding around, the Irvings weren't amused and threatened to move away. A horrified Geoff said, 'What? You wouldn't leave me here alone, would you?'

It didn't take long for word to spread about the Irvings and their talking mongoose. Journalists beat a path to the farmhouse door. Almost literally in fact: so remote was the dwelling that it was a fair old hike uphill through bracken and foliage, but when they arrived Geoff always kept out of their way and each left disappointed. The renowned ghost hunter Harry Price even came to Dalby in 1933 but left with only a couple of grainy, indistinct photographs. Given that the Irvings were the only ones ever to see Geoff, most people wrote off the tale as a hoax. But why they would construct such a hoax is unclear; although they were struggling financially there's no record of the family ever selling their story. In fact, sightseers were a regular blight on their lives; one contemporary newspaper report quotes James as saying that 'ruffian sightseers' had climbed on to the roof and blocked the chimney, choking the place with smoke and soot. James is also well portrayed in newspaper profiles, many making a point of mentioning what a straight-up, level-headed guy he was, with nothing to suggest he was a master of hokum. If anything the story made their life a misery, so why construct and prolong such an elaborate hoax?

By 1935 the Irvings had had enough and left Dalby and the Isle of Man. Geoff was never seen nor heard again, but in 1947 another local farmer shot and killed a strange-looking animal that was 'neither stoat nor weasel'. Some say that this was Geoff, others contend that the creature had left with the Irvings which, given the mutual affection between family and mongoose, would seem likely.

I wanted to believe that Geoff existed, particularly when I learned that in 1912 a neighbouring farmer had imported several mongooses from India to keep down the local rabbit population, and that many Indian legends attribute to the mongoose the ability to speak. The Irvings for their part disappeared until in 1996 an American investigator of the paranormal finally tracked down an elderly Voirrey. She said that she'd been labelled mentally disturbed and a gifted ventriloquist. If the latter was the case, she wondered, why hadn't she gone into ventriloquism as a career and made some money? She was fed up with the whole business, which was why she had never talked about Geoff. He had existed, she insisted, but she wished he hadn't, and that's all she would ever say on the matter.

I drove to Dalby in search of, well, I didn't know. As far as I knew, the house the Irvings lived in had been demolished years ago, and only one wall remained. There must be something there though, I thought; this was a tale that had fascinated the world at the time. And it still does: search for the Dalby Spook on the Internet and all sorts of paranormal and poltergeist message boards pop up with explanations from the considered to the crackpot.

Dalby isn't a big place. It sits on the south-western

coast looking out towards Ireland and I'd driven through it before I'd realised I was even there. Looking to turn around, I headed left down a narrow road signposted 'Niarbyl' that turned into a track down into a tiny cove. At the end of the track, beneath tall cliffs, were two low, thatched cottages, single-storey whitewashed buildings that faced out to sea. It felt like the most secluded place in the world. There was no sign of life, but the cottages were too well tended to be abandoned. Just around the headland was another building, a tiny house clearly only big enough to contain one room. Again it was whitewashed, and even had a little garden to the side. Lobster pots were piled up against the back wall, while the cliff rose high above the roof and the Irish Sea lapped against the rocks in front.

I made a vow that one day I'd come and live here in one of these cottages. Nobody would know they were here; it was only by sheer chance that I'd stumbled upon them. Later, I mentioned to Daphne that I'd found this extraordinary remote place with its fishermen's cottages and its own little bay. I expected her eyebrows to shoot skywards and a multitude of enquiries to pour forth, which I would deflect with a knowing tap to the side of my nose and an infuriating, 'Sorry, my secret.' Instead Daphne said, 'Oh, that must have been at Niarbyl.' Before I could deflate fully, she added, 'That's a very famous place. Have you ever seen the film *Waking Ned*? That's where a lot of it was filmed. Those cottages were used as Ned's house, where they find him dead with the winning lottery ticket.' One day, I really will find somewhere completely undiscovered. Then I shall live there completely alone and not tell anyone, just to spite you all.

The Isle of Man is popular with filmmakers, hence the presence of Scary and a bunch of other faces you'd know but couldn't put a name to in the Sefton (it's usually reasonable to assume that they've been in *The Bill* or *Casualty*, programmes which keep the entire acting profession going by themselves). Indeed Roy, the avuncular, faintly military, Cointreau-dispensing barman at the hotel, had reeled off an impressive list of names who'd graced the premises. Clearly he wanted it known that Scary Spice didn't impress him. 'That David Jason,' he told me loudly in order that Scary might hear, 'now there's a real gentleman. They don't make them like him any more.' Man's varied landscape, not to mention its tax advantages, has led to the islanders actively marketing the place as a film location. To the makers of *Waking Ned*, the Isle of Man looked more like Ireland than Ireland did.

A haven though Niarbyl undoubtedly was, there was no mongoose here. Heading back out of Dalby I passed a grand but deserted-looking hotel. A tin sign swung by the roadside giving the name of the hotel, over which peered the cheeky face of what had to be a mongoose. I swerved into the car park and strode eagerly through the doors. Eventually a man appeared. 'Can I help you?' he asked. I smiled my biggest smile and announced, 'I've come in search of a talking mongoose.' Now, I confess that at the time I'd thought I was one of very few people in the world still privy to Geoff's legend and rather hoped that those of us who knew about Geoff were like some secret society. I'd assumed that mention of his name would have this hotelier, whose sign is the only visible acknowledgement of Geoff in his erstwhile locality, grasping me in a firm handshake, clapping me on the shoulder and announcing, 'Go and sit down, my mongoose-savvy friend. I shall prepare coffee and cakes and we will talk long into the night.'

Instead, the man perceptibly rolled his eyes, said, 'Well, we've got a page about it on our website, the address is on that card there,' turned around, walked through a door and closed it behind him. I'd drawn a blank on Geoff. An afternoon of investigations had thrown up nothing more than a roll of the eyes and a drawing on a tin sign. Mind you, the sign meant I'd seen more of Geoff than Harry Price ever did, and he was a proper ghost hunter.

We eschewed the Sefton bar that evening. Partly because neither of us could look a bottle of anything in the eye after the night before, but mostly because I had an important mission the next day that didn't involve talking animals of any kind.

I think it was the moment my vision turned from colour to black and white when I realised that cycling the Isle of Man TT course on a push-bike was probably not the greatest idea I have ever had. Barely halfway around the course my legs felt as if the muscles were on the outside and being twanged by small children, my lungs were trying to batter their way out through my ribs and my drumming heart was fighting its way up into the back of my throat, wanting to strangle me. Yet only a few weeks earlier, in the warm comfort of my own home, it had seemed such a fantastic idea. The 37 3/4-mile course, used in its current format since 1911, is run entirely on public roads allowing a perhaps unique opportunity for the hapless amateur like myself to emulate, or at least imitate, the sporting greats. How often do you get the opportunity to curl a free-kick into the top corner at the San Siro? Or heave an enormous six into the Mound Stand at Lord's? These legendary venues are out of bounds to us mortals, but the TT course, home to one of the world's greatest motorcycle races, was there to be conquered. By me.

Now motorbikes are, I confess, a mystery to me. I don't know a spark plug from a bath plug, and until recently thought Kawasaki was a Japanese drink. Yet here was a rare opportunity to follow in the footsteps of some of the greatest names in sporting history, men like Joey Dunlop, Mike Hailwood and Carl Fogerty. And, in the absence of a purring beast of engineering beneath my rear end, I would do it on a pushbike. It was nearly forty miles, certainly, but surely no bother on a bike? After all, 2002 TT-winner Dave Jefferies had lapped the course in eighteen minutes dead. I used to cycle the one and a half miles to school in about fifteen minutes – how hard could it be?

So it was that I found myself on a hired mountain bike on the start line of the world famous TT course one damp, blustery morning. There was even a grandstand alongside me as I psyched myself up, but unlike on race days it was inhabited only by a snootily aloof seagull. Within seconds of my pressing my first pedal, the wind was forcing my hair back from my forehead and I was hurtling down Brae Hill at an impressive velocity. Feeling exhilarated and instantly high on adrenalin I tucked in aerody-namically like the pros. Then the traffic lights changed and I skidded inelegantly to a shuddering halt, wobbling alarmingly to a standstill like a small boy whose stabilisers have just been removed. Curses, I thought, there goes my assault on the lap record. I glanced to my left into a cemetery, an appropriate sight for the start of the TT course as more than two hundred people have been killed during or while practising for the race since its inception a century ago. There was one of those Day-glo posters outside the church that bore the message 'How great thou art' and, for a moment, I believed it.

Incidentally, is there just one person who writes the scripts for all those posters you see outside churches? They've fascinated me for years. Some are just barefaced exhortations to get your backside through the door ('God – worship him here, now!'), while others are more subtle, employing plays on words, or reflecting current trends in popular culture. During the last World Cup, for example, I spotted a poster outside a church near me that read in black letters on a bright pink background, 'Football – the greatest game. Jesus – the greatest . . . name'. The idea I think was to attract my attention with the topical football reference. By crikey, I'd think, football *is* the greatest game, whoever's behind this poster clearly knows their onions. Then I would read the second half of the rhyming couplet and think, Oh, I say, that's a terribly clever thing. I like the way the three dots emphasise just what an ingenious piece of work that is, making me wait for the pay-off for maximum effect. Until now I'd thought that Chatsworth Musters, the pioneering bird man of Utsire, had the greatest name and I'd even construct an argument in favour of Willibrod of Heligoland, not to mention Sir Cloudesley Shovell, but no. Jesus. It's a great name, I'd never really realised that before until my attention was drawn to the fact by this poster. And with that, I'd be through the portals and signing up for every service going.

On this occasion, however, the sign was nothing

more than an ill-timed boost to my inflated ego. If someone had thought to erect a sign there that read 'Connelly, you fat git, the last time you took any exercise of note it was a brisk walk to the Co-op because you'd heard a rumour they were making roast beef Monster Munch again. Forget it, go back to the Sefton. Scary Spice is staying there, you know. Oh, and it's going to rain', then maybe the Church would have been on to something. Instead, I puffed out my chest and when the lights turned to green set off again. The slope bottomed out and became a steady but arduous climb and hence the theme of my trek was established. I had told people in the hotel on our first night on the island what I was going to do and they were impressed. 'Doing the mountain course on a pushbike, eh?' they'd said as I cockily explained my plans while throwing another measure of Cointreau down to hotfoot it after the Jameson's that had gone before. But now a small alarm bell began to ring at the back of my mind, the source of which I couldn't quite put my finger on. As I puffed uphill past the two-mile marker, the word 'mountain' suddenly came hurtling back to me.

The Isle of Man TT course goes up a mountain.

Hence within a few miles of the start I was really struggling. I was well out of Douglas and into the countryside and the wind was whipping across me; with classic timing I'd chosen a day when

385

Britain was being lashed by gales, sending roof slates flying and trees tumbling across the country. And I was halfway up a mountain, ill-equipped without even a bottle of water, alone, and on a pushbike. Nobody knew where I was.

It was when I'd reached the monochrome limits of my endurance and the hailstones began flinging themselves out of the grey sky to sting my rosy face that I betrayed the basic ethics of sport. Out in the Manx hills with a storm brewing and only a temperamental set of *dérailleur* gears between me and death from exposure, my Corinthian principles deserted me completely. I cheated. I phoned Jo and summoned her from the warmth of the hotel to the middle of nowhere to rescue me. Having expected an easy day of drinking coffee, reading the papers and popping out to take the occasional snap, Jo was not too impressed at my breathless pleas to prevent me from dying of exposure and exhaustion by coming to find me in the car. But hats off to her, she played the role of the St Bernard dog to perfection, lacking only the little barrel of brandy or, at a push, Cointreau around her neck for the full effect.

There is a gossamer-thin line between honourable defeat and cheating. If I'd packed it in there and then and spent the rest of the day lying on my hotel bed watching Sky Sports I would have been nothing more than the classic British sporting loser. That's certainly what I had in mind when I threw the bike in the boot and prostrated myself along the back seat of the car. But for some reason something told me to press on. Rest up for a couple of miles and then, as the saying goes, put me back on the bloody bike. In terms of cycling prowess I may be more Homer Simpson than Tommy Simpson, but somewhere deep down a flame flickered into life, a message to myself that I shouldn't give in so easily. As I lay staring up at my car ceiling among the accumulation of crisp packets and drinks cartons tossed over my shoulder during a period of several months, a voice told me that I wasn't a quitter. It told me that I wasn't a loser. It also told me that if I bribed Jo to keep shtum by paying for dinner that evening, no one would be any the wiser and I could just lie and say I completed the whole thing on the bike.

So that's exactly what I did, and a pattern soon developed for the rest of the course. I would wobble my way up the mountainside for as many miles, or more usually yards, as my jellied legs would carry me, then recover in the car for a bit. I passed warm, welcoming houses where people with far more sense than me were doing sensible things, like staying indoors and not trying to cycle up a mountain with a monsoon imminent. Just before Ramsey I took a spectacular wrong turn after which it took Jo some considerable time to locate me again, but I knew by then that I had reached the halfway point. It was a landmark which logic suggested would mean the rest of the course being downhill; but this was the Isle of Man where logic doesn't come into it and any hopes of a legs-akimbo, blurry-pedalled descent from there to the finish line were soon dashed. Ahead was the arduous climb up Snaefell Mountain, the highest point on the entire island.

In my defence I could have just packed it in and still pretended I'd done it. No one would have been any the wiser and at least I was making a token effort. Was it my fault that I'd underestimated the course and overestimated my physical capabilities? Well, okay, yes I suppose technically it was my fault, but nevertheless I tried to proceed with a reasonably clear conscience. At the back of my mind, however, a nagging voice kept whispering, 'Cheat.' And it was there on the top of Snaefell Mountain, with the island beneath obscured by mist, that I felt the true extent of my shame. I stood buffeted by the gale in front of the statue erected in memory of arguably the TT's greatest ever rider, Joey Dunlop. The Ulsterman had taken the Manx chequered flag a record twenty-six times before his death racing in Estonia in 2000. He'd been sculpted leaning back on his machine with a cheery grin but, up there in the misty silence, his smile mocked me. And with good reason.

There are numerous memorials to fallen riders around the course, from heroes like six-times winner from the thirties Jimmy Guthrie, who has an impressive cairn dedicated to him on Snaefell, to the weekend bikers killed while living the TT dream, their passing marked by tiny plaques screwed to nondescript walls. I stood before Joey Dunlop feeling utterly ashamed to have taken my task so lightly. The TT course is not a playground for half-baked buffoons like me to muck around on. A few weeks after my visit, Dave Jefferies, who had won three titles at the 2002 TT and held the lap-speed record, left the road at 160mph, crashed into a telegraph pole at Crosby and was killed, during practice for the 2003 race. As I stood there in front of Joey Dunlop, I realised that by taking the TT heritage so lightly I was mocking the memory of people like him, Jimmy Guthrie and Dave Jefferies, people driven by a thirst for challenge and danger, people who are genuine heroes to the motorcycling fraternity. From Dave Jefferies to weekend bikers, people had died riding the course I was ineptly navigating for a bit of a laugh. I was chastened by the bronze Joey Dunlop's broad grin. The reason I'd never curled an exquisite free-kick into the top corner at the San Siro nor heaved a mighty six into the Mound Stand at Lord's is because I'd no right to. These sporting meccas are for the people who earn the right to be there through talent, dedication and that extra indefinable something that makes the great truly great, and that goes for the TT course too. They may be public roads for fifty-one weeks every year, but put them together in a certain order and they become another great sporting venue where the gifted compete. My sporting pedigree went no further than that hat-trick of own goals for Westhorne Colts Under 11s and smiting the odd cricket ball around the grounds of south London for a wandering team whose prime physical specimens included a thirteen-year-old Charlie Connelly and a seventy-two-year-old called Harold and once went two years without winning a match. I had no right to be here, no right to attempt this course in such a flippant manner.

It was mostly downhill for the final three or four miles, which I managed to complete on the bike despite being engulfed in a fierce hailstorm, and I crossed the finish line a wiser and far more humble man than when I had last been there some seven hours earlier. Many riders had cheated death on this course. I had just cheated.

As Jo drove us back to the Sefton, the early-evening shipping forecast came on the radio. 'Irish Sea,' said a familiar voice, 'south-westerly six to gale eight, increasing gale eight to storm ten, perhaps violent storm eleven later. Rain or squally showers, moderate or good, occasionally poor.' That night fierce storms battered the island. In the darkness outside the Sefton, the strings of lightbulbs between the lampposts along Douglas seafront swung violently in the gale, looking from my rattling window like a ceilidh for fireflies. As torrents of rain hurled themselves out of the darkness at this historic piece of rock once grumpily discarded by Finn MacCool, the Isle of Man hunkered down to sit out the worst storms locals could remember for decades. As I pulled the bedclothes around me and was about to drop off to sleep, above the howling wind I heard the throaty sound of a motorcycle roaring along the esplanade.

The River Shannon is the longest in Britain and Ireland, a fact that caused me to raise a surprised eyebrow and prepare a solid argument for Old Father Thames. A little research revealed, however, that the Shannon is a clear winner. Rising in County Cavan in the north of the island, the river flows a haphazard course of around two hundred miles to the sea on the west coast, splitting Counties Clare and Kerry. It's a symbolic and evocative waterway which features prominently throughout Ireland's turbulent history, a great barrier dividing Leinster from Connaught, east from west. The river is named for the mythical Sionan, who is said to have drowned after feeding on the very Salmon of Knowledge that had blistered the giant digit of Finn MacCool. The salmon and the knowledge contained within its pink flanks was intended for male stomachs only, and poor Sionan paid the price for her inquisitive gluttony. It may have been an untimely and chauvinistic demise, but it did result in her immortality through having the river in which she perished named after her.

The significance of the Shannon has been noted ever since it was mapped by Ptolemy. The Vikings sailed up it, allowing them to make deep inroads into Ireland. Brian Boru deployed his fleet there before the crucial Battle of Clontarf. The Normans, unable to subdue Connaught, fortified it to protect the rich plains of Leinster. Following his victorious and murderous campaign in Ireland, Cromwell banished the defeated Irish with the choice of going either 'to hell or to Connaught'. Hence for thousands of Irish people the crossing of the Shannon meant the surrender of and eviction from their homelands. The river became an early symbol of the division of Ireland – east–west this time rather than the north–south split that exists today.

In the ensuing centuries the Shannon has led a more peaceful existence. As it was an important trading and transport route, it's perhaps appropriate that Ireland's most significant international airport other than Dublin is named after it. Once I'd passed through the airport it was to the northern side of the Shannon estuary that I was headed, destined for the Clare marina town of Kilrush. As I waited at Limerick station for my connecting bus I picked up a newspaper and learned that I was heading for the second-tidiest town in the whole of Ireland. I also learned that I was sitting in the nation's second-filthiest station. When the Bus Éireann service deposited me in Kilrush town square a couple of hours later I could see why this little town on the northern bank of the Shannon estuary had earned its title. Brightly coloured buildings surround the central island of the square in which sits the town hall. All the shops seemed to have their original signage, beautifully restored, while a wide boulevard rolled gently downhill to where the Shannon itself twinkled in the sunlight among the masts of boats lolling gently in the marina. It was an image familiar from thousands of posters and tourist leaflets – it was postcard perfect, and the owners of the Irish theme pubs that have sprung up around Europe would have killed for this kind of authenticity. And most of all, it was tidy. I can't remember the name of the town that actually scooped the tidy title, but by jiminy, if it was any cleaner than this they must have been hoovering the pavements on the hour, every hour. So tidy was Kilrush in fact that the first thing I did after checking into the Kilrush Creek Lodge at the marina was go and have my hair cut in order that I might not make the place look untidy.

The Creek Lodge was a splendid and remarkably empty place. I'd been given one of the most delightful rooms of my entire journey: simple, bright, clean and with a view out into the marina. As a single traveller I had become used to being parked in broom cupboards with evocative views of the bins. Here, though, I had a choice of vistas: the marina through the French windows that opened on to my balcony, or the fields of Clare through the side window. I stepped through the French windows and into the sunshine.

Beneath me, the only thing disturbing the mirrored water was a canoe containing an Englishman speaking with a refined home-counties accent. There were three local men within hailing distance of their seventh decade on and around a bench next to the water, and I deduced that the man in the canoe had given them his camera and asked them to take his picture as he rolled his craft over in the water. I also deduced that the three men had decided to have a bit of fun at the expense of the pompous arse in front of them. Canoes are buoyant things that aren't supposed to turn over, particularly when their occupant is wearing a lifejacket. So the man really had to struggle to overturn himself and the canoe, thrashing away at the water with his paddle in the effort to get under the water. It took quite a while for him to achieve this, and he was under-standably elated when his dripping head popped up again from the drink. The local in charge of the camera, I noticed, had not even lifted it to his eye.

'Did you get it?' gasped canoe man, hopefully.

'Ah, sure, I don't think I did that time, sorry,' said the man with the camera.

'Oh, really? Okay, well, I'll have another go.'

Again, after much floundering and general thrash-ing around, the canoeist managed to submerge himself and I noticed that the shoulders of all three men by the bench were quaking with laughter.

'What about that time?' said the canoeist eagerly as he emerged from the water again.

'Do you know what? I think I just missed you again. You were very quick, see.'

This happened twice more as I stood and watched, with the shaking of the men's shoulders increasing every time the Englishman forced himself beneath the water, before he finally gave in.

I'd hoped to visit Scattery Island while here, an ancient and historic lump of rock in the estuary reached by boat from Kilrush. However, public transport links out here in the wilds of Clare are such that, although I'd allowed myself two days, the vagaries of the timetables meant that I'd actually get about forty waking minutes of time not on or waiting for buses. I walked around the edge of the marina to the Scattery Island visitor centre in the vain hope that there might be a boat going over in the brief time I'd be in Kilrush. The man in the centre spoke at a million miles an hour and used the word 'actually' in place of punctuation.

'Actually you might be able to go out actually,' he said in response to my query. 'Actually if you go over to the marina they'll be able to tell you actually actually I think they might just have gone for the day actually but I think they'll have stuck the times up in the window actually so you might be able to see them there actually but feel free to have a look around here actually.'

Actually, I did. Scattery has an eventful history, situated as it is at the end of Ireland's most significant river. It has always been a holy place, and though now uninhabited, there are the ruins of many churches and cathedrals across its surface. According to legend it used to be inhabited by a fearsome monster called Cathach. Indeed, the island's name in Gaelic is Inis Cathargh, the Island of Cathach. It took a sixth-century saint by the name of Senan to banish Cathach from the island, and Senan's legacy still pervades. At one time there were seven monastic orders, until the Vikings arrived in the early part of the ninth century and killed most of the monks. The Norsemen held the island for two hundred years until Brian Boru showed up with his army and slaughtered a thousand Vikings, leaving their bodies unburied as a lesson to others thinking of invading Ireland via the Shannon.

It was during the eighteenth century that Scattery islanders became renowned for their pilotage and would be seen paddling their curraghs furiously in the direction of any ships nosing into the estuary. The first to the ship claimed the lucrative right to give it safe passage up the river so the competition was fierce. By 1881 the population of the island had reached 141, its highest ever, but economic decline set in and in 1979 brother and sister Patti and Bobby McMahon, the last residents of Scattery, left the island for the last time to bring to an end around sixteen hundred years of continuous occupation. Scattery islanders and their descendants are still some of the most respected pilots in Europe, however, while one islander, appropriately named Senan, is now a bishop in Nigeria. Today Scattery is a low-key tourist destination notable for its 120-foot fifteenth-century tower, which still stands complete despite centuries of storms and gales. I thanked my new friend at the island centre and made to leave.

'Actually, would you like to sign the visitors' book, actually?' he asked. 'Actually I would,' I replied, picked up the pen, wrote my name and added the comment 'Very interesting, actually'.

I was not destined to visit the island, however, at least not this time; the notice in the window of the marina revealed that the next boat to Scattery wasn't for another couple of days and would depart after I'd left. As the sun began to go down I took a walk around the headland to the nearby village of Cotta. I nipped around the side of the lifeboat house and walked down to the foot of the slipway that bisected a pebble beach. Scattery lay ahead of me, low in the water, the medieval tower being its highest point. To my right the estuary opened out towards the Atlantic. On the horizon, a container ship sat motionless between the Clare and Kerry headlands. It was very quiet and the water was mirror still. The Shannon was a motionless mass of

397

silver beneath a yellow stripe of sky between the horizon and a thick grey band of cloud. The only sound came from two young children in a nearby playground. I dabbled a tentative trainer in the clear, calm water that lapped almost imperceptibly over the thick pebbles that made up this immaculate beach. The only litter I could see on the entire strand was a slightly rusty tin badge protruding from between two rocks that read 'I don't litter! Blue Flag Beach'.

I sat down on the slipway and looked across to Scattery as the sun began to set. In the gathering gloaming it wasn't hard to imagine the Viking longships sailing up the Shannon, or the Scattery pilots' curraghs beetling around the waters at the first sign of a sail. The holy island had a faintly ethereal quality in the twilight and I had no desire to go anywhere but this beach for the time being. It was one of the most peaceful settings in which I had ever passed an evening. The sinking sun peeped out through a gap in the clouds and sent a shaft of rippling yellow light across the surface of the water to my feet and then disappeared, before flaring again between the cloud and the horizon, making the pebbles and sea wall to my left glow a rich pinky orange, one of the most beautiful colours I've ever seen. The monks on Scattery would have watched sunsets like this a millennium and a half ago, and little, if anything, of the vista would have changed since then. Maybe before the arrival of St Senan people saw sunsets like this as the fiery breath of Cathach warning them away from his island. The sun slipped below the horizon and the light turned from warm orange-pink to blue-grey. The clouds were tinged briefly with purple and pink fringes, and then the colours disappeared.

As darkness began to fall and the air to turn chilly, I took a reflective walk back to Kilrush for an evening in Crotty's. While generations of people had gone to Scattery on religious pilgrimages, Crotty's pub represented for me a pilgrimage of a musical nature.

I am a big fan of Irish music. It could be something to do with the Irish blood that sloshes around in me, but I am a sucker for it and Clare is the perfect place for suckers like me to go and find it. A decade or so ago I worked in the music industry and struck up a strong friendship with a band from Donegal called Goats Don't Shave. They were a folk-rock outfit of some repute, with a substantial following in Ireland, Britain and America. I'd worked as a tour manager for them for a while (a job that required little more than finding the cheapest flea-pit bed and breakfast in whichever town we happened to be, and booking rooms).

Open any book on traditional Irish music and the name of Elizabeth Crotty will crop up sooner rather than later. Her tunes were covered by The Chieftians among others and her death in 1960 caused widespread mourning across Ireland and prompted a telegram of condolence from the Irish president Eamon De Valera at a time when Ireland was a totally male-dominated society. If I'd bumped into a real-life Spice Girl in Douglas, then Elizabeth Crotty was her pioneering equivalent in Ireland, only without the navel piercings. Or so I assume.

Born in 1885 in the village of Cooraclare, Elizabeth Markham grew up in a musical family, developing an aptitude for the concertina. In 1914 she married Jim Crotty and the couple took over a new pub in Kilrush which they named Crotty's. Elizabeth would frequently play in the bar, demonstrating a finely honed technique and sensitivity to the tunes of the west-Clare tradition. During the 1940s and 1950s Elizabeth Crotty's fame spread across Ireland, particularly when archivists began travelling the country armed with recording equipment. She became and remains one of the leading names in Irish music, an early exponent of what Mel B and her cohorts would later claim as their own and label girl power.

A woman's place in Ireland had always been in the home. It certainly wasn't in the pub and it certainly wasn't playing music in the pub. And it certainly wasn't as president of the Clare branch of Comhaltas Ceoltóiri Éireann, the association of Irish musicians. But Elizabeth Crotty broke the mould, and she did it mainly in the pub that still bears her name. There's an annual music festival here, the 'Eigse Mrs Crotty', and most nights of the week Crotty's has a session comprising local players. The session is the mainstay of Irish music (although the pub session only developed when ex-pats in London began gathering in hostelries because their boarding houses did not allow music), and Clare is arguably the best place to find them. Doolin, a coastal town in west Clare, could stake a confident claim to be the musical capital of Ireland while Lisdoonvarna, a tiny village inland from Doolin, was the scene of a massive annual festival that attracted the biggest names in Irish music before it outgrew its location.

But Crotty's is the place to go in this part of the county. It's a proper old-fashioned pub, full of dark corners, tiled floors and snugs where reels, airs, single jigs, double jigs, slip jigs and slides tumble from assorted fiddles, accordions and whistles, just as they did when Jim and Elizabeth Crotty lived here. It was a lively night in the dim light to a soundtrack of extraordinary musicianship. Fiddle bows shot back and forth while fingers blurred over fingerboards, digits skipped over accordion buttons and beaters skittered over goatskin *bodhrans*. Flushed faces shone in the dim light in the same way they had in the Old Schoolhouse on Utsire months earlier. There are people across Ireland who display a musical dexterity and talent that should be earning them a fortune. No disrespect to my erstwhile fellow guest at the Sefton but there's little question that musical success these days comes in inverse proportion to musicality.

I walked back down to the Lodge with the reels still ringing in my ears. The boats bobbed in the marina and out on Scattery the ghosts danced a merry ceilidh beneath the sweeping beam of the lighthouse.

I was sad to leave Kilrush the next morning. Walking up the street towards the town square and the bus out of town, I saw dozens of people sitting on ground-floor windowsills passing the time of day. I waited for the bus as the shops opened for business, their fronts a vivacious combination of yellows, pinks, reds and blues picked out by the morning sunshine. In true local fashion, I parked my backside on the windowsill of Patrick Bourke Ltd, Gents' Outfitters, and looked across the square to the Central Shoe Store, Coffey's and O'Doherty, O'Kelly & Co., Solicitors. The dark façade of Crotty's loomed away to my left with its ancient Guinness signs. If I didn't know better, I'd have thought I'd walked into another film set.

I wasn't able to visit the next sea area on the list, but then until relatively recently more people had been to the moon than had been to Rockall. For a guano-streaked, uninhabitable lump of rock sticking out of the north Atlantic, the pebble thrown by Finn MacCool has had a turbulent old time of it. On the face of it Rockall, which sits miles from any major shipping route, is a pretty insignificant thing. It pokes out of the sea in the middle of nowhere. It's sheer on one side and sloping on the other, and with its grey shape striped with white droppings it can look as though someone has sunk a giant statue of Don King into the Atlantic foam. Despite this, Rockall has had nations at logger-heads, been the focus of global environmental protests and was even a pawn in the Cold War.

One legend suggests that the rock, some eighty feet across and seventy feet high, is the extremity of the ancient kingdom of Brazil, while scientists claim that it's the tip of a volcano that last erupted fifty million years ago. I'm sticking with the Finn MacCool story myself, given that he's a giant and therefore much bigger than me.

Not surprisingly given its remote location, it's only relatively recently that Rockall has even been mapped accurately, let alone visited. Its first possible mention is on a Portuguese chart dating from 1550, although whatever the cartographer marked on there he did just before getting up to go to the pub as the word was smudged. It looks like 'Rochol', although the position is very approx-imate when compared to Rockall's true location. A Norwegian chart from a century later marks 'Rocol' in a reasonably accurate position, while the first recorded shipwreck on the rock and its attendant reef came in 1686. A rowing boat full of bedraggled French sailors turned up on the remote Scottish island group of St Kilda, their gestures indicating that their ship had been wrecked against a large rock to the south-west.

As shipping traffic grew, so did the sightings and accurate positioning of Rockall. Indeed, with its distinctive shape and its coating of sea bird droppings, many ships mistook the rock for another vessel in full sail. One such hoodwinked craft was HMS *Endymion*, which was patrolling the waters north-west of Ireland in September 1811. The ship's Lieutenant Basil Hall wrote in his journal that it wasn't a ship at all, but 'a solid block of granite growing, as it were, out of the sea at a greater distance from the mainland than, I believe, any other island or islet or rock of the same diminutive size is to be found in the world. Its name is Rockall.'

Intrigued, the *Endymion* sailed close to Rockall, where Hall led a small landing party, becoming in all likelihood the first person ever to set foot there. Indeed, the treacherous nature of the rock and its environs almost caused Hall's party to come a cropper. A significant swell meant that the men were forced to jump from the rock into their dinghy, and once aboard noted that because of the thick fog which had come down suddenly they had absolutely no idea where the *Endymion* was. The *Endymion*, meanwhile, had managed to lose sight of Rockall in the murk. The men had no option but to sit tight by the rock while being buzzed by resident sea birds 'in notes most grating to our ears'. Hall posted a scout on top of the rock to look for the *Endymion*'s masts above the fog, which eventually lifted enough for the ship to be sighted. Unfortunately, by the time the scout had made the perilous journey down from the rock and back into the boat, the fog had closed in again and they were back to square one. After several hours, and just when Hall had taken the decision to spend the night on the inhospitable surface of the rock, the fog lifted and the party was rescued. It was an appropriately fraught first visit to one of the world's most remote and unwelcoming places. Hall's ordeal had its compensations, however – the ledge near the top that represents the only flat area is known to this day as 'Hall's Ledge'.

What Rockall does boast is an incredibly fertile fishing ground, and with the coming of the steamships in the 1860s the area became popular with trawlers. In 1862 the *Porcupine* became the second ship to visit the rock, while taking soundings in preparation for the laying of the first transatlantic telephone cable. According to the ship's log, a bosun named Mr Johns succeeded in gaining a footing, 'but not at the part where the summit is accessible'.

While the volume of shipping increased, so did the risks and in 1904 Rockall suffered its worst ever tragedy. The three-thousand-ton liner *Norge* was en route from Copenhagen to New York with eight hundred people on board when it struck the reef of which Rockall itself is the only visible part. So rough were the seas that nearly half of the *Norge*'s lifeboats were smashed to matchwood on launching, and six hundred people drowned. The surviving lifeboats drifted for a week, and the incident prompted discussion about erecting a lighthouse on the rock. Clearly, however, the logistics of such a project were prohibitive, and the combination of luck and the absence of busy shipping lanes in the vicinity has conspired to make the *Norge* the last significant shipwreck on the reef.

It took the Cold War for Rockall to acquire any great significance beyond a motel for itinerant guillemots. In the early days of the Iron Curtain the British were using South Uist in the Hebrides as a firing range, which prompted then defence secretary Harold Macmillan to fear that the Russians could use Rockall as a base for spying on their Hebridean pyrotechnics. Thus the British decided to formally claim Rockall as their own. The whole thing was done with a quintessentially British attention to detail and ceremony. Three soldiers and a civil servant were taken by helicopter from HMS *Vidal* and lowered on to Hall's Ledge with a Union flag, a plaque, a bucket of cement and a couple of trowels. The inscription on the plaque, which remains there to this day, reads:

By authority of Her Majesty Queen Elizabeth the Second, by the Grace of God of the United Kingdom of Great Britain and Northern Ireland and of her other realms and territories Queen, Head of the Commonwealth, Defender of the Faith etc, etc, etc, and in accordance with Her Majesty's instructions dated the fourteenth day of September One Thousand, Nine Hundred and Fifty-Five, a landing was effected this day upon this Island of Rockall from HMS *Vidal*. The Union Flag was hoisted and possession of the Island was taken in the name of Her Majesty. (Signed) R.H. Connell, Captain, HMS *Vidal*, 18th September 1955.

The four men stood to attention as the flag was raised, with Lieutenant-Commander Scott announcing, 'In the name of Her Majesty Queen Elizabeth the Second, I hereby take possession of this island of Rockall.' At that, the *Vidal* sailed past and unleashed a twenty-one-gun salute.

And so Rockall stood, a British outpost in the Atlantic, a Gibraltar for puffins, uninhabited and largely unloved for another twenty-five years until things got really interesting. By 1971 there was strong reason to suggest that Rockall was sitting on top of a great big bubbling cloud of natural gas. The Danes, Icelanders and Irish, who'd nudged each other and sniggered behind their hands at the Brits playing empires in 1955, suddenly got interested and made noises regarding sovereignty themselves. Just for fishing, you understand, nothing to do with the potential billions in gas revenue. Oh no, that wasn't it at all. In response to this, however, the British government passed the Rockall Act of 1972, which made Rockall officially part of Inverness-shire (which presumably makes the guillemots liable for council tax. The fact they haven't paid might explain why they've never had their bins emptied).

Events after this became increasingly farcical, especially when Britain imposed a fifty-mile exclusion zone around the rock and began issuing petrol-drilling rights and licences. The best bit though was when, in a terrifically British move to demonstrate sovereignty, it lowered a sentry box and two Royal Marines in ceremonial dress and bearskins on to the rock while a helicopter flew around them taking pictures. And this, folks, is what our taxes are paying for. When the Danes and Icelanders had stopped laughing, they reinforced their claim to the region by arguing that Rockall was uninhabitable and therefore couldn't be called an island, something that would prevent the British imposing their exclusion zone. So in 1985 the British government flew former SAS man Tom McClean out to the 'island' and had him live there in the middle of the Atlantic in a pod for just over a month to a constant soundtrack of screeching birds. And David Blaine thought he had it tough in a box over the Thames. There, said the British, one of our subjects lives there. It's an island, it exists, and it's ours. Take that, you chunky-knitwear-sporting, pickled-herring eaters.

With these events descending rapidly into farce I can't help wondering what Prince Roy of Sealand made of it all. The Danes and Icelanders decided that they really weren't into playing silly buggers and, like the Irish, kept a dignified silence without actually withdrawing their claims to sovereignty. In June 1997, however, Rockall hit the headlines again when three Greenpeace activists were lowered on to Hall's Ledge with a life pod and occupied the rock for a total of forty-two days. By British criteria, they argued, they'd stayed on the island longer than Tom McClean, and this made Rockall theirs. They asserted their claim by renaming the rock Waveland and declaring it a global state committed to worldwide environmental protection.

At first the British responded with the political equivalent of sticking their fingers in their ears and chanting, 'La la la, can't hear you,' but within weeks had decided to finally comply with the international law of the sea by giving up their claim to fishing rights of the sixty thousand square miles of water around the rock. While Britain had to cede to international law in this case, it did point out that as Rockall lies within two hundred miles of St Kilda it is still a British possession.

For me, though, Rockall will never truly be

British until it boasts a branch of Costcutters, half a dozen estate agents and a residents' association complaining that the police presence isn't visible enough.

MALIN, HEBRIDES, BAILEY

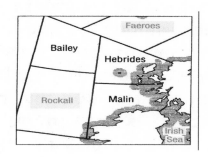

Area Malin appeared in 1949, covering half of what used to be Area Hebrides. Malin's coastal boundary stretches from Slyne Head around to Belfast, where it meets Area Irish Sea. Its northern boundary stretches due west from Tarskavaig on the Sleat peninsula in Scotland until it meets Area Rockall. In 1924 Area Hebrides covered a vast swathe of sea from the Donegal coast up to north of Cape Wrath; today it's a much smaller area bordered to the north by Area Fair Isle and Area Faeroes. Area Bailey, a 1949 addition, is a completely seabound area to the west of the Hebrides.

Driving through Derry in a hired car, I headed north from Northern Ireland and crossed into southern Ireland. It's a confusing directional conundrum, one thrown up

411

by the partition of the island in 1922. The name Donegal, Dún na nGall, means 'foreigner's fort', a title foisted on the north-western county by the English after the Flight of the Earls in the early seventeenth century. It's a curious name inasmuch as Donegal, stuck among the wild hills and mountains in the far north-west of Ireland, was never comprehensively conquered by the English. Hence the strong Catholic tradition that remains there, the second largest county in Ireland, and the reason why it was left out of the partition treaty. The Protestant-dominated counties to the east feared that any future vote on the reunification of Ireland would be swayed by the Catholics in the north-western hills.

Malin Head is Ireland's northernmost point, the tip of the Inishowen peninsula. Like Finisterre and Land's End, it's a place for solitude and reflection where the Atlantic crashes against the shore. From Malin it's a long, dramatic drive around the coast, through Creeslough, Dunfanaghy and Falcarragh, from where you can see Tory Island eight miles out into the Atlantic. Around a hundred people live on the little island, a community that fought against Donegal County Council's evacuation plans in the late seventies. The arrival of a new priest, Father Diarmuid Ó Péicin, galvanised the islanders into fighting to preserve their community and, despite the hardships associated with such a remote location, avoided its becoming another St Kilda.

Around the Bloody Foreland I drove until I reached my lodgings, a guesthouse on the Derrybeg road. The wind that seemed to be following me around the shipping forecast had ropes clanging against the flagpoles outside.

It was around 2 a.m. when the shrill sound of an alarm roused me from my slumbers. A high-pitched electronic chirrup, it went on for a good half an hour before I swung my legs out of bed and went to the window. It didn't seem to be a car alarm, it must have been coming from inside the hotel. I pulled on a pair of shorts and a t-shirt and padded down to reception. There was no one behind the desk, but on the wall next to it a small plastic box was giving it plenty, an oscillating shrillness which felt as if it were actually coming from a point just behind my eyes. I prodded at a couple of buttons but nothing happened. I went back to the room. Surely I wasn't the only one to hear it? Or had everyone else been evacuated and was now wrapped in blankets in a draughty community hall somewhere while the hotel burned down around me? I picked up the phone and dialled reception, even though I knew there was nobody there. Not surprisingly nobody answered. I pressed the button for an outside line and dialled the hotel number. After a couple of rings a woman's voice answered sleepily. I didn't know the etiquette for rousing a hotelier from their bed in the middle of the night, but surely they'd heard the alarm.

'Hi,' I said, sounding as apologetic as I could,

413

'I'm in room 110 and can hear an alarm going off.'

'Ah, sure, that'll be a car in the car park.'

'No, it's coming from inside the hotel.'

'No, it does sound like it, but it's a car.'

'I promise you it's inside the hotel. I've just been down and had a look. It's coming from the box on the wall next to reception, and it felt like someone was driving knitting needles into my ears.'

'Really? Okay, thanks, we'll check it out.'

I replaced the receiver and lay back on the pillow. Around five minutes later the alarm finally stopped, leaving a marvellous, silent void in the air. Just as I was dropping off, the phone rang. I looked at the time; it was now nearly three. I picked up the receiver.

'Erm, hello?'

'Hello, is that room 110?' It was the same woman I'd spoken to about the alarm.

'Er, yes.'

'Ah, that's grand. Just wanted to let you know the alarm's gone off.'

'Yes, I'd noticed, thanks.'

'Well, thanks for letting us know about it. Sleep well now.'

I replaced the receiver, and slumped back on to the pillow again. I'd just reached that point of almost no return, the one where you sometimes start dreaming you're falling over and jerk awake, kicking your bedfellow in the process, when there was a knock at the door. At first I thought I was dreaming and ignored it, but no, there it was again. I climbed out of bed and stumbled to the door. The light from the hallway flooded in, I blinked a couple of times and saw that there was a man in his fifties standing there in a vest and tracksuit bottoms. His wispy hair was smeared all over his cranium and his eyes had that puffiness of a man recently awakened from a deep sleep.

'Sorry to disturb you,' he said, 'but was it you that reported the alarm?'

'Yes, it was me.'

'Ah, that's grand, well I've stopped it now.'

'Yep, I'd noticed.'

'Yes, well, I just wanted to come and say thanks very much for letting us know, and sorry that it disturbed you.'

'That's no problem. Thanks for dropping by,' I said, gently closing the door.

'You're welcome. Sleep well now.'

On a clear day it's conceivable that I could have seen my next destination from the tip of Malin Head. The Outer Hebrides have long been used as an allegory for somewhere so remote as to be practically cut off from civilisation. 'You're going to live in Sidcup? Christ, you might as well move to the Outer bloody Hebrides.' A curved chain of islands facing into the Atlantic, the Western Isles represent Scotland's last frontier. Storm-lashed and wild, the isles have fascinated travellers since Martin Martin published his *Description of the Western Isles of Scotland* in 1698. From Lewis, whose northern tip lies on the same latitude as John O'Groats, to the southernmost isle of Mingulay, roughly level with Aberdeen, the Western Isles have provided a constant barrier against the weather and waves of the Atlantic for the west coast of Scotland.

Each of the islands has its own distinct character and landscape, but my destination was inspired by celluloid rather than scenery. The Isle of Barra is the southernmost inhabited island of the Western Isles chain, and was the filming location of the classic 1949 Ealing comedy *Whisky Galore!*. I've always been a fan of the Ealing films, not least because my dad was in some of them. He went to school next door to the studios, so whenever they needed some kids running around in the background of a scene, Pa Connelly and his mates would get the call. He's too self-effacing about it, though. If it had been me I'd have opened every conversation in the half century since with, 'Of course, I've worked with Alec Guinness, Stanley Holloway and Peter Sellers, you know,' followed by something suitably crass like, 'It's true what they say: there really *is* no business like showbusiness.' I may even have affected a smoking jacket and a cravat.

Whisky Galore! probably doesn't get the recognition it deserves. For a start it gave a new word to the English language: galore, *gu leoir*, the Gaelic word for 'plenty'. It also gave the French the name of a legendary club, the Whisky-A-Go-Go. *Whisky Galore!* is a tale of David against Goliath, Celtic ingenuity against stuffy, upper-class English rule. The islanders of Great Todday find that wartime austerity has exhausted their supply of whisky when by chance the SS *Cabinet Minister* runs aground and sinks on rocks near by, carrying a cargo of a quarter of a million bottles of whisky. The island's English laird, Captain Paul Waggett, played by Basil Radford, has the insurmountable task of preventing the *faux-naïf* islanders from squirrelling away the cases, a task that finally breaks him and leaves the islanders celebrating two impending weddings and the end of their drought. It's typical Ealing, gentle, on the side of the little guy, and very funny. Behind the film, however, based on then Barra resident Compton MacKenzie's novel of the same name, is a true story. For Great Todday read Barra's closest neighbouring island, Eriskay, and for the SS *Cabinet Minister* read SS *Politician*. The true story was not quite as whimsical, however, with many Eriskay islanders ending up in prison after the affair, often on the flimsiest evidence.

Beautiful as Barra is, its history is tinged with hardship and tragedy. From 1427 until the 1830s the island had been the property of the Clan MacNeil, their castle sitting on a rock in the middle of Barra's natural bay at Castlebay. They must have been up all night coming up with that name for the settlement. In 1838, clan chief Roderick MacNeil's debts grew to such an extent that he lost the island to creditors, who sold it on to

Lieutenant-Colonel John Gordon of Aberdeenshire, who also acquired North Uist, Benbecula and South Uist for a total of £120,000. This meant that Gordon now owned the southern half of the Western Isles, which he planned to turn into enormous sheep farms and hence make a great deal of money. There was only one problem though. There were people inconsiderate enough to be living and working exactly where he wanted his sheep to roam. There was only one thing for it: they had to go.

These days Gordon would have had to come up with a substantial relocation package. Display boards full of artists' impressions of soon-to-be-built mock-Tudor semis, and tables smothered with brochures shouting 'We pay your deposit!' in big letters would be set up in a community centre. Bookish men in suits would go from door to door offering residents twice the going rate for their properties. But this was the 1830s when there was no such namby-pamby shilly-shallying. Instead Gordon just sent the boys in. A ship was moored in the harbour while big blokes went around hammering on doors and manhandling islanders on to the boat. Old people were given the choice of leaving or being stranded on the island with the roofs of their houses removed. Men, women and children were prodded aboard with guns. More than two thousand people found themselves suddenly on board a creaky old hulk bound for Quebec, where they would arrive homeless, jobless and penniless. It was an extraordinarily brutal clearance of a quiet fishing and farming community by an absentee landlord, one that ensures the name John Gordon will ring down the centuries on Barra for a long time to come.

The sheep farms failed, news that might have cheered the exiled Hebrideans across the Atlantic. Or perhaps not. In one final attempt to profit from his disastrous, inhuman venture, Gordon offered his islands to the British government for use as penal colonies. They were, after all, nearer than Australia; but the government turned him down. In the ensuing years the community gradually began to rebuild, but it took until the 1930s for Barra to restore anything like its former glory, only for the outbreak of the Second World War to see a return to austerity. Hence when one night in February 1941 a ship went down in Eriskay Sound between Barra and its neighbouring island, the islanders saw it as another example of the providence of the sea, *cuile Mhaire*, Mary's treasure chest.

The eight-thousand-ton SS *Politician* had been steaming between Liverpool, Manchester, New Orleans and the West Indies for most of the war. German U-boats patrolled the southern waters, but the northern route through the Hebrides meant that cargo ships had a decent chance of crossing the Atlantic if they went like the clappers. When the *Politician* left Liverpool on February 4, 1941 she had more than a quarter of a million bottles of whisky on board bound for

America, and as the shipment was for export only there was no excise duty payable. In the middle of the night, with the crew thinking they were further south than they actually were, the ship ran aground. Once the men had been taken off the stricken ship to safety, the islanders began to explore the hold and before long cases of whisky began disappearing. The salvage question was murky – it took weeks to decide that the ship that became affectionately known to locals as the *Polly* could not be refloated and repaired. During this period it was unclear whether the local population could claim salvage rights. However, they had no concern with receivers of wrecks and endless paperwork.

Local customs chief Charles McColl, on whom the Waggett character is loosely based in the film, saw it differently, however. To him, the local men sailing away from the *Politician* in boats laden with crates were thieves pure and simple, and he commenced a single-minded, merciless campaign to recover the contraband and bring the culprits to justice. McColl raided nearly every house on Eriskay, confiscated boats and patrolled the waters around the forlorn ship, until thirty-five men and one fourteen-year-old boy were arrested and charged. Even being found wearing oily clothes – the hold in which the whisky was stored was drenched in spilled oil – was, in McColl's eyes, enough to prove guilt. In the end, to the horror of the community, twenty Barra men were sent to prison in Inverness for periods of between twenty days and three months. Most of the whisky was never discovered, having been secreted in every possible nook and cranny of the island. Under floorboards, down rabbit holes, sunk in tidal pools, the stuff was everywhere.

That would have been the end of the story were it not for the fact that the English novelist Compton Mackenzie had set up home on Barra. His fictional account of the tale was published as *Whisky Galore!* in 1948, and the Ealing film version followed a year later.

It's a five-hour ferry crossing to Barra from Oban, one of the longest in the British Isles. Britain was experiencing unseasonably fine weather, and as the Caledonian MacBrayne ferry picked its way between the Inner Hebrides, the sun brought out the bright green of the hillsides and the sparkling blue of the water. A dolphin swam alongside us for a considerable time, with us passengers oohing and aahing at its plunges and tumbles, totally failing to interpret them as 'Stop applauding, you gormless twats, there's a child trapped in a well over there'.

If ever a journey needs a soundtrack of slow airs played on the bagpipes, and let's face it, most of them do, sailing into Castlebay Harbour is one of them. The island rises up behind the little town of grey stone buildings, but what makes the panorama so special is the castle built on a big rock in the middle of the bay: Kisimul Castle, the ancient seat of the MacNeils. I was booked into the imposing Castlebay Hotel, overlooking the harbour. Being a lone traveller of course, instead of having a room with a sweeping maritime vista dominated by an ancient castle, I was at the back of the building with a sweeping refuse vista dominated by wheelie bins. I also noted for the first time another unwritten rule of hotel rooms: the further the television is from the bed, the less likely it is that there'll be a remote control.

I took a quick walk around the town, and rounding the corner of the main street down to the harbour couldn't work out at first why I recognised it. I'd never been here before yet the row of old buildings sloping down towards the quay, looking out to the bay and the castle beyond looked very familiar. Then it dawned on me. Of course, stupid: *Whisky Galore!*. Where I was standing was almost exactly where the camera had been set up for the opening shots of the film, over which a booming voice intones, 'Whisky. *Uisge beatha*, the water of life. And to a true islander life without whisky is just not worth living.' Walking down past the shopfronts I noticed a plaque dedicated to the film's producer, Alexander Mackendrick. Perhaps appropriately given the success of the film in the half century since its release, the plaque is affixed to the wall of the Barra branch of the Royal Bank of Scotland.

The next morning I was up and away early to catch the ferry to Eriskay. Eriskay, the location of the real whisky galore story, is a short ferry trip across the sound from Barra. The ferry leaves from the other end of the island, and if you're up and about early enough you can get a lift in the van with the island's postman. Of course, this got me to the ferry terminal an hour and a half early. Not to worry, I thought, it's a ferry terminal. There'll be a café, I'll be able to buy a paper, it's a nice day, I'll sit outside in the shade sipping a latte and catching up with world events.

Me and my fancy city ways. The postman, who'd raised his eyebrows slightly and glanced at his watch when I'd said where I wanted dropping off, roared off into the distance having left me on a big patch of gravel by a concrete slope that led down into the sea surrounded by a big old silence. No latte, no newspaper, no nothing. There was a locked Portakabin nearby, with a notice taped to the door announcing a planning application for a building, but that was it. The only buildings in view adjoined the airstrip about a mile away. I sat down on the gravel and waited, with nothing to do but watch the slow progress of the sun across the sky. After a few minutes, maybe even hours, I don't know, there was a buzzing overhead and a Twin Otter plane came lolloping out of the clouds. I watched as it banked right and commenced its final approach to the most unusual runway in Britain. Barra's is an airport like no other, for its runway is a cockleshell beach. Aircraft have been landing on the vast white expanse of crushed shells since the thirties, and Barra is believed to be the only beach airport serving scheduled passenger flights in the world. The plane descended with frankly alarming speed and touched down in a swirl of spray. A second or two later, the sound of the landing reached me, a sound reminiscent of the backwash of a wave that's just broken on to a pebble beach. The chances are that that plane had left Glasgow after I'd left Castlebay, covering 140 miles to my five. The chances are that the people disembarking from the plane had got out of bed later than me that morning too.

Somehow I passed the time before the ferry chugged around the headland (did you know that there are 3,763,461 pieces of gravel by the Ardmore jetty on Barra?) and we departed for Eriskay. There's a community of around 150 people on Eriskay, an island boosted by the construction of a causeway to nearby South Uist and the intro-duction in 2003 of the ferry service to Barra. Once practically cut off from the other islands, Eriskay (which mean's 'Eric's Isle', although no one's exactly sure who Eric actually was. My money's on Sykes) is now linked to its neighbours to the north and south, and after an almost catastrophic decline during the twentieth century the population is beginning to rise significantly again. There were around a dozen of us sitting in the sun on the upper deck and about half a dozen cars on the main deck below. Only a few months before we would have had to take a ferry up to South Uist and a bus down along the causeway; a journey of hours now cut to forty minutes.

For such a small island Eriskay has a disproportionately significant place in history. As well as the whisky galore saga, Eriskay was also the place where Bonnie Prince Charlie first set foot on Scottish soil. The ferry from Barra pulls in next to a beautiful white sandy beach called Coilleag a Phrionnsa, the Prince's Beach. It was here on July 23, 1745 that Prince Charles Edward Stewart disembarked from the French ship *D'Oueteille* and set about raising an army for the Jacobite rebellion. Having grown up in Rome, speaking no Gaelic and very little English, let alone having any military experience, he was an unlikely leader. The nickname 'Bonnie' probably didn't exactly strike fear into the heart of adversaries either. It's easy to imagine him hiding in a cave somewhere with Flora MacDonald one cold night before returning to exile, a small warming fire lighting his pained expression as he lamented not being nicknamed 'Mad Dog' or 'Bad Mo-Fo'. Yet after his arrival on Eriskay he managed to assemble a Highland army and march on London before inexplicably turning back at Derby. I've been to Derby, and while it would never make my list of top ten groovy places I didn't think it was that bad. Crushing defeat at Culloden in 1746 put an end to the young pretender's claims to the throne and he spent the ensuing years on the run, eventually returning to France and dying in Rome, leaving a string of aggrieved lovers in his wake.

There's a stone cairn on the beach now to mark the spot where the Bonnie Prince came ashore. There's also a rare pink flower that grows there known as Prince's Flower; according to legend it first grew from seeds that fell from the royal pockets as he alighted. I thrust my hands into my own pockets and reflected that this particular Charlie (if I say so myself, I do have a fairly regal bearing and in certain lights can appear distinctly bonnie) had no exotic flora to contribute to Eriskay, just some small change, a Boots receipt for insect repellant and an empty packet of wine gums.

It's a steep climb from the jetty to the cluster of houses that make up the nameless 'Village' (it briefly crossed my mind to decamp to Eriskay and start up a newspaper purely so I could call it the *Village People*), a walk that leads eventually to the island's community centre. It was a hot, dry day so the sign outside that read 'Teas' drew me inside. I sat at a table facing a giant framed photograph of the *Politician* while three children played a noisy game of pool near by, drank a refreshing cup of tea and looked aimlessly out of the open door across the scrubby *machair*, the sandy grassland that covers most of the Outer Hebrides. I wondered how many of the bottles liberated from the *Politician* were still out there somewhere. One thing's for sure: in the unlikely event that I'd stumble across one on my short visit to Eriskay I could clean up – eight bottles went for £4,000 at Christies, and that was back in 1987. And bear in mind the stuff's now undrinkable.

Revitalised by the tea, I set off in search of stronger sustenance. Despite its boozy heritage, the island's pub, inevitaby named the Politician, opened as recently as 1988. If there was nothing to see of the original incident – the *Politician* itself is on the sea bed, invisible even at low tide – I would at least have a whisky on the island of *Whisky Galore!*.

It was mid-afternoon when I pushed open the door of the Politician and presented myself at the bar. A young girl appeared and gave me a smile so lovely I might never have left the island. 'What can I get ye?' she asked, as I stroked my stubbly chin and perused the line of single malts upturned on optics behind her. I've never been a particular connoisseur of *uisge beatha*. In the past, if it was the colour of unmilked tea and had a figure of forty or above in front of a percentage sign, that was good enough for me. I'd drunk some horrendous stuff in my time. During a period of unemployment in the mid-nineties I splashed out a whole £5.99 on a bottle of Canadian whisky, apparently matured expertly to perfection over finest beechwood. Wow, I thought, that sounds like quality gear, what a bargain. Back at the flat I poured myself a hefty splash, switched on the television to a cable station whose weather forecasts were for some reason broadcast in Norwegian by a woman wearing a bikini, and assumed my customary pose on the sofa. The blinding headache came on about an hour later and didn't go away until nightfall. Three days later.

Hence, confronted with rows of the stuff, all looking the same but with different labels, I was at a total loss what to do. Single malt, grain, or a blend of the two? How many years should it be aged? Fortunately for the smiling vision before me, I was the only customer. 'Sorry,' I said, 'I'm not really sure which one to go for.'

My eye was suddenly caught by a square-shaped bottle on the shelf below the optics. It had no label and its contents looked cloudier than one of Diego Maradona's urine samples. It couldn't be, could it?

'That bottle there,' I said, pointing, 'it wouldn't be . . . ?'

'This one?' said the girl laying a hand on it. 'Oh, aye, this one came off the *Polly*.'

My jaw travelled downwards at precisely the same velocity as my eyebrows went in the other direction. She took it from the shelf and placed it on the counter in front of me. 'It's the only one still on the island, apparently,' she said. 'At least, the only one we know about.'

'Can I . . . ?' I asked, wondering if I could pick the bottle up.

'Sure.'

I lifted it off the counter. The contents were

opaque; the glass itself tarnished. In the neck of the bottle was a cork, cracked, broken and black.

'Have a sniff of the cork,' said the girl.

I lifted the bottle to beneath my nose and breathed in gently. There was a general musk of old age, but in there somewhere was the definite tang of the water of life. A liquid over half a century old that had survived the bombings of warehouses in Glasgow and Leith, been hoisted aboard the *Politician*, had slopped around inside this very bottle when the ship ran aground and then been surreptitiously removed by oil-smeared men at the dead of night.

'I think that one was found under the floor-boards when an old house was being renovated about ten years ago.'

'Wow,' I said.

'The whisky itself is ruined now; a lot of it was contaminated by seawater and the cork went bad too. But it's an original all right, from hold number five of the *Polly*.'

'Wow.'

Eventually I came to my senses and chose a shot of single malt from the Hebridean island of Islay (pronounced eye-la), an island that boasts seven distilleries. It was smooth, musky and a far cry from the Canadian stuff that had poisoned me a few years before. I thought of the story of the forced repatriation of the Barra and Eriskay islanders to Quebec and wondered whether that head-cracking rotgut I'd consumed in south

London had been the whisky-loving emigrants' idea of revenge.

While I sipped my whisky at the bar, the barmaid pointed out other features connected to the stricken old ship that had inspired one of my favourite films of all time. At the end of the bar was a porthole, mounted in dark wood and apparently rescued from an outside urinal somewhere on South Uist. On the wall was a Jamaican ten-shilling note, a less drinkable item that was also contained in the hold of the *Polly*, and over the door was a machete salvaged from the wreck. In the corner by the pool table was a giant oval of iron, a link from the ship's anchor chain. I ordered another whisky, a large one; I was celebrating. I reached into my pocket and pulled out Harry's picture. I ordered a large one for him too. We were both celebrating. I'd come to Eriskay not expecting to see anything in particular of the historic event that had prompted my visit, just wanting to see the home of the true story. Instead I was surrounded by relics, and even had the smell of some of the whisky in my nostrils. I half expected to look up and see a young Gordon Jackson propping up the bar in his fisherman's sweater with his shock of blond hair, and James Robertson Justice taking a dram in his tweed suit, allowing himself a wry smile as Basil Radford marched in, his back as ramrod straight as his determined but frustrated expression. When the girl behind the bar started to look like Joan Greenwood, I knew it was time to go.

I boarded the ferry, took a seat up top and lost myself in a Hebridean summer reverie. A Swiss geologist called Necker had made the same trip in 1821, when it was a lot more dangerous, 'But the beauty of the weather, the serenity of the sky and the perfect calmness of the sea removed all idea of danger,' he said, and I knew exactly how he felt. About halfway across, however, my vision suddenly went cloudy and I began to shiver. Crikey, I thought, that hangover's kicked in quick. Looking around me, though, I noticed my fellow passengers pulling on coats and sweaters and realised that it wasn't the whisky, rather it was the weather. A thick sea mist had come down without warning, sending the temperature plummeting, reducing visibility to practically nothing and producing an oppressive silence that had me thumping my ears in an attempt to unblock them. The mist had come from nowhere, literally out of the blue. Where once there had been sharp, clear views of distant islands across the sparkling water, now we could see no further than ten feet beyond the handrails. My teeth began chattering and tiny crystals to appear on my clothes. The ferry rattled my fillings with its foghorn and the engines slowed to a low rhythmic purr. It was very spooky. I half expected to see a ghostly ship appear out of the murk, all ragged sails and slack rigging, sweeping past us without a sound. Our progress back to Barra was slow and careful.

Back in Castlebay gusts of fog blew gently between the buildings. The castle in the bay appeared and disappeared with each tiny breeze. As I walked towards the hotel, a man loomed out of the murk. 'Bit foggy,' I said, cheerily. 'Aye,' he said, 'I've just come in on my boat. Everywhere outside a three-mile radius of Barra is in brilliant sunshine.'

I popped into the Castlebay Bar next to the hotel, where a big screen was showing Glasgow Celtic playing a Lithuanian team in a Champions' League qualifying game. There were around thirty people in the room, most of them wearing Celtic's green-and-white hooped shirts. It struck me that I'd never seen so many Celtic shirts outside Glasgow as I had in Barra. Every washing line seemed to have the hoops hanging from a couple of pegs. Barra, like most of the southern Western Isles, is staunchly Catholic, with the huge Our Lady Sovereign of the Seas church dominating Castlebay. Had I been in the northern part of the isles, where Protestantism dominates, everyone would have been wearing the blue shirts of Rangers and becoming honorary Lithuanians for the evening.

The reason for the sharp religious divide between north and south dates back to the seventeenth century, when Father Dermit Duggan set out from the southern tip of the isles on a mission to convert the locals to Catholicism. From Mingulay, he travelled up through Barra, Eriskay and South Uist, successfully selling the Catholic faith. He'd got as far as Benbecula by 1657 when he died suddenly, and the divide has been there ever since.

Celtic laboured to a 1–0 victory. I joined the locals in a celebratory Islay whisky and retired to bed. It had been a long day and I had to be up early to catch a flight off the islands from the famous cockleshell runway. As I made the short jaunt from bar to hotel, a large lifeboat glided silently into the harbour.

In the morning, the island was still held in the cold, clammy palms of the thick fog. It was still very chilly; on the ferry the fog had caused the temperature to plunge so fast I actually heard it thump on to the deck and bounce a couple of times. On breakfast television that morning, one of the presenters held up a newspaper which had 100F! plastered across the front page. Record-breaking temperatures were expected during the day. I opened the window. It was bloody freezing outside. Nutritionists and skin experts were wheeled on to the screen giving earnest advice about drinking liquids and staying covered up. In my case that meant Bovril and a layer of thermals.

I checked out of the hotel, ploughed through the fog to wait for the postman again, hopped into the van and headed for the airport. The cockleshell beach was even more fogbound than the rest of the island. Naturally I was ridiculously early for my flight to Glasgow and as I strolled in, the previous flight was in the process of being cancelled. Someone had kindly printed out the shipping forecast from the Internet and pinned it to a noticeboard. 'Hebrides,' it said, 'south-easterly three or four, fair, moderate with fog patches.' Which didn't sound good.

Gradually my fellow Glasgow passengers began to trickle in, all receiving the news that our flight was doubtful with a resigned exhalation and roll of the eyes. We walked aimlessly in circles, raising our eyebrows at each other and puffing out our cheeks. We lined up by the plate-glass window facing the runway, straining our eyes to detect any landmarks that might indicate the fog was lifting. Occasionally a hint of a dark shape that might be a building would threaten, but was soon swallowed up again in the white wall of murk which, coupled with the white of the beach, made a pretty stark vista.

Out there somewhere beyond the fog was Bailey, a landless sea area about which I could find out not a thing beyond the fact it was named after a sandbank. I'd be passing over it on my way back from Iceland at the very end of my journey, allowing it the final tick on my mental checklist, but below me would be empty sea. No territorially interesting lumps of rock, no mad Russian admirals taking pot shots, nothing. And nothing was exactly what I was looking at as I mused upon the nothingness of Bailey.

'Why don't we all line up at the end of the runway and just blow really hard?' I speculated out loud. No one answered. I thought I was funny. I was mistaken.

After an hour of hanging about, word came through that the Glasgow flight had been cancelled. We queued resignedly to put our names down for the next one, which departed the following morning. In the meantime I'd made a new friend called Helen, who'd been booked on to a Benbecula flight in order to meet her parents in Stornoway. We caught the bus to Castlebay and checked back into the hotel where a man and a woman whom I recognised as fellow Glasgow-flight refugees followed us in. We all exchanged raised eyebrows, rolled eyeballs and a puff of the cheeks before Helen and I headed down the main street to take the little boat over to Kisimul Castle. The ferryman brought his craft alongside the quay and we hopped in.

'Were you waiting on the quayside this morning?' he asked me.

'Yes.'

'Did ye miss your lifeboat then?'

After learning of the deeds of Henry Blogg and meeting the Cromer lifeboat crew, I'd joined the RNLI, and that day I was wearing a fleece bearing the RNLI logo. It turned out that the lifeboat I'd seen nosing into the harbour the previous night was a new one en route to Tobermory from the RNLI centre in Poole. The boat had left early in the morning, and apparently once I'd been seen on the quayside in my branded leisurewear I'd been identified as a lost lifeboatman.

'Everyone's been talking about it all morning. They thought you must have had a big night on the bevvy or, ye know . . .' he glanced at Helen, '. . . got lucky, and your mates had sailed wi'oot ye.'

I'd never been the talk of a town before and, while my circumstances were nowhere near as exciting as those the villagers had come up with, I jumped out of the boat at the castle with a definite spring in my step.

Kisimul derives from the Gaelic for 'the rock in the bay'. The current clan leader, Ian MacNeil, occasionally resides there in a spartan, draughty apartment, but most of the time it's open to the public – MacNeil having leased the castle to Historic Scotland for a thousand years in return for a bottle of whisky and £1 a year. I made a mental note to approach the building society with a similar offer to replace our mortgage. His generosity didn't stop there, though. A couple of weeks after my visit, MacNeil transferred the lease of almost the entire island to the people, again a thousand-year arrangement, but this time without even the peppercorn rent. The residents of two nearby islands, Gigha and South Uist, had recently bought the leases on their isles too, but at a cost

436

of millions of pounds. On Barra, not a penny would change hands.

'He's always had the best interests of the islanders at heart, but this is quite a dramatic move for which he can really be complimented,' said Western Isles MSP Alasdair Morrison after the announcement, which MacNeil released to the island's community newspaper before telling the rest of the press. 'It's not very often you find me praising a landowner but I will certainly do so now; he's done a very decent thing.'

'He could have put the island on the open market at a time when Scottish estates are changing hands for millions of pounds,' Barra resident Jessie MacNeil told the BBC. 'That in itself speaks worlds about the man and how we see him.'

As we made to leave the castle, which dates back to 1427 and was skilfully restored by the present clan chief's father, our two fellow airport refugees arrived. This time we supplemented the eyebrow raising and cheek puffing with actual conversation, and learned that they were two civil servants from the Scottish Executive over to hear the crofters' general grievances. Had they come a few weeks later when Ian MacNeil had announced that they could have the 440 crofts on the island for free, the meeting might have gone better.

The next day the fog was, if anything, worse, but breakfast television still insisted upon what a scorcher it was going to be again, all hot sun and clear skies. Over breakfast, civil servants Douglas and Emma announced an alternative plan to get off the island, which they were prepared to let Helen and me in on. They'd booked a taxi to take them to the airport. If the flight looked likely to be cancelled, they'd race around to the jetty to hopefully make the early ferry crossing to Eriskay. At Eriskay they'd have another taxi waiting which would rocket them across South Uist to the airport on Benbecula where the connecting flight to Glasgow on to which we'd all been booked would take us off the islands. It was a good plan. On paper. Things started to go wrong immediately when the taxi didn't show up, leaving the four of us standing outside the hotel in the fog slapping at the hundreds of midges that had descended on us as soon as we'd stepped outside. How on earth, we asked as we flailed around like extras in a Chuck Norris film, had they seen us in the fog?

The taxi clearly wasn't going to show, but fortunately, just as we were about to give up hope of ever leaving Barra, a bus did. At the airport the fog was as bad as the previous day and a fresh lot of disgruntled passengers had arrived, so we hotfooted it to the ferry and just made it before they drew up the gangplank. One high-speed taxi ride to fog-free Benbecula Airport later (where the presence of a film crew served only to strengthen my suspicion that we were actually a part of some reality game show) and, hard as it had been to believe, we were actually leaving the Outer Hebrides.

One thing's for sure, it wouldn't have happened in Sidcup.

FAIR ISLE, FAEROES, SOUTH-EAST ICELAND

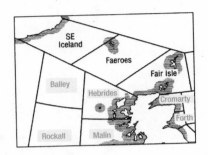

On the original 1924 map, the seas around Orkney and Shetland were marked as Area Shetland. In 1932, the area was divided into two, Orkney and Shetland, before combining again to become Area Fair Isle in 1949. Area Faeroes first appeared on the map in 1932, taking its current dimensions seventeen years later when Area Iceland was introduced. Iceland was renamed the more specific Area South-east Iceland in 1956.

My year was nearly up, and I'd timed things perfectly. So perfectly, in fact, that I would arrive home from South-east Iceland, the final area on the list, on the afternoon of October 17, deadline day. That evening I would be at my table in the Cutty Sark with Icelandic air still in my lungs, having breakfasted in Reykjavik. There would be a rosy glow of satisfaction on my cheeks and a pervading air of smugness about my person. Even more so than usual. I made my way through the streets of Lerwick early one autumn morning with a definite sense of entering the home straight.

I've often arrived ludicrously early for flights, but never so early that I've been able to get a lift to the airport from the pilot, let alone a pilot who had two other flights to make before I jumped into the plane behind him. But that's what I achieved one blustery morning in the Shetland Isles when I turned up at Lerwick bus station on Mainland, the largest of the Shetlands, en route to Fair Isle.

It was clearly too early for the man behind the counter inside the bus station, who had found me waiting patiently outside for him to open up. He switched on the automatic doors, which swept apart and allowed me in, by which time he was inside his little office donning a high-visibility jacket. His skin was pale and there were blood vessels popping in his eyes – the previous night had clearly been a good one.

'Can I get a bus to Tingwall Airport?' I asked. Tingwall was barely five miles away and I was so ridiculously early that the odds had to be good. The man behind the counter exhaled expansively, sending out a gust of last night's whisky under the window whose metallic tang almost sent me reeling across the room. One more lungful would have been enough to preclude me from driving for the rest of the day.

'Aye,' he said. 'Er, no,' he said. 'Hang on, aye, you can,' he said. 'Ah, no,' he said. Fortunately I had plenty of time to allow him to have an argument with himself. Then a thought struck him. 'Are you flying somewhere today?' he asked. Yes. 'Well, you see that guy over there?' He was pointing at a bored-looking man also wearing a high-visibility jacket walking towards the bus station in a manner that suggested he really didn't feel like going to work today. 'He's the pilot waiting for his lift; why don't you just jump in with him?'

Tingwall Airport made Land's End Aerodrome look like Heathrow. There was no Choxaway Café here, and certainly no waffles. It was nothing more than a hut containing an office, a toilet and a waiting room. The waiting room had plastic chairs around the edge, posters of nice landscapes on the wall, a desk in the corner and a low, wood-effect table on which sat copies of *Reader's Digest* and *People's Friend*. For a moment I thought I'd gone to the dentist by mistake. Inter-island flights like these are more laid-back affairs than the international ones most of us are used to. There's just one plane serving the islands from here, and before my flight to Fair Isle it had to go to the nearby island of Foula and back. Then the Islander would take me to Fair Isle and return to Tingwall before going out to the Skerries, a tiny archipelago to the east of Shetland, and returning. Then it was Foula again and finally another round trip to Fair Isle, the last leg of which would bring me back here to Mainland. Check-in times are a little more relaxed here too, hence the funny look I got from the woman who appeared at the desk in the corner when I presented my ticket.

'Ye're going to Fair Isle?' she said, face agog and holding my ticket as if I'd just handed her a two-week-dead macaw.

'Yes.'

'Not Foula?'

'No, Fair Isle.'

'This next flight's for Foula.'

'So I gather.'

'You know the Fair Isle flight's not for another hour and a half?'

'Yes.'

'So ye'll have a good hour and a half to wait, ye know.'

'I know.'

'Did ye think the Fair Isle flight went an hour earlier?'

'No, nothing like that. I'm just a twat.'

Eventually the pilot came through the door and called everyone for the Foula flight. The other half a dozen people in the room stood up and filed out to the aircraft. I sat there, flicking through a *People's Friend*. 'You coming, mate?' asked the pilot in a broad Australian twang.

'No, I'm waiting for the Fair Isle flight.'

'Fair Isle? That's not for about an hour and a half. You're a bit early, aren't you?'

'Yeah, I know.'

'Did you think the Fair Isle flight was earlier?'

'No, I'm just a twat.'

'Okay, see you back here then.'

And off he trotted to the plane, climbed into the pilot's seat, turned the plane around and took off for Foula. I could be imagining it but I'm sure that as the plane buzzed overhead I heard an Australian voice saying, 'That guy in the waiting room, guess what time his flight is?' Half a dozen peals of laughter were carried to me on the Shetland breeze. I'm pretty convinced that he actually flew around again, just so the passengers could get a good look at the back of my stupid head through the window.

I killed time by rummaging through the pile of magazines until I found one called *Scottish Islands Explorer*, edited by Linda Grieve, who it turns out is one of the seventy people who make up Fair Isle's population.

When I had heard the shipping forecast as a child, as well as conjuring the smell of crispy pancakes, the names of the areas would prompt pictures in my mind. The very sound of the words would invoke an image, usually weather-related. I'd never been to these places, I didn't even know where most of them were, but the careful enunciation of the BBC announcers would give me an impression of the area, or rather the prevailing

444

weather there. Some were obvious: German Bight would make me think of an icy, biting wind. Fastnet meant fierce gales, whipping the surface from the sea. Some were a little more obscure. For some reason Shannon meant the sun shining on a blue sea, Hebrides a drenching summer rain with the hint of a rainbow, Forth a murky morning struggling towards daylight, and Faeroes a bright, thick covering of cloud moving slowly across the sky.

Fair Isle, you'd have thought, would have been a sunny vista, a blue sky with the odd smoky tuft of white cloud. But no, despite its name Fair Isle suggested the foulest of weather, clouds as dark as night, high winds and icy raindrops flying through the air at bullet velocity. The impression I had of Fair Isle was of a weather-lashed rock surrounded by foaming seas, its handful of people hard-bitten, ruddy and suspicious of strangers.

Fair Isle is actually Britain's remotest island community. Three miles long and barely one and a half wide, it sits twenty-five miles south of the Shetlands and roughly the same distance north of the Orkneys. It's a green plateau raised vertically from the sea on sheer cliffs and, until the airstrip was built in the mid-seventies, the only way on and off was by sea. Rough sea. Very rough sea. Today, as well as the British Airways route to and from Tingwall (the national carrier's only single-pilot service incidentally, fact fans). Fair Isle is served by its own ferry, the *Good Shepherd IV*, which traverses one of the roughest crossings in European ferry dom. It puts in at the north end of the island, the only place feasible to land despite most of the community living in the south, and is heavily subsidised, a foot passenger paying just a couple of pounds for the two-hour journey. The air service is frequently disrupted by bad weather, the little propliner being easily tossed around in the wind, and when even the hardy *Good Shepherd* is confined to harbour by mountainous seas, the islanders are on their own.

Faced with the hardships of Fair Isle life, the same economic conditions which had the historic community of St Kilda far out in the north Atlantic asking to be moved to the mainland in the 1930s, the population shrank gradually from the nineteenth century until the National Trust for Scotland took over the island in the fifties. There had been as many as four hundred people on Fair Isle before the notorious Highland clear-ances in the nineteenth century, but by the 1950s that number had dipped below fifty. Total evacu-ation, as had happened in St Kilda, seemed almost inevitable until the intervention of the NTS. Since then conditions and transport links have improved dramatically, and the community today is a happy, hard-working one.

Linda's editorial in *Scottish Islands Explorer* reflected upon the changes she'd witnessed in recent years on Fair Isle. From her home she can see the south lighthouse, which in March 1998 became the last in Britain to be automated. The lighthouse has accommodation for five families, but had stood empty and dark for nearly five years. A recent renovation has seen new tenants move in, and now, she says, it's reassuring to see lights showing in the building again. Improvements have been made to agriculture, while the Fair Isle Bird Observatory continues to be a vital source of tourist income. Not only that, they are able to keep a close eye on bird numbers; global climate change has meant puffins, terns, guillemots, kitti-wakes and skuas have had trouble breeding in recent years, providing a new challenge on the traditional haven for feathered friends.

Linda wrote:

> To those not party to the detailed unfolding of life here it may seem that little changes, but the isle is not a museum piece set in time. All our actions along with outside developments and influence have an effect; some beneficial, some maybe not so. It is witnessing these changes that makes living here so wonderful.

It's around twenty-five minutes to Fair Isle by plane, and I was lucky enough to arrive on a gorgeous autumn day. The island loomed up before us, a rich green in the white-flecked blue of the sea, as we swooped in over the eastern cliffs and landed on the dirt runway which serves as

Fair Isle airfield. Fair Isle has an even more spartan airport than Tingwall: just an unmanned hut which also garages the island's brand-new, shiny red fire engine which is rolled out every time the aircraft is due to appear in the sky. A minibus was waiting to escort the five twitchers on board to the bird observatory, but I struck out on foot with the intention of finding Linda and chewing the fat of Fair Isle life.

I walked the short distance from the airstrip to the south, where most of the island community lives. The plane took off again, banking around the southern end of the island to head back north to Tingwall, the buzz of its engines diminishing into the background and leaving just the sound of the breeze rustling the grass and the odd 'baa' of a nearby sheep. Eventually I found the shop and realised that with the absence of a pub or café this was the only chance of sustenance during my few hours on the island. I bought a couple of bags of crisps, a few bars of chocolate and a bottle of water, and asked the nice woman behind the counter if she knew where I might find Linda. 'Of course,' she said, escorting me to a large map of the island pinned to the wall, which didn't just show significant landmarks, it showed every building on the island. 'Here's her house,' she said, laying the pad of her index finger below a black square on the map. 'Just carry on in the direction you're going, turn left at the cemetery and Linda's house is on the right. You can't miss it.'

She was right, I couldn't. And I didn't.

'After university I travelled around the country working as a field archaeologist,' Linda told me when I asked how she came to be on the island. 'I lived, in the Hebrides for a while, where I got a taste for island living, and moved to Fair Isle when the property that I am now living in was advertised by the NTS.

'Some of the best things about living here are the sea, which is always beautiful in all its many moods, no pollution, no traffic and no time devoured by commuting to work every day. There's no crime or vandalism; I have never locked my door in the twelve years I have lived here, and you have a feeling of worth in the community, that what you think and do has value.

'On the downside there is no secondary education for children, necessitating them staying in a hostel in Lerwick during term times.'

To many people, being stuck out on a windy rock in the North Sea would be their idea of hell. Surely there must be something special about the place to make the islanders stay?

'There is implicit trust between neighbours, and the safety to walk out alone at midnight and not worry. We're all in the same boat, so to speak, so most people try to get on with each other and not have a lot of issues circulating between them.

'You could still live traditionally from a croft but there would be no money for all the little luxuries that we now like. Most working adults have at least one job such as teaching, nursing, postmen and shop-keepers. We also have a silversmith, Fair Isle knitters, and, of course, a magazine editor. I don't think many youngsters really want to move away as most have a deep love of the island. Some return after higher education if they can make a living and get somewhere to live, while others get caught up in life elsewhere.'

As this is Britain's remotest community, I wondered whether the islanders regarded themselves as Scottish, or even British.

'Fair Isle's strongest links are with Shetland. There is remarkably little contact with Orkney as there are no direct transport links in that direction. There's not much feeling of being Scottish and even less of being British.'

Leaving Linda's house I walked back towards the lighthouse on the southern tip of the island almost with reluctance, aware that the constant procession of islands and coastal communities I was visiting had produced a mental checklist which I was wearily ploughing through in each place. Lighthouse. Check. Sea birds. Check. Dandruffy twitchers. Check. Sit on a rock and watch the waves crashing against the shore. Check. Highly agreeable sunset. Check. Struggling traditional industry and economic mainstay. Check. Notable historic shipwrecks. Check.

On St Agnes in the Scillies I'd seen the site of one of Britain's first ever lighthouses, in Arbroath I'd heard the story of the Bell Rock and on

Plymouth Hoe had scared myself half to death atop the old Eddystone Light. Since the *fyr* on Utsire I'd seen dozens of lighthouses, but I had time to kill before the plane returned to take me back to Shetland so I took a slightly grumpy stroll towards the whitewashed tower, hands thrust deep into my pockets, kicking the odd pebble into the undergrowth. On the wall was a plaque that had me chastising myself for the reluctance of my visit, for once again I'd found a local tale that put global events into perspective. I had naively assumed that an outpost like Fair Isle would not have been greatly affected by the Second World War. What use to Hitler was a three-mile lump of rock between Orkney and Shetland? I'd forgotten that the northern seas around Britain had been used as a base for warships, and that they were an important artery for shipping routes ferrying supplies to Britain, and that lighthouses like this one provided a vital navigation service as well as warning of the presence of Fair Isle and its outlying rocks. So I shouldn't have been surprised to read that in December 1941 German aircraft attacked it, killing the wife of an assistant lighthouse keeper. The following month a bomb fell on the housing block, killing the lighthouse keeper's wife, their ten-year-old daughter and an anti-aircraft gunner. The bomb also knocked out the lighthouse; a Fair Isle man hacked his way through snowdrifts in a fierce gale with aircraft still circling in order to restore the beacon, for

451

which selfess act he earned himself the George Cross.

A car pulled out through the gate and a woman smiled and waved at me from the driver's seat as the wheels crunched over the gravel and the car moved away around the corner. The housing block had been beautifully renovated by the National Trust for Scotland; it looked like a mews you'd find in Kensington only with a much nicer view. The lighthouse itself had been recently white-washed and the sun glinted off the windows of the light room. It was hard to imagine that little more than a generation earlier this had been the scene of such devastation and tragedy.

Before long it was time for me to head back to the airfield, which was deserted when I got there only half an hour before the plane departed. Admittedly, there's no check-in system, you just get on the plane and go, but I thought there might be somebody around. After a while a couple of fellow passengers appeared bearing rucksacks. The plane was due to land and take off again within ten minutes, and as the arrival time drew nearer I walked to the top of a mound and stood by the windsock, looking out into the blue sky to spot the plane as it approached. Nothing happened. Arrival time came and went, soon followed by departure time, and I was still standing there by the runway, staring into the distance like an extra from *Reach for the Sky*. There was still no sign of the plane when I heard a phone ringing inside the building somewhere. It rang and rang off the hook. A short while later one of the backpackers hailed me from outside the building. 'I say,' he called. 'I managed to find that phone which was ringing and dialled 1471. I got through to Tingwall Airport. Apparently the plane also serves as the air ambulance for the northern isles and it's been called away to take an emergency patient to Aberdeen. They're hoping to get to us today, but it might be tomorrow instead. Apparently our best bet is to sit tight and wait.'

The first thought that ran through my head on hearing this was 'There's no pub here'. Not 'Where will I stay?', 'I've got no clean trolleys with me' or even 'Crivens, I hope the person is all right', but 'There's no pub here'. I chastised my shallow subconscious as I descended from my mound and joined my fellow strandees in the little waiting room. Nick and Ellie were a couple from the Peak District who had been staying with friends in Shetland and popped over to Fair Isle for a spot of camping. Every winter they rent out their house and head off to Asia or South America, and for the ensuing hours they regaled me with tales of being airlifted out of several South American countries when armed insurrection had broken out around them. They were a gentle, softly spoken couple, but rebellion just seemed to follow them around. I realised that I could probably keep track of their movements during the coming winters just by noting the whereabouts of global *coups d'état*.

As we sat there in the little airport hut I half expected the door to burst open and a renegade band of cigar-toting militant crofters to enter and announce they had taken Fair Isle by force and were imposing martial law. A group to put the 'baa' back into Baader-Meinhof.

The hours ticked by. Tingwall had told Nick that if the plane was coming it would have to be there by the time it got dark. The sky was beginning to bruise and there was still no sign of anything beyond a few bad-tempered gulls. There was a crunching of gravel outside – a car was pulling up. I had learned from Nick that as Fair Isle had no roll-on roll-off ferry service, the cars here were exempt from road tax. No wonder everyone in a car smiled and waved at outsiders; there was an unspoken 'Hiya, suckers' behind every grin. A middle-aged woman pushed open the hut door. 'Are you waiting for the plane?' she asked, and was answered by three nodding heads expecting bad news. 'Aye, well, it should be here in twenty minutes.'

If I'd had my hat with me I would have thrown it in the air. A man with a mop of curls and matching beard so unruly it could surely only be cropped by shears climbed out of the passenger seat, disappeared into the garage and emerged pulling on a fireman's jacket. I recognised him as the man I'd sat behind on the flight out this morning, when he'd been wearing a similar jacket marked 'HM Coastguard'. When your community

454

is just seventy strong I guess a certain amount of doubling up has to be done when it comes to sharing out duties. Another car arrived. Suddenly the airfield was humming with activity. Two more men got out and joined their colleague in donning firemen's jackets. They climbed into the fire engine, started it up and sped off up the runway in a cloud of dust. They did two full circuits of the airfield at high speed, during which I asked the man with the beard whether it was really a good idea to mess about like that with a plane due at any moment.

'Och, no,' he replied, 'they're scaring away the sheep. A couple of years ago the plane hit a lamb that had run on to the runway as it made its final approach. Buckled the front wheel completely, it did. Cost twenty grand to repair the damage, not to mention the disruption to the service. Didn't do the sheep much good either. The Civil Aviation Authority made us build that new fence on the other side of the runway there to keep them off.'

Before long, a light appeared in the murky sky. As it drew nearer the light sprouted wings and soon came into land. Within ten minutes we were airborne and heading away from Fair Isle in the gathering gloom.

Back in Lerwick, Nick, Ellie and I decided to get something to eat and opted for a fish and chip shop near the harbour. I noticed that there was no cod on the menu. I wondered aloud whether this was connected to the crisis in the fishing industry which had sowed the seeds for the journey that brought me here. 'No,' said Nick, a veteran of visits to Shetland, 'it's just that cod's a bottom feeder, so they won't eat it here. They prefer healthier fish.' I nodded sagely, impressed at the dietary habits of the Shetlanders but wondering how this tallied with the 'deep-fried pizza' listed just below the haddock and plaice on the neon-lit menu.

Later that evening I headed for an upstairs bar by the harbour where a traditional Shetland music session was cranking itself into action. I was soon captivated by the flying fiddles, accordions and piano in the corner of the room. My rapt gaze and the way my jaw hung open presumably heralded how stunned I was by the playing, because an old man with wispy white hair leaned over and said, 'You think this is good? Are you going to see Calvin tomorrow night?'

The only musical Calvin I knew of was the rapper Snoop Doggy Dog, and somehow I didn't have the old man down as a disciple of da hood, let alone one on first-name terms with the Snoopster. Calvin, it turned out, was Calvin Vollrath, a Canadian fiddle player who was stopping off in Shetland en route to a tour of Sweden. He had played in the islands a couple of years earlier and had been captivated by the Shetlands and their astonishing fiddle players.

It's the remoteness of Shetland that has led to its distinctive music and culture. You'll see the

Shetland flag – a white cross on a light blue background – far more often around the place than the Scottish saltire. There's a definite Norse influence here, after all the Shetlands are closer to Bergen than they are to Aberdeen, while London and Reykjavik are practically equidistant from Lerwick. Later that evening I got hopelessly lost on my way back to the guesthouse and while squinting at a streetmap beneath a lamppost noticed that most of the roads have Norse names: King Harald Street, St Olaf Street, St Magnus Street, Thorfinn Street. Indeed, the islands were a Norse possession for around six hundred years until being given to the Scots in 1469 to finance a Norwegian royal marriage dowry.

Lerwick itself was established in the seventeenth century when Dutch herring fleets put into the natural harbour, and it soon developed into a major fishing centre. It was Hanseatic traders who first introduced the violin to the islands in the eighteenth century, which the islanders adapted to their ancient Norse musical traditions rather than, as you might expect, Celtic ones. The isolation enabled Shetland musicians to develop their own style of playing, with the Scottish influence of the accordion, piano and guitar arriving only with the expansion of shipping in the nineteenth century.

By the 1960s, however, the proliferation of rock 'n' roll meant that the fiddle tradition in Shetland was in serious danger of dying out. It took the concerted efforts of a fiddler named Tom Anderson to cajole young people into taking up the instrument, travelling to schools in order to teach local kids, and it was one of Tom's old pupils, Aly Bain, who catapulted the Shetland fiddle on to the international stage. Bain moved from Lerwick to the mainland and began by accompanying Billy Connolly around the folk clubs of Glasgow before forming the Boys of the Lough, a band still going strong more than twenty-five years later. In addition Bain took his fiddle on television, travelling the world making documentaries that gave a global aspect to a style of music that once existed among only a few old men gathering in draughty village halls. Today, music is thriving in Shetland, with young bands like Hom Bru and Fiddlers' Bid emerging as natural successors to Bain. Indeed, if you only buy one album of traditional music in your life, make it Fiddlers' Bid's *Da Farder Ben Da Welcomer*.

As I meandered through the streets trying to find my bed, I vowed to secure myself a ticket to see Calvin Vollrath the following day. Lerwick is a comparatively small town of around eight thousand people, roughly half the islands' population, but its network of tightly packed streets and steep *closes* – the sharp, narrow inclines that stream away from the harbour providing shelter from the elements – are easy places in which to lose your bearings. No wonder Lerwick was once a smugglers' haven; the customs men didn't stand a chance in these streets.

Admittedly I had taken a drop or two during the evening, but it still took me forty minutes to find a destination that was actually barely five hundred yards from the tapping feet in the pub.

The next morning I was out early into the drizzle destined for High Level Music, the instrument and CD shop above a chemist that's the first port of call for any Shetland music enthusiast. They had no tickets for Calvin Vollrath left. The man in the shop even produced an empty plastic tub from beneath the counter to prove this. Either ice-cream gluttony is seen as an acceptable substitute for an evening of music in Shetland or this was where he had kept the tickets before he'd sold them all.

'Try the camera shop across the street,' he suggested, having shown me the ice-cream tub from all angles, 'they might have a couple left.'

I drew a blank at the camera shop too. 'We had a phone call that a lady had returned a couple of tickets to the Shetland Hotel,' said the girl behind the counter. 'You could try there.'

I walked around the harbour to the Shetland Hotel, a modern, boxy construction which was clearly a product of the oil boom of the seventies. This was where the gig was happening, but the rumours of returned tickets proved unfounded. 'You could try the Shetland Accordion and Fiddle Club,' said a helpful young man in a tartan waistcoat at reception. 'They're the organisers. I think the guy who runs it is at Leask's, the travel agent by the harbour.'

So, I'd tried a music shop, a camera shop and a hotel in search of tickets, now a travel agent represented my last hope. I threw myself on the mercy of Peter Leask, pleading to be admitted as a member of the press. 'Aye, you'd be more than welcome,' he said. 'Can't promise you a seat, but feel free to come down.'

I could have kissed him. I didn't though – his beard looked all prickly for a start – but it was with some degree of relief that I repaired to the Havly Centre, a community-centre-cum-café for the vast number of Norwegians who pass through Lerwick either on business or for pleasure. Once I'd stepped into its warm interior I could have been back on Utsire. The wood panelling around the walls, the tapestries, the photographs of old Norway, the warm smell of treated wood and strong coffee, even the tablecloths could have been straight from Dalanaustet. When I presented myself at the counter I heard Norwegian voices chattering from the kitchen beyond until eventually a woman appeared and served me with a steaming mug of coffee. 'Not a very nice day,' I said as she handed me my change.

'Oh, it is a nice day,' she beamed, 'it's a lovely day.'

Norwegian humour, I thought above the spatter of the rain on the window.

'Every day is a nice day,' she said. 'Every day is a lovely day because the Lord made it.'

That evening it might still have been a lovely

day as far as the Lord was concerned, but from my point of view it was wet, windy and miserable. Fortunately, for the next few hours I would be in a nice warm room containing a bar, three hundred people and a rotund Canadian fiddler called Calvin. Having used that classic gatecrasher's line 'Peter said it was okay', to secure entry, I struck up a conversation with one of the organisers. Earlier that week he'd been to Edinburgh where the Shetland Accordion and Fiddle Club had picked up the award for Best Folk Club at the Scottish Traditional Music Awards. 'We're quite a small club,' he said, 'and we were up against some fierce competition from big clubs in the Scottish central belt so we're delighted, as you can imagine.' He nestled the engraved silver dish in the crook of his arm as if it were a newborn baby; I got the impression that this was an achievement on the scale of Torquay United winning the FA Cup.

'The fiddle-playing revival has been a remarkable success in recent years,' he added. 'In fact next week we've got our annual Young Fiddler of the Year competition. The only drawback is that the growth in fiddle playing has been at the expense of the accordion.'

Eventually I took up a position at the back of the room and prepared to be assailed by the sounds produced by horsehair on catgut and leathery bellows. Now, I consider myself to be a reasonably hip and groovy kinda guy. I'll never be a high priest of fashion, granted, but I select my trainers carefully, never buy clothes in Burtons and saw Blur when they were just the best band in Colchester. I once skilfully avoided being the drummer in a Sigue Sigue Sputnik offshoot band (it was close for a while there though, I have to admit). An evening of fiddle and accordion music should, by rights, have had me leaving the Shetlands on principle, stuffing pages from the *NME* in my ears as I went. When I once scratched a living playing bad guitar and caterwauling around the pubs of Hackney and Stoke Newington, accordion jokes would soon appear whenever fellow musicians gathered. What's the difference between an accordion and a trampoline? You take your boots off to jump on a trampoline. How do you get two accordionists to play in tune? Shoot one of them. What's the definition of an optimist? An accordionist with a pager. Oh, how we'd laugh as we'd sit on our amps exchanging such ribaldry while waiting for somebody, anybody, to come into the pub so we could start. Yet here I was at a concert of accordion and fiddle music that I had spent most of the day ensuring I'd be able to get into and I didn't feel like a geek.

Maybe it was because these people weren't English. I don't know why, but the English have a curious, heartfelt disdain for their traditional music. Mention folk music to most English people and phrases like 'chunky jumpers', 'finger in the ear' and 'a right load of old wank' won't be long in following behind. Yet up here, as in the rest of

Scotland and most of Ireland, there is at worst a genuine respect and at best a rampant enthusiasm for indigenous music. The support acts that night were mostly groups of local teenagers in tracksuits and baseball caps, the same kids I'd seen hanging sullenly around the chip shop the night before, probably debating whether to have another slice of deep-fried pizza. Yet when they finish listening to Eminem, they unhitch the clasps on their accordion and fiddle cases, rosin up their bows and belt out a few rollicking tunes. Not only that, they then go up on a stage in a local hotel and do it in public. I can't for the life of me imagine that happening where I live – say the word 'bow' to the pasty, Burberry-capped youths of my neighbourhood and they'll probably reply 'selecta', then spit on your shoe and tag your garage door with a spray can. A squeeze-box to them is most likely to be something a local girl of a certain reputation might allow them round the back of the chemist if they play their cards right.

Yet for a full hour a procession of young Shetlanders trooped to and from the stage with accordions and fiddles and produced some breathtaking playing that combined technique, passion and sensitivity. And these were no nerds with their top shirt buttons done up and their school shoes on, these were normal, everyday kids with the labelled sportswear to prove it.

Just before the break, a band led by twin accordions (a phrase that until recently would have had me scrabbling at the window to escape) took to the stage, led by a balding man with catfish lips. He was outstanding; a true virtuoso. I always think that a musician has mastered his or her instrument when it seems to become part of them rather than a separate entity. A master player can, having perfected their technique, concentrate on the emotion and passion of the piece, coaxing notes from the instrument as readily as breathing, treating it as an extension of their own body. His playing held the crowd, a cross-section of society from white-haired pensioners to toddlers, via men with Glasgow Rangers shirts stretched over their beer bellies and teenage girls in crop tops, completely enthralled. When he pulled a solo slow air from the bellows that dripped with melancholy, I looked out of the window into the darkness of the harbour. A solitary trawler chugged past, heading out into the North Sea, the tune seeming to encapsulate the hardships and perils of life around Shetland.

Calvin Vollrath had several tough acts to follow, and he succeeded. A big, bespectacled man, his size and girth made the fiddle look tiny, as if he had a wooden spoon under his chin. The nimbleness of his fingers as they drummed over the fretboard belied the frying-pan size of his hands, while his right arm flew backwards and forwards with a languidness out of keeping with its velocity. Accompanied by a pianist and guitarist, the giant Canadian played for two hours. Although he comes from the North American fiddle tradition that encompasses old time and swing, his repertoire covered most of the northern hemisphere. Several times he expressed his deep awe of Shetland music, and when he called local champion fiddler Brian Gear up to the stage for a duet their styles combined perfectly; a coming together of cultures and musics from both sides of the Atlantic.

The tunes still filled my head as I descended the stairs for breakfast the next morning, my last on Shetland. A cock-up in my transport arrangements – for once not my fault – had meant that instead of strolling to the harbour to catch a boat to the Faeroes (a perambulation described as a 'lang whack' by the woman running the guesthouse – it took a couple of days for the penny to drop that she meant 'long walk'), I had to fly to London. As I tucked into a breakfast heartier than Papworth General, a voice on the television news in the corner said, 'And now we go live to our correspondent in the Shetland Isles.' Someone turned up the volume and a man in a wax jacket holding a microphone stood leaning into a wind that made his carefully lacquered hair look like that of Medusa.

It turned out that fierce storms in the south of the islands had caused several landslips during the night and the road south was completely blocked for about five miles. The road south, of course, being the road to the airport. Things were worse for people in south Mainland though. The land-slips had not only cut off the main artery through the slim island, they had also fractured water mains, not to mention the damage to fences and the sheep that had been swept into the sea. The storm hadn't been forecast; perhaps if it had, the devastation might have been less extensive. But there had been nothing, not even in the late-night shipping forecast, to suggest what was on its way. (Incidentally, listeners to the shipping forecast would have had a better idea that the great storm of 1987 was approaching than those who watched Michael Fish's televised forecast.)

The following day the road had somehow been made passable, and the bus down to Sumburgh Airport could at last get through. The landslips had been the result of some of the worst weather conditions the islands had seen for a very long time. For three hours in the middle of the night, ferocious storms had lashed the area, with many of the slides believed to have been caused by lightning striking the ground. Bottled water had been airlifted in to the stranded residents of the south and a bridal party had to be taken to Lerwick by coastguard helicopter in order to make the nuptials. The bus snaked around the hills, and I lost count of the landslips when they reached double figures. It was a remarkable sight. Huge brown gouges in the hillsides, muddy smears that produced vast hillocks of earth and rock at the bottom of the slopes and in the sea itself. It was such a jaw-dropping vista that I failed even to raise a smile as we passed the direction sign for a village called Twatt. In Sandwick, the largest village in the south, hundreds upon hundreds of bottles of water stood stacked on pallets in the car park. Giant, blue, bell-shaped containers had been placed near by, from which locals filled plastic containers with fresh water. Everywhere mud-spattered Land Rovers and diggers skidded around the slimy roads. Giant clods of earth, many six feet across and still topped with turf, lay by the side of the road, often with wire fences tangled around them that had been swept away as easily as cobwebs. The bus edged through the gaps dug by earthmovers and diggers, sliding gingerly over the caterpillar-track imprints. Having this road open within twenty-four hours of such a major incident was a remarkable achievement on the part of the Shetland authorities and emergency services. 'It's a complete disaster,' one elderly Shetlander had said on breakfast television news that morning, 'I've not seen anything like it in my life.' As the bus rounded the headland beyond the worst-hit area, I looked back at a landscape scarred with deep brown furrows hundreds of feet long, an ancient view changed for ever by just three hours of weather.

The airport that serves the eighteen Faeroe Islands is located on the remote western island of Vágar, a considerable distance from the capital Tórshavn. This is because it's the only island with a piece of flat ground long enough to accommodate a runway, and even then it's one of the shortest in Europe. When flying with the national carrier, Atlantic Airways, for the first time, you may be struck by the frequency and enthusiasm with which the cabin staff ply you with free booze. Once you catch a glimpse of the tiny stretch of tarmac towards which you're barrelling out of the heavens, you soon realise why. From Vágar it's more than an hour by bus to Tórshavn, a journey that passes among green hills and vast basalt rock faces down which thin waterfalls tumble.

The Faeroes are roughly halfway between the Shetlands and Iceland, and legend has it that they were created when God cleaned out his finger-nails after creating the earth. It's a tough place to live, the terrain is so rocky that it's almost impossible to grow any vegetables other than a few potatoes, but the Faeroese are a hardy bunch and the population of a little under forty-eight thousand has created a thriving, vibrant nation, albeit one under Danish protection. In fact, the vegetables you buy in Faeroese supermarkets are shrink-wrapped and imported from Denmark. If you live in the Faeroes and want to buy fresh fruit and vegetables, your best bet is probably to move to Copenhagen.

I've had a soft spot for the Faeroes ever since their national team caused one of the biggest ever upsets in world football in their first competitive game. It was September 1990 and the part-time team of teachers, students and fishermen were up against an Austrian side just back from the World Cup finals. While Austria had recently played the likes of Italy and Czechoslovakia, the Faeroes had warmed up with matches against the Shetlands and Iceland reserves. Although the Faeroes were nominally at home, the match took place in Landskrona, Sweden, because at the time the islands didn't even have a grass pitch. Austria's star striker, the dubiously permed Toni Polster, had predicted double figures for his side, so of course the Faeroes played out of their skins and won 1–0; the goalscorer, a timber merchant from Sandavagur called Torkil Nielsen, has not had to buy a drink since. Which is probably a considerable relief to him given the price of booze in the Faeroes.

Being in such a remote location, the Faeroese have had to rely upon the sea for subsistence and around a quarter of the population are employed in fishing or fish processing. Just about all of what they catch and process goes abroad; in 2002, 99.6 per cent of Faeroese exports were fish or fish-related (incidentally, when I checked this with Faeroese government statistics I learned that in 2002 there were 2.5 suicides in the Faeroes. How can you have half a suicide? Couldn't they decide whether he'd really meant to do it?).

Tórshavn is a picturesque little town that lacks the frenzy of most European capitals. It's a jumble of brightly coloured buildings which seems to be expanding almost by the day. As it is the centre of

Faeroese trade, commerce and culture, people tend to gravitate towards the capital: the population of Tórshavn is around 16,500; the next largest town, Klaksvík, boasts less than a third of that figure.

I was staying in a self-catering guesthouse on the fringes of town (although at the rate Tórshavn was growing, by the time I checked out it was on the fringes no more). I was sharing my apartment with three middle-aged Danish couples who developed the frankly annoying habit of laying the table for their breakfast the previous evening and doing likewise for dinner before they left for their day's walking each morning. It struck me as rather territorial given that we were sharing the place, and I was disappointed to find that my cheery greetings were met with tight-lipped nods and terse hellos. But then if I'd had a nice apartment with a magnificent view across the harbour and found it suddenly invaded by a scruffy English bloke, I'd have got a bit huffy too. That probably didn't excuse my licking a couple of plates and replacing them on the table ready for their dinner every afternoon though.

A walk around Tórshavn is one of Europe's more pleasant urban strolls. The Tinganes peninsula to the south of the harbour is where the town began and where the ancient parliament the Alting met for the first time in 825. Indeed, until a century ago Tinganes was all there was to Tórshavn, a finger of land with a couple of quiet streets of ancient Faeroese buildings. The buildings, including the

Faeroese parliament, are of dark wood and like many buildings on the islands are topped with grass roofs to provide insulation in cold weather. 'I'm just popping out to mow the roof' may sound like a convoluted euphemism for a visit to the toilet, but it's a phrase heard in many Faeroese households during the summer months. In contrast, Faeroese gardens don't have lawns; they're covered in roofing slates. They're not really, I just made that up.

Around the harbour from Tinganes is Café Natur, the islands' first pub. Until as recently as 1992 alcohol was strictly rationed in the Faeroes, something that according to folklore dates back to the seventeenth century. Apparently, unscrupulous Danes would come over to the islands, get farmers drunk and take advantage of their inebriation to have them sign documents handing over their land, so the sale of alcohol was banned outright. Eventually you could apply to the government to buy alcoholic drink but, and this is a stroke of genius by the Faeroese authorities, you could only apply if your taxes were all paid up to date. It was the Faeroese equivalent of the Inland Revenue taking over Oddbins and only handing over a bottle of Jacob's Creek on presentation of your latest P60. But you couldn't have it straight away: the booze would arrive by boat from Denmark every three months and the country would grind to a halt for days afterwards, leaving the streets full of prostrate, pie-eyed, pissed-up but paid-up Fareoese.

Warm and welcoming though Café Natur is from the changeable local weather ('four seasons in one hour' is a popular local saying, and it's not unknown to experience sun, rain, snow, hail, dense fog and gale-force winds in the time it takes to put the bins out), the beer prices aren't. Which is a shame because the local brew, Føroya Bjór is magnificent.

As I sat and watched darkness fall over the harbour, the colourful fishing boats turning monochrome and then disappearing into the darkness, I ruminated to myself that the Faeroes are probably the closest thing we have to the shipping forecast in miniature. They certainly have the weather. On average there is rainfall, or at least some kind of precipitation, on 280 days every year in the islands. Effectively that means it's raining for nine months of every year. It's permanently windy too, as the local phrase 'he who waits will get wind' illustrates. Or maybe that's a reference to the Faeroes' meat-based diet, I don't know. The clash of cyclones means that the wind rarely comes from the same direction for long, which is how the islands earned their self-devised nickname of 'The Land of Maybe': it was almost impossible to make firm arrangements with people on other islands as the wind could tie you down for weeks at a time. Despite the wind, fog is an almost permanent fixture with a thick blanket known as *mjørki*, pronounced 'myurky', descending and lifting without warning all year round.

The Faeroes also have a closer relationship with the sea than almost anywhere in the northern hemisphere. 'The sea is our marketplace,' one Faeroese told me, a concept that has got them into trouble in recent times. People who don't know the Faeroes through football will probably know them for the controversial slaughter of pilot whales called the *grindadráp*. A few times a year when a pod of pilot whales is spotted close to the islands, boats are launched, the whales are ushered into the nearest harbour and set about with knives. The first time I heard this I found it as appalling as that simple description sounds. Photographs of blood-red water with Faeroese wading in waist deep, the surface broken by the smooth backs of dying pilot whales had me wondering what sort of primitive, backward people these were.

And then I went to the Faeroes and found out the truth for myself.

'The *grindadráp* is a tradition that dates back hundreds of years,' a Faeroese told me in Café Natur, 'but that's not why we do it. Tradition is important, obviously, but the tradition arose because of the hardships of living out here in the middle of the north Atlantic. The whales are caught for food, the hunts are strictly regulated and the meat is divided out equally among the entire population. A higher proportion of each whale is consumed than of an Atlantic cod. Pilot whales are not an endangered species: there are around 850,000 in the north Atlantic and last year the *grindadráp* accounted for around six hundred of them, so we're not even making significant dents in the population. In fact the population is rising slightly.

'The kills are made quickly and humanely with minimum suffering to the animals, and to be honest the criticism we received, which isn't as bad as it used to be, was rather misplaced. Some environmental organisations were even giving out false information about the hunts, which led to a damaging boycott of our produce in the early nineties when our economy was already suffering quite badly. Unemployment in Tórshavn was up to one in five at one stage and even banks were going out of business. It's not so bad now, and the media have started reporting on the whale hunts in a more balanced way. It's easy for people to sit in, say, London and criticise, and set up a direct debit to an environmental group to ease their conscience, but they don't know anything about us or our life here. These animals have a good life in the sea before being killed swiftly and used for food. That surely has to be better than keeping animals in cages, injecting them full of chemicals and then slaughtering them in horrible conditions, which happens in many countries but not here.

'In an ideal world this wouldn't happen. But this isn't an ideal world and life out here can be pretty hard. We're basically living on big lumps of rock at the mercy of the elements. The sea is our marketplace and we have to make the most of it. And that includes the *grindadráp*. In fact, people who object should maybe look a little closer to home. Pregnant women here are advised not to eat the whalemeat now because of high levels of mercury present, and it's not us polluting the seas and poisoning the whales.'

The next day I hired a car and drove to one of my favourite places in Europe, Tjørnuvik on the northern tip of Streymoy, the largest of the Faeroe Islands. It's a pleasant drive, but you have to keep an eye out for the sheep. The Faeroese name for their islands, Føroyar, derives from the Norse meaning 'Isles of Sheep', and even today there are thought to be nearly three times as many sheep in the Faeroes as there are people. There is a DKK1,000 fine for anyone hitting a sheep with their car, accidentally or otherwise, so I was on my guard. Faeroese sheep are notoriously litigious creatures, and what you might interpret as cute bleating actually means 'Nice car. Wouldn't it be a shame if the front wing got damaged?' Believe me, those innocent, quizzical ovine faces mask sharp financial minds fully conversant with compensation law. Where do you think the verb 'to fleece' comes from?

Sea birds are another staple of the islands and feature strongly in the Faeroese diet to this day. The bird cliffs at Vestmanna, on the western coast of Streymoy, are the Faeroes' most popular tourist attraction. The islands boast over three hundred different species of sea bird, and roast puffin remains a popular local dish. Puffins stuffed with sawdust are also proving to be a thriving cottage tourist industry for ornithological taxidermists. Faeroese law states that you can't shoot puffins. You can, however, twat them with a big stick. Skilled puffin catchers scale the treacherous cliffs twatting puffins with big sticks and fastening them to their belts for safe passage like a feathery black-and-white sporran.

Guillemots are also rife in the islands but you're not allowed to catch Faeroese ones, not even with big sticks. You are, however, allowed to catch those that have come over from Iceland. How you can tell which is which is a moot point. You could ask them, but Icelandic guillemots are canny creatures and can do a convincing Faeroese accent.

Tjørnuvik is a tiny settlement of houses facing north to the Arctic. It's surrounded on three sides by steep hillsides that form a vast natural amphitheatre of grassy layers of ancient rock, bisected by half a dozen streams of natural water that bounce down to the tiny village below. The settlement was almost entirely wiped out by landslides in both the seventeenth and nineteenth centuries, and its remoteness caused it to be used as a place of exile for Faeroese women convicted of 'immoral behaviour' in the 1600s.

I'd been to Tjørnuvik in summer a few years earlier, arriving at midnight. The Faeroese don't quite get the midnight sun (although it's light enough to dispense with the lighthouses for two months every year), and between the sea and a thick ridge of cloud viewed from Tjørnuvik was a deep-orange stripe of fiery colour. It was daylight when I arrived this time, and I sat for a while on the beach, my coat pulled around me against the wind as the waves crashed on the shore. It's quiet in Tjørnuvik; it feels as though the rest of the world is far, far away. It's so quiet, in fact, that it feels as though the rest of the Faeroes are far, far away. Nearby are the remains of a medieval Viking settlement. Tjørnuvik's sheltered harbour made it a popular place for ships to put in, and it appears the Vikings used it as a base. Twelve Viking graves were found at Tjørnuvik and in the remains of a Viking building were found traces of hazelnut shells. Hazelnuts were a popular medieval hangover cure, so Tjørnuvik was clearly once a centre for all sorts of drunken Viking royster-doystering. Shame they'd have had to wait nearly a millennium for the girls to turn up.

The Vikings had a strong influence on Faeroese history and culture, and the islands' remoteness has led linguists to believe that modern Faeroese is about as close as you get to the language spoken by the ancient Norse hordes. It took a concerted nationalist campaign to save the language from dying out when Danish proliferated, and it wasn't until 1938 that Faeroese became the language of instruction in schools. The Home Rule Act of 1948, which gave the

Faeroes a large degree of autonomy from Denmark, made Faeroese the first language of the islands, and a real effort was made to turn the echoes of the ancient past into everyday speech. This even extended to placing handy grammar hints and verb declensions on the sides of milk cartons. It's a curious, strangely poetic language, which, according to the glossary in the back of a 1948 book I found about the islands, contains a number of useful words and phrases. *Brenna krakk*, for example, means 'burning the three-legged stool after turning down a suitor'. *Fjall* is a useful verb meaning 'to go into the hills to work among the sheep', whilst *skadahvalur* is 'whalemeat sold at auction to defray the cost of damages to boats'. *Vevlingur* is 'a cord worn around the sleeve when digging for puffins' and there's also my favourite, the *skeinkjari*: that popular chap, the 'man who goes among wedding guests, offering them drink'.

As I sat on the beach at Tjørnuvik, off to the right I saw the two huge standing stones known as Risin og Killingin which emerge from the sea just beyond the headland and are the subject of one the most popular pieces of Faeroese mythology. The story goes that an Icelandic giant and a witch once visited the Faeroes and liked the place so much they decided to tow the islands back to Iceland with them. So one night they attached a rope to the northern tip of Streymoy and began to heave. Predictably it was pretty hard work, but so determined were the pair that they lost track of the time. They were so engrossed in their task that they failed to notice the sun coming up from behind the hills. Of course, being a giant and a witch, as soon as the sun's rays hit the dastardly pair they were turned to stone and have remained there ever since. At low tide you can even see the rope. As I pulled my coat tighter around myself I hoped that my journey to Iceland, the final leg of the shipping forecast odyssey, would not be nearly so arduous. Nor its outcome quite so geological.

While I wasn't actually turned entirely to stone, I did become pretty stony-faced as I waited to board the plane for Reykjavik. Stonier-faced than Mount Rushmore, in fact. They weren't going to let me into Iceland, apparently on the grounds that I had a perfectly valid passport.

'Your passport expires in December,' said a nice lady at the departure gate.

'I know,' I replied.

'Well, it's October now.'

'Mmm-hmm.'

'That means we shouldn't let you go to Iceland. If they send you back then we get fined a lot of money.'

'Why would they send me back?' I asked. I wasn't, after all, planning on seeking asylum, nor did I recall washing down any condoms stuffed with high-grade class-A drugs with my preflight coffee.

'Your passport expires in December.'

'Yes, I know.'

'It's October,' she said with a shrug.

'So they might not let me into Iceland because I've got a valid passport?'

'Well, there's only a couple of months left on it,' she replied with an almost audible derisive snort, as if I was trying to use a passport that I'd just made from the pages of my notebook with felt-tipped pens and a picture of Shirley Bassey torn from a magazine.

'I know. It's a good job I'm going home on Thursday really then, isn't it?'

She made a phone call, holding my passport as if it had a stick of dynamite and ticking alarm clock attached. A couple of minutes later an important-looking man arrived, took the passport from the nice lady and examined it for a few moments.

'Mr Connelly?'

'Hello there.'

'Your passport expires in December.'

'Yup.'

'It's October.'

'Mmm-hmm.'

'They might not let you into Iceland.'

'So I gather.' I resisted a strong urge to yank the epaulettes from his shirt and throw them down the stairs. By now most of the other passengers had edged past me and boarded. Any second now the pilot would be tapping on the inside of the cockpit window and pointing at his watch through the glass.

'Why don't we phone Iceland?' said the nice lady. So she did. After a brief conversation she put the phone down and told me, 'Iceland says it's okay.'

'Well, what a surprise that is, what with me having a valid passport and everything,' I said. Actually, I didn't say that, but I thought it. Really loudly. In fact she'd hardly finished speaking before I was hotfooting it down the tunnel to the plane in a swirling cloud of the highest dudgeon.

When I got to my hotel in Reykjavik it was past midnight. I flopped on to the bed, switched on the television and found an old black-and-white Alec Guinness film just starting. In the opening scene Sir Alec was clearly departing for foreign climes as he drove his open-topped car up to a shed that bore a big sign reading 'Immigration'. 'Morning, sir,' said a chirpy immigration officer, taking Sir Alec's proffered passport. 'Did you know your passport expires in December, sir?' he asked. The speed and accuracy with which I threw the remote control at the set was such that the off button had gone 'clunk' before the great actor could even draw breath to answer.

Surprisingly for one of the longest coastlines of any shipping forecast area, South-east Iceland didn't present me with a great number of options. A cursory glance at the Icelandair destination map before I'd left revealed that the town of Höfn was my only choice, but guidebook research suggested Höfn, which means 'harbour', might not be the most fascinating place to end my journey around the shipping forecast. 'Höfn is a fairly modern fishing and fish-processing town' was the most exciting description I could find. 'If you want to know about glaciers, this is the place to come,' I read in another guidebook. I didn't particularly want to know about glaciers, but as I wouldn't be in town for the highlight of Höfn's year, the annual lobster festival, I rather feared that I was going to. Höfn it would have to be.

Before I'd left the Faeroes I'd done a quick Internet search and found this tantalising description:

> Höfn is the main town of the municipality of Hornafjordur, one of the largest in Iceland. The area is dominated by Europe's biggest glacier, Vatnajökull. It is inhibited by approximately 2,500 people. No more information is available about Höfn at this time.

What had the place done to deserve being 'inhibited by approximately 2,500 people'? And why the sudden information blackout?

In order to keep my options open I'd decided not to book internal flights in advance. This meant that having battled my way through the sleet and strong winds of a murky Reykjavik morning I arrived for the first time in my life at an airport that did not have my name anywhere on its passenger lists intending to fly out of it. I presented myself at the ticket desk and asked the price of a return flight to Höfn.

'And when will you be travelling, sir?'

'Today please.' Ooh, I felt so delightfully spontaneous.

'I'm afraid that won't be possible.'

'Look, if it's about that passport business, it was all sorted out.'

'Passport? No, sir, this is a domestic flight, you don't need a passport.'

'Oh, okay, good, right. So why can't I go to Höfn then?'

'I'm afraid today's flight has been cancelled, sir, because of the terrible weather we're having.'

'Cancelled? Oh, s . . . suffering succotash.'

'You're suffering with what, sir?'

'Oh, nothing. In fact I don't even know what a succotash is, let alone why it might be suffering. Can I book for tomorrow instead?'

'I'm afraid not, sir.'

'Why not? I explained about the passport thing. Is it the succotash?'

'There are no scheduled flights to Höfn tomorrow, sir.'

Hmm, and the day after that was deadline day, before the end of which I had to be in Greenwich. I'd all but collected the set. I'd visited every area I could and, if I was to be a strict completist, had either sailed through or flown over Viking, Forties, Dogger and Rockall and would be flying through

Bailey on the way home from Iceland. South-east Iceland was the only area not accounted for even by my own elastic standards. The man behind the desk, probably curious as to why a foreigner might be so desperate to visit this 'fairly modern fishing and fish-processing town' in an obscure part of his country, particularly at a time when the locals weren't even dancing around a bemused lobster, had a suggestion.

'There may be a bus you could take.' He'd never be the receptionist from the Vier Jahreszeiten, but he was making a decent fist of things with little to go on. 'The bus station is about fifteen minutes' walk from here.'

Fifteen minutes later I was for the second time that day presenting myself, windswept, bedraggled and not a little squelchy about the feet, at a ticket office enquiring about going to Höfn.

'I'm afraid you missed the bus to Höfn today,' said a young woman with blond hair.

'What about tomorrow?'

'Yes, there is a bus tomorrow. It's a long journey though; have you considered flying?'

'I have considered it long and hard, but it ain't gonna happen, unfortunately. How long is the bus journey?'

'A little over eight hours.'

Eight hours on a bus. And then eight hours back. All for the opportunity to see the location of a lobster festival and look around a place about which, apparently, no further information is available at this time. What a glamorous end to my journey. I looked at the timetable. The bus back from Höfn arrived in Reykjavik several hours after I was due to land in London for a Phileas Fogg-style welcome from friends and family ('I'll be working late the night you get back so you'll have to feed the cat as soon as you get in,' Katie had told me on the phone. 'I'll try and remember to take a bolognese out of the freezer for you'). I was stuck. In Reykjavik. In the rain. And I couldn't get to Höfn.

There have been greater travelling dilemmas than this throughout history. When St Brendan and his monkish chums set out from Ireland in their coracle and rowed all the way to Iceland, bus timetables to a fairly modern fishing and fish-processing town not suiting his schedule probably wouldn't have bothered him that much. Would Stanley have reached a bus terminus, perused the timetable and said, 'Drat, if I wasn't supposed to be dining at my club on Wednesday I could have got on that bus and found Dr Livingstone'? But cold, wet and hundreds of miles from home, I was almost resigned to spending another couple of frustrating nights killing time in Reykjavik. I was cross with myself. Höfn is not exactly the African interior. There are daily buses and (usually) flights. There's a tourist office. There's a small selection of places to stay. Icelandair even has a hotel there that does a pleasant seafood buffet in its restaurant, apparently. But I couldn't get there.

In any case, I tried to console myself, Höfn, with all due respect to what's probably quite a lovely fairly modern fishing and fish-processing town, was unlikely to be Utopia. I will probably now never ever go there in my life, and I don't consider my life will be much the poorer for it. But I had spent two days short of a year chugging to and from thirty sea areas and the thirty-first and final was thwarting me. The fact that a combination of time and weather was thumbing its nose at me was quite appropriate given the place where this journey began and the broadcasting institution at its heart. But I felt a little bit pathetic as I squelched down on to a plastic seat in Reykjavik bus station. People have tried great escapades and failed – balloonists crossing the Atlantic, folk going over Niagara Falls in barrels, finding the right exit from Leicester Square tube station – and have felt no need to be ashamed of their failure. And me? Despite numerous public transport links I couldn't even get to bloody Höfn.

For the first time on the entire shipping forecast journey I felt completely dejected. I'd had low moments: getting soaked to the skin on Tennyson Down, the muddy, blood-spattered bathroom in Arbroath, the horrendously pukey trip to Lundy, but I'd never felt as low as this.' I was letting the bloodline down.

Only I could find myself marooned at the central point of a nation's transport infrastructure at such a crucial time in my journey. The clock was ticking.

Time was running out. There had to be something I could do, somewhere I could go. 'Take the *Herjólfur* ferry to Vestmannaeyjar.' I'd followed pioneering explorers like FitzRoy and Cook, and heroes like Henry Blogg, but I couldn't get to South-east Iceland even though I was actually in Iceland and sitting at the central node of its public transport system. 'Take the *Herjólfur* ferry to Vestmannaeyjar.' I was a sopping wet, windswept failure at a loss as to what to do next. 'Take the *Herjólfur* ferry to Vestmannaeyjar.' If only Harry, or someone or something could give me a sign. A pointer as to my next . . . huh?

I was sitting facing a rack of timetables and brochures. Along one shelf was a row of blue-and-yellow leaflets bearing the instruction 'Take the *Herjólfur* ferry to Vestmannaeyjar' in big letters on the front, above a photograph of a sleek-looking white ferry gliding past a rocky island on a millpond-smooth blue sea. I stood up, picked up one of the leaflets and opened it.

'Take the *Herjólfur* ferry . . .' yes, I've got that now thanks, '. . . for a new view of Iceland,' it said. Given that my view of Iceland until now had been largely though a sheet of rain from a dark sky and the inside of Reykjavik's transport centres, this was a promising start. 'The ferry *Herjólfur* is an attractive option for those who want to visit Vestmannaeyjar (the Westman Islands) off Iceland's south coast.' Off Iceland's south coast? That sounded promising.

I pulled out my guidebook and looked at the map. Sure enough, what I had previously assumed to be a grease mark left by an errant crisp crumb was in fact a small cluster of islands. I looked at the page closely. I didn't have a shipping forecast map with me so couldn't be sure these islands were inside the tramline that began at Cape Wrath and formed the western boundary of Fair Isle, Faeroes and South-east Iceland. But it was at least closer than Reykjavik; I had little choice but to go for it. The weather and transport fates had conspired against me thus far – surely I was due a slice of luck? From within my pocket I sensed Harry rolling his eyes, shaking his head and calling me a silly bugger.

I ran over to the ticket office again, the wholly inadequate and thoroughly soggy canvas basketball shoes I was wearing squeaking across the tiles as if I were standing on the tail of a small terrier with every step. I waved the leaflet at the girl behind the counter.

'I want to go here. Can I go here? Please tell me I can go here.'

'To Vestmannaeyjar? Today?' She tappety-tap-tapped at her computer keyboard. 'Yes, there is a bus leaving here in an hour that connects with the ferry at Thorlakshofn. The crossing is about two and three quarter hours, so you would be in Vestmannaeyjar by late this afternoon. What did you say? No, I'm afraid I can't marry you, I'm sorry.'

The bus ride to Thorlakshofn was treacherous. The bus was a full-sized coach that the driver struggled manfully to control in the face of giant gusts of rain-spattered wind which swept ferociously over the bleak volcanic plains. We swayed this way and swerved that way as the wind roared around the bus's extremities. It would probably be a rough crossing, I thought, remembering my Lundy experience. I consulted my guidebooks. 'The crossing can be notoriously rough,' confirmed one. 'The ferry affords a spectacular arrival (if you aren't being sick),' said the other. Oh, great.

We finally arrived at Thorlakshofn Harbour, where the *Herjólfur* was moored with her hinged bow pointing at the murky sky to facilitate the entry of cars. The scamper to the little terminal building was only about twenty yards but it was straight into the howling wind and rain. My holdall was actually lifted off my shoulder at one point, while the rain attacked the half dozen of us making for the terminal like a hail of machine gun fire. I bought my ticket, boarded the ship and took a seat in the cafeteria. Beyond the harbour wall, through the spray, I could see massive waves smashing against the rocks in giant fantails of spume. Torrents of rain spattered the windows. The wind screamed past. A seagull flew slowly by the window, flapping its wings desperately, but something appeared slightly amiss. It took me a moment to realise that it was actually going backwards.

We cast off. Even the waters in the harbour were choppy, but when we passed between the two flashing buoys that marked the harbour mouth and chugged into the Atlantic itself, the *Herjólfur* listed alarmingly to port. The sound of smashing crockery came from the kitchen behind me. Just when it seemed as though the ferry had to tip over completely, it listed hard to starboard, almost pressing my dopey, pale face against the window next to me. And so commenced the most hair-raising, nauseous and undulating maritime crossing of my entire life. No sooner had the ship completed its first alarming tilt out of the harbour than a familiar cold clamminess oozed from my skin. I knew what this meant. I scanned the walls for racks of sickbags, but instead they had only cardboard cartons, the sort that Americans eat noodles out of. They appeared to be exactly the right size to prevent them fitting into the bins, nor was there any kind of lid. No place for British reticence about bodily functions here. There was no crew member to subtly relieve you of your carefully closed sickbag like a couple of shoplifters moving merchandise among themselves. No, here you clearly had to sit with your open carton on the table while that morning's breakfast slopped around inside it, grinning sheepishly at passers-by.

As the ship, which must have been a good three or four times the size of the *Oldenburg*, was tossed around the north Atlantic in stomach-churning pitches and plummets, I remembered that laying my head on the table and trying to sleep seemed to help on the way to Lundy. I tried it, folding my cold, clammy arms and resting my cold, clammy forehead on them. It worked for about half an hour, but I soon found myself running for the gents and renewing my acquaintance with the pickled herring, cheese and cold meats on which I'd break-fasted unawares in Reykjavik that morning. I would make two further visits to shout for Hughie on the big white telephone. Oh boy, I felt ill. This was a crossing that made Bideford to Lundy seem like rowing a boat around the pond in Greenwich Park. Nearly three lurching, thumping, undulating, stomach-wrenching hours later we finally entered the calm waters of the harbour at Heimay, the only inhabited Westman island, and my stomach could start the long process of forgiving me.

I disembarked feeling, and presumably looking, like death. I was chilled to the marrow, my stomach was sore from the retching, my limbs were shaking and my clammy flesh felt as though it were hanging loosely from my bones. My rapid dehydration had given me the beginnings of a really dreadful headache. The rain had eased a little but the island was wrapped in fog (although that could just have been my eyes) and I set off from the ferry terminal in search of somewhere to stay. There were two guesthouses on the way to the tourist office and both were closed for the winter. It didn't look good. I felt ill, I was freezing cold and wet and all I wanted to do was go into a warm room, throw my bag on the floor and fall face first on to a comfy bed.

After twenty cold, damp minutes I found the street where the tourist office was. I walked up and down it three times but there was no tourist office. I checked the building number in the guidebook – 38. I found number 38. It was an empty shopfront with only a solitary carpet tile on the floor and an empty cola bottle on the windowsill to show it had ever known human habitation. The tourist office was no more. I was now even colder, wetter, clammier, headachier and generally shakier than ever; I was alone, hundreds of miles from home, and I had nowhere to stay and nowhere to go. I trudged aimlessly around the corner. There stood the Hotel Thorshamar, meaning 'Thor's hammer', something I suspected was being applied to the inside of my head at that very moment. I rummaged through the guide: it was Heimay's most salubrious and most expensive accommodation. By this time I didn't care. I went inside and enquired after a room. The friendly woman behind the reception desk quoted me a figure that would have wiped out the national debt of several west African countries. There was no way I could afford it. Crestfallen? My crest had fallen so far it was now tunnelling through the earth's crust and was last seen heading for the Mohorovic Discontinuity. The receptionist exuded a genuine air of pity and concern. I was pale, bedraggled, thoroughly fed up and now so shaky that my whole body was vibrating gently at her.

'We do have a self-catering guesthouse behind the hotel, you're welcome to stay there,' she said, quoting a rate that I could just about afford. She picked a key off a hook and bade me follow her to a building beyond the hotel dustbins and an open door from which steam and the noise of giant washing machines emerged. 'You'll be the only one here, I'm afraid, but you should be comfortable.' And with that she was gone. My mood improved immediately as soon as I set foot inside. A rush of warmth gave me a big cuddle as I closed the door behind me. I had an entire house to myself: eight bedrooms, three bathrooms and a fully equipped kitchen. I selected a warm room, threw down my bag and fell face first on to a comfy bed.

An hour's kip helped to restore the humours and immediately I awoke I felt much better. Revitalised by a couple of swigs of water and an old cereal bar I'd found in the bottom of my bag, I plundered the guidebooks for knowledge of the islands that would be my final shipping forecast destination.

The Westman Islands are among the youngest landmasses in the world. Situated a few miles from the southern coast of Iceland (on a clear day the mainland is highly visible), they are an archipelago with a remarkable recent history. Formed only around five thousand years ago by underwater volcanic activity, most of the sixteen islands are small, steep-sided and rockily uninhabitable. Heimay, where I now lay in my holiday mansion, is the largest and the only one to support a human population. It's also one of Iceland's most important fishing ports. Although there are only four thousand people living here, Heimay provides nearly one fifth of the total Icelandic catch.

Legend has it that the first settlers on Heimay were five Irish slaves who murdered their master on the mainland and fled to the islands believing they'd be safe. They weren't, and two weeks later they were chased down and killed. The islands were named Vestmannaeyjar, the Islands of the West Men, in strange tribute to the incident, strange not least for the fact that Ireland is east of Iceland. In the ensuing centuries Heimay found itself raided and plundered repeatedly. English pirates used it as a base in the early sixteenth century until they were usurped by the Danes. The most serious incident occurred in 1627 when Algerian pirates arrived under a Dutch captain named Jan Janzten. Finding little of value, the pirates turned their attention to the population. The 242 men, women and children of the Westman Islands were either murdered, raped, kidnapped or sold into slavery, with only thirteen people remaining on the island by the following year. Life on Heimay was hard. Fresh water was scarce, and with a diet consisting of seabirds and fish, illnesses like dysentery were common. In

1783 disaster struck when lava from a volcanic eruption on the mainland poured into the sea and poisoned all the fish in Westman waters.

The most famous disaster to befall the island, however, occurred at around two in the morning one night in January 1973 when the island itself blew up. Almost without warning a huge explosion opened a giant fissure along the eastern half, and fountains of orange lava began spraying into the night sky just a few hundred yards from Heimay town. Fortunately for the unsuspecting population, bad weather the previous day meant that the entire fishing fleet was in port and the island could be evacuated quickly and easily. Everyone, all 5,200 islanders save a couple of hundred people who remained to tackle the situation, went to the mainland to sit out the eruption. A few years earlier an eruption in the sea south of the Westman Islands had created a whole new island called Surtsey. Alarmingly for the islanders, who were roused in the middle of the night and dispatched to the mainland in little more than the clothes they stood up in, that eruption had lasted four years.

Fortunately the wind was coming from the west, meaning that most of the lava was directed away from the town. The initial explosion had still buried around a third of it in ash, however, while pyroclastic fragments, some weighing up to 250kg, smashed through roofs and windows, setting light to buildings. A week after the eruption, a volcano five hundred feet high had appeared in the east of the island, two million tons of ash had fallen on Heimay and a cloud of steam and gases rose five miles into the sky. It was then that some of their luck ran out. The western side of the volcano cone collapsed, sending thousands of tons of lava, at temperatures as high as 2,000° Fahrenheit, into the harbour and towards the village. Sixty homes were destroyed on the night of the collapse alone.

This was a serious problem. An isthmus of land in the north of the island had created a marvellous natural sheltered harbour. The way the lava was flowing into the sea and solidifying, the harbour was in danger of being closed up completely, not to mention the potential destruction of the entire village itself. The rescue workers had to come up with something, and fast. It was a geologist called Thorbjørn Sigurgeisson who had the idea of spraying the lava with seawater, suggesting that this would be enough to cool the moving, vibrating wall of molten rock by a couple of hundred degrees and solidify it enough to arrest its movement. It worked. Thirty-eight pumps and nineteen miles of pipe deposited six million tons of seawater on to the lava, cooling it enough to stop its progress. It was just in the nick of time too – where the harbour mouth had once been half a mile wide, now it was just two hundred yards across.

After five months scientists announced that the

eruption had fini...
begin returning to
four thousand people
apocalyptic scene. H
buried under the lava v
feet deep. In all three
completely buried wi
burned out by the vol
the fissure. But most
remarkably only one p
drug addict who died c
attempting to loot a
had effectively fought the vo...
the solidified lava meant that the islan...
grown in size by nearly one fifth. The narrower
harbour mouth even made for a better anchorage.
Not only that, scientists and engineers managed
to harness the energy from the lava to heat the
entire island for a full twelve years after the eruption. The Vestmannaeyjar landscape had been
changed for ever, with a new volcano appearing
in its midst named Eldfell, Fire Mountain, a bit
of a dull, predictable choice if you ask me.
Personally, I'd have called it Brian after a placid,
unassuming bloke I used to play cricket with who
was also prone to unexpected fiery eruptions after,
say, a hotly disputed clean-bowled decision had
gone against him. There are probably still cricket
pavilions across the South-east that have one of
Brian's bats on their roof after he'd gone off like
a volcano at some perceived cricketing slight.

vision. The only channel
ve coverage of the Icelandic
moned the strength to go out
misty and murky. A thick band
overed about sixty feet above the
ering the tops of the hills and neigh-
ts invisible. The harbour was deserted.
ólfur sat high in the water next to the
rminal, and it was then that I noticed the
d-new tourist office attached to the terminal
t I had gone straight past the minute I'd got
off the boat. The streets were as deserted as the
harbour and I walked for around twenty minutes
without seeing another soul.

After dining on pizza in an Icelandic restaurant
done out like a Greek taverna and run by Bosnians,
not to mention a glass of wine for a price that
would have got me three whole bottles of the stuff
in my local off licence, I slept long and soundly,
the best night's sleep I'd had in the entire shipping forecast.

The next morning the wind had dropped
slightly but fog the consistency and opacity of
cream cheese still clung to the hills. I set out for
the volcanic eastern part of the island, keen to
see the crater that produced the 1973 eruption.
The east side of Heimay town has a curious look
to it. Roads seem to disappear suddenly into a
steep hillside. The main road along from the
harbour rises so sharply that it looks as though
it's standing up at a right angle. This is the new

part of the island. I strolled around the edge of the lava that provides the new shoreline adjoining the harbour. Waves lapped against a fine-grained beach, while scrubby hills rose up behind and disappeared into the fog. It could have been a wintry beach scene anywhere in the northern hemisphere other than for the fact that everything was completely black. This wasn't sand, it was a strand of volcanic ash which made for a surreal spectacle. I walked along the beach with the steep cliffs opposite vanishing into the murk. When I'd gone as far as I could go I had to rub my eyes to make sure they were still working properly. With the sea grey beneath a misty sky and the beach a monochrome kaleidoscope of blacks and greys, it really seemed as if I was seeing in black and white. It was faintly unsettling: my brain was telling me I should be seeing golden yellow beneath my feet and blue sea beyond. But no, there was no colour at all. I was walking along a black beach by a grey sea under a grey sky. It started to drizzle slightly and the cloud was now so low I could almost reach up and touch it. I commenced a lonely trudge up Eldfell, soon being wrapped in the fog until I could see nothing above or below me. Damp black dust covered my ill-advised canvas shoes and clung to the hem of my jeans. Tufts of fog occasionally fell out of the sky and tumbled down the hillside, and everything was still all in black and white.

Finally I reached the rim of the crater, where

suddenly there was colour: igneous rocks of red and yellow, and the floor of the crater was a mixture of yellow and black dust. Then I noticed that the crater was still steaming. The steady drizzle increased and more steam emerged from the ground in response because, somewhere deep below, the Fire Mountain was still burning. In fact you don't have to dig too deep to find temperatures in three figures: islanders frequently impress visitors by coming up here and baking bread in hollowed-out recesses. I remained up there for a while, alone in the mist and rain, just me and the volcano, and scraped at the ground with my foot, sending up new clouds of steam from just below the surface. Then it struck me: I was walking on land that was younger than me. Believe me, you truly know you're getting on a bit when you're older than a flipping volcano.

Near the edge of town, still quite a way up the hill, I found a large stone, polished and mounted on cement. An inscription had been painted on to its face and, although I speak not a word of Icelandic, I deduced that it was a memorial to a house swallowed up by the lava. From what I could gather, the inscription referred to a house that was built in 1908. There was also the date January 23, 1973, the night the island blew up, and it seemed the stone marked the spot where the house had once stood, seventeen metres below.

In the afternoon, with all the museums shut for the winter and nothing to do, I just walked. For a good three or four hours I wandered in the rain, feeling strangely lonely and, as the afternoon wore on, a little depressed. I had no real idea why. Maybe it was because my journey was coming to an end, or maybe I was getting some kind of seasonal affective disorder, a condition rife in Scandinavia's dark winters. After all I'd not seen the sun or even the sky for several days. I'd been rained on constantly ever since I'd got to Iceland, and with the streets of Heimay generally deserted I'd not had a conversation with anyone for a long time. At lunchtime I'd dined alone in a restaurant whose English menu advertised 'deep-friend shrimp'. It was an appealing prospect. We could have sat by the harbour while I poured out my troubles to my new crustaceous chum and told him all about the shipping forecast, we could have thrown stones into the water and then maybe I'd have had him for my dinner with a little salt and pepper.

After some more aimless meandering I found myself back on the black beach. I was absolutely wet through. Rainwater poured off the brim of my hat in front of my eyes. The huge coat that had absorbed most of the Isle of Wight's annual rainfall had now done the same on the Westman Islands. My footprints from the morning were still in the ash as if they'd been made five minutes earlier. I looked out to the grey sea, the horizon invisible in the rainy mist beyond a couple of small islets. Out there was South-east Iceland. Out there was the entire shipping forecast map, vast, choppy, usually soggy, and I'd conquered it. I'd finished. In the morning I'd get back on the ferry and start a long journey home. I stood looking out to sea while the rain pitter-pattered on my hat and for the first time on the entire odyssey I just felt miserable. I'd reached the end of my voyage around the shipping forecast, and I was cold, sopping wet and lonely, my feet ached like hell and I couldn't get the nauseating smell of fish guts, which drifted from the processing plants, out of my nostrils.

I went back to the guesthouse, heaved off my sodden coat, peeled off my hat, slumped on to a chair in the kitchen and levered off my wet shoes. It was late afternoon. I had nothing to do. I certainly couldn't afford another meal at Icelandic restaurant prices. Here I was, supposed to be celebrating the end of my odyssey and I was facing a dark evening of lonely boredom, watching the rain on the windows and listening to the wind rattling the panes. I should perhaps have felt some sort of fulfilment, even the approving gaze of my grandfather, great-uncle and great-grandfather, but instead all I felt was the chafing of my saturated jeans and a wave of morose, self-pitying boredom.

And then, after staring forlornly at the floor for a good while, I became conscious of something. The light was changing. Where all had been grey and blue, there was a yellowness in the air. Black splodges slowly formed on the ground. Shadows. It was the sun. The sun was coming out. It was low in the sky and casting weak streams of pale yellow light, but it was the sun all right. Finally it had battered through the mist, rain and cloud and was shining down on the Westman Islands. I laughed out loud and clapped my hands, an act that echoed around the empty house and made me suspect I'd gone a bit nuts. I grabbed my soggy shoes which, since I'd removed them, had shrunk a little to the same degree that my feet had expanded. I skipped out of the door as lightly as a slightly overweight man in tight shoes can. I felt bright. The sun on my face may have been watery and wintry but it was warm. I walked into the centre of Heimay beneath a blue sky. For the first time I saw the tops of the hills. There were colours on them, vivid greens. For the first time I noticed the gaily coloured roofs of Heimay's houses, all blues, reds and oranges. My hat was still back in the kitchen, dripping forlornly into the sink, but if I'd been wearing it it would have been at the jauntiest of angles and beneath it I would have been humming a selection of hits from the shows. I realised that I had nothing to mark the end of my voyage, so plunged into the nearest open shop and cheerily bought a small piece of volcanic rock with a flagpole sticking out of it, atop which was a little Icelandic flag. The woman who sold it to me spoke with a North American accent and wore an 'I survived the Toronto blackout 2003' t-shirt. She even invited me for coffee at her and her husband's house that evening. I agreed heartily, feeling so full of relaxed bonhomie that I would later go back to the guesthouse, nod off in the kitchen and not stir until 2 a.m., hence missing out on the coffee and having them think I was really terribly rude.

I trotted into the supermarket and bought some snacks to see me through till morning. I looked into my shopping basket and thought of Utsire, my first destination, and how I'd bought almost exactly the same things on my first night on the shipping forecast map as I just had on my last. As I stepped out of the supermarket a car pulled up with a scarf in the back window that said 'Everton Football Club'. I laughed so hard I nearly dropped my groceries.

I rose long before dawn the next morning, the final day of my trek, in order to catch the ferry. It was very dark and there were no lights in any of the surrounding windows. I bagged up my rubbish, made my bed and let myself quietly out of the guesthouse. Then I felt a pang of guilt, let myself back in, removed the toaster from my bag and replaced it in the kitchen. The rain-shiny streets were dark and empty. The previous night I'd seen the weather forecast on the television, read by a man with a voice so lugubrious that a couple of times I thought he'd actually dropped off. On the map right over Vestmannaeyjar was a blue circle with an arrow pointing to the north-west. In the middle of the circle was a big fat number nine. That's nine as in 'severe gale nine'.

My last journey on the shipping forecast map would be a suitably turbulent one. Back at Broadcasting House, Jane wouldn't have been able to breathe any 'calm' into South-east Iceland that morning. The rain began to fall, picked out like fireflies in the lighthouse beam that swept over-head. The wind howled in my ears. It really was going to be another terrible crossing. Still, I hadn't eaten much and I surely had to get my sea legs sometime. Maybe I'd be all right this time.

The bright lights of the ferry shone in the distance.

TRAFALGAR

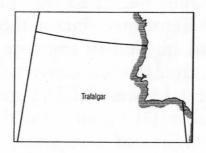

Area Trafalgar was introduced in 1956 and extends from the west of southern Portugal to north-west Africa. It is the only region not to feature in every broadcast, appearing only in the 0048 bulletin. The Trafalgar Tavern meanwhile is a pub on the Thames at Greenwich that stands around twenty feet to the west of the Prime Meridian.

The sun streams through the trees, their leaves turning golden before fluttering to the ground with an almost audible sigh. It's a chilly late afternoon in Greenwich Park and there are just a few tourists left drinking in the views of London from beneath Wolfe's statue. I've just left the observatory and seen all four of the clocks John Harrison made to eventually claim the longitude prize, still in perfect working order. A stroll down through the park, past a French couple kissing across the Meridian in a snog straddling the eastern and western hemispheres, and I'm at the National Maritime Museum. It's been tarted up a bit since my last visit, and behind the ticket desk, facing me as I enter the building, is a giant video screen. On it there are images of the sea; now and again a windswept seafront with a lone walker passing from right to left, hands thrust deep in pockets and collar turned up against the wind. Then there's a fish market. The footage has a certain familiarity. As I get nearer I notice there's a soundtrack and I allow myself a chuckle. It's not the ambient new-age noodling over a background of crashing waves that makes me laugh but the voiceover that drifts in and out.

> . . . North Utsire, north-westerly three or four, occasionally five, becoming variable three, showers, good . . . Fair Isle, westerly three or four backing southerly five or six, veering southwesterly four or five later, showers then rain, good becoming moderate, occasionally poor later . . .

When you enter the nation's museum of maritime history the first thing you see and hear is the shipping forecast. I take the lift to the very top floor of the museum, to the Nelson room. As Trafalgar warrants a mention in the forecast only once a day, and that in the wee small hours, I decided to stay a little closer to home to officially complete my journey. I'd call in and see Admiral Lord Nelson, then settle into a chair in the Trafalgar Tavern overlooking the Thames. The Nelson room is packed with exhibits that chart the life of the famous admiral killed at the Battle of Trafalgar, brought home and laid in state in the Painted Hall about six hundred yards north-east of where I stood.

Towards the back of the room, in a dimly lit glass case, is the uniform he died in, picked off by a sniper at the height of the battle in 1805. His dress coat, still a vibrant blue, bears the hole just below the left shoulder made by the bullet that killed him. His stockings lie at the bottom of the case, still showing the fading brown patches of blood that seeped from his body in the three hours it took him to die below decks on the *Victory*. What strikes you most is just how small he must have been. The uniform looks as though it would barely fit a ten-year-old child. This is belied by the copy of his head and shoulders from Nelson's column, which stands at the very end of the room. It's massive, and reminds me of an old *Blue Peter* item where John Noakes once climbed the column in order to help clean off the accumulated pigeon shit. Being so close to something I'd only seen from the ground makes me feel a bit woozy, as if suddenly I was John Noakes, a couple of hundred feet above the ground armed with only a wire brush and a bottle of bleach. The staring, sightless eyes are also a bit unsettling and

I feel almost obliged to draw in a pair of crossed pupils looking towards the bridge of the giant nose.

Leaving Nelson, I wander through the grounds of the old naval college, now part of the University of Greenwich, to the riverside gates where the admiral's body was unloaded from the *Victory*. The Thames flows slowly by; the tide's high and the water laps on to the footpath. I follow the river for a few hundred yards until I reach the Trafalgar and spend a quiet couple of reflective hours in flickering candlelight while watching the odd boat sail past the window. It's something I've done in several places around the shipping forecast map, but this time I'm not alone. I've got Katie with me and she's looking more beautiful than ever in the candlelight. I'm telling her stories of my travels, most of which she's already heard. Several times.

We move on to the *Cutty Sark*, walking along the riverbank in the darkness, go through the heavy doors, climb the long, sweeping wooden staircase and approach the table by the big window where this voyage had begun exactly a year earlier. I now know where Utsire is. I've sailed over Dogger Bank. My coat is still marinated in rain from Wight and South-east Iceland. I've done it. I've been to every area on the map. I skip down the stairs to the bar, and return with three drinks. One for Katie, one for me and one for old Harry, whose picture lies on the table in front of me. Well, he had asked that

'If you see this young chap wandering in London, treat him well.' Cheers, Harry. My journey may not have been as fraught, nor indeed as inadvertent, as his, but I'd done it. Not only that, I felt I understood my heritage a little better, my maternal cockney roots and my paternal Irish ones. Most of all, I understand the shipping forecast better. No longer is it a strange conglomeration of odd phrases that once preceded my fish fingers, chips and peas, it is now something different. Something far, far deeper than a random collection of words. My meteorological knowledge isn't much improved – I'd certainly experienced plenty of weather but still don't know a millibar from a Milky Bar – but I understand other things. The fringe communities of our islands. Our near neighbours across the sea. Thanks to the solemn, rhythmic intonation of the shipping forecast I feel like a wiser man. I raise my glass and clink it with Katie's and Harry's.

When we get home, although it's been a long, long day, I wait up awhile, turning the radio on quietly so as not to disturb the sleeping form in the next room. At the appointed time a soothing, familiar voice says, 'And now before the shipping forecast, here's *Sailing By*.' I close my eyes as Ronald Binge's lilting arpeggios and brilliantly simple melody fill the room.

And now the shipping forecast issued by the Met Office at 0015 . . .

As each area is named I'm back there. Skidding around the dancefloor on Utsire, stunned by the beauty of the oil platforms in the Cromarty Firth, in Cook's attic in Whitby, among Norwegian drunks en route to Hanstholm. I'm crashing through the North Sea with facefuls of salty spray on the way to Sealand, then walking on the White Cliffs of Dover in the sunshine. There's the crunching beneath my feet of the old quarry in Portland, the smell of strong coffee in Bilbao, and the eerie presence of the ancients as the sun went down over Finisterre. I'm racing the sun along the horizon on the way back from St Agnes, then on a little ship being thrown around the Bristol Channel. I'm in a hailstorm astride a pushbike high on a Manx mountain, then watching an extraordinary sunset over the Shannon estuary. There's the smell of the turf fires on the Atlantic coast of Donegal, then the sound of a fiddle in a busy Lerwick pub.

. . . Faeroes, South-east Iceland, occasionally seven, squally wintry showers, good . . .

FURTHER READING

There have been, to my knowledge, three previous books based on the shipping forecast. Photographer Mark Power visited the sea areas and produced a terrific book of photographs titled simply *The Shipping Forecast* (Zelda Cheatle Press, 1996). Peter Collyer also trekked around the sea areas producing the marvellous watercolours that make up his book *Rain Later, Good* (Thomas Reed, 2000). As well as the thirty-one sea areas, Peter went on to visit all the coastal stations (which is just showing off, if you ask me). The third book, *Faeroes to Finisterre: Stories From the Sea Areas* (Frederick Muller, 1952) by John Merrett, was based on a children's radio series of the same name and, not surprisingly considering its year of publication, concentrates heavily on the Second World War.

To list every book and website that I found helpful would be exhaustive and require a level of personal organisation that is far beyond me. So here are a few highlights in no particular order. *FitzRoy: The Remarkable Story of Darwin's Captain and the Invention of the Weather Forecast* (Headline,

2003) by John and Mary Gribbin is a new and highly readable biography of the main man. George Morey's *The North Sea* (Frederick Muller, 1968) and *The Narrow Sea: Barrier, Bridge and Gateway to the World: The History of the English Channel* (Headline, 2003) by Peter Unwin are excellent studies of their eponymous bodies of water. George Drower's *Heligoland: The True Story of German Bight and The Island That Britain Betrayed* (Sutton Publishing, 2003) gives the fullest account of Heligoland's history that anyone could wish for, and is notable for the passion and outrage that leaps from every page. For Drake and Cook I drew mainly on *Sir Francis Drake: The Queen's Pirate* (Yale University Press, 1998) by Harry Kelsey and *Captain Cook: Obsession and Betrayal in the New World* (Ebury, 2002), Vanessa Collingridge's highly personal account of Cook and his legacy.

Henry Blogg of Cromer: The Greatest of the Lifeboatmen (Poppyland Publishing, 2002) by Cyril Jolly is a brilliant, brilliant book. First published in the 1950s, it's a biographical classic that I can't recommend highly enough, while Adam Hart-Davis and Emily Troscianko's *Henry Winstanley and the Eddystone Lighthouse* is a pacy account of the events that led to my bout of vertigo on Plymouth Hoe.

Roger Hutchinson's *Polly: The True Story Behind Whisky Galore* (Mainstream, 1998) outlines the shadowy events on Eriskay that inspired a classic novel and Ealing film, while *Rockall* (Country Book Club, 1957) by James Fisher details the remarkable history of that big lump of rock in the north Atlantic. Charles Jennings's *Greenwich: The Place Where Days Begin and End* (Little, Brown, 1999) is in my opinion the best book yet written about my favourite place in the whole wide world, while Mark Kurlansky's *Cod: A Biography of the Fish That Changed the World* (Vintage, 1999) details the remarkable story of the species that occupies our waters in decreasing numbers.

As for the web, the shipping forecast itself can be found at http://www.bbc.co.uk/weather/ukweather/shipping.shtml and http://www.meto.gov.uk/datafiles/offshore.html. Martin Rowley's excellent website can be found at http://homepage.ntlworld.com/booty.weather/metindex.htm – anything you ever wanted to know about meteorology you can find here thanks to one of the people who write the shipping forecast.

Try an Arbroath smokie for yourself (I can also heartily recommend the smoked salmon) via Campbell Scott's website, http://www.arbroath-smokie.co.uk, while you can find out more about the Bell Rock Lighthouse at David Taylor's fantastic all-singing, all-dancing website, http://www.bellrock.org.uk.

There's more about the Cromer lifeboat at http://www.cromerlifeboats.org.uk, while the official website of the government of the Principality of Sealand is at http://www.sealandgov.org/index.

html. There's more on the talking mongoose of Dalby at http://www.ballacallin.com/mongoose. asp, while Roger Lapthorn provides probably the best cyber port of call for Rockall at http://www.geocities. com/rlapthorn/rock.htm. Http://www.therockalltimes.co.uk. is a very, very funny site. Fair Isle resident Linda Grieve's excellent *Scottish Islands Explorer* magazine has a website at http://www.scottishislandsexplorer.com.

Linda Sgoluppi is an abstract painter from Northampton who has created a series of images based on the sea areas. More at www. lindasgoluppi.com.

SeaBritain 2005 is a year-long festival of the sea taking place across the nation; it's designed to remind us of how important the sea has been and continues to be to these islands. More information can be found at www.seabritain2005.com.

Finally and, of course, most importantly, don't forget to stop by at http://www.charlieconnelly. com and I'll get the kettle on.